Learning Foreign
and Second Languages

Teaching Languages, Literatures, and Cultures
MODERN LANGUAGE ASSOCIATION OF AMERICA

Chair
Guadalupe Valdés

Series editors
J. Michael Holquist, Sumie Jones,
Claire J. Kramsch, Yvonne Ozzello

Learning Foreign and Second Languages: Perspectives in Research and Scholarship. Ed. Heidi Byrnes. 1998.

Learning Foreign and Second Languages

Perspectives in Research and Scholarship

Edited by
Heidi Byrnes

THE MODERN LANGUAGE ASSOCIATION OF AMERICA
New York 1998

For information about obtaining permission to reprint material from
MLA book publications, send your request by mail (see address below),
e-mail (permissions@mla.org), or fax (212 477-9863).

Library of Congress Cataloging-in-Publication Data
Learning foreign and second languages : perspectives in research and
    scholarship / edited by Heidi Byrnes.
        p.   cm. — (Teaching languages, literatures, and cultures,
    ISSN 1092-3225 ; 1)
      Includes bibliographical references and indexes.
      ISBN 0-87352-800-X. — ISBN 0-87352-801-8 (pbk.)
      1. Language and languages—Study and teaching. 2. Second language
    acquisition. I. Byrnes, Heidi. II. Series.
    P51.L39   1998
    418'.007—dc21   98-39497

Set in Stone Serif and Univers 45 Light. Printed on recycled paper

Published by The Modern Language Association of America
10 Astor Place, New York, New York 10003-6981

CONTENTS

PREFACE TO THE SERIES   vii

Introduction: Steps to an Ecology of Foreign
Language Departments   1
   Heidi Byrnes

Constructing Second Language Acquisition Research
in Foreign Language Departments   23
   Claire Kramsch

Sociohistorical Perspectives on Language Teaching
in the Modern United States   39
   Elizabeth B. Bernhardt

Linguistics, Applied Linguistics, and
Second Language Acquisition Theories   58
   Thom Huebner

Approaches to Empirical Research
in Instructional Language Settings   75
   Kathleen M. Bailey

Cognitive Characteristics of Adult Second
Language Learners   105
   Bill VanPatten

Acquiring Competence in a Second Language:
Form and Function   128
   Catherine Doughty

Constraints and Resources in Classroom Talk:
Issues of Equality and Symmetry   157
  Leo van Lier

Interlanguage Pragmatics   183
  Gabriele Kasper

The Role of Technology in Second Language Learning   209
  Robert J. Blake

Evaluation of Learning Outcomes in Second Language
Acquisition: A Multiplism Perspective   238
  Elana Shohamy

Constructing Curricula in Collegiate Foreign
Language Departments   262
  Heidi Byrnes

NOTES ON CONTRIBUTORS   297
NAME INDEX   301
SUBJECT INDEX   309

PREFACE TO THE SERIES

The Teaching Languages, Literatures, and Cultures series was created in response to recent transformative changes in the three areas of language teaching: language, literature, and culture. By curricular necessity or personal choice, many teachers teach in more than one area of specialization. At the same time, current theories and methodologies encourage teachers to incorporate multiple perspectives in their courses. This series aims to help secondary and postsecondary school practitioners come to grips with new challenges by examining the ways different languages, literatures, and cultures intersect in theory, research curricula, and program design. The series is intended to reach specialists and nonspecialists alike and to create cross-specialty dialogue among members of the profession engaged in what have previously been considered vastly different efforts.

Learning Foreign and Second Languages: Perspectives in Research and Scholarship, the first volume of the series, provides an overview of the field of second language acquisition (SLA) to members of foreign language departments whose primary area of interest is literary research. The book's purposes are to enlarge the range of thinking about the learning and teaching of foreign languages and to call into question the conventional separation of language and literature. The contributors to the volume offer their literature colleagues an important tool for addressing the issues that currently face traditionally constituted foreign language departments. We hope that a clear and incisive presentation of the epistemological presuppositions and major theoretical stances of the field of second language acquisition will support a dialogue between language and literature specialists that can contribute not only to the managing of the teaching mission of their departments but also to the development of a new institutional identity for foreign language departments in higher education.

Series Editors

Introduction: Steps to an Ecology of Foreign Language Departments

Heidi Byrnes

It is well known that any scholarly project is marked by the period and place in which it was conceived and nurtured into being, that it is shaped by the environment into which it is launched, and that its future impact is subject to many variables that lie outside its narrowly defined scholarly agenda. But although these truths are well known, I make them the focus of my introductory comments to this volume because the volume is unusual with regard to all three: unusual in its impetus and intellectual parentage, in the larger context of its publication, and in its potential for bringing about change in areas that lie beyond its scholarly focus.

My assertion implicitly refers to an issue of great concern to the authors of the volume, namely, the difficulty of introducing a highly specialized field—the vibrant field of second language acquisition research (SLA)—to a nonspecialized audience, to readers who share only an interest in foreign language teaching and learning at the collegiate level. In other words, while I welcome the likelihood of a range of readings of the essays in this volume, it does seem appropriate that readers be given some preliminary interpretive framework beyond the implicit and explicit references the authors provide in their texts. I hope readers find my comments useful as they set out to uncover, from their varied perspectives, the volume's scholarly interests and significance; as they evaluate its topic treatment and manner of presentation, consider its larger goals and purposes, and apply its many implications to their professional situations.

BACKGROUND

In 1990 the MLA Executive Council established a new Advisory Committee on Foreign Languages and Literatures, a committee I was privileged to chair for three years. The charge to the committee specifically stated that it was to give "particular attention to foreign language and literary studies at all levels of the educational system and in society at large" ("Meeting" 944). Though that charge appears ordinary to a fault, it was motivated by an increasing sense of the nonordinary state of affairs in United States foreign language education. Not surprisingly, that assessment did not generally originate with those members of the profession who were engaged in literary scholarship, by far the most influential group—influential because of numbers and, even more important, because of prestige in the academy and particularly in foreign language departments. Instead, the assessment originated with a much smaller group of professionals, those who had direct experience with foreign language education, experience that ranged from teaching duties to administrative tasks to research in second language learning and teaching. But few in either group were ready to be as bold as Dorothy James, who in a seminal 1989 article designated the United States "system as it stands . . . a recipe for disaster" ("Re-shaping" 81). On the one hand, colleagues might not have agreed with that stark designation, seeing from their vantage point no immediate reason for radical change. On the other hand, they might merely have been reluctant to express themselves quite as bluntly, because they then would have been obligated to tackle a problem that, in view of prevailing realities in the academy, seemed overwhelmingly, hopelessly complex.

The broadly constituted MLA committee, however, chose to be optimistic. In part that optimism stemmed from the fact that the MLA, the country's largest and most influential professional organization focused on foreign languages, was reasserting a role that, over time, had become subdivided—ACTFL had assumed the task of attending to issues of language learning and teaching, while the MLA's membership, coming almost exclusively from the collegiate level, was interested primarily in literary scholarship. As a result the MLA did not represent the concerns of noncollegiate levels of foreign language instruction unless it explicitly chose to engage in such bridge building.

Against that background, the committee's mandate reflected a new thinking, an approach that keen observers inside and outside the MLA's organizational structure had gradually come to identify as crucial if a substantive future for foreign language study in this country was to be assured: that the field of language education needed to be conceptualized in its entirety, though without undermining the differentiation of practice in different environments. For example, the field needed to transcend the traditional and powerful native—nonnative distinction, which, given the increasing realization of the special place of heritage language users in the United States, was becoming not only obsolete but potentially counterproductive (see Valdés). The field needed to examine the relation between native language literacy and foreign language study. Perhaps ultimately it could even promote a mutually supportive and complementary relation between the work accomplished in English departments and the concerns addressed in foreign language departments. The field needed to deal with the place of content and subject matter in the acquisition and use of a second language. Finally, the field needed to work assiduously toward establishing intellectual linkages between scholarship and practice, between literary-cultural studies and language acquisition. Facile claims of harmony ("We already incorporate the other side") and either ignoring the important differences or declaring them essentially unbridgeable were no longer satisfactory strategies. It seemed appropriate for the MLA to work to develop the encompassing representation on the national scene that would address the vexing issues that faced foreign language study at all levels of instruction.

The committee's goal was to help overcome the marginalization that had limited foreign language professionals in many of their activities and, by implication, in the success and influence their field could have in American education overall. The committee, as James had done in her signal article, intended to narrow the gap between the two distinct but complementary areas of language acquisition: language teaching-learning and literary research. These specific objectives were agreed on: (1) professionalization of teaching languages through preservice education and in-service development and support; (2) assistance for faculty members in the language teaching profession who, neither playing the roles nor receiving the rewards of their literary colleagues, were marginalized in their departments; (3) greater professional recognition of scholarly work in the area of language learning and teaching; (4) in-depth exploration of the issues confronting language learning and teaching in the United States; (5) recognition of outstanding teaching; and (6) diverse survey activities.

The committee considered as a key project the publication of a unique volume of essays that would take a second language acquisition perspective toward the issues and dilemmas that foreign language departments face. When committee members became aware of the absence of such a volume, they agreed to that proposal. If nonspecialist colleagues found it difficult to inform themselves of these issues though they were deeply affected by them, then the volume could accomplish two goals: to explain the current situation and to lay out a possible future direction for foreign language departments. The volume would not offer specific recommendations but would help formulate thoughtful proposals, which would subsequently have to be shaped in and by a particular institutional setting (Swaffar, "Mission").

THE SHIFTING GOALS OF FOREIGN
LANGUAGE LEARNING

An understanding of the foreign language field in the early 1990s requires a more detailed look at the goals, approaches, and pedagogies for language learning that had become established in diverse instructional contexts.

Learning Foreign and Second Languages was planned at a time when second language teaching had regained strength at the secondary level and was beginning to show some rejuvenation in the primary grades (particularly through innovative immersion programs in a remarkable range of languages) as well as at the collegiate level. This improvement can be attributed to a felicitous combination of outside funding (e.g., by NEH, the United States Department of Education, FIPSE) that became available then and of the nation's consideration of foreign language educational goals, pedagogical approaches, and curricula at all levels of instruction. This tremendous activity, uniquely American, has come to be known as the proficiency movement. It engendered an optimism and an innovation that, in a short period of time, came to affect all aspects of K–12 foreign language teaching (curriculum, instructional approaches, materials, assessment, teacher education) and included entire state systems (e.g., Texas, Minnesota, New York). The proficiency movement was rightfully connected in the late 1980s, and even now is connected, with a welcome enrollment growth in precollegiate foreign language programs in many parts of the country.

In some instances the rejuvenation reached the beginning levels of collegiate foreign language instruction and led to important changes in language programs (at the University of Pennsylvania, at the University of

Minnesota). A rethinking of the presuppositions and the praxis of the field even inched forward to the heart of the matter, namely, an articulated foreign language curriculum made up of a well-considered sequence of courses that would span all levels of education based on a comprehensive conceptualization for foreign language learning (see Welles, *Articulation*). Articulation efforts were formulated with much personal and professional commitment both at the regional level (e.g., the effort spanning six New England states [*Articulation and Achievement*]) and at the state level (e.g., Minnesota). Indeed, the 1996 document released by the National Standards in Foreign Language Education Project is a direct extension to the national level of these professional collaboration initiatives that focused on an articulated sequence of instruction that would eventually encompass grades K–16 (*Standards*).

What supported these bustling activities and the optimism they both generated and required for their sustenance is itself an exciting though by no means uncontroversial chapter in American foreign language education. The support came from motivations and historical roots that were amazingly diverse: a set of five task forces convened by the MLA and the American Council of Learned Societies with the goal of finding a unifying principle and sense of mission for language study; the 1979 report of the President's Commission on Foreign Language and International Studies, *Strength through Wisdom*, which urged the creation of a common yardstick for establishing national requirements in foreign languages and specifically urged the acceptance of descriptors of language ability that were based on real-life performance rather than on years of study; the subsequent creation, under the auspices of ACTFL, of proficiency guidelines (1982 [*ACTFL*], revised in 1986 ["ACTFL"]); the collaboration among diverse governmental agencies and the academy, particularly in oral proficiency assessment; and, ultimately, the extensive revisions of curricula and instructional approaches under the proficiency banner, which began to dominate professional discussion in the late 1980s and early 1990s.

Developments in second language acquisition theory and empirical research also supported the shift toward communicative language teaching. Some antedate the proficiency movement; others run parallel to it, with or without explicit connections. Some developments have been antithetical to each other regarding the role of accuracy in learner language and, more important, regarding the best way of fostering accuracy. Yet, despite their differences, both the proficiency movement and communicative language teaching are part of an extraordinary shift, a shift that has been justified by increasingly rich SLA research evidence.

One can hardly imagine a more dramatic swing of the pendulum: from an emphasis, before 1970, on language as a system of linguistic forms to be acquired by the study of grammar to an emphasis, beginning in the 1970s and continuing to the present, on language as a means of communication, where students learn not by studying rules but by engaging straightaway in the use of language to convey meanings. In the traditional, grammar-based syllabus and teaching methodology, the linguistic forms themselves are the object of study, a study typically accomplished in highly elaborated inflectional sets; in the communicative approach, it is not the language but the content that is important. In this volume the essay by Catherine Doughty and my discussion of curriculum address this shift, though from slightly different angles.

A number of decisive insights provided by research are worth mentioning. Not only is knowing the rules of a language different from communicative ability, it seems even to put learners at a disadvantage when they are asked to take that route. Furthermore, the rules in structuralist grammars are not the rules that are necessary to acquire competence in a language. The mastery of grammar rules, though a formidable feat in itself, leads to a "classroom language" that lacks important characteristics of target language use. There is another problem with the standard sequence of grammatically driven syllabi: certain aspects of second language learning seem unalterable no matter what their sequencing in instruction (see VanPatten, this volume). Finally, "learned" forms, even overlearned forms, can disappear under the influence of the complex interlanguage systems that learners generate themselves. These systems, moreover, differ from the grammatical systems of both the native language and the language to be acquired.

It is not surprising, given such shortcomings, that the traditional goals and methods of language learning came under serious scrutiny. Diverse societal, sociopolitical, and socioeconomic pressures and changes in means of communication, in possibilities for travel, in available technologies, in student population, and in learner goals all contributed to making the communicative approach the prevalent one—though recently that approach has been seen to have its own shortcomings. Second language acquisition research is now carefully analyzing those shortcomings, so that they may be overcome (see VanPatten, Doughty, van Lier, and Byrnes, this volume). The lines of argumentation put forward in the contributions of *Learning Foreign and Second Languages* are best understood against this background.

INSTITUTIONAL CONTEXTS

Another set of considerations frames this volume's contributions: academic and institutional contexts for foreign language education. Although one would expect the bustling language learning activity at the precollegiate level to have worked its way into the college curriculum, such has generally not been the case, at least not in mainstream curricula. On the contrary, nearly all proficiency initiatives come to a halt at the curricular places that are definitional for foreign language study in this country: undergraduate content courses, mostly literature courses, and graduate curricula that orient graduate students toward an understanding of language, language teaching, and language learning that is considered most appropriate for future faculty members. This is not to say that changes have not taken place. They have, but they tend to remain changes at the margins, with no serious reconsideration of the whole. The communicative approach is often viewed skeptically and thought to undermine essential goals of collegiate foreign language departments.

Many reasons for this state of affairs can be given. If proficiency is understood as the American version of the far-reaching communicative language teaching revolution that during the 1970s rose to prominence in Europe, then one could say that departments failed to realize the deeper implications of the dramatic shift from observing, analyzing, and replicating language as a largely invariant and normative system to learning to understand language in terms of creative use across a range of communicative contexts that are highly variant according to their different sociocultural embeddings, though by no means random.

But for all its vitality on the local level, the proficiency movement has not sufficiently articulated a larger agenda. It might have stated its intellectual aspirations more comprehensively instead of expressing them in terms of context-dependent oral proficiency for daily interactions. A focus on everyday conversational language skills disregards the legitimate demands in education to foster extended monologic skills. As Catherine Snow and other researchers have shown, it is not conversational interaction but the ability to produce extended monologue that predicts literacy and school achievement (Snow 98). Or the proficiency movement might have given less weight to a testing practice, the oral proficiency interview (OPI), that at times became prescriptive. In other words, the movement should have developed a different frame of reference, a different constitutive narrative, a different focus in its practice, and a different vocabulary—a vocabulary whose concepts would resonate better with the dominant self-image of language departments that continue to be preoccupied with literature and cultural studies.

But that did not happen. The result has been a particularly contradictory situation: foreign language teaching and learning in the United States, under the larger rubric of student-centered communicative language teaching, is confined to the precollegiate sector and cannot be recognized by, indeed seems difficult to reconcile with, the intellectual and institutional goals that characterize collegiate foreign language departments (see Kramsch, this volume). Departmental faculty leaders, usually from the literature ranks, staunchly defend the status quo and prefer inaction or stalling actions—although many realize that far-reaching changes in the intellectual environment, in the practices and organizational contexts of the academy, and in resource allocations call for a thorough rethinking of the conduct of our lives. William Massy, Andrea Wilger, and Carol Colbeck, who coined the term *hollowed* collegiality in their analysis of faculty behavior in a range of disciplines, show that such a response is not unusual. But for foreign language departments the repercussions of an inability to change have become particularly destructive in the last few years.

It is most ironic that communication, which should have been everyone's goal, instead became a highly disputed notion, because the communicative approach demonstrated that even after long instructional sequences learner language, when actually used, remained noticeably flawed. It was natural to place the blame on use-oriented communicative teaching, which had replaced form-focused, grammar-based teaching. In reality, flaws are definitional for learner language, a phenomenon that SLA theory and practice captures by the term *interlanguage*. But the traditional approach, emphasizing knowledge about language and literature as opposed to the current demand for performance of language and literature, had concealed that fact. To use a well-known analogy: students' crimes of linguistic inaccuracy had not suddenly increased, only their reporting. In addition, an emphasis on speaking in daily life—surely the preponderance of communicative instruction and interaction in the first four semesters—was seen as hopelessly inappropriate preparation for the study of literary texts, which was the central concern of the so-called upper-level language courses. Indeed, if communicative instruction is confined to speaking in daily life, students' literate abilities in the third and fourth years of the undergraduate curriculum will suffer. But a communicative approach does not inherently need to be so constricted.

In sum, while the proficiency movement seriously questioned traditional practice, it was unable to gain the intellectual momentum that would have been necessary for it to mobilize the entire field of foreign languages in this country, all the way through graduate study. This unexpected weakness is most tellingly illustrated by the fact that the notion of proficiency did not address, as it should have been able to do, the painful gap that exists among a department's diverse missions in literature, culture, and language teaching and did not further speak to the traditional hierarchy among those missions and, consequently, among faculty members. Instead, the idea of communicative competence really did not reach the heart of the curriculum, therefore did not touch the great divergence in status between faculty members who teach language and faculty members who teach content courses. One might initially be grateful that it didn't. But the communicative revolution, by stopping short of the real institutional power as it exists in foreign language departments, failed also to impress on departments the need to face a host of other central problems and to find a solution for them.

FUTURE ISSUES IN FOREIGN LANGUAGE DEPARTMENTS

Foreign language and literature departments are beleaguered these days. In a remarkably short time, a few years, the climate for foreign language study has deteriorated dramatically. Powerful forces, having moved to the fore, are relentlessly restructuring higher education and, in particular, traditionally constituted foreign language departments. Although planned in much more optimistic times, *Learning Foreign and Second Languages* now joins a chorus of voices outside and inside the academy that are critically examining nearly all aspects of the conduct of collegiate foreign language departments (e.g., Byrnes, "Future" and "Governing"; James, "Teaching"; Kramsch; Kurth; Roche and Salumets; Swaffar, "Using"; Webber; Welles, *Articulation* and *Education*). Calls are made for examining undergraduate and graduate curricula; philosophies of education in the United States; assumptions about adult foreign language learning; faculty members' responsibilities, roles, and reward structures; research and scholarship in foreign languages; student recruitment, retention, and position; and outcomes in terms of a liberal education and in terms of language competence. Much soul-searching and forthrightness is demanded in the face of the increasingly corporate, legalistic, and financial lines of argumentation that dramatically challenge the kind of scholarly inquiry and the cooperative interaction that have traditionally characterized, or at the very least were considered to characterize, the academic ideal.

Even as enrollments are surging in some languages (numerically in Spanish, but on a percentage basis in Arabic and Chinese ["Results"]), departments seem to be experiencing a loss of their center and vitality. The stark realities of enrollment shifts and drops overall in the foreign languages cast an ominous hue of crisis on the following picture:

Departments run the risk of losing their identity as foreign language departments if they move into the institutional curriculum at large and give up the unique connection to their languages.

Departments can make themselves irrelevant as American language departments if they continue to cling, even subtly, to a debilitating standard of nativeness in their hiring (with job searches that require near-native language ability); in their graduate student selection (with no support provided for upper-level, academic language acquisition); and in their curricula (with courses and text selections that are a reduced version of native canons instead of being informed by an American context).

Departments' traditional humanistic engagement with literature is in danger of being carelessly thrown overboard when departments interpret student demand for a greater range of ways to become engaged with other cultures and languages as a dismissal of literature as a way to know oneself and others.

Departments' presence as an intellectually valid contributor to the academy is jeopardized when departments are unable to see the difference between a broadened but demanding curriculum and a broadened but essentially service-oriented curriculum that exists largely for the benefit of other programs across the campus, particularly in professional schools (e.g., programs in business German, Japanese for international relations majors, Spanish for health care providers).

Departments encounter curtailment of curricular options—the extreme curtailment being the closing of a department—regarding the central problem of United States foreign language departments, namely, how to bridge the gap between the language teaching component and the literary and cultural studies component of their enterprise.

Departments face serious faculty resource mismatches when senior and experienced faculty members, who typically are educated in a literary field, teach few students, while novice graduate TAs teach the bulk of students in language classes.

Finally, the long-term programmatic viability of departments is in jeopardy when their faculty makeup does not match student demands and furthermore has no generational staggering to ensure both programmatic continuity and smooth renewal. The lack of staggering is further aggravated by the uncapping of retirement age.

Small wonder that administrations everywhere are contemplating and putting into place major realignments in faculty positions (in tenure, multiple-year contracts, adjunct and part-time hiring, position cuts or redesignations) and in governance. The recent creation of language centers is only one of the more visible among a range of developments (Patrikis), all of which expose what was previously an internal split in departments by outsourcing language instruction in various ways, ways that threaten a department's intellectual presence, not to mention physical existence. We need to see very clearly what is happening here lest we respond with misguided measures. While these realignments typically occur as administrative and fiscal moves, they are just as often the result of—and quite decidedly precipitated by—administrative frustration with the nonseriousness of faculty responses to departmental and, beyond, to institutional crises.

But there is no need for gloom. As I hope this volume will make clear, our current environment also contains remarkable potential for far-reaching, perhaps even exuberant rejuvenation—in intellectual orientation as well as in the myriad educational practices of foreign language departments. Promising linkages from SLA research to the field of literature seem possible. Foreign language literature programs in the United States might find the construction of alterity a particularly felicitous theoretical point of departure and organizing principle (Berman, "Thinking" and "Reform"; Peck). The notion of foreign cultural literacy strongly recommends itself not only because it is a deeply humanistic contemporary response that nevertheless goes back to the central project of the American university—namely, liberal education—but also because it has the pragmatic ability to unite the traditional three goals of foreign language departments: to teach language, to engage in the study of works of literature, and to convey general cultural knowledge. Just what a focus on foreign cultural literacy might mean for a department is revealed in questions such as these: Can a cultural studies focus on otherness be accomplished through traditional disciplinary channels, or does it require interdisciplinary approaches? If it requires interdisciplinary approaches, how are the epistemological and methodological issues to be addressed? Finally, could interdisciplinarity itself, though much hailed, be merely a vehicle toward a redefinition of goals and norms for the new field (Berman, "Reform")? Since recent developments in SLA research take a social constructivist view of language, of language learning, and of literacy, much common ground for further exploration seems to exist (see Byrnes, this volume).

We are surely sober and wise enough to know that such a rosy picture is far from inevitable. Indeed, circumstances beyond our control as well as our inappropriate actions or inaction may already have created structural realities that undercut a comprehensive conceptualization and an encompassing humanistic practice for foreign language learning in the United States at all levels. Even so, we should not lose hope but, instead, work to avoid further devastation of our academic landscape. The questions are these: Can we, at this time, discern and plan courses of action that will revitalize collegiate foreign language departments? Will we be able to understand and decisively use the enormously liberating potential of a number of intellectual developments in our field? Are there steps we might take to create an ecology, long overdue, of foreign language departments?

I offer the concept of multiple literacies as a candidate for connecting the diverse strands of foreign language departments and suggest a strategy toward realizing that goal. The MLA plays a pivotal role. Just as this professional organization has figured prominently in foreign language education in the past, it should once again assume organizational responsibility—and its individual members should assume personal responsibility—for the future of foreign language departments. The agenda should include not only our exposing students to foreign language literatures but also our seeing that students learn a foreign language to some comfortable level of use. It will take more than simply reminding the foreign language literary scholars in the MLA of their obligations to the health of their entire departments. English literature faculty members too should help foreign language departments perform substantively in a collegiate curriculum. This matter has received essentially no attention in the organization, notwithstanding the otherwise increased sensitivities to the cultural embeddedness and multiple interpretive contexts of all texts. It is for this professional environment that *Learning Foreign and Second Languages* presents its insights from SLA research and scholarship, and to an audience that includes scholars in literature, English and non-English, so that together we may effect changes toward an internal ecology of foreign language departments and a larger ecology of foreign language and English departments in American colleges and universities.

The primary aim of this volume is to provide an overview of the field of second language acquisition through instruction, as distinct from both first language learning and naturalistic second language acquisition. The volume divides its subject matter into eleven topics. The in-depth essays can be read independently, but together they show important conceptual and practical linkages. Readers may experience these linkages simply by taking the essays in sequence. The authors also make implicit and explicit connections among the central issues in the field that have become crystallized since roughly 1975.

The volume also strives to accomplish two additional tasks. One, it must make clear that the findings it relates are not final and fixed but, instead, marked by their intellectual time and place as well as by the institutional context of the researchers and the educational settings or learning environments that were investigated. Two, it must make clear that the research reported does not exist in isolation but, instead, speaks to the problems of foreign language education in the United States that urgently need to be resolved.

It is hoped that readers will become familiar enough with the field of second language acquisition to be able to discern and critique its epistemological presuppositions and major theoretical stances, to appreciate both the opportunities and limitations of its constructs, and to interpret the meaning of some of its most salient descriptive and explanatory details. It is hoped that readers will come to appreciate that the field's insights about second language learning merit serious consideration, which those insights have not received in the past, given the politics surrounding foreign languages in this country. SLA research strongly supports a major shift in intellectual and institutional academic practice regarding second language learning and teaching—a shift in the political landscape, as it were. By continuing a dynamic examination of the field's theoretical, methodological, and pedagogical assumptions, scholars will make possible the kind of open dialogue that will be necessary for us to tackle the tasks all foreign language departments face. SLA researchers will then be able to build strong alliances not only with colleagues who are interested in language pedagogy but also with literature faculty members who, in turn, will commit themselves to explore interdisciplinary approaches to foreign language studies. Such exploration will effect critically needed changes in foreign language departments in higher education.

More and more scholars are reflecting on the field of second language acquisition: on the role and nature of SLA theorizing (Beretta; Block; Brumfit; Firth and Wagner; Hall; Hatch, Shirai, and Fantuzzi; Kamil; Klein; Long; Spolsky); on the relation between theory and practice (Clarke; Ferguson); on the possibility, desirability, even necessity, at times, of different metaphors, which might ultimately mean different theories (Lantolf; Larsen-Freeman; Reddy; van Lier); on different research methodologies (Kasper and Grotjahn; Davis and Lazaraton); on different pedagogies and educational goals (New London Group); and on the concept that pedagogical method as interested knowledge perpetuates inequities (Pennycook).

All these issues are of course wrapped up in the difficult question of the delimitation of the field (Kramsch). But the continued reconsideration of the intellectual moorings of SLA research and of the extension of its boundaries already supports a rich dialogue with the other field of inquiry that centrally deals with foreign language, namely, foreign literature.

In sum, the agenda of *Foreign and Second Language Learning* is to provide professionals from neighboring fields with access to SLA research. By enlarging the range for thinking about the learning and teaching of foreign languages, the volume should also contribute to the development of a new academic identity for foreign languages and to a new institutional identity for foreign language departments in higher education.

The first two essays give the context of language learning and teaching in collegiate foreign language departments, the second two discuss theoretical and methodological considerations in SLA research, the next four provide an overview of current thinking about the process of instructed foreign language learning as seen from perspectives that focus on the learner, and the last three examine applied areas for SLA research.

Both Claire Kramsch and Elizabeth Bernhardt show the intimate connection between SLA research and scholarship and the practices of American higher education, a connection at times fraught with debilitating paradoxes. The authors also point to hopeful developments that, if identified and seized on, afford opportunities for building up a trust and a mutual respect between SLA research and literary-cultural studies that have long been absent. That result would enable the humanistic inquiry that is claimed to be the hallmark of foreign language study and would make possible for our students border crossings and multiple social identities.

Kramsch describes the academic environment: the language curriculum in foreign language departments, the increasingly close relation between SLA research and neighboring intellectual pursuits in literary-cultural studies, and language program coordination. To varying degrees these areas are both supported and challenged by new developments in the production and transmission of knowledge, developments that not only reconfigure what constitutes an academic pursuit but also affect disciplinary status, disciplinary boundaries, and attributions of prestige. Adopting a sociocultural perspective, Kramsch uncovers beneficial exchanges between literary-cultural studies and second language acquisition.

Bernhardt goes beyond the foreign language department and discusses language teaching in the United States since 1865 against the backdrop of social, political, and historical events. She encourages us to understand language teaching as an element in the evolution of a distinctively American education, not as a set of unrelated bandwagon phenomena. She urges us to become familiar with the basic chronology of landmarks in American language teaching and to see how these relate to national policy and legislation in the context of different real and imagined crises. By taking a comprehensive view of American education, she shows that the fate of collegiate curricula is inevitably intertwined with K–12 education, a connection that until quite recently has been overlooked. The sometimes distressingly poor results of language learning and teaching efforts on the national scale, in other words, are explained not only by America's unsophisticated stance toward other peoples, cultures, and languages. The poor results can also be explained by the profession's inability or unwillingness to understand that its history is affected by its unique American context. Without that understanding, the profession cannot shape its own destiny creatively and successfully.

The next two essays locate SLA research intellectually and methodologically. Thom Huebner discusses the field in the environment of the disciplines of applied linguistics and linguistics. Such connections are by no means the only ones possible. Indeed, many of the problems foreign language study currently faces are the result of the strong affinities of SLA toward the empirical sciences, including psychology, and of the accompanying interruption of its old ties, signaled by the term *philology*, to the humanities. The often disturbed relation of SLA to pedagogy and educational issues further complicates the picture.

But the SLA-linguistics connection—the emphasis of SLA on models of formal syntax—is itself far from unproblematic. In fact, much of the dynamic in both applied linguistics and SLA research results from the attempt to loosen these previously defining bonds and develop separate theoretical models and methods. SLA research, inherently interdisciplinary, has difficulty finding theoretical metaphors that will satisfy disparate fields. Whether it will someday no longer primarily be the beneficiary of theoretical and empirical contributions from other disciplines but will be able to develop its own distinguishing characteristics depends on the continued openness and vitality of SLA theorizing and modeling.

Claims to "normal science" status, as Thomas Kuhn describes it, are of course best developed and substantiated through the articulation of research methodologies. Kathleen Bailey offers an overview of three major approaches to empirical research in the foreign language field: experimental research, naturalistic inquiry, and action research. Important differences among them are the extent of control the researcher has over the variables, the a priori selection of variables and structuring of data, and the degree of intentional intervention by the researcher. The setting for empirical research can itself become an object of investigation, as happens with classroom-centered research. The collection and analysis of data (quantitative and qualitative) in terms of four major research traditions (the psychometric tradition, interaction analysis, discourse analysis, and the ethnographic tradition) are increasingly seen as variable according to the purpose empirical research serves. The result is a rich palette of research alternatives for getting at the phenomenon of instructed second language learning but also a greater demand to maintain principled ways of investigating and interpreting individual research results and to compare results across different kinds of studies.

Against that background the essays by Bill VanPatten, Catherine Doughty, Leo van Lier, and Gabriele Kasper offer four perspectives on second language learners. VanPatten emphasizes the universal aspects of second language acquisition, particularly the notion that a second language is strongly constrained and individuals do not simply create unique and idiosyncratic versions of it during acquisition. He discusses orders of acquisition, developmental stages, common processing errors, the absence of possible errors or possible stages of development, and the limited effects of explicit grammatical instruction. He then reviews proposals about the nature of the underlying processes and mechanisms that could explain those constraints in the process of language acquisition. Important perspectives are provided by Universal Grammar theory, by investigating the learners' processing capacity of available linguistic input in terms of competing resources, and by considering possible processing constraints for producing output, that is, the learners' second language speech.

For Doughty contemporary emphases on communicative language use and content-based language learning provide a fertile environment in which to investigate a number of dichotomies in language pedagogy. Although language is a system of linguistic forms and functions, all the research evidence indicates that mastery of a second language does not occur structure by structure but is a complex process involving interrelated systems that develop in nonlinear fashion. In contrast with the form-focused classrooms of the past, contemporary communicative classrooms offer the clear benefit of exposing learners to real language and motivating them with relevant content. But they cannot guarantee that learners will acquire targetlike language norms. Focusing only on meaning has implications for ultimate attainment of the formal features of a language, even after learners had the benefit of long periods of study. How to facilitate targetlike accuracy while not stifling fluency is currently a key research question, and answering it will further our understanding of the processes of instructed second language learning. The question is also of importance to adult collegiate classroom learners, many of whom wish to be able ultimately to use a second language in academic and professional settings.

Van Lier examines the prevalent assumption that social interaction plays a central role in learning processes. This approach makes the investigation of second language learning even more daunting. A purely linguistic focus, for all its acknowledged complexity, does not submerge the determinants of learning in the fluid dynamics of a real-time context; sociocultural theory does. As a consequence a major research tradition, considered scientific, is being called into question (see also Hall; Firth and Wagner). Causes and effects, generalizations, and predictions that were presumed to govern second language learning now turn out not to be statable with the kind of certainty that was previously assumed. More serious, they are less than useful for a contemporary understanding of learning, one that involves the social setting for learning as a complex adaptive system. Adopting the sociocognitive perspective of the Russian psychologist Lev Vygotsky, van Lier submits instructional discourse to a close analysis through the concepts of equality and symmetry in interaction. He makes the assumption that interaction, particularly interaction that is symmetrical and thereby naturally contingent, is beneficial for learning. But fostering more contingent interactions in the classroom is not enough. One must also ensure that learners have access to the more official aspects of the language, those mandated socioculturally and institutionally. That accessing typically occurs through expert-novice interactions. The goal is for learners to become autonomous language users by developing their own voice, which will be different for different occasions.

Kasper delineates the basic concepts of interlanguage pragmatics and shows how pragmatics and the study of language acquisition intersect. Here, too, communicative competence is located in a societal context that is understood as interactive since it is taken to contain the knowledge "as to when to speak, when not, and as to what to talk about with whom, what, where, and in what matter" and the ability "to accomplish a repertoire of speech acts, to take part in speech events, and to evaluate their accomplishment by others" (Hymes, qtd. by Kasper). According to Kasper, the challenge interlanguage pragmatics faces in its research theories and practices is to uphold the fundamental assumption of the situational and textual embeddedness of all linguistic action and the assumption of the interactiveness of linguistic action. Pragmatics must uphold these assumptions even though authentic discourse is rarely investigated directly, the findings of the field being based largely on elicited data.

The volume's remaining essays apply these insights to three areas: the role of technology in second language learning, the assessment of learning outcomes, and curriculum construction. Since assessment and curriculum in particular must carefully consider the institutional context of language learning, the closing contributions complete the conceptual circle of the volume, which began by situating foreign language learning in departments of foreign languages in American higher education.

Robert Blake's essay vividly demonstrates that incorporating technology into the foreign language classroom today bears little resemblance to the technically clumsy, methodologically unimaginative, physically restricted, and pedagogically ancillary uses of the equipment of yesterday. He gives an overview of the state of the art in computer-assisted language learning and discusses the use of multimedia materials, particularly in a microcomputing environment. Readers are likely to find his in-depth account of a few exemplars both convincing and inspiring.

The communicative revolution in language teaching has also affected testing. Only when one has defined what it means to know a language—and the redefinition of that is the essence of the communicative, sociocultural perspective on language—can one begin to prepare valid tests of language proficiency. Elana Shohamy's multiplism principle in assessment requires both a broader understanding of outcomes and new procedures for measuring those outcomes. It allows for "multiple purposes of language assessment, multiple definitions of language knowledge, multiple procedures for measuring that knowledge, multiple criteria for determining what good language is, and multiple ways of interpreting and reporting assessment results." The statement strongly signals the end of the era of "one size fits all" standardized testing in the instructional context. Shohamy expands the construct by suggesting multiple ways of designing test items and tasks, administering assessment, determining the quality of procedures, and interpreting, reporting, and using assessment results. But language assessment need not be restricted to language knowledge; it can include other aspects that affect language learning, such as learner attitudes toward various components of instruction.

The concluding topic is the potential impact of SLA research on the construction of curricula in collegiate foreign language departments. I frame my essay with the claim that recent SLA research has indeed produced a body of knowledge that can overcome the unproductive curricular division in those departments between language courses and content courses. I propose the concept of multiple literacies and offer an intellectual focus around which four crucial goals for foreign language departments can be achieved: (1) undergraduate program comprehensiveness and coherence, which thus far have eluded departments; (2) an intellectually sound answer to the question of whether foreign language instruction in the customary sense belongs in colleges at all; (3) an overarching curricular concept that can resist the increasingly powerful centrifugal forces departments experience when language becomes a mere tool for a host of disciplinary and professional interests across the academic spectrum; and (4) a bridging of the deep discontinuities between the diverse scholarly interests in departments.

I critically assess the current state and status of curricular thinking in the foreign language field and point out problems, particularly institutional impediments to any kind of curricular change. It would be delusional to think that the results of SLA research could be directly and magically translated into curricular practice without being severely tested by institutional realities. One can nonetheless express the wish that the stresses departments are experiencing will not engender despairing inaction but will lead eventually to facilitation. SLA research can now propose an intellectual focus for the multiple goals residing in foreign language departments that is compatible with proposals that have been proffered by colleagues in literature. May the linkage of language and literature be, as Alfred North Whitehead describes it, not only one of romance that explores heretofore unconsidered connections but also one that does not shy away from the precision needed for all colleagues in foreign language departments to engage in the desired, rigorously academic, and educationally sound reorientation of programs for the benefit of their students' humanistic education.

WORKS CITED

"ACTFL Proficiency Guidelines 1986." *Defining and Developing Proficiency: Guidelines, Implementations, and Concepts.* Ed. Heidi Byrnes and Michael Canale. Lincolnwood: Natl. Textbook, 1987. 15–24.

ACTFL Provisional Proficiency Guidelines. Hastings-on-Hudson: ACTFL, 1982.

Articulation and Achievement: Connecting Standards, Performance, and Assessment in Foreign Language. New York: College Board, 1996.

Beretta, Alan, ed. *Theory Construction in SLA.* Spec. issue of *Applied Linguistics* 14 (1993): 221–321.

Berman, Russell A. "Global Thinking, Local Teaching: Departments, Curricula, and Culture." *ADFL Bulletin* 26.1 (1994): 7–11.

———. "Reform and Continuity: Graduate Education toward a Foreign Cultural Literacy." *ADFL Bulletin* 27.3 (1996): 40–46.

Block, David. "Not So Fast: Some Thoughts on Theory Culling, Relativism, Accepted Findings, and the Heart and Soul of SLA." *Applied Linguistics* 17 (1996): 63–83.

Brumfit, Christopher. "Theoretical Practice: Applied Linguistics as Pure and Practical Science." Eleventh World Congress of Applied Linguistics (AILA 96). U of Jyväskylä, Finland. 8 Aug. 1996.

Byrnes, Heidi. "The Future of German in American Education." *Die Unterrichtspraxis* 29.2 (1996): 251–59.

———. "Governing Languages: Is Form Function?" Do We Know Where We Are Going? Patterns of Change in Departments of Foreign Languages. MLA Convention. Washington Hilton, Washington. 28 Dec. 1996.

Clarke, Mark A. "The Dysfunctions of the Theory/Practice Discourse." *TESOL Quarterly* 28 (1994): 9–26.

Davis, Kathryn A., and Anne Lazaraton, eds. *Qualitative Research in ESOL*. Spec. issue of *TESOL Quarterly* 29 (1995): 423–626.

Ferguson, Charles A. "Language Teaching and Theories of Language." *Language Teaching, Testing, and Technology: Lessons from the Past with a View toward the Future*. Ed. James E. Alatis. Georgetown Univ. Round Table 1989. Washington: Georgetown UP, 1989. 81–88.

Firth, Alan, and Johannes Wagner. "On Discourse, Communication, and (Some) Fundamental Concepts in SLA Research." *Modern Language Journal* 81 (1997): 285–300.

Hall, Joan Kelly. "A Consideration of SLA as a Theory of Practice: A Response to Firth and Wagner." *Modern Language Journal* 81 (1997): 301–06.

Hatch, Evelyn, Yasuhiro Shirai, and Cheryl Fantuzzi. "The Need for an Integrated Theory: Connecting Modules." *TESOL Quarterly* 24 (1990): 697–716.

James, Dorothy. "Re-shaping the 'College-Level' Curriculum: Problems and Possibilities." *Shaping the Future: Challenges and Opportunities*. Ed. Helen S. Lepke. Middlebury: Northeast Conf. Reports, 1989. 79–110.

———. "Teaching Language and Literature: Equal Opportunity in the Inner-City University." *ADFL Bulletin* 28.1 (1996): 24–28.

Kamil, Michael L. "Some Alternatives to Paradigm Wars in Literacy Research." *Journal of Reading Behavior* 27 (1995): 243–61.

Kasper, Gabriele, and Rüdiger Grotjahn, eds. *Methods in Second Language Research*. Spec. issue of *Studies in Second Language Acquisition* 13 (1991): 109–304.

Klein, Wolfgang. "A Theory of Language Acquisition Is Not So Easy." *Studies in Second Language Acquisition* 12 (1990): 219–31.

Kramsch, Claire. "Introduction: Making the Invisible Visible." Kramsch, *Redefining* ix–xxxiii.

———, ed. *Redefining the Boundaries of Language Study*. Boston: Heinle, 1995.

Kuhn, Thomas S. *The Structure of Scientific Revolutions*. 2nd ed. Chicago: U of Chicago P, 1970.

Kurth, Awino. "Reinventing a German Studies Department: The Stanford Chronicle." ACTFL-AATG Annual Conf. Philadelphia Convention Center, Philadelphia. 22 Nov. 1996.

Lantolf, James P., ed. *Sociocultural Theory and Second Language Learning*. Spec. issue of *Modern Language Journal* 78 (1994): 418–527.

Larsen-Freeman, Diane. "Chaos/Complexity Science and Second Language Acquisition." *Applied Linguistics* 18 (1997): 141–65.

Long, Michael. "The Least a Second Language Acquisition Theory Needs to Explain." *TESOL Quarterly* 24 (1990): 649–66.

Massy, William F., Andrea K. Wilger, and Carol Colbeck. "Overcoming 'Hollowed' Collegiality." *Change* July-Aug. 1994: 10–20.

"Meeting of the MLA Executive Council." *PMLA* 105 (1990): 940–46.

New London Group. "A Pedagogy of Muliliteracies: Designing Social Futures." *Harvard Educational Review* 66 (1996): 60–92.

Patrikis, Peter C. "The Foreign Language Problem: The Governance of Foreign Language Teaching and Learning." Kramsch, *Redefining* 293–335.

Peck, Jeffrey M. "Advanced Literary Study as Cultural Study: A Redefinition of the Discipline." *Profession 85.* New York: MLA, 1985. 49–54.

Pennycook, Alastair. "The Concept of Method, Interested Knowledge, and the Politics of Language Teaching." *TESOL Quarterly* 23 (1989): 589–618.

President's Commission on Foreign Language and International Studies. *Strength through Wisdom: A Critique of US Capability.* Washington: GPO, 1979.

Reddy, Michael J. "The Conduit Metaphor: A Case of Frame Conflict in Our Language about Language." *Metaphor and Thought.* Ed. Andrew Ortony. 2nd ed. Cambridge: Cambridge UP, 1993. 164–201.

"Results of the MLA's Fall 1995 Survey of Foreign Language Enrollments." *MLA Newsletter* 28.4 (1996): 1–2.

Roche, Jörg, and Thomas Salumets, eds. *Germanics under Construction: Intercultural and Interdisciplinary Prospects.* München: Iudicium, 1996.

Snow, Catherine E. "Understanding Social Interaction and Language Acquisition: Sentences Are Not Enough." *Interaction in Human Development.* Ed. M. Bornstein and Jerome Bruner. Hillsdale: Erlbaum, 1989. 83–103.

Spolsky, Bernard. "Introduction to a Colloquium: The Scope and Form of a Theory of Second Language Learning." *TESOL Quarterly* 24 (1990): 609–14.

Standards for Foreign Language Learning: Preparing for the Twenty-First Century. Yonkers: Natl. Standards in Foreign Lang. Educ. Project, 1996.

Swaffar, Janet. "Institutional Mission and Academic Disciplines: Rethinking Accountability." *Journal of Education* 45.1 (1996): 18–38.

———. "Using Foreign Languages to Learn: Rethinking the College Foreign Language Curriculum." *Reflecting on Proficiency from the Classroom Perspective.* Ed. June K. Phillips. Lincolnwood: Natl. Textbook, 1993. 55–86.

Valdés, Guadalupe. "The Teaching of Minority Languages as Academic Subjects: Pedagogical and Theoretical Challenges." *Modern Language Journal* 79 (1995): 299–328.

van Lier, Leo. "From Input to Affordance: Social-Interactive Learning from an Ecological Perspective." Eleventh World Congress of Applied Linguistics (AILA 96). U of Jyväskylä, Finland. 7 Aug. 1996.

Webber, Mark J. "The Metamorphosis of the Foreign Language Director; or, Waking Up to Theory." Kramsch, *Redefining* 3–38.

Welles, Elizabeth B., ed. *Articulation.* Spec. issue of the *ADFL Bulletin* 26.3 (1995): 1–66.

———. *Graduate Education and Undergraduate Teaching: Juncture and Disjuncture.* Spec. issue of the *ADFL Bulletin* 27.3 (1996): 1–77.

Whitehead, Alfred North. *The Aims of Education.* New York: Free, 1957.

Constructing Second Language Acquisition Research in Foreign Language Departments

Claire Kramsch

Current shifts in disciplinary boundaries in the humanities (Greenblatt and Gunn) and the emergence of second language acquisition as a legitimate subject of research are calling for a reappraisal of the traditional areas of scholarship in foreign language departments (Swaffar, Arens, and Byrnes; Kramsch "Foreign Languages" and "Introduction"). If language learning is a field of research in its own right, how does it relate to the scholarship in literary or cultural studies conducted in the same department? What is the relation of language learning research to the teaching of foreign languages in that department? Are the teaching of a foreign language and the teaching of a foreign literature related in any way? How should we envision the collaboration of language learning researchers, language teachers, literature scholars, and literature teachers in one department? Does the emergence of SLA research call for rethinking traditional departmental structures?

Before we can attempt to answer these questions, several dimensions of the academic context need to be constructed: the nature and role of the language curriculum in foreign language departments; the place of second language acquisition research in the present intellectual configuration of language, literary, and cultural studies; and the relation between SLA research and language program coordination.

The traditional curriculum of language instruction and literary and cultural studies in foreign language departments in the United States shows the general characteristics of the American college and university curriculum, of which Frederick Rudolph wrote:

> The curriculum has been an arena in which the dimensions of American culture have been measured, an environment for certifying an elite at one time and for facilitating mobility of an emerging middle class at another. It has been one of those places where we have told ourselves who we are. It is important territory.   (1)

The curriculum of foreign language departments bears the mark of this double historical mission. The first two years of language study are usually viewed as the language program per se, the delivery of the basic skills necessary for one to be a member of the middle class; everything beyond that, with the exception of advanced conversation and composition courses, is viewed as falling in the domain of literature or cultural studies broadly conceived, the domain of the intellectual elite. Whereas the first two years are usually designed for a general audience, the third and fourth are mostly, albeit not exclusively, designed for those concentrating or majoring in the language.

This distinction implies a fundamental dichotomy not only between language and literature but also between the teaching of linguistic proficiency and the teaching of ideational content. While the teaching of language has traditionally been viewed as a marginal activity, the remedial inculcation of skills, administered by graduate students or professionals for the general education of unspecialized undergraduates, the teaching of literature is viewed as serving the more specialized needs of society or as replenishing academic ranks through majors and, later, through graduate students (Brecht and Walton 140–41). The teaching of content has always carried more prestige in academia than the teaching of linguistic skill; ideas, not skills, are considered central to the intellectual mission of the university and consonant with a faculty member's scholarly work.

Thus, before we describe the various aspects of second language acquisition research, it is important for us to define its place vis-à-vis other, more established scholarly endeavors in foreign language and literature departments. Most SLA research takes place outside foreign language departments: in programs and departments of linguistics, applied linguistics, and English as a second or international language; in schools of education; or in interdepartmental MA and PhD programs. There are also multiple strands of research related to the way people acquire a foreign language, and not all those strands fall under SLA proper. Taking a language learning perspective on the entire foreign language enterprise cuts across traditional disciplinary boundaries. It may exact a toll from readers who are used to dealing with language pedagogy or with literary and cultural studies but not with psycho- and sociolinguistics, pragmatics, discourse analysis, social psychology, educational theory, and psychometric research. For example, a department chair in charge of appointing and promoting faculty members may have difficulty situating the field of a young language learning researcher: Does the candidate's research come under the rubric "linguistics," "applied linguistics," "foreign language methodology," or "foreign language education"? Where should the department chair recruit the referees? Who are the candidate's peers?

This book is about research in second language acquisition, but it is likely to be read by scholars from other fields who may have a way of talking about language learning that is quite different from that of second language acquisition researchers or applied linguists. SLA researchers in foreign language departments often have to reach out to audiences across multiple discourse boundaries—a much more difficult task than to seek recognition and legitimation in a traditional field of research, such as eighteenth-century French literature, which has its distinct disciplinary practices and gate-keeping criteria. Literature scholars, SLA researchers, and language teachers don't share the same discourse, because they don't occupy the same subject positions in the academic hierarchy. Indeed, there are forces at work to keep each group within its own discourse boundaries. If language teachers start using the discourse of SLA research, they may be reminded by the literature professoriat that their job is to teach conjugations and declensions, not to "foster the development of L2 interlanguage." And if literature scholars venture an opinion about language teaching, their opinion might be contested by second language acquisition researchers who adduce experimental data to support the pedagogic practices they advocate. That traditional discourses are currently being challenged places the debate about the disciplinary base of foreign language study in a new intellectual context.

In this essay, I adopt a sociocultural perspective on second language learning research, attempting to stay clear of both exclusively linguistic and exclusively literary forms of exposition.

THE STUDY OF LANGUAGE IN FOREIGN
LANGUAGE DEPARTMENTS

The traditional lines along which power and legitimation are distributed in the general discourse of academia are being put into question through four recent developments: the intrusion into academia of nonwritten forms of knowledge, the proliferation of alternative modes of knowledge delivery, the advances made in information-processing technologies, and the rise of the social sciences (see Kramsch, "Introduction"; Patrikis; Noblitt). These four areas of change challenge traditional academic discourse in its four distinct characteristics: literacy, schooling, interpretation, canonicity. The following discussion examines the nature of these challenges and how each affects current perceptions about language learning and teaching in foreign language departments.

Academic Literacy versus Vernacular Orality

The academic domain has traditionally been written, literate knowledge, which is viewed as superior to orally preserved and transmitted wisdom (see Havelock; Ong; Goody). We are all familiar with the effects this historical legacy of monastic scholarship has had on the learning and teaching of foreign languages. The text-based classical languages Latin and Greek were for a long time the only languages deemed worthy of academic study. "Living" foreign languages were accepted as legitimate academic subjects only much later, and those among them that had a respected literate tradition were considered more acceptable than those that did not. In France, for example, English, German, and Spanish are regularly taught in schools, but until the 1960s there was a definite preference among the educated elite for German over English—not because German was a more difficult language and therefore more meritorious to learn but because it was perceived as the language of thinkers and philosophers, whereas Anglo-Saxon culture was perceived to be more orally, that is, pragmatically, oriented.

Things have changed. The dominance of belles lettres is on the decline; the access to higher education of generations of students raised with television and video has given oral and visual modes of learning a new respectability (Kress; Schwerdtfeger). The spread of electronic media further contributes to breaking the monopoly of written texts as the source of knowledge (Noblitt). This progressive shift from a purely literate to an increasingly oral, visual, and electronic academic culture has worked in favor of foreign languages. It is now academically respectable to learn a foreign language not only to read and translate foreign texts but also to actually speak that language with native speakers in natural environments, and to communicate with them by satellite, e-mail, and World Wide Web technologies. However, by accepting orality and electronic communication as legitimate forms of knowledge, academia faces the difficult problems of responsibility for and control over unschooled knowledge.

Schooled versus Unschooled Forms of Knowledge

Academia has always been reluctant to give academic credit for knowledge that could as well be acquired on the street—for example, oral fluency in a foreign language. If, as Stephen Krashen maintains, oral fluency is a matter of unconscious acquisition whereas learning is the conscious internalization of rules and if no amount of learning by itself can ever lead to acquisition, where does schooling come in? If oral fluency is the goal, then schools must teach, *horribile dictu,* unschooled knowledge. But how can schools then guarantee the quality of their product? The acquisition-versus-learning dichotomy goes to the heart of academic legitimation. Hence the virulence of Krashen's critics in some sectors of the academy (Gregg; Barasch and James). The controversy echoes the debates that have characterized academic discourse since the time of Plato and Socrates.

This controversy takes on various forms in foreign language and literature departments, from the fear of a Berlitz takeover by proficiency-oriented language teachers to misgivings about the appropriateness of teaching "natural" communication in a schooled setting. In a 1982 review of a German communication-oriented textbook, Ruth Sanders expresses an opinion that is shared by many literacy-oriented scholars today:

> The authors reject the traditional academic view of foreign language teaching . . . and substitute a pragmatic goal for the learner: ability to use the language at work and in personal life.   (319)

> However . . . for better or worse, many Americans perceive [foreign language] speaking ability as peripheral to their lives. Unlike immigrants in West Germany, American students do not need to use German for communication. They are not simply "adult learners," but are also members of an academic community. For these students, the cognitive, humanistic, less immediately pragmatic values of [foreign language] learning may be more significant.   (321)

Reading is the skill most likely to develop critical thinking and sen-
sitivity to language as a tool of rhetoric and argument. If we slight
reading for an approach that catches students' interest through attractive visuals rather than with intellectual content, we may do
them a disservice. . . . What we should not do is to allow ourselves
to be captivated by a communicative ideology (or any other) until
we have measured it against our own educational goals. These, I believe, we ought to set as liberally as possible, especially in a time
when the appeal of vocationalism threatens the existence of general
education.   (322; see also Kramsch, "Commentary")

Such a statement illustrates well the challenge posed by demands for communicative competence and for the transmission of information in natural,
that is, unschooled, settings instead of in traditional forms of academic literacy and institutional responsibility.

Interpretation versus Information

The argument that "reading is the skill most likely to develop critical thinking" is academic, but the notion of skill itself is not of academic origin. Historically, the teaching of skills belongs in professional schools, not in
universities. Indeed, many would say that universities are supposed to help
students discover, through example and emulation, the universal truths by
which humankind may choose to live. Such discovery is a matter of analysis
and interpretation, not a transferable skill.

This view is, of course, no longer valid. What might have been true of
European universities — their academic exclusivity — never really applied to
American universities, who have always had the double role of providing for
the timeless reproduction of an educated elite and of giving students the
professional training necessary to enter the job market. Foreign languages,
at the intersection of the education of the mind and the education for the
workplace, bear the brunt of this contradictory mission. Currently, the pressures of the United States job market are giving foreign languages an immediate and universal purpose; they are putting new demands on the
orientation of upper-division curricula and undergraduate major programs.

But the perception of what skills are needed in the workplace is very
much influenced by the ever-growing encroachment, in all walks of life, of
an information-processing view of language and language use. This view,

which values the transmission, retrieval, and exchange of information, is not always compatible with the belief that what academia does best is critical analysis and interpretation.

Canonical Culture versus Everyday Culture

Whereas the traditional academic discourse of language study was linked to the literary and artistic canon of culture with a big *c*, the more recent discourse of language study has been permeated by "utilitarian" (Scollon and Scollon) or "commodified" (Fairclough, *Discourse*) ways of talking and thinking about knowledge that have changed both the form and the content of foreign language programs. Research into how speakers use language for everyday social transaction has had an important influence on the way applied linguists view the acquisition of a foreign language (see Kasper, this volume). The new discourse parallels the rise of the social sciences and the interest in the study of everyday practices (Goffman; Bourdieu; Certeau), including the practice of a foreign language. That such forms of culture with a little *c* clash with the more established, canonical "high culture" is nothing new. Three hundred years ago, Charles Perrault, the advocate of the moderns in the debate between the "ancients" and the "moderns," which ignited French intellectual circles at the end of the seventeen century, would have probably argued, unlike his colleagues Racine and Boileau, for the value of speaking a foreign language rather than just writing it, however clearly and elegantly.

In sum, four new developments in the production and transmission of knowledge have challenged traditional academic scholarship: oral forms of knowledge have challenged the exclusivity of text-based scholarship; unschooled knowledge has challenged the educational monopoly of schools; information-processing technologies have challenged the humanities' exclusive concern with critical thinking and interpretive abilities; real-life practices and everyday culture have challenged the literary and artistic canon as the only intellectually valid object of research.

The question seems to be, How can schools fulfill their educational mission if they have to transmit such forms of knowledge as how to order a cup of coffee in a French bistro, how to write a letter of complaint to a German landlord, how to get information from an Italian train schedule, or how to understand a Spanish fiesta? To state the question another way, What form must knowledge take to become the responsibility of schools? Clearly what is at stake is not the notion of real-life skills but, rather, the amount of reflection and critical thinking that one should apply to the use of those skills. Traditionally, forms of orality have been made academically acceptable by being reflected on, written about, and so on, by being textualized in some way. This textualization, a secondary orality of sorts, is the hallmark of schooled literacy.

It is in this context that we have to view the emergence of the new field of second language acquisition research and the role it has played in revitalizing language instruction and research in foreign language departments.

THE EMERGENCE OF SECOND LANGUAGE ACQUISITION RESEARCH

In the late 1960s, as the nature of academic scholarship was starting to change, language teachers and literature scholars responded differently to the challenges described above. Literary study left the domain of pure philology and broadened its literate interests to include real-life phenomena — actual readers and communities of readers, actual speech acts, and oral stories and discourses. It allied itself with critical theory and found common interests with such relevant disciplines as sociology, feminist studies, and psychoanalysis. Language study, in contrast, allied itself with linguistics. The call for a less exclusive focus on the grammar of written language and on the translation of written texts and for more relevance of language study to the practice of everyday life occurred at roughly the same time as linguists were turning their attention to phenomena of first language acquisition by children and second language acquisition by children and adults (see Kramsch, "Language Acquisition").

At that crucial junction, language pedagogy found its natural ally not in the field of literary and cultural theory but in the burgeoning field of applied linguistics, especially second language acquisition research, which was born around 1967, following the influential article by S. Pit Corder "The Significance of Learners' Errors." Language pedagogy found in SLA not only a research base that was more suited to its oral orientation and to the early levels of acquisition of most American students but also a methodological approach perceived as less elitist, because more exact, than the subjective forms of inquiry of literary interpretation. Thus language learning and teaching came into its own through association with a scientifically respectable and empirically testable field of research instead of with the traditional forms of literary scholarship.

Since its beginning, SLA research has been interested mostly in the acquisition of English as a second language by immigrants to Anglophone countries or by residents of former members of the British Commonwealth. The field of English as a second language was born in the wake of World War II, and the growing demand for English as an international language spawned a host of studies on the conditions of (mainly English) language learning and teaching. Because the demand for English was linked primarily to the job market, not to the reading of representative works of any high or low culture, SLA research was almost exclusively focused on the acquisition of the spoken language by children and adults, mostly in untutored host environments. Interest in the development of classroom second language acquisition in foreign environments and of second language literacy skills emerged only in the 1980s.

In the 1970s and 1980s SLA research dealt mostly with learners' acquisition of morphology and, to a lesser extent, of syntax and vocabulary. The research was heavily influenced by linguistics and psycholinguistics, both of which fields used predominantly quantitative methods not only to explain phenomena but also to predict them. Accordingly, results of SLA research were often used to predict the success of this or that teaching method or approach. In the 1980s in Germany, there was virulent controversy over who should have control of foreign language pedagogy: linguists working in the tradition of Universal Grammar, like Sascha Felix and Angela Hahn; psycholinguists with a more developmental orientation, like Jürgen Meisel and Manfred Pienemann; or psycholinguists and discourse analysts with a more educational bent, like Richard Bausch and Frank Königs (for a sense of the controversy, see Bausch and Königs, "(Er)Werben" and "Lernt"). Since then, SLA researchers have become more cautious in making direct links between SLA theory and language teaching practice (Lightbown; Kramsch "Politics"; Huebner this volume; Byrnes, this volume).

Interest in other approaches has grown. Psycholinguistics and SLA research proper have been broadened by their inclusion into the more general field of applied linguistics, which covers also sociolinguistics, language policy and planning, translation, discourse analysis, pragmatics, stylistics, comparative rhetoric, language testing, and other areas of language use (Huebner, this volume). Today applied linguistics has emerged as an interdisciplinary field of inquiry that brings together researchers and practitioners of language use at annual conferences such as those of the American Association of Applied Linguistics (AAAL), Teachers of English to Speakers of Other Languages (TESOL), the American Council for the Teaching of Foreign Languages (ACTFL), the American Educational Research Association (AERA), and specific language teaching associations like the American Association of Teachers of German (AATG) and the American Association of Teachers of French (AATF). The scholars and teachers meet according to whether their inclination is more theoretical or practical, more acquisition-generic or language specific, and according to how interdisciplinary their interests are. Researchers in applied linguistics and second language acquisition publish in such journals as *Applied Linguistics, Language Learning, Studies in Second Language Acquisition, Modern Language Journal, TESOL Quarterly, Language in Society, Canadian Modern Language Review,* and *Foreign Language Annals.* (For a larger list of relevant journals, see the section In Other Professional Journals in *Modern Language Journal.*)

What is the relation of SLA research, given its history, to scholarship in literary-cultural studies? While the field of English composition has become theoretically and pedagogically closer to literary-cultural studies, SLA research has not. The reasons, as I see them, are the following:

Until now, SLA research has studied mostly the conditions under which nonnative speakers first begin to speak a language. It deals therefore with a level of linguistic competence far below that needed to talk about sophisticated topics of a literary or cultural nature.

Second language reading research has focused on the development of beginning or low-intermediate readers and writers, whose ability to analyze and interpret foreign cultural texts is different from that of composition students who are native speakers of the language. And until now second language reading research has not been concerned with the development of second language textual competence of a literary kind.

Literary scholarship is valued for the richness of its textual interpretations, for its verbal eloquence, theoretical sophistication, and broad erudition. In contrast, SLA research, empirically based, is valued for the rigor of its methodology, the integrity of its data collection and interpretation, the soundness of its measurements, the well-foundedness of its claims. Each field has its own metalanguage: for example, literary-cultural theory talks about "voice," "subject positioning," the "boundaries between self and other"; second language acquisition theory talks about "individual differences," "route and rate of acquisition," "input, intake, and output," "strategies and procedures."

SLA research ultimately strives to enhance our understanding of a learning process, that is, the acquisition of knowledge through another language. But because this knowledge has been viewed until now purely in linguistic and psychological terms, as researchers focus on the individual language learner in a largely asocial and ahistorical way, there has been little common ground between the issues of relevance to SLA research and the poststructuralist, postmodern concerns of critical theory (but see Peirce; von Hoene; see also Kramsch, "Redrawing").

WHAT SLA AND LITERARY-CULTURAL STUDIES CAN GAIN FROM EACH OTHER

There is a growing mutual respect between second language acquisition research and literary-cultural studies scholarship, but it comes with a tinge of mistrust on both sides. Literary scholars know little about SLA research and often confuse it with foreign language pedagogy and methodology; SLA researchers know little about the diversity of approaches and interests among literary scholars and often don't see the relevance of literary or cultural theory to second language acquisition (Webber). However, as SLA enters the study of written competency; stresses the role of consciousness, reflection, and metalanguage in language acquisition; and takes learner social and cultural differences seriously, both literary criticism–cultural studies and SLA may move toward common theoretical interests. Similarly, as literary-cultural studies scholars turn their attention to pedagogy and the language classroom (Peck; Worth; Marks; Berman), the classroom is becoming a meeting place for SLA theory and literary-cultural theory.

A rapprochement is conceivable through a discourse-based language pedagogy that is currently being advocated by applied linguists in Great Britain (Carter and Simpson; Widdowson, *Practical Stylistics* and *Stylistics and the Teaching;* Fowler; Fairclough, *Language* and by feminist-literary-cultural studies scholars in the United States (von Hoene; Kramsch and von Hoene).

What SLA Research Can Gain from Literary-Cultural Studies

Until now, SLA research has cautiously limited itself to what it views as ex-perimentally and theoretically tenable, despite some isolated voices in the 1970s that called for more humanistic SLA research (e.g., Clarke; Ochsner). It has had to stake out a domain for itself that allows it to make scientific claims about how and under what conditions people learn languages. But the 1990s have witnessed a push to broaden this tradition. In the fall 1995 issue of the *TESOL Quarterly,* both Kathryn Davis and Anne Lazaraton advocate adding to the quantitative search for universal rules of linguistic behavior a greater role for qualitative research methods. They call for sociolinguistic and ethnographic types of inquiry, for analyses that include the participants' per-spective on the data rather than give only the researcher's interpretation. They encourage types of inquiry that attempt to uncover general patterns of language use across social contexts rather than seek to establish universal rules of interlanguage usage (Davis; Lazaraton).

The current inclusion of SLA research proper into the larger context of applied linguistics research is bringing about a better understanding of the relation of SLA to sociocultural theory (Lantolf), discourse theory (McCarthy; Hatch; Gee; Cook, *Discourse*), and stylistics and linguistic criticism (Fowler; Widdowson, *Practical Stylistics;* Cook, *Discourse and Literature;* Carter and Simpson). This better understanding should make it easier for literary stud-ies scholars and SLA researchers to talk to each other. The progressive incor-poration into language acquisition research of the processes of socialization and social identity formation that accompany the acquisition of another per-son's language (Peirce; van Lier, this volume) should enable cultural studies and feminist scholars to find common areas of interest with SLA researchers.

What Literary-Cultural Studies Can Gain from SLA Research

The study of a foreign literature has traditionally assumed that, once the lin-guistic hurdles have been overcome, there is really no difference between a native reader and a nonnative one, because literary reading skills are univer-sal. SLA research, with its focus on learner variability, can confirm psy-cholinguistically what is already suggested by feminist and sociocultural criticism: that every reading is socially situated and that there is no au-tonomous learner or reader of a foreign literary text (Kramsch and von Hoene, "Emergence" and "Re-thinking").

The classroom is becoming increasingly attractive as the locus of humanistic research. SLA classroom research can provide intriguing examples of "cultural fault lines" masquerading as grammatical or lexical errors (Kramsch, *Context*); these examples can support postmodern theories of cultural border crossings and the development of multiple social identities.

SLA research is initiating a return to the value of language in literature. After decades of separation between language studies and literary studies, SLA is focusing attention once again on the word itself and on language learning as the apprenticeship into a foreign culture (Byrnes, this volume). In particular, increasing SLA research on the acquisition of non-Western languages and literatures directs our attention to cultural traditions in which the split between orality and literacy is less pronounced than in the West.

The Applied Linguist Who Is
Also a Professional Language Teacher

Because in many foreign language departments the applied linguist or SLA researcher may also be teaching in the language program and may even be the language program director, in charge of the language curriculum and the training of teaching assistants, it is worth reflecting on the role of the researcher who is at the same time an educator. We have already noted that the majority of SLA researchers are not professional language teachers. The converse is also true: The majority of professional language teachers are not SLA researchers. Some are methodologists: they develop teaching materials and write textbooks based on SLA researchers' findings. Some are empirical or theoretical linguists: they work in the tradition of socio- or psycholinguistics, gathering data and subjecting them to quantitative or qualitative analyses, or they work on spoken or written texts and subject them to various kinds of discourse analysis. Whatever their research background, professional language teachers-researchers are in a particularly vulnerable position, because they are likely to be isolated on both sides of the foreign language department's language-literature divide. Therefore, language program coordinators seek intellectual sustenance in other, relevant fields on campus—education, psychology, linguistics, anthropology, the sociology of language. But it is vital for them not to lose sight of the unity of language and of the crucial role they can play in acting as intermediaries between the two halves of their department's curriculum. The irony is that foreign language and literature departments often wish to have, in their language program director, a person that graduate schools in this country have long ceased to produce. As one French literary scholar remarked recently, "What foreign language departments are looking for in the language program director is someone from another era, who was trained in philology and in literature, and is equally at home in language and in literary study. They are looking for the hinge (*la cheville ouvrière*) between the two halves of the department." If that is so, then foreign language departments should help their language program directors develop their scholarly potential in precisely that direction, by fostering in the literature faculty members an interest in second language acquisition and applied linguistics and by showing graduate students the links between language study and literary-cultural studies.

Constructing the place of second language acquisition research in foreign language departments has entailed reviewing the historical split between the teaching of language and the teaching of literature, examining the emergence of the specific field of second language acquisition research and its relation to scholarship in literary-cultural studies, and ultimately considering the role of the language teacher-researcher in the intellectual reward structure of foreign language departments. In view of the growing concerns about the nature and role of foreign language study in the United States today, the time may have come to circle the wagons around the only thing that makes foreign language and literature departments unique, namely, the language they study in all its forms — linguistic, literary, cultural (Berman). By seeking links between second language acquisition research and textual scholarship, we hope to find intellectual bridges between the two halves of our common foreign language ground — the language department, "cette patrie désunie en deuil de la langue" 'this divided homeland in mourning for language' (Coste 225; my trans.).

WORKS CITED

Barasch, Ronald M., and C. Vaughn James, eds. *Beyond the Monitor Model*. Boston: Heinle, 1994.

Bausch, Karl Richard, and Frank Königs. "(Er)Werben und (Er)Lernen. Eine Antwort auf zwei Antworten." *Die neueren Sprachen* 84 (1985): 218–33.

———. "'Lernt' oder 'erwirbt' man Fremdsprachen im Unterricht? Zum Verhältnis von Sprachlehrforschung und Zweitsprachenerwerbsforschung." *Die neueren Sprachen* 82 (1983): 308–36.

Berman, Russell. "Global Thinking, Local Teaching: Departments, Curricula, and Culture." *ADFL Bulletin* 26.1 (1994): 7–11.

Bourdieu, Pierre. *Outline of a Theory of Practice.* Cambridge: Cambridge UP, 1977.

Brecht, Richard D., and A. Ronald Walton. "The Future Shape of Language Learning in the New World of Global Communication: Consequences for Higher Education and Beyond." *Foreign Language Learning: The Journey of a Lifetime.* Ed. Richard Donato and Robert M. Terry. Lincolnwood: Natl. Textbook, 1995. 110–52.

Carter, Ronald, and Paul Simpson, eds. *Language, Discourse and Literature. An Introductory Reader in Discourse Stylistics.* Boston: Unwin, 1989.

Certeau, Michel de. *The Practice of Everyday Life.* Berkeley: U of California P, 1984.

Clarke, Mark A. "Second Language Acquisition as a Clash of Consciousness." *Language Learning* 26 (1976): 377–90.

Cook, Guy. *Discourse.* Oxford: Oxford UP, 1989.

———. *Discourse and Literature.* Oxford: Oxford UP, 1994.

Corder, S. Pit. "The Significance of Learners' Errors." *International Review of Applied Linguistics* 5 (1967): 161–69.

Coste, Daniel. "Analyse de discours et pragmatique de la parole dans quelques usages d'une didactique des langues." *Applied Linguistics* 1 (1980): 224–52.

Davis, Kathryn. "Qualitative Theory and Methods in Applied Linguistics Research." *TESOL Quarterly* 29 (1995): 427–54.

Fairclough, Norman. *Discourse and Social Change.* Cambridge: Polity, 1992.

———. *Language and Power.* London: Longman, 1989.

Fowler, Roger. *Linguistic Criticism.* Oxford: Oxford UP, 1986.

Gee, James. *Social Linguistics and Literacies: Ideology in Discourses.* London: Falmer, 1990.

Goffman, Erving. *The Presentation of Self in Everyday Life.* New York: Doubleday, 1959.

Goody, Jack. *The Interface between the Written and the Oral.* Cambridge: Cambridge UP, 1987.

Greenblatt, Stephen, and Giles Gunn, eds. *Redrawing the Boundaries: The Transformation of English and American Literary Studies.* New York: MLA, 1992.

Gregg, Kevin. "Krashen's Monitor and Occam's Razor." *Applied Linguistics* 5 (1984): 79–100.

Hatch, Evelyn. *Discourse and Language Education.* Cambridge: Cambridge UP, 1992.

Havelock, Eric. *Preface to Plato.* Cambridge: Harvard UP, 1963.

Kramsch, Claire. "Commentary to the Editor." *Die Unterrichtspraxis* 16.2 (1983): 313–14.

———. *Context and Culture in Language Teaching.* Oxford: Oxford UP, 1993.

———. "Foreign Languages for a Global Age." *ADFL Bulletin* 25.1 (1993): 5–12.

———. "Introduction: Making the Invisible Visible." *Redefining* ix–xxxiii.

———. "Language Acquisition and Language Learning." *Introduction to Scholarship in Modern Languages and Literatures.* Ed. Joseph Gibaldi. New York: MLA, 1992. 53–76.

———. "The Politics of Applied Linguistics." Plenary address delivered at the Annual Convention of the American Association of Applied Linguistics, Long Beach, CA, 1995.

———, ed. *Redefining the Boundaries of Language Study.* Boston: Heinle, 1995.

———. "Redrawing the Boundaries of Foreign Language Study." *Language and Content: Discipline- and Content-Based Approaches to Language Study.* Ed. Merle Krueger and Frank Ryan. Lexington: Heath, 1992. 203–17.

Kramsch, Claire, and Linda von Hoene. "The Dialogic Emergence of Difference: Feminist Explorations in Foreign Language Learning and Teaching." *Feminisms in the*

Academy. Ed. Domna Stanton and Abigail J. Stewart. Ann Arbor: U of Michigan P, 1995. 330–57.

——. "Re-thinking the Teaching and Learning of Foreign Languages through Feminist and Sociolinguistic Theory." *Cultural Performances: Proceedings of the Third Women in Language Conference.* Ed. Mary Bucholtz, A. C. Lian, Laurel Sutton, and Caitlin Hines. Berkeley: Berkeley Women and Lang. Group, 1995. 378–88.

Krashen, Stephen D. *Principles and Practice in Second Language Acquisition.* Oxford: Pergamon, 1982.

Kress, Gunther, ed. *Communication and Culture: An Introduction.* Kensington, Austral.: New South Wales UP, 1988.

Lantolf, James P., ed. *Sociocultural Theory and Second Language Learning.* Special issue of *Modern Language Journal* 78 (1994). 418–577.

Lazaraton, Anne. "Qualitative Research in Applied Linguistics: A Progress Report." *TESOL Quarterly* 29 (1995): 455–72.

Lightbown, Patsy. "Great Expectations: Second-Language Acquisition Research and Classroom Teaching." *Applied Linguistics* 6 (1985): 173–89.

Marks, Elaine. "Memory, Desire, and Pleasure in the Classroom: La Grande Mademoiselle." *MLA Newsletter* 25.4 (1993): 3.

McCarthy, Michael. *Discourse Analysis for Language Teachers.* Cambridge: Cambridge UP, 1991.

Noblitt, James S. "The Electronic Language Learning Environment." Kramsch, *Redefining* 261–90.

Ochsner, Robert. "A Poetics of Second-Language Acquisition." *Language Learning* 29 (1979): 53–80.

Ong, Walter. *Orality and Literacy.* New York: Methuen, 1982.

Patrikis, Peter C. "The Foreign Language Problem: The Governance of Foreign Language Teaching and Learning." Kramsch, *Redefining* 291–333.

Peck, Jeffrey M. "Toward a Cultural Hermeneutics of the 'Foreign' Language Classroom: Notes for a Critical and Political Pedagogy." *ADFL Bulletin* 23.3 (1992): 11–17.

Peirce, Bonny Norton. "Social Identity, Investment, and Language Learning." *TESOL Quarterly* 29 (1995): 9–31.

Rudolph, Frederick. *Curriculum: A History of the American Undergraduate Course of Study since 1636.* San Francisco: Jossey-Bass, 1977.

Sanders, Ruth H. Rev. of *Deutsch Aktiv* and *Übungstypologie zum kommunikativen Deutschunterricht,* by Neuner et al. *Die Unterrichtspraxis* 15.2 (1982): 318–22.

Schwerdtfeger, Ingeborg C. *Sehen und Verstehen: Arbeit mit Filmen im Unterricht Deutsch als Fremdsprache.* Berlin: Langenscheidt, 1989.

Scollon, Ron, and Suzanne Scollon. *Intercultural Communication: A Discourse Approach.* Oxford: Blackwell, 1995.

Swaffar, Janet, Katherine Arens, and Heidi Byrnes. *Reading for Meaning: An Integrated Approach to Language Learning.* Englewood Cliffs: Prentice, 1991.

von Hoene, Linda. "Subjects-in-Process: Revisioning TA Development through Psychoanalytic, Feminist, and Postcolonial Theory." Kramsch, *Redefining* 39–57.

Webber, Mark J. "The Metamorphosis of the Foreign Language Director: or, Waking Up to Theory." Kramsch, *Redefining* 3–38.

Widdowson, Henry G. *Practical Stylistics.* Oxford: Oxford UP, 1992.

——. *Stylistics and the Teaching of Literature.* London: Longman, 1975.

Worth, Fabienne. "Postmodern Pedagogy in the Multicultural Classroom: For Inappropriate Teachers and Imperfect Spectators." *Cultural Critique* 9.23 (1993): 5–32.

Sociohistorical Perspectives on Language Teaching in the Modern United States

Elizabeth B. Bernhardt

Historians maintain that there is no such thing as history; rather, there are versions of history reconstructed from different events, interpretations, and perspectives. Which events are chosen for emphasis, which are ignored, which get interpreted as positive or negative—and how one perceives their import—are all judgments of the historian, not facts for a time line. This essay on the development of language teaching in the United States is inevitably colored by the point at which I stand—the latest years of the twentieth century—and by my belief in the value of language study. More important, my essay is written with a concern for a profession that self-admittedly has never been in the mainstream of American education. Framed by this concern, it examines the social and historical factors (both internal and external to the profession) that have led to and then contributed to the marginalization of language teaching in the United States.

Claire Kramsch argues that language teaching is a dialectic process. I believe that the profession of language teaching in the United States has been in a dialectic with itself from the first. The profession holds opposing viewpoints about the content and mission of language teaching, which force the profession into circular patterns; the profession is haunted by questions of self-worth. Why does our professional literature, for example, fail to describe language teaching as an important element in the evolution of American education? Why does our profession see its history as a set of unrelated, bandwagon phenomena, when even the framers of the Constitution concerned themselves with issues of language? How is it that older as well as newer members of our profession are unfamiliar with the basic chronology of major landmarks in American language teaching and with related national policies and critical pieces of legislation? Further, why is audiolingualism, which stemmed from the Army Language Training Program, almost always portrayed in a negative light, even though much of what was written about the program at the time is indistinguishable from contemporary writings on communicative language teaching? How are we to understand the role of such professional organizations as the Modern Language Association or the role of the federal government in decisions regarding the infrastructure for language teaching? It is a bitter irony in our profession that *context* is an important word, and yet our own context seems to be foreign to us.

This essay is organized chronologically but should not be considered as adhering to a time line. An extensive and important chronology is currently available in chapter 6 of H. H. Stern's *Fundamental Concepts of Language Teaching*. That chapter sketches, in timetable format (i.e., date, brief comment), major events in language teaching in the English-speaking world. I take a different approach, focusing on language teaching events in terms of the wider social and historical context. I ask these questions: How has language teaching been conceived since the earliest days of the American common school? How has immigration legislation affected language teaching? What role have key military events such as the world wars played? Do world economic patterns influence language teaching? And what are the repercussions in the language teaching profession of the different versions of social justice and of schooling?

EARLY AMERICA, 1620–1800

Although in the late twentieth century there is undeniably social and economic repression, the principle on which the United States was established was freedom from repression. In their fascinating account of early America, Lorraine Pangle and Thomas Pangle remind us that the Founders were aware of the "problematic heritage" of a Europe signified by Christianity and hereditary nobility and how unsuited a landed gentry and a State-imposed religion were to a democratic system (11, 13, 14). David Simpson remarks that in the Founders' discussions of establishing the American republic, "the notable point is perhaps that the politicians were interested at all in the question of language; and they surely were" (41). Benjamin Franklin, Thomas Jefferson, John Adams, and Noah Webster all maintained public opinions about the role of language, that is, of English and other tongues ancient and modern, in the development of the new republic.

A tension about the role of modern languages is present even in the earliest writings that could be construed as American. In helping to establish a "distinctively American path in education" (Pangle and Pangle 75), Franklin called for the establishment of an academy that was a precursor to the notion of a secondary school. He commented that after completing the academy's curriculum, graduates would

> be fitted for learning any Business, Calling, or Profession, except such wherein Languages are required; and tho' unacquainted with any antient or foreign Tongue, they will be Masters of their own, which is of more immediate and general Use; and withal will have attain'd many other valuable Accomplishments; the Time usually spent in acquiring those Languages, often without Success, being here employ'd in laying such a Foundation of Knowledge and Ability, as, properly improv'd, may qualify them to pass thro' and execute several Offices of civil Life, with Advantage and Reputation to themselves and Country.   (108)

Franklin's words are indeed marked by a vision of language teaching and learning that can only be called wasting time for those who seek economic security. As Pangle and Pangle write, "Americans turned from the second-hand, ornamental or scholarly, study of classic texts to a reenactment—in a wholly new setting, and with a much-changed script—of a portion at least of the civic spirit those texts depicted. That spirit, the Americans insisted, was sufficiently available in translations and resumes" (89). Franklin's hostility toward languages other than English is also exemplified by his opposition to German schools in Pennsylvania. Joel Spring notes that Franklin was a proponent of Anglicization and further implies that a press owned by Franklin was responsible for anti-German propaganda.

Jefferson, in contrast, did not view language learning as time wasting; nor do his writings display any particular hostility toward ethnicity. In fact, as Pangle and Pangle show, Jefferson was much more conservative than Franklin on the matter of languages, believing in the preservation of Latin and Greek. Jefferson states:

> The learning of languages being chiefly a work of memory, it seems
> precisely fitted to the powers of this period [ages 8–16], which is
> long enough too for acquiring the most useful languages antient
> and modern. I do not pretend that language is science. It is only an
> instrument for the attainment of science. But that time is not lost
> which is employed in providing tools for future operation. (147–48)

Jefferson's education proposals of 1817 and 1818 included modern languages in the curriculum and a continuation of the learning of Greek and
Latin. The utilitarian implications of these proposals prefigure a twentieth-
century view of functionalism in language use.

Contemporaries of Franklin and Jefferson, among them Adams and
Webster, also devoted considerable attention to language. Webster held a
utilitarian notion of language study, and many of his educational writings
are strongly vocational, as are Franklin's and Jefferson's writings. He notes
that college study is for the "learned professions" and that "four years, with
the most assiduous application, are a short time to furnish the mind with
the necessary knowledge of the languages and of the several sciences. . . . It
may be worthy of consideration whether the period of academic life should
not be extended to six or seven years" (qtd. in Rudolph 56–57).

These views do not represent the major thrust of the Founders' attitude
toward language, which was the astute recognition of language's political
role in the new American republic of immigrants. During the Revolutionary
War, Adams called for the establishment of a language academy. In a 1780
letter to Congress, he contended:

> The honor of forming the first public institution for refining, cor-
> recting, improving, and ascertaining the English language, I hope is
> reserved for congress. . . . It will have a happy effect upon the union
> of the States to have a public standard for all persons in every part
> of the continent to appeal to, both for the signification and pro-
> nunciation of the language. The constitutions of all the States in
> the Union are so democratical that eloquence will become the in-
> strument for recommending men to their fellow citizens, and the
> principal means of advancement through the various ranks and of-
> fices of society.   (249–50)

Adams believed that a standardized language would help deliver citizens
from the ancient yoke of the system of landed gentry and would permit
advancement unhindered by linguistic prejudice. Further in his letter to

Congress, Adams articulates the desire to outdo England, England having failed to establish an English standard.

This theme is more forcefully articulated by Webster. In a 1789 paper, Webster writes:

> As an independent nation, our honor requires us to have a system of our own in language as well as government. Great Britain . . . should no longer be *our* standard. . . . It must be considered further, that the English is the common root or stock from which our national language will be derived. All others will gradually waste away — and within a century and a half, North America will be peopled with a hundred millions of men, *all speaking the same language.*   (20–21)

At the end of the paper Webster notes that all Americans, having won independence, need to "embrace any scheme that shall tend, in its future operation, to reconcile the people of America to each other" (36). For Webster that scheme was obviously a common language.

Adams's dream of an American language academy did not come true. Libertarianism among the people — a result of their escape from monarchism in its many forms in Europe — made Congress reject the idea of establishing a national language by fiat and resist the establishment of any "national sponsored cultural institutions" (Heath 11). In contrast, Webster's vision and prediction proved correct. His comments chillingly foretell the constructs and consequences of linguistic imperialism (Phillipson).

In the early United States, there was a dialectic between a utilitarian view of language study and the messianic establishment of American English as a manifest destiny. This opposition of forces provides a backdrop for the sociohistorical views of language held today. It is important that the question of language has always been tied to the question of nationhood. Although the language teaching profession may feel cursed by the legacy left by the Founders, surely it should appreciate the democratic principles on which they based their views of language. The profession should also remember that, when a nation was created that rejected the old ideas of class and religion, many people came to America to escape cultures that were oppressive socially and economically. These cultures were and still are representative of what the profession, in twentieth-century America, is trying to teach. The very essence of America therefore contradicts the concept and goals of the teaching of foreign language and culture.

EARLY MODERN AMERICA, 1800–1920

The "intellectual revolution . . . in the seventeenth and eighteenth centuries that changed the purposes of education and made possible a secular school system" (Spring 17) clearly set the stage for the American public school system. According to Spring, this revolution was marked by freedom of personal expression and the utilitarian idea that education could improve the human condition. How did the concepts of freedom and utilitarianism play out in the nineteenth and early twentieth centuries?

During the nineteenth century, the public school gained increasing prominence. There were enormous regional differences in public schools, with the "South lag[ging] behind the North" (17). The English Classical School in Boston was established in 1821—it was called the first public high school—and during the 1830s and 1840s a relatively well developed organization for the "common," or public, school evolved.

"By 1850," Daniel Tanner and Laurel Tanner write, "it was recognized in all northern states and some of the southern states that 'common schools,' that is, free schools for all children, not just for poor children, were necessary for the well-being of a society with universal manhood suffrage" (39).

Curricular offerings suggested for the common school included reading, writing, orthography, grammar, geography, history, elocution, composition, physiology, botany, mineralogy, geology, agriculture, vocal music, drawing, penmanship, and spelling. There is no mention of a language either "antient" or modern in any reports of early-nineteenth-century common school curricula. This absence reflects the utilitarian foundation of the common school, whose purpose was to educate citizens in a democracy, not prepare them for advanced study in the traditional European sense.

It is important to remember that a separate, religious track of schools did exist at the time. Although these schools were usually Irish Catholic, many were for immigrants from other linguistic backgrounds and used ethnic languages for instruction. That is to say, learners of languages other than English existed, but by and large such learning was not supported by the public system. In fact, when reformers in New York suggested in 1842 that parochial schools be supported by public funds, riots broke out. Similar riots occurred in Philadelphia (Spring 111).

Despite occasional reports of ethnic schools in the Midwest and of the use in those schools of German or Swedish as a language of instruction, the education literature from the post–Civil War period is virtually silent on the issue of foreign language, as it is on many other academic subjects. Tanner and Tanner provide an explanation: from the close of the Civil War until 1893, education was focused on social responsibility. They note, "There was no theoretical framework for curriculum development beyond the objectives of meeting student and societal needs and realizing the promise of democracy" (66).

The last decade of the nineteenth century was pivotal for American education in general and foreign language education in particular. In 1890 a commission called the Committee of Ten was created by the National Education Association to examine the secondary school curriculum. Its charge was to make recommendations for college entrance requirements. According to Edgar Wesley:

> The period preceding the appointment of the Committee of Ten [was] a period of war between the high schools and colleges. The opening battle had been won by the high schools; they refused to teach Greek even though the colleges demanded it as an admission requirement. Their refusal, however, was not based on any principle concerning the usefulness of knowledge. It was, rather, a matter of circumstances: Teachers of Greek were scarce and so were students who wanted to study Greek.   (70–75)

The committee made recommendations in nine areas: Latin, Greek, English, modern languages other than English, mathematics, the physical sciences, natural history, history, and geography. Perhaps most importantly, the committee argued that these nine areas were of equal value. In the curricular offerings proposed, the modern languages other than English were German and French, in a four-year sequence. German and French now seemed to have been put on a level with Latin, Greek, and mathematics. But in additional recommendations providing four versions of a high school curriculum acceptable for college admission, the committee characterized as "distinctly inferior" a program that emphasized modern languages and did not have Latin as a requirement (*National Education Report* 625–37).

There is no question that the Committee of Ten's recommendations regarding modern languages did much to advance the language teaching profession in the twentieth century. One cannot help wondering, however, how different the profession might have been if the committee had not stigmatized modern languages from the beginning.

In a broader societal context, another critical force was at work: the massive immigration of Europeans who were not speakers of English. This turn-of-the-century phenomenon signaled the change from an agrarian rural society to an industrial urban one. The immigration made necessary an array of social services and ultimately a welfare state; it laid the foundation for what was to become the United States' superpower status, and it provided the human capital necessary to enrich the few and create a middle class. Although the Founders had called for a single language to unify citizens, that call was a whimper compared with the cry for nationalism from politicians at the beginning of the twentieth century. These politicians, too, discussed the importance of language for national unity, but in a different spirit. Their word for unity was "Americanization."

John Higham says that "as an organized, articulate movement, Americanization did not receive its primary impetus from educators. The impulse came from two civic-minded groups who had little in common with one another except a felt need for closer social unity" (236). Higham attributes this impulse to the increased need for unity among peoples who were living in greater proximity in urban centers. The first civic-minded group that supported Americanization consisted of social workers, who, according to Higham, "faced the problem from a humane perspective" (236). The social workers wanted to provide the new immigrants with a feeling of home, to give them a sense of personal value (read: to show respect for their native language and culture) but also of personal empowerment (read: to provide them with access to the benefits of American society through a knowledge of English). Records of Hull House in Chicago, the best known of the settlement houses, demonstrate that instruction was given to recent immigrants both in their native language (e.g., Italian) and in English (Moore 43). Jane Addams, founder of Hull House, stressed throughout her memoirs the importance of language instruction for immigrants. She wrote: "Even a meager knowledge of English may mean an opportunity to work in a factory versus nonemployment. Or it may mean a question of life or death when a sharp command must be understood in order to avoid the danger of a descending crane" (*Twenty Years* 438). Immigrant services in New York City provided special night classes for immigrants. The thousands who were served in major metropolitan areas are a tribute to the commitment to furthering ethnic unity through a social service structure that emphasizes, in modern terms, additive bilingualism.

The second civic-minded group advocating Americanization consisted principally of the "patriotic hereditary societies" (Higham 236). These societies, such as the Daughters of the American Revolution and the Society of Colonial Dames, fed the fire of Americanization not from the motive of reform but from "nationalist anxieties" about disunity and foreign radicalism (236). They spent considerable personal and monetary resources to provide civics classes that would turn immigrants into Americans. School boards, the YMCA, the United States Chamber of Commerce, and the (eventual) Ford Motor Company all participated in and contributed to Americanization efforts to school new immigrants in the American language and culture. Businesses considered that their Americanization efforts paid off in industrial productivity and worker attitude. Higham gives the anecdote that the first ESL dialogue line in Henry Ford's English School was "I am a good American" (248).

One of the fiercest proponents of Americanization was Theodore Roosevelt, who declared:

> We must have but one flag. We must also have but one language.
> . . . We cannot tolerate any attempt to oppose or supplant the language and culture that has come down to us from the builders of the Republic with the language and culture of any European culture. . . . Whatever may have been our judgment in normal times, we are convinced that today our most dangerous foe is the foreign-language press.   (129, 130, 131)

With victory in World War I and the economic depression that followed, the fervor and the resources spent on Americanization efforts declined. In fact, what resources remained were frequently directed at keeping immigrants out instead of remaking them when they arrived. Perhaps the most stunning manifestation of this new direction was the 1921 Quota Act, which seriously restricted immigration, particularly from southern Europe and Russia. Addams likened the Quota Act to the cruelty of the Spanish expulsion of the Moors and Jews in the sixteenth century (*Second Twenty Years* 264).

MIDDLE MODERN AMERICA, 1920–58

The middle modern period began and ended in the same way—with victory for the United States over foreign foes. It is interesting that the country's isolationism at the beginning of this period, a response to foreignness often characterized as "fanaticism" (Coleman and Fife vi), left the United States with a vulnerability that had to be overcome quickly for both World War II and the cold war. Two key influences on foreign language teaching in the middle modern period are the Coleman Report and the Army Specialists' Training Program (ASTP).

A person attending a meeting in the profession might reflect on the hundred years of meetings that came before and hundreds of people who sat at those meetings. All committee members are products of their sociohistorical time. So it must have been with the members of the committee on modern foreign languages supported by the National Education Association and chaired by Algernon Coleman. One wonders if they were influenced by nationalism, Americanization, and the idea of rejecting immigrants or if they were social reformers who saw schooling as pulling people up by their bootstraps. We can only speculate about the social attitudes held by the twelve men, most of them professors from private institutions such as Yale University and the University of Chicago, who sat on Coleman's committee. What is not speculation but fact was the decision of the committee, by an overwhelming majority, that foreign language instruction in American schools should be for reading only.

Coleman's book-length report of 1929 discusses the findings of the Committee of Ten and then gives a list of suggested modifications for the foreign language curriculum (I have abbreviated the following quotation):

1. Reduce considerably the amount of time devoted to oral work.
2. Require considerably more reading outside the classroom.
3. Adopt an extensive reading course.
4. Exclude from modern language classes all but superior students.
5. Demand a three-year period [of instruction].

Coleman concludes with a set of recommendations for assessing whether the students "have attained the ability to read the foreign language in a manner approximating reading ability in the mother tongue" (Coleman and Fife 167).

Stern believes that the Coleman Report is the "*bête noire* of American language teaching" (101). It is indeed difficult not to view it negatively. But the report has a positive side. In contemporary and honest language it comments on teacher oral proficiency and on the importance of cultural knowledge, takes up the issue of length of study, and in an appendix offers a complete research agenda that reveals dilemmas and concerns still with us at the end of the twentieth century—about assessment, high school–college articulation, authentic materials, and placement.

One can imagine what it was like to teach in the years after the stock market crash. In the Great Depression, teachers must have been struck by the luxury of schooling, when so many of their pupils left because their families needed them or moved in search of work. Was a college education a reality for even the superior student? What purpose did the reading of French or German serve in a community that could not feed its members? It is little wonder that the stigma of elitism is still with the foreign language profession today.

The reading legacy left by Coleman virtually ensured monolingualism for a few generations. In times of peace and isolation, monolingualism is unproblematic. But within ten years of the declaration that the purpose of language teaching was reading, the United States found itself in a critical deficit that had to be remedied essentially overnight. Hence the Army Specialists' Training Program was established.

Paul Angiolillo provides an excellent account of the ASTP. Using words like "disaster" and "failure" to describe American language instruction at that time, Angiolillo explains why the armed forces had to become involved in it. He cites reports from the armed forces that expressed the need for soldiers to work in spoken languages and writes, "Schools and colleges failed to teach much of anything in foreign languages but particularly neglected the oral phase of language learning. . . . Among the few [people] who qualified immediately for language work in the armed services [were not the] school and college majors in German or French or even the teachers of languages" (13–14). Angiolillo further notes that the army's intention went beyond the romance of training spies and undercover agents. The objectives were to improve communication with allies and with the enemy (such as prisoners) and simply to make common soldiers feel more confident in foreign situations.

Clearly, the army rejected the traditional notion of American language teaching based on the reading method. It asked for the help of noted linguists, who developed a program using the idea of intensive practice; ten hours a day, six days a week. The principal sources for both the theory and practice of the intensive program were Leonard Bloomfield's *Outline Guide for the Practical Study of Foreign Languages* and Bernard Bloch and George Trager's *Outline of Linguistic Analysis*.

A late-twentieth-century look at Bloomfield and at Bloch and Trager tempts one to say that they advocated mindless, behavioristic structuralism. But each approach is a carefully documented structural conceptualization of language. Admittedly, there are statements, particularly in Bloomfield, that modern second language research has rejected. It is important to keep in mind, however, that these two books were used as guides only and by no means constituted the curriculum of the Army Specialists' Training Program. The curriculum, in fact, at least as reported by Angiolillo, was quite modern: there was a substantial emphasis on area studies (47, 139), a dedication to the practice of language in real-life situations through role playing (91), the use of authentic reading materials to provide the basis for conversation (106), and a concentration on the cultural knowledge and patterns external-ized through language (230). One could argue that the ASTP foreshadowed the modern notions of form-focused and meaning-focused instruction.

Coleman and Robert Fife note that the 1942 initiation of the ASTP in languages was a milestone. They write, "The immense interest in the mili-tary experiments in the foreign-language field, belated and incomplete as it was, had an effect, not only on the teaching profession, but on all circles of the public. For the first time the American people became really foreign-language conscious" (vii). As bibliographers, Coleman and Fife contend that there was an enormous increase in the number of articles and monographs written on the subject of language teaching and that these appeared in the popular press as well as in academic journals. But they continue on a slightly sour note:

> From this outburst, which put foreign languages on the front page, the professional teachers stood somewhat apart. They welcomed the opportunity to play a leading role in the patriotic task of inten-sive instruction and the belated recognition of the vital importance of their work for the national cause. As a whole, however, they were not inclined to share the extravagant predictions of expansion of foreign language study in postwar years, realizing that peace-time conditions would bring back the old problem of curricular jamming.   (vii)

The middle modern period began with the Coleman Report and ended with the Army Specialists' Training Program—no more concrete example exists of the language teaching dialectic, no better demonstration of Stern's characterization of language teaching history as a series of "claims and counterclaims" (30). This thirty-year period foreshadowed the language teaching schizophrenia with which the profession ends the century: the tension between the traditional, humanities-based, reading-oriented study of belles lettres and views advocating functionality and oral proficiency; the paradoxical image of language as part of the humanities but simultaneously in the service of government and the military; the social problematic of maintaining and valuing a cultural identity while encouraging people to assume another; and the economics of promising in a short term what can be delivered only in the long term.

LATE MODERN AMERICA, 1958–97

Generally speaking, the period of 1958 to 1997 is characterized by the linguistic and learning theories that have dominated it. Hardly any account of modern language teaching fails to include a discussion of behaviorism; of its supposed language teaching outgrowth, audiolingualism; of the cognitive reactions to behaviorism and of cognitive code, which is the version of language teaching based on cognitive reactions, of the academic acceptance of such hyphenated linguistics as sociolinguistics and psycholinguistics; of the development of the field of second language acquisition; and, finally, of communicative or, to use the American term, proficiency-oriented teaching approaches. Such discussion often includes condescending references to the rapid growth and decline of language laboratory use, disparaging remarks about the large-scale method comparison in the Pennsylvania Project, self-conscious mentions of the eclectic approach to teaching methodology, and allusions to the development of different course designs for different student populations.

In this period, a different set of key sociohistorical phenomena influenced the development of language teaching: the cold war, worldwide emigration for political and economic reasons, and the decline of the American economy. The specific language teaching links to these phenomena are the centers and programs in language teaching sponsored by the National Defense Education Act; the growth of TESOL and of political movements such as English Only, US English, and English Plus; and, finally, the President's Commission on Foreign Language and International Studies appointed by

President Jimmy Carter in 1979 as well as the federal push for enhanced standards demanded by President George Bush and developed by President Bill Clinton in America 2000.

In September 1958 Dwight Eisenhower signed the National Defense Education Act. That legislation devoted substantial federal dollars to the improvement not only of mathematics and science instruction but also of foreign language learning. A superficial explanation for the NDEA was the Soviet launching of Sputnik, an event that supposedly terrorized the American populace with the threat of worldwide communism. But Joseph Axelrod and Donald Bigelow provide a different perspective: "Although Sputnik was thought to be immediately responsible for the passage of the law, legislation of this kind was discussed in government circles before Sputnik blasted off, and the law represented the combined result of many influences at work, among them the Modern Language Association" (*Inventory* 7).

Axelrod and Bigelow cite an official of the United States Office of Education who declared, "It is no exaggeration to say that without the MLA there might never have been an NDEA" (7). Referring to a six-year Rockefeller-funded project of the MLA that ended in 1958, they state that it provided the intellectual leadership for including foreign languages in the national defense commitment. They also believe that the "reading aim" established in 1929 was the primary force against which language teaching in the United States had to react during World War II and against which it had to continue reacting during the cold war (4). Whatever brought the NDEA into being, and surely there were several causes, the NDEA provided monies for study abroad, supported language and area centers in less commonly taught languages, and financed the teacher training and graduate programs of many prominent language teaching professionals whose influence will be carried into the twenty-first century. In some sense, NDEA monies, financing the profession of language teaching, contributed to the language-literature split.

The mention of the Modern Language Association in connection with the NDEA is fascinating when one considers the perception of the MLA in the last few decades of the twentieth century. The MLA is frequently criticized for being interested only in literature, not in language teaching. Who has not heard the quip that MLA means Modern Literature Association, not Modern Language Association? Yet historical records about the NDEA legislation show the concern that the MLA has had for language teaching and teachers. Axelrod and Bigelow note:

> The influence of the Foreign Language Program of the MLA on language training . . . is complex and crucial. No other professional group has played so important a role. The condition which the MLA was seeking to improve—a condition which beset all foreign language teaching in this country—was grave. . . . The Modern Language Association was doubling its efforts in combating the woeful inadequacy of the conditions and methods of language instruction in the United States.   (11–12)

The commitment to language teaching that the MLA had in the late 1950s and early 1960s is best demonstrated by the seed money and support that the MLA gave to the establishing of a separate teacher-oriented organization, the American Council on the Teaching of Foreign Languages (ACTFL). If history could not speak, one might conclude that the MLA was (and is) uninterested in foreign languages. What actually happened is that the MLA was so interested that it divested itself of language teaching concerns by supporting the creation of a separate group of language teachers. The inaugural issue of *Foreign Language Annals* reports both the procedural and the financial support offered by the MLA toward the establishing of ACTFL in 1968.

The role and power of language teaching and learning in the 1970s paralleled those in the 1920s in a number of ways. In the 1920s, the social welfare system responded to massive immigration with the creation of language teaching resources; the political system responded with programs for Americanization. The 1970s were also influenced by massive emigration, globally and nationally. Globally, guest workers (Gastarbeiter) sought homes in lands where they needed to learn a new language. This movement, principally into northern Europe, produced educational responses, for example, the unit-credit module system enacted by the Council of Europe (Trim). In the wake of the Vietnam War, the United States experienced the pressure of enormous numbers of refugees from Southeast Asia, and that pressure led to a massive marshaling of resources for English language teaching.

These sociohistorical events forced the United States once more into a linguistic dialectic: social service agencies advocated increased resources for immigrant groups, especially language services in both the heritage languages and English; political groups on the right, crying out against the potential harm to the nation of linguistic diversity, created action groups like English Only. But the left, too, worked to the detriment of other-than-English language teaching: the agencies pushing for more resources for immigrants frequently found themselves arguing against the foreign language resources in order to receive more funding. As the division between foreign and second language learning increased, the purpose for teaching a foreign language diverging more from the purpose of teaching a second language, second language learning gained prominence and foreign language learning received even less attention and was decried for its elitism. Meanwhile, those agencies opposed to linguistic diversity fomented intolerance toward languages other than English, creating an environment for language teaching and learning more hostile than ever before in the United States.

During World War II, the crisis had been military; in the 1970s, it was economic. In both cases, language teaching suddenly had a role to play. Thirty-five years after the establishing of the Army Specialists' Training Program, President Jimmy Carter marshaled federal resources to begin again to solve the language problem in the United States. The solutions came from the report of the President's Commission on Foreign Language and International Studies, *Strength through Wisdom*.

The report is quite clear about which language skills are vital to national needs: functional, oral ones. In powerful parallel to the federal government's stated objectives during World War II, the report considers that the purpose of language study is to acquire language in use, not some abstract knowledge that does not relate to what one can *do* with it. There is little wonder that language teaching organizations, especially ACTFL, gladly embraced the federal government's infrastructure for language teaching. That framework, based on the Foreign Service Institute's Oral Proficiency Interview, probably did as much to change the course of language teaching in the United States as the NDEA monies did thirty years before. The framework provided an alternative conceptualization for language programs across the nation. But by rejecting the reading aim in the same manner as the ASTP had, it also contributed to the rift between language teaching and literature teaching.

After weathering many opposing forces across the century, the profession faces its final challenge of the decade: standards. Encouraged as federal policy by Presidents Bush and Clinton, standards are seen as the solution for both educational and equity problems. The logic is that if everyone knows what should take place on both sides of the desk, then learning will improve. Whether the creation of standards for both teachers and students will lead to better learning is the open question for all content areas in the twenty-first century.

This discussion of the recent past and present was written with trepidation and risk—trepidation, because with modern history there are many people alive who have a version of "what really happened"; risk, because no interpretation of "what really happened" will be received with gladness. We can smugly criticize Coleman and his committee and not have to worry about offending them; the same cannot be said of the participants in more recent events. And the more recent the picture, the more it will be colored by political perceptions. Did Coleman and his committee think they were writing just one more report that would get filed and collect dust, or did they suspect that their work would live on after them? Did the people on the president's commission in 1979 realize the impact their report would have on the future of language teaching? Do we in 1998 know whether teacher and student standards, recommended by Goals 2000, will become just another report or indeed set the pace for language teaching in the twenty-first century? Only future scholars can answer this question.

It is not uncommon at language teaching conferences or other professional meetings to hear members of the profession lament the sorry state of education in America and, specifically, to decry the American lack of sophistication about other peoples and cultures. Heard with these lamentations are references, overt or covert, to the superior language learning and general educational experiences of Europeans. Whenever I hear such a conversation, the song from *My Fair Lady* resounds in my ears, paraphrased: "Why can't an American be more like a European?" And I answer, in my thoughts, Americans are not Europeans; they carry with them a two-hundred-year history of specific egalitarian attitudes toward education in general and language in particular. They come from a country that for all its flaws has accepted and, if not welcomed, at least tolerated the culturally different. The United States has compelled foreigners to assimilate linguistically, but there are many countries that have compelled a more total assimilation.

Historically, Americans have been born into a linguistic schizophrenia, for which I have attempted to provide some explanations. Clearly, a more complete history of the profession is necessary. Other academic areas, such as science and mathematics, are also products of the social and historical forces around them. But they, unlike language learning, would never be considered marginal in a curriculum—they are at the core. Our profession must engage in a powerful discussion of who we are and whether we should accept a position at the periphery of education. But such a discussion demands that we thoroughly explore and understand the context in which we find ourselves.

WORKS CITED

Adams, John. *The Works of John Adams.* Vol. 7. Boston: Little, 1852.

Addams, Jane. *The Second Twenty Years at Hull-House, September 1909 to September 1929, with a Record of a Growing World Consciousness.* New York: Macmillan, 1930.

———. *Twenty Years at Hull-House, with Autobiographical Notes.* New York: Macmillan, 1910.

Angiolillo, Paul F. *Armed Forces' Foreign Language Teaching: Critical Evaluation and Implications.* New York: Vanni, 1947.

Axelrod, Joseph, and Donald N. Bigelow. *Inventory of NDEA Title VI Language and Area Centers: Final Technical Report.* Washington: Amer. Council on Educ., 1961.

———. *Resources for Language and Area Studies.* Washington: Amer. Council on Educ., 1962.

Bloch, Bernard, and George L. Trager. *Outline of Linguistic Analysis.* Baltimore: Linguistic Soc. of Amer.; Waverly, 1942.

Bloomfield, Leonard. *Outline Guide for the Practical Study of Foreign Languages.* Baltimore: Linguistic Soc. of Amer., 1942.

———. *The Teaching of Modern Foreign Languages in the United States.* New York: Macmillan, 1929.

Coleman, Algernon, and Robert Herndon Fife. *An Analytical Bibliography of Modern Language Teaching, 1937–1942.* New York: King's Crown, 1949.

Franklin, Benjamin. *The Papers of Benjamin Franklin.* Vol. 4. Ed. Leonard W. Labaree. New Haven: Yale UP, 1961.

Heath, Shirley Brice. "A National Language Academy? Debate in the New Nation." *International Journal of the Sociology of Language* 11.1 (1976): 9–43.

Higham, John. *Strangers in the Land: Patterns of American Nativism, 1860–1925.* New Brunswick: Rutgers UP, 1988.

Jefferson, Thomas. *Notes on the State of Virginia.* Chapel Hill: U of North Carolina P, 1955.

Kramsch, Claire. *Context and Culture in Language Teaching.* Oxford: Oxford UP, 1993.

Moore, Dorothea. "A Day at Hull-House." *One Hundred Years at Hull-House.* Ed. Mary Lynn McCree Bryan and Allen F. Davis. Bloomington: Indiana UP, 1990. 42–49.

National Education Report of the Committee of Ten on Secondary School Studies. New York: Amer. Book, 1894.

Pangle, Lorraine Smith, and Thomas L. Pangle. *The Learning of Liberty: The Educational Ideas of American Founders.* Lawrence: U of Kansas P, 1993.

Phillipson, Robert. *Linguistic Imperialism.* Oxford: Oxford UP, 1992.

President's Commission on Foreign Language and International Studies. *Strength through Wisdom: A Critique of US Capability.* Washington: GPO, 1979.

Roosevelt, Theodore. "Children of the Crucible." *Annals of America.* Vol. 14. Chicago: Encyclopaedia Britannica, 1968. 129–31.

Rudolph, Frederick, ed. *Essays on Education in the Early Republic.* Cambridge: Belknap–Harvard UP, 1965.

Simpson, David. *The Politics of American English, 1776–1850.* New York: Oxford UP, 1986.

Spring, Joel. *The American School, 1642–1990.* New York: Longman, 1990.

Stern, H. H. *Fundamental Concepts of Language Teaching.* Oxford: Oxford UP, 1983.

Tanner, Daniel, and Laurel Tanner. *History of the School Curriculum.* New York: Macmillan, 1990.

Trim, J. L. M. *Some Possible Lines of Development of an Overall Structure for a European Unit/Credit Scheme for Foreign Language Learning by Adults.* Strasbourg: Council of Europe, 1978.

Webster, Noah. *Dissertations on the English Language.* Boston: Thomas, 1789.

Wesley, Edgar Bruce. *NEA: The First Hundred Years: The Building of the Teaching Profession.* New York: Harper, 1957.

Linguistics, Applied Linguistics, and Second Language Acquisition Theories

Thom Huebner

FOREIGN LANGUAGE EDUCATION AND THE (APPLIED) LINGUIST

Traditionally, in foreign language departments at American universities, especially in departments of the more commonly taught languages (e.g., Spanish, French, German), linguistics has had a relatively circumscribed role. Among colleagues who have developed their scholarly expertise in areas of literature, the resident linguist has been expected to provide scholarship on the structure and history of the language or languages of the department.

The applied linguist in foreign language departments has been an even rarer entity. Although important work in applied linguistics, both on learning and teaching theory and on the development of instructional materials and methodologies, has come from scholars in foreign language departments, most often the teaching of the foreign language itself (as opposed to literature) is relegated to graduate students, lecturers, or those faculty members lacking the seniority to teach their specializations.

This essay explores the relation between linguistic theories and empirical research in second language acquisition, particularly as those theories and research findings pertain to foreign language departments. While the research reviewed here may not directly impinge on issues of curriculum and materials design, classroom methods and procedures, and models of assessment, it is relevant to the foreign language department in that "sound pedagogical practice must be anchored in in-depth knowledge of the capabilities of second language learners and the processes and strategies that they need for language learning to take place" (Gass and Schachter 3). The intersection of linguistic theories and theories of second language acquisition can also shed light on the very nature of a language, its use and history, how it is acquired as a first language, and its relation both to other cognitive processes and to its social context. All these areas are central to an understanding of the subject matter of foreign language departments.

THEORIES AND THEIR APPLICATIONS

The construction of theories of language and the construction of theories of second language acquisition are clearly not the same kinds of activities. Furthermore, they are both quite different from the teaching of foreign languages. Each has its own set of assumptions, goals, and methods. But because each assumes a "notion of 'a language' as a total system of some sort, a set of knowledges and skills shared by a social group and acquired by the individuals in it" (Ferguson, "Language Teaching" 81), one can look for areas relevant to all three enterprises.

Application of theory entails the use of a theoretical construct for the solution of a problem. With language, the problem may be of a very practical, how-to nature. How, for example, can one structure a classroom activity to maximize learning? But the utilization of the findings that emerge from theory building in one field may be required to solve problems that arise in the construction of theory in another field. How, for example, can the acquisition of second languages be described, explained, and predicted in a systematic manner?

I now examine some goals of theories of language, explore meanings that have been associated with the term *applied linguistics,* and briefly outline important developments in second language acquisition research. Then I focus on a few of the areas of overlap between the construction of theories in linguistics and second language acquisition, with possible implications for foreign language teaching.

Linguistic Theory and Theories

In the narrowest sense, the term *linguistic theory* is often used in contemporary linguistics to refer to a number of models of formal syntax and to a lesser degree models of phonology, morphology, and semantics. The overriding goal of many such models is to characterize in a formal way the properties of grammar that are true of all languages.

Some models eschew any claims of pertinence for language acquisition:

> We make no claims . . . that our grammatical theory is *eo ipso* a psychological theory. . . . Our general theory is not a theory of how a child abstracts from the surrounding hubbub of linguistic and non-linguistic noises enough evidence to gain a mental grasp of the structure of a natural language. Nor is it a biological theory of the structure of an as-yet-unidentified mental organ.
>
> (Gazdar, Klein, Pullum, and Sag 5)

Nevertheless, to the extent that these models are useful or necessary for an understanding of the structure of, for example, French or German or Japanese, there is a place for them in the foreign language department. For other models, however, the connection between linguistic theory and first language acquisition is of central concern: "In a highly idealized picture of language acquisition, universal grammar is taken to be a characteristic of the child's pre-linguistic state" (Chomsky, *Lectures* 7). While no model, to my knowledge, makes any specific claims about second language acquisition, any theoretical claims about first language acquisition deserve examination from the perspective of SLA theory.

In the plural, the term *linguistic theories* is used to refer to any number of theories, formal and functional, about language at all levels of organization (phonological, morphological, semantic, discourse-pragmatic, as well as syntactic) and from a variety of perspectives (synchronic, diachronic, sociolinguistic, psycholinguistic, etc.). In this sense, the goal of linguistic theories is to search not only for a universal grammar but also for principles underlying the ways language is conventionalized in particular speech communities and for the factors that contribute to individual differences in language acquisition and use.

When one looks for relations between theories of language and theories of second language acquisition, particularly when one considers how developments in theories of language might be brought to bear on problems of language pedagogy, a more inclusive use of the term *linguistic theory* obviously provides a richer vein to mine.

Applied Linguistics

The term *applied linguistics* is generally used to refer to "the application of linguistic science to various practical problems" (Ferguson, "Linguistic Theory and Pedagogical Application" 29). But over the last half century, it has taken on several meanings and become increasingly broad in scope.

From the 1950s and into the 1970s, the (sub)field of applied linguistics was almost exclusively associated with language teaching, specifically with contrastive analyses of learners' native and target languages in order to predict and address areas of difficulty. A major focus was on foreign language teaching methodology and materials development. This use of the term is reflected in the first of two definitions provided in the *Longman Dictionary of Applied Linguistics:* "the study of second and foreign language learning and teaching" (Richards, Platt, and Weber 15).

A broader definition of applied linguistics can be found in *Applied Linguistics.* First appearing in 1979, this journal perceives the aim of the field as exploring the "relation between theory and practice" and lists among areas included in the field "first and second language learning and teaching, bilingualism and bilingual education, discourse analysis, translation, language testing, language teaching methodology, language planning, the study of interlanguages, stylistics and lexicography" (policy statement on inside back cover). The statement represents a view of applied linguistics not limited to the application of linguistic theory to foreign or second language teaching. Nonetheless, the major priority remains the "links between theoretical linguistic studies, educational research and the planning and implementation of practical programs."

Recent investigations into language from other disciplinary perspectives have spawned such fields as speech-act theory, the ethnography of communication, pragmatics, conversational analysis, accommodation theory, and variation analysis. Insights from these fields have been applied to the study of cross-cultural communication, communication across genders and social class, doctor-patient communication, therapeutic discourse, and the language of the law, advertising, and the workplace. This expanded scope of applied linguistics is reflected in the second definition given in the *Longman Dictionary:*

> [Applied linguistics is] the study of language and linguistics in relation to practical problems, such as lexicography, translation, speech pathology, etc. Applied linguistics uses information from sociology,

psychology, anthropology, and information theory as well as from linguistics *in order to develop its own theoretical models* of language and language use, and then uses this information and theory in practical areas such as syllabus design, speech therapy, language planning, stylistics, etc.   (15; emphasis added)

In this definition, applied linguistics is committed to theory construction. Among the areas of applied linguistics germane to foreign language departments, perhaps most central are theories of how people acquire a second language.

Second Language Acquisition

Second language acquisition is a relatively recent field of inquiry. A milestone date for its inception is 1967, with the publication of S. Pit Corder's "The Significance of Learners' Errors." In that article, Corder states what has since become axiomatic in second language acquisition research: that learners, in the process of learning a second language, create a system consisting of elements from both the target language and the native language, but also of elements that cannot be traced to either. At the time, Corder referred to this concept as the learner's "transitional competence." Subsequently, this concept has been referred to as the learner's "approximative system" (Nemser), "idiosyncratic dialect" (Corder), and "interlanguage" (Selinker). It is the last term that has found most common currency. One can frame all SLA research in terms of the nature and extent of interlanguage systematicity.

On the one hand, this research is interdisciplinary: it takes theories and research methodologies from a number of disciplines and uses them to solve problems in the acquisition of second and foreign languages. Policy statements of some of the journals in the field show the interdisciplinary nature of SLA research. *Language Learning* "publishes research articles that systematically apply methods of inquiry and theories from linguistics, psycholinguistics, cognitive science, ethnography, ethnomethodology, sociolinguistics, sociology, semiotics, educational inquiry, and cultural or historical studies to address fundamental issues in language learning, such as bilingualism, language acquisition, second and foreign language education, literacy, culture, cognition, pragmatics, and intergroup relations" (inside front cover). *Studies in Second Language Acquisition* is "devoted to problems and issues in second language acquisition and foreign language learning, defined broadly to include problems of language contact—interference, transfer, pidginization" (inside front cover).

On the other hand, the existence of the journals is itself one indication of an emerging discipline (see Huebner, Introduction). Another indication is regularly scheduled conferences, such as the annual Second Language Research Forum, which facilitate communication among members of this new research community. Courses and textbooks (e.g., Ellis, *Understanding*; Klein; Larsen-Freeman and Long; Cook; Ellis, *Study*; Gass and Selinker) transmit the field's growing body of research to future generations of researchers. Some universities even offer degrees in the field (though where those degrees are housed and the names of the degrees reflect the interdisciplinary nature of the field). Finally, this emerging discipline can be identified by the development of various schools, models, and theories to explain its investigative focus.

Although a single unified theory of second language acquisition has yet to emerge, the indexes of the above-mentioned textbooks make reference to nativist theories, variationist theories, environmentalist theories, interactionist theories, functional-typological theories, the monitor model, the acculturation model, the multidimensional model, the pidginization hypothesis, and the teachability hypothesis. The root of many of these theoretical constructs can be traced to developments in linguistics.

THE INTERFACES BETWEEN LINGUISTIC
THEORY AND SLA RESEARCH

The application of linguistic theory to SLA research represents the traditional view of the link between the two fields, an extension of the connection that held in the 1950s and 1960s between linguistic theory and applied linguistics: the application of contrastive analysis theory to the teaching of second and foreign languages. Implied is the belief that theories of language have much to offer SLA research and foreign language teaching but that the reverse is only incidentally true. From this perspective, to the extent that theories of language can be used to explain patterns of second language acquisition, the linguistic theory would be incidentally supported.

Another view holds that SLA research can make more direct and substantive contributions to linguistic theory. For example, SLA data that contradicted a proposed linguistic construct could force the reformulation or abandonment of that construct. In the process, the theory of SLA would be incidentally supported, by virtue of the fact that it is consistent with a theory of language in general. This view is not a new one, but little if any progress has yet been made in that direction. Before examining why, I look at some typical ways in which theories of language have enriched both SLA theory construction and foreign language teaching.

Contributions of Linguistic Theory to SLA Research

The development of second language acquisition theory has drawn heavily on theoretical developments in linguistics. A sampling of contributions of theories of register and discourse, speech acts, variability, and universal grammar provides a selective overview of the field of SLA research.

REGISTER AND DISCOURSE ANALYSIS

Register refers to a speech variety associated with a specific communication situation. Sports announcing, for example, employs a register that is distinct in its phonology, syntax, and lexicon from speech varieties used in other communication situations (see Ferguson, "Sports"). The identification of "simplified registers," such as talk addressed to babies or to foreigners (baby talk, foreigner talk; see Ferguson "Absence"), together with advances in discourse and conversational analysis, has motivated research into the effect of input on SLA.

Charles Ferguson's initial observation that foreigner-talk simplification often resulted in the use of ungrammatical forms to address second language learners was supported in early research on SLA (e.g., Wong-Fillmore; Clyne; Andersen; Heidelberger Forschungsprojekt). Subsequent research, however, suggested that while foreigner talk resulted in adjustments not made to native speakers (see Hatch for a review of the research), ungrammatical utterances addressed to nonnative speakers were not as common as originally believed.

Furthermore, developments in discourse analysis and conversational analysis made it possible to look at accommodations in conversational structure between native speakers and nonnative speakers (see Hatch, Shapiro, and Wagner-Gough; Long, "Input"). Conversations between native speakers and nonnative speakers involve more confirmation checks, comprehension checks, and clarification requests than do conversations between native speakers. Such adjustments have been found to aid comprehension by second language learners (Parker and Chaudron). These findings have seen pedagogical application in the current emphasis on communication in foreign language classrooms.

SPEECH-ACT THEORY

Speech-act theory, arising from work in the philosophy of language, proposes that speech acts consisting of a single utterance may incorporate three kinds of meaning or force (Austin; Searle). The locutionary force of an utterance is the propositional content of the utterance. The illocutionary force of an utterance is the effect the utterance is intended to have. The perlocutionary force refers to the actual effect the utterance has. Speech acts are said to be direct when the relation between the locutionary force and the illocutionary force is transparent. For example, "Open the window" would be a direct speech act, since the locutionary force (an imperative form of an action verb and an object) matches the illocutionary force (a request or command). When the relation is less transparent—for example, "It's hot in here," a declarative observation of fact intended as a polite request to open the window—the speech act is said to be indirect.

The focus of speech-act analysis in SLA research has been at the level of illocutionary force; specifically, the focus has been on the differences in the ways native speakers and nonnative speakers construct and use such speech acts as requests, apologies, and refusals. Lack of knowledge of target language norms is certainly one reason for the differences, as is the lack of command of target language forms needed to perform speech acts in a targetlike manner. The linguistic identity that the learner wants to establish or maintain may be another reason.

Investigation into the performance of speech acts by second language learners has shown that learners have a couple of options: they can transfer speech-act patterns from their first language or, on the basis of their limited knowledge, overgeneralize about speech-act patterns in the target language. Different factors take precedence at different stages of interlanguage development (see Blum-Kulka, House, and Kasper; Blum-Kulka). In the pedagogical domain, the focus on functions of language can be viewed as an application of research on speech acts.

VARIATION THEORY

Work within sociolinguistic paradigms has been concerned with the nature of variation found in language use. William Labov's work on social and stylistic factors in variation (e.g., *Patterns*) has shown that much of what had previously been thought to be random variation was indeed patterned and determined by social class or style shifting. The work of variationists such as C. J. Bailey and Derek Bickerton tied language variation to language change.

The assumptions and research methodologies of variation theorists have been applied to second language acquisition (e.g., Ellis, "Sources"; Tarone; Young; Bayley and Preston), although it has been pointed out that sociolinguists investigate variation in speech communities whereas SLA researchers apply their insights to individual learners (see Preston).

Nevertheless, SLA applications of variation theory have found that learners use forms more or less targetlike depending on the phonological (Dickerson), morphological (Wolfram), or syntactic (Hyltenstam, "Implicational Patterns") context, on the relationship of the learner to the interlocutor (Beebe and Zuengler), and on the nature of the task (Dickerson and Dickerson). Furthermore, what appears to be random variation among forms in the interlanguage turns out to be highly systematic in terms of the functions served by the forms (Huebner, *Analysis.*) Finally, free variation between targetlike and nontargetlike forms may be a manifestation of second language development—the language acquisition counterpart to diachronic linguistic change (Ellis, *Understanding*).

Patterns of variability can be determined only by our examining a range of possible factors. How factors affect variability may change depending on the stage of second language development a learner is at. Facts about variability in SLA call for a reevaluation of the significance of mistakes and highlight the importance of multiple means of assessing student foreign language proficiency.

LANGUAGE UNIVERSALS

One approach to language universals that has been useful in predicting the forms that interlanguages will take is to make the cross-linguistic comparisons of the surface structures of the world's languages in order to propose "typological universals" (Greenberg). For example, it has been found that languages with verb-subject-object word order always have prepositions while languages with subject-object-verb word order have postpositions.

Typological universals can also be implicational: that is, if a language has feature A, it will also have feature B. An example is the accessibility hierarchy, which articulates a number of implicational relations, in languages of the world, among relative clause types. At one end of the implicational continuum are subject-focus relative clauses and at the other are object-of-comparison relative clauses. The continuum goes from subject to direct object to indirect object to object of preposition to genitive to object of comparison. Here are illustrations of the types:

subject → direct → indirect → object of → genitive → object of
object   object   preposition   comparison

That is the man who *bought the knife.*	(subject)
That is the man whom *we saw at Bundy.*	(direct object)
That is the man to whom *we gave the vial of*	
blood.	(indirect object)
That is the man with whom *she fought.*	(object of preposition)
That is the man whose *glove we found.*	(genitive)
That is the man whom *Ron is smaller than.*	(object of comparison)

It is an interesting fact that if a language has relative clauses of any one of the types in the continuum, it will also have relative clauses of all the types to the left of that type, but not necessarily to the right.

This theoretical construct has been used to help identify patterns of second language acquisition. Susan Gass found that among a mixed group of learners of English as a second language, the percentage of correct relative clause types could pretty much be predicted by the accessibility hierarchy ("Investigation," "Language Transfer"). That is, the subject-focus relative clause was the one formed correctly most frequently among this population, followed by the direct-object relative clause, with the object-of-comparison relative clause correctly formed the least frequently.

Kenneth Hyltenstam found that among a mixed group of learners of Swedish as a second language, resumptive pronouns (for example, "That is the man whom Ron is smaller than *him*"), which are ungrammatical in Swedish as well as English, were more likely to be found among relative clause types at the right end of the continuum than at the left, a pattern that is also true for all languages ("Use").

Several studies have used the accessibility hierarchy to look at learners' capacities to generalize (Gass "From Theory"; Eckman, Bell, and Nelson). The general findings of these studies were twofold. First, students who were given instruction on the formation of relative clauses at the right (difficult) end of the continuum were able to generalize that knowledge to form subject- and direct-object-focus relative clauses on their own. Second, the opposite was not true: students given instruction in the formation of relative clause types at the left (easy) end of the continuum were less likely to be able to generalize that knowledge to form relative clause types at the right end.

Both Hyltenstam ("Use") and Susan Gass and Josh Ard point out that while typological universals may help predict the forms that interlanguages will take, they don't necessarily explain them. Although explanations for typological universals have generally been in terms of discourse constraints, ease of processing, functional considerations, or pragmatics, no theory provides a principled set of criteria or procedures for investigation into the sources of typological universals.

Contributions of SLA Research to Linguistic Theory

That second language acquisition research should be able to inform and influence linguistic theory is a point made long ago:

> Scholars whose chief intellectual interest has been in the development of linguistic theory have generally looked on the problems of language learning either as of little concern to them or as an appropriate field for the application of linguistics. . . . I should like to present the view that language learning is of great interest to the linguist and that the application can work the other way: the study of language learning has value for the construction of linguistic theory. (Ferguson, "Linguistic Theory and Language Learning" 115)

More recently the point has been made again, and repeatedly, by those working in SLA (see Bolinger; Comrie; Lightbown; Flynn and O'Neal; Gass and Schachter; Ferguson, "Language Teaching"; Huebner, "SLA").

To be sure, SLA research has created and fed back into source disciplines — including linguistics — knowledge about "language contact and change, language variation, language proficiency, sensitive periods in human maturation, ethnic identity, developmental sequences in language acquisition, cross-cultural communication, and relationships among language, learning, and cognition" (Long, "Scope"). Nevertheless, it is still difficult to find theoretical linguists who draw on SLA data for theory construction. It is equally difficult to identify any example of how SLA research has substantively changed any theory of linguistics.

Two factors contribute to this situation. The first factor rests in the nature of second language acquisition. Unlike first language acquisition, SLA is complicated by the fact that learners have additional knowledge sources to draw on, including their knowledge of a first language and a more highly developed set of cognitive processes. In addition, the social context of SLA is, if not more complex than, certainly different from that of first language acquisition. The second factor concerns the current state of theory development, both in linguistics and in SLA. The predicament can be illustrated with an example from the interface between theory building in SLA and a theory of language known as Universal Grammar.

Universal Grammar theory proposes a "system of principles, conditions, and rules that are elements or properties of all human languages" (Chomsky, *Reflections* 29). These rules and principles form the mental representation of language and are said to be hard-wired into the brain. The most compelling argument for this idea is what has been called the logical problem of language acquisition, which states that input alone is insufficient for the child to acquire a system as complex and abstract as language in as short a time as language acquisition takes place.

The most widely held model of Universal Grammar theory, called government-binding theory, distinguishes between principles and parameters. Principles are highly abstract properties of language that underlie the grammar rules of all specific languages. A parameter is the degree to which a principle of language can vary among different languages (Crystal 249). For example, a principle called subjacency constrains the extent to which a constituent may be moved within a sentence. It states that a constituent can move over no more than one bounding node. This principle explains why the question 1 below is grammatical whereas question 2 is not, although both have moved the tense from within the sentence to the front of the sentence (the asterisk in linguistics is a convention to denote ungrammatical sentences; the blank denotes the place in a sentence from which a constituent has been moved).

The man who was wearing the earring heard the noise.

1. *Did* the man who was wearing the earring hear ___ the noise?
2. **Was* the man who ___ wearing the earring heard the noise?

While subjacency, a principle that applies to all human languages, states that a constituent can move over no more than one bounding node, what constitutes a bounding node is a parameter that may vary from one language to another.

In the government-binding model of the Universal Grammar theory, parameters involve clusters of features. For example, the pro-drop parameter, one of the most fully investigated, is said to have two settings. Pro-drop languages, like Italian or Spanish, share a number of features: null-subjects (*voy a ir* instead of *I'm going to go; hace fresco* instead of *it is cool*); variable subject-verb word order in declarative sentences (*la policia llega* and *llega la policia*); and resumptive pronouns (leaving a pronoun in a subordinate clause from which a noun phrase has been moved, e.g., "That is the man whom Ron is shorter than *him*"). Languages like English or French, which are not pro-drop, have just the opposite values for this cluster of features.

Applying the government-binding model to second language acquisition, researchers have not determined whether second language learners have access to universal grammar. One tack has been to look for patterns of acquisition of clusters of features associated with a given parameter. For example, Lydia White and Usha Lakshmanan both examined the features associated with the pro-drop parameter among second language learners of different language backgrounds. Their studies found that the learners did not observe the patterns of acquisition predicted by the pro-drop parameter.

This finding, if we accept its methodological validity and reliability, could have a substantive impact on the development of linguistic theory, in particular on the shape of the government-binding model. It suggests that the parameters proposed by the model are incorrect. White in fact offers this as a possibility, and there is subsequent research to support her position. Sharon Hilles assumed a different set of features associated with the pro-drop parameter (obligatory use of subject pronouns, dummy subjects *it* and *there,* and uninflected modals) and found, in a reanalysis of an earlier, longitudinal study, that the acquisition of these features seemed to be temporally related. She hypothesized that the acquisition of one feature triggered the acquisition of the others as the learner moved from a language that was pro-drop to a language that was not.

But the complicated nature of the phenomenon of second language acquisition, together with the newness of SLA theory, has prevented this kind of evidence from being brought to bear on the formulation of such theoretical constructs in linguistics as the notion of parameters. Learners, at least hypothetically, do have access to the additional knowledge sources of a first language and other cognitive processes. And so it may be that in acquiring this cluster of features, second language learners are not relying on universal grammar at all. Until the role of cognitive and social factors in second language acquisition can be convincingly distinguished from the role of universal grammar, theoretical linguists are unlikely to pay much attention to SLA data. The task of sorting out those factors is, of course, one of the motivations for doing SLA research.

The connection between theories of language and second language acquisition has traditionally been a close one. Until now, the benefits of this connection have been one-sided, with SLA research the beneficiary. As theories of SLA develop, the connection will become increasingly reciprocal. What has become apparent over the past quarter century or more of SLA research, however, is that second language acquisition is a field worthy of empirical research, both for the development of theory and for the practical implications it promises for language pedagogy. For these reasons, the field deserves a place at the table in foreign language departments.

NOTE

I am grateful to the Mellon Foundation and to the National Foreign Language Center at Johns Hopkins University for supporting my work during the time that this paper was written, and to Norine Berenz for having read and responded to an earlier draft of this paper.

WORKS CITED

Andersen, Roger W. "The Impoverished State of Cross-Sectional Morphology Acquisition/Accuracy Methodology." *Working Papers on Bilingualism* 14 (1977): 47–82.
Austin, John L. *How to Do Things with Words.* Oxford: Clarendon, 1962.
Bailey, C. J. *Variation and Linguistic Theory.* Washington: Center for Applied Linguistics, 1973.

Bayley, Robert, and Dennis Preston, eds. *Second Language Acquisition and Linguistic Variation.* Amsterdam: Benjamins, 1996.

Beebe, Leslie M., and Jane Zuengler. "Accommodation Theory: An Explanation for Style Shifting in Second Language Dialects." *Sociolinguistics and Second Language Acquisition.* Ed. Nessa Wolfson and Elliot Judd. Rowley: Newbury, 1983. 195–213.

Bickerton, Derek. *Dynamics of a Creole System.* Cambridge: Cambridge UP, 1975.

Blum-Kulka, Shoshana. "Interlanguage Pragmatics: The Case of Requests." *Foreign / Second Language Pedagogy Research: A Commemorative Volume for Claus Færch.* Ed. Robert Phillipson, Eric R. Kellerman, Larry Selinker, Michael Sharwood Smith, and Merrill Swain. Multilingual Matters, 64. Clevedon, Eng.: Taylor, 1991. 255–72.

Blum-Kulka, Shoshana, Juliane House, and Gabriele Kasper. "Investigating Cross-Cultural Pragmatics: An Introductory Overview." *Cross-Cultural Pragmatics: Requests and Apologies.* Ed. Blum-Kulka, House, and Kasper. Norwood: Ablex, 1989. 1–34.

Bolinger, Dwight. Introduction. *Language Structures in Contrast.* Ed. Robert J. Di Pietro. Rowley: Newbury, 1971. vii–ix.

Chomsky, Noam. *Lectures on Government and Binding.* Dordrecht: Foris, 1981.

———. *Reflections on Language.* New York: Pantheon, 1975.

Clyne, Michael, ed. *Foreigner Talk.* Spec. issue of *International Journal of the Sociology of Language* 28 (1981): 1–115.

Comrie, Bernard. "Why Linguists Need Language Acquirers." *Language Universals and Second Language Acquisition.* Ed. William Rutherford. Amsterdam: Benjamins, 1984.

Cook, Vivian J. *Linguistics and Second Language Acquisition.* New York: St. Martins, 1993.

Corder, S. Pit. "Idiosyncratic Dialects and Error Analysis." *International Review of Applied Linguistics in Language Teaching* 9 (1971): 149–59.

———. "The Significance of Learners' Errors." *International Review of Applied Linguistics in Language Teaching* 5 (1967): 161–69.

Crystal, David. *A Dictionary of Linguistics and Phonetics.* 3rd ed. Oxford: Blackwell, 1991.

Dickerson, Lonna. "The Learner's Interlanguage as a System of Variable Rules." *TESOL Quarterly* 9 (1975): 401–07.

Dickerson, Lonna, and Wayne Dickerson. "Interlanguage Phonology: Current Research and Future Directions." *The Notions of Simplification, Interlanguages, and Pidgins and Their Relation to Second Language Learning.* Actes du 5ème Colloque de Linguistique Appliquée de Neufchâtel. Ed. S. Pit Corder and Eddie Roulet. Geneva: Didier; Librairie Droz, 1977. 18–29.

Eckman, Fred, Lawrence Bell, and Diane Nelson. "On the Generalization of Relative Clause Instruction in the Acquisition of English as a Second Language." *Applied Linguistics* 9 (1988): 1–20.

Ellis, Rod. "Sources of Variability in Interlanguages." *Applied Linguistics* 6 (1985): 118–31.

———. *The Study of Second Language Acquisition.* Oxford: Oxford UP, 1994.

———. *Understanding Second Language Acquisition.* Oxford: Oxford UP, 1985.

Ferguson, Charles A. "Absence of Copula and the Notion of Simplicity: A Study of Normal Speech, Baby Talk, Foreigner Talk, and Pidgins." *Pidginization and Creolization of Languages.* Ed. Dell Hymes. New York: Cambridge UP, 1971. 141–50.

———. "Language Teaching and Theories of Language." *Language Teaching, Testing, and Technology: Lessons from the Past with a View toward the Future.* Ed. James E.

Alatis. Georgetown Univ. Round Table 1989. Washington: Georgetown UP, 1989. 81–88.

———. "Linguistic Theory and Language Learning." *Report of the Fourteenth Annual Round Table Meeting on Linguistics and Language Studies*. Ed. Robert J. Di Pietro. Washington: Georgetown UP, 1963. 115–22.

———. "Linguistic Theory and Pedagogical Application." *Report on the Second Annual Round Table Meeting on Linguistics and Language Teaching*. Ed. John De Francis. Washington: Georgetown UP, 1951. 28–51.

———. "Sports Announcer Talk: Syntactic Aspects of Register Variation." *Language in Society* 12 (1983): 153–72.

Flynn, Suzanne, and Wayne O'Neal. Introduction. *Linguistic Theory in Second Language Acquisition*. Ed. Flynn and O'Neal. Dordrecht: Kluwer, 1988. 1–24.

Gass, Susan M. "From Theory to Practice." *On TESOL '81*. Ed. Mary Hines and William Rutherford. Washington: TESOL, 1982. 129–39.

———. "An Investigation of Syntactic Transfer in Adult Second Language Acquisition." Diss. Indiana U, 1979.

———. "Language Transfer and Universal Grammatical Relations." *Language Learning* 29 (1979): 327–44.

Gass, Susan M., and Josh Ard. "L2 Acquisition and the Ontology of Language Universals." *Second Language Acquisition and Language Universals*. Ed. William Rutherford. Amsterdam: Benjamins, 1984. 33–68.

Gass, Susan M., and Jacquelyn Schachter. Introduction. *Linguistic Perspectives on Second Language Acquisition*. Ed. Gass and Schachter. Cambridge: Cambridge UP, 1989. 1–9.

Gass, Susan M., and Larry Selinker. *Second Language Acquisition: An Introductory Course*. Hillsdale: Erlbaum, 1994.

Gazdar, Gerald, Ewan Klein, Geoffrey K. Pullum, and Ivan Sag. *Generalized Phrase Structure Grammar*. Oxford: Blackwell, 1985.

Greenberg, Joseph H. *Language Universals, with Special Reference to Feature Hierarchies*. The Hague: Mouton, 1966.

Hatch, Evelyn. "Simplified Input and Second Language Acquisition." *Pidginization and Creolization as Language Acquisition*. Ed. Roger W. Andersen. Rowley: Newbury, 1983. 64–86.

Hatch, Evelyn, Rina Shapiro, and Judy Wagner-Gough. "Foreigner Talk Discourse." *I[nstituut voor] T[oegepaste] L[inguistiek] Review of Applied Linguistics* 39–40 (1978): 39–60.

Heidelberger Forschungsprojekt. "The Acquisition of German Syntax by Foreign Migrant Workers." *Linguistic Variation: Models and Methods*. Ed. David Sankoff. New York: Academic, 1978. 1–22.

Hilles, Sharon. "Interlanguage in the PRO-drop Parameter." *Second Language Research* 2 (1986): 33–52.

Huebner, Thom. Introduction. *Sociolinguistic Perspectives: Papers on Language in Society by Charles A. Ferguson*. Ed. Huebner. New York: Oxford UP, 1995. 3–15.

———. *A Longitudinal Analysis of the Acquisition of English*. Ann Arbor: Karoma, 1983.

———. "SLA: Litmus Test for Linguistic Theory?" *Crosscurrents in SLA and Linguistic Theories*. Ed. Huebner and Charles A. Ferguson. Amsterdam: Benjamins, 1991. 3–22.

Hyltenstam, Kenneth. "Implicational Patterns in Interlanguage Syntax Variation." *Language Learning* 27 (1977): 383–411.

———. "The Use of Typological Markedness Conditions as Predictors in Second

Language Acquisition: The Case of Pronominal Copies in Relative Clauses." *Second Languages: A Crosslinguistic Perspective.* Ed. Roger W. Andersen. Rowley: Newbury, 1984. 39–58.

Klein, Wolfgang. *Second Language Acquisition.* Cambridge: Cambridge UP, 1986.

Labov, William. *Sociolinguistic Patterns.* Philadelphia: U of Pennsylvania P, 1972.

Lakshmanan, Usha. "The Role of Parametric Variation in Adult Second Language Acquisition: A Study of the 'Pro-Drop' Parameter." *Papers in Applied Linguistics—Michigan* 2 (1986): 97–117.

Larsen-Freeman, Diane, and Michael H. Long. *An Introduction to Second Language Acquisition Research.* London: Longman, 1991.

Lightbown, Patsy M. "The Influence of Linguistic Theory on Language Acquisition Research: Now You See It, Now You Don't." *Developments in Linguistics and Semiotics, Language Teaching and Learning, Communication across Cultures.* Ed. Simon P. X. Battestini. Georgetown Univ. Round Table 1986. Washington: Georgetown UP, 1987. 130–42.

Long, Michael H. "Input, Interaction, and Second Language Acquisition." *Native Language and Foreign Language Acquisition.* Ed. H. Winitz. Spec. issue of *Annals of the New York Academy of Sciences* 379 (1981): 259–78.

———. "The Scope of Applied Linguistics." ESL Dept. Lecture Ser. U of Hawaii, Manoa, 31 Aug. 1994.

Nemser, William. "Approximative Systems of Foreign Learners." *International Review of Applied Linguistics in Language Teaching* 9 (1971): 115–24.

Parker, Katherine, and Craig Chaudron. "The Effects of Linguistic Simplifications and Elaborative Modifications on L2 Comprehension." *University of Hawaii Working Papers in English as a Second Language* 6 (1987): 107–33.

Preston, Dennis. *Sociolinguistics and Second Language Acquisition.* Oxford: Blackwell, 1989.

Richards, Jack C., John Platt, and Heidi Weber. *Longman Dictionary of Applied Linguistics.* Essex, Eng.: Longman, 1985.

Searle, John. *Speech Acts.* Cambridge: Cambridge UP, 1969.

Selinker, Larry. "Interlanguage." *International Review of Applied Linguistics in Language Teaching* 10 (1972): 209–31.

Tarone, Elaine E. *Variation in Interlanguage.* London: Arnold, 1988.

White, Lydia. "The 'Pro-Drop' Parameter in Adult Second Language Acquisition." *Language Learning* 35 (1985): 47–62.

Wolfram, Walt. "Systematic Variability in Second-Language Tense Marking." *The Dynamic Interlanguage: Empirical Studies in Second Language Variation.* Ed. Miriam R. Eisenstein. New York: Plenum, 1989. 187–97.

Wong-Fillmore, Lilly. "The Second Time Around: Cognitive and Social Strategies in Second Language Acquisition." Diss. Stanford U, 1976.

Young, Richard. *Variation in Interlanguage Morphology.* New York: Lang, 1991.

Approaches to Empirical Research in Instructional Language Settings

Kathleen M. Bailey

It is the main purpose of this essay to provide an overview of three major approaches to empirical research in the foreign language field: experimental research, naturalistic inquiry, and action research. (The emphasis is on instructional settings in the United States, and examples are drawn primarily from research on foreign language teaching and learning.) The second purpose is to introduce basic concepts and vocabulary associated with these three approaches. The third purpose is to provide guidance to interested readers on resources for learning more about research on language learning and teaching in such settings.

Research in instructional settings is sometimes collectively referred to as classroom-centered research, or simply as classroom research—that is, research "all or part of whose data are collected in classrooms" (Long, "Box" 3). Or, as Richard Allwright has put it, "Classroom-centered research is in fact research that treats the language classroom not just as the setting for investigation but, more important, as the object of investigation. Classroom processes become the central focus" ("Classroom-Centered Research" 191). Descriptions of the findings and procedures of classroom research on language education are available in several articles (e.g., Bailey, "Classroom-Centered Research"; Gaies; van Lier, "Classroom Research") and books (Allwright and Bailey; Brumfit and Mitchell; Chaudron, *Second Language Classrooms;* Edge and Richards; Ellis, *Learning;* Freed; van Lier, *Classroom*).

I define empirical research as research based on the collection and analysis of primary data (as opposed, say, to library research, or literary criticism, or linguistic introspection, which theorizes in the absence of data). Data, according to Gregory Bateson, are records of events. They may be quantified (as in measurements, frequencies, and test scores) or not quantified (as in journal entries, observational field notes, think-aloud protocols, and transcripts of interactions). Nonquantified data are often referred to as qualitative data because they deal with the qualities of the people or processes being studied.

The three broad approaches to empirical research are experimental research, naturalistic inquiry, and action research. This simple division provides a convenient way to compare research approaches (Allwright and Bailey; Bailey, Omaggio-Hadley, Magnan, and Swaffar). Other authors draw the lines in different ways. For example, in 1980 Michael Long categorized language classroom research as taking either the interaction analysis approach or the anthropological approach ("Box"). Later, in 1984, he discussed process research, product research, and process-product research ("Process"). However, John Smith and Lois Heshusius argue that in general education research, the positivist quantitative approach and the relativist qualitative approach are essentially incompatible. Craig Chaudron discusses four traditions in classroom research: the psychometric tradition, interaction analysis, discourse analysis and the ethnographic tradition (*Second Language Classrooms* 13–15). James Brown, in his description of statistical language studies, avoids terms such as *empirical* and *experimental,* for the following reasons:

> First, there are other, nonstatistical studies that could be called empirical (e.g., ethnographies, case studies, etc.) since, by definition, empirical studies are those based on data (but not necessarily quantitative data). Second, there are statistical studies that are not exactly experimental in the technical sense of that word (e.g., quasi-experimental studies, post-test only designs, etc.). Third, there are statistical studies that have little or nothing to do with experimentation (e.g., demonstrations, survey research, etc.).
>
> ("Statistics . . . Part 1" 569–70)

Rüdiger Grotjahn describes eight possible research paradigms using three parameters: qualitative versus quantitative data, interpretive versus statistical analysis, and type of research design (59–60). It should be clear, then, that there are many different ways to classify approaches to research. In fact, as John Lett has pointed out, "A problem in understanding and discussing educational research is that there are so many ways to categorize it and so little agreement on nomenclature" (15).

In discussing the advantages and disadvantages of the experimental tradition, naturalistic inquiry, and action research, this essay shows the different goals and uses of each approach. None of these approaches is superior or inferior to the others. A researcher simply must choose the research designs and procedures appropriate to the issues under investigation.

The experimental tradition is the most familiar and historically has been the dominant approach. But it is not without problems, especially in attempts to address language-related phenomena. As a result, the so-called alternative paradigms of naturalistic inquiry and action research are quickly gaining ground and are certain to be more widely used in the future.

EXPERIMENTAL RESEARCH

Imagine that the administrator of a German program wants to know if a particularly costly set of new audiovisual materials will improve students' mastery of German enough to justify the expense of the materials. Before deciding to order them for the whole program, the administrator conducts an experiment: a sample of students uses the new materials, and their learning is compared with that of a group of learners who use the existing materials.

Suppose the two groups of learners were tested with identical examinations and the administrator found that the students who used the expensive new materials performed significantly better. But the administrator would want to have confidence in the outcome of the study before purchasing the new materials; she would want to be sure that the students in the group that used the new materials (the experimental group) were not substantially better language learners to begin with than those who used the regular materials (the control group). So before doing the experiment, she might first administer some form of language aptitude measure to all the students. Likewise, unless the students were true beginners at the language, she would want to make sure that one group did not know more German than the other prior to the experiment. (This could be determined by administering a

pretest in German to both groups at the beginning of the study and checking to see that the two groups were equal at the outset.)

Such preexisting conditions are considered threats to the validity of the
study, since they can influence the results. (Did the students in the experimental group really perform better because the new materials were superior
to the old ones, or was it because those students were inherently better language learners, or because they already knew more of the target language
than the control group?) The situation I am describing is of course highly
idealized. Educators can seldom exert control over all relevant variables
needed to rule out the possible competing hypotheses that might explain
observed behaviors.

In the experimental tradition, a researcher wants to be sure that it is the
treatment (in this case, using the new materials) that has caused the observed effect, rather than some other, uncontrolled variable or variables. To
the extent that the observed differences between the two groups' performances can be attributed unambiguously to the treatment, the study is said
to have internal validity. In our German example, perhaps part of the reason
the experimental-group students did well was not that the new materials
were superior but just that they were new. After the novelty wears off, the
students might be less motivated to use the expensive materials to study. In
that case, their performance would drop back down to where it was before—
in other words, to the level of the control group. When this sort of thing occurs, a study is said to lack internal validity.

The experimental research tradition really consists of a family of research designs and analytic procedures underpinned by the theory of probability. Research designs are essentially standardized plans for conducting
research that are laid out before the investigation is started. The greater the
control over the variables that might influence the outcome of the study,
the stronger the design. The so-called true experimental designs (which include randomization of subjects, control groups and experimental groups,
and a high degree of control over variables) are considered the strongest because they control for most threats to validity. In the ex post facto designs, a
researcher studies preexisting conditions but does not administer a treatment. (For example, a researcher might compare the performance of male
students and female students on a particular test or task.) In the quasi-
experimental designs, a single group of subjects serves as its own control
group, as the researcher alternately applies the treatment to and withholds it

from the group over time. The quasi-experimental designs are used when there is no control group available. (For instance, with a single class of French learners, a teacher might use a film with every other instructional unit and then compare the students' performance on the material that included films with their performance on the material that did not.) Finally, the preexperimental class, which is often used in preliminary studies, or pilot studies, lacks both randomization and a true control group. (A teacher might assess the students' knowledge or skills before a unit, teach the unit, and then measure the students' skills and knowledge again. But even if the students' performance improves, we cannot say for sure that the improvement has been caused by the instruction, since we cannot compare the results with those of an equivalent control group that has not received the treatment.) Thus, in these less powerful designs, a researcher exerts less control over variables and therefore cannot make the strong causal claims that are possible with true experimental designs.

This relation of control and causality is directly tied to the goals of experimental research. In this tradition, there are typically three main goals: to build theory by testing hypotheses or answering research questions; to discover relations, especially causal relations; and to generalize results beyond the research sample to the wider population it represents. This last goal is referred to as generalizability, or external validity: the extent to which the findings of the experiment will obtain under nonexperimental conditions. For example, suppose that, in our hypothetical study of the costly new German materials described above, the students selected for the experimental group are atypical in some way. Suppose they are more intelligent than the rest of the learners in the German program. In that case, the same positive results found in the experiment might not occur when the materials are used on a wider scale. The study would therefore lack generalizability.

The experimental approach to research is characterized by numerous statistical analytic procedures, which use primarily quantified data, such as measurements (including test scores) or frequency counts. Typically researchers use statistical procedures to look for significant relations among variables, or for significant differences among groups. It is beyond the scope of this essay to discuss these procedures or the mathematical logic that underlies them. However, in the section on resources below, references are made to works that language professionals can consult to learn more about statistics and the experimental tradition.

Advantages and Disadvantages

Advocates of experimental research feel that this approach has several advantages. First, given that it is a highly codified approach to science, it allows us to test hypotheses with widely accepted standardized procedures. The existing metalanguage and codified procedures provide an elaborate "reconstructed logic" (Kaplan 8) that is shared by researchers worldwide. The experimental approach also uses agreed-on criteria for determining statistical significance, and it attempts to replicate the objectivity of the physical sciences (a desire some have referred to as physics envy). Perhaps because this tradition has value, prestige, and political clout in academe, preservice teachers can easily access training in the experimental approach at their universities.

Another advantage to this approach is that, given the experimental emphasis on clear definitions and control over variables, comparisons across studies and sites are often possible. And to the extent that all variables except the treatment can be held constant across groups, proponents of experimental research claim that investigators can make causal statements to explain the differences observed between groups. To return to our German example, if there were no threats to validity, the administrator could attribute the experimental group's higher scores to the use of the new materials and would therefore be able to justify the cost with confidence. But we will see that language learning is too complex to be reduced to simple causal claims (see van Lier, "Ethnography") .

There are also numerous disadvantages of experimental research. The experimental paradigm has been applied to educational research with varying degrees of success, as noted by Smith and Heshusius: "Positivist social and educational inquiry has not achieved the same intellectual and practical mastery of subject matter as has been the case for natural science" (7). As Leo van Lier has pointed out, "Even in the physical sciences, causality has been put on trial by complexity theory. . . . Positivism, the search for causal laws, the iron-clad generalization, and the forced choice between *either* objectivity *or* subjectivity, have been left behind in the critical approaches to the social sciences ("Forks" 342). This statement applies particularly to research on language teaching and learning, since one can seldom control all the variables influencing the outcome of a treatment designed to "cause" language learning. Previous language learning experience, aptitude, motivation, attitude toward the target language and culture, and intelligence are just a few of the potentially confounding variables involved. Well-known examples of such research are the Pennsylvania Project (Clark; Otto; P. Smith) and the University of Colorado comparative methods research program (Scherer and Wertheimer).

Other disadvantages are related to the data in experimental research. Widely used statistical procedures require quantifiable data, but many linguistic phenomena are not easily or validly measured or counted. Furthermore, many of the most commonly used statistics require that individual items of the data be independent of one another. (The achievement of this condition is possible with many multiple-choice language test items, but it is highly questionable when working with discourse-length data, such as conversations or transcripts of classroom interaction.) Most statistical procedures work better with large numbers of subjects. Such numbers may not be available to language classroom researchers. Likewise, the most powerful designs require a level of control over variables that is not typically available in language research with human subjects, for both ethical and practical reasons. In addition, conducting experimental research on human subjects, or even interpreting such research, requires extensive training and experience. But there is another, more philosophical problem with the experimental paradigm; it concerns the researcher's stance toward truth. The key question here is: What constitutes convincing evidence? For many people, if a phenomenon is not measurable, it is not worth studying. In the pursuit of "hard data" and objectivity, however, we may miss important issues. We may overlook or trivialize key variables because they are not easily quantified. Describing research on affective factors, Keiko Samimy and Jennybelle Rardin write:

> There are two critical issues of concern in applying the quantitative paradigm to the investigation of affective variables. First, since quantitative studies necessitate a researcher to be particularistic . . . in his/her a priori hypotheses, it might artificially or prematurely isolate interrelated variables, thus distorting the data. Second, in order to maintain objectivity, a researcher is removed from the subjects and/or the data. . . . Being detached from the context and ignoring the personal and dynamic nature of the subjects involved in the study, there is a danger that the researcher will interpret what is happening in a narrow and limited way.   (380–81)

And since the research data in foreign language education are often derived from people, the propensity to quantify seems to lead to a stance where individual learners are represented only by test scores. Their individuality is even further obscured when the test scores are averaged to find the mean. In this approach to research, critics note, human beings are reduced to the status of experimental subjects.

Resources

There are a number of useful methodological references on the experimental research approach in language education and applied linguistics. One user-friendly test designed primarily to prepare teachers to be consumers of such research is James Brown's *Understanding Research in Second Language Learning.* Brown's two-part article "Statistics as a Foreign Language" is intended specifically to enable language teachers without prior background to understand statistical reporting in language research.

Evelyn Hatch and Anne Lazaraton's *Research Manual* and Anthony Woods, Paul Fletcher, and Arthur Hughes's *Statistics in Language Studies* are somewhat more technical; they are intended to help language professionals conduct original research and analyze data using statistical procedures. Two surveys of research methods in our field, David Nunan's *Understanding Language Classrooms* and Donna Johnson's *Approaches to Research in Second Language Learning,* contain chapters on the experimental approach.

Some helpful references from general education are Richard Jaeger's *Statistics: A Spectator Sport,* which was written for nonspecialists and includes many clear illustrations drawn from education; Richard Shavelson's *Statistical Reasoning for the Behavioral Sciences,* which gives detailed examples and step-by-step procedures; and Bruce Tuckman's *Conducting Educational Research,* an overview of educational research methods. A classic description of research designs can be found in Donald Campbell and Julian Stanley's *Experimental and Quasi-Experimental Designs for Research.* In their book *Naturalistic Inquiry,* Yvonna Lincoln and Egon Guba provide an excellent critique of experimental research.

NATURALISTIC INQUIRY

Whereas experimental research ideally entails collecting data from control and experimental groups composed especially for the study (and selected through randomization), naturalistic inquiry works with naturally occurring settings and groups. Unlike experimental research, it does not typically seek to exert external control over variables or preselect them. Describing the essential characteristics of naturalistic inquiry, Lincoln and Guba stress these two points: "What is salient to us is that, first, no manipulation on the part of the inquirer is implied, and, second, the inquirer imposes no a priori units on the outcome" (8). As Smith and Heshusius have pointed out, the philosophical foundations and the purposes of naturalistic inquiry and experimental research are quite different.

The main goals of naturalistic inquiry are to describe or explain phenomena and thereby discover patterns or systems underlying behavior. "Naturalistic inquiry does not normally try to find causes of phenomena. Instead, the general goal of naturalistic inquiry is to understand the phenomena under investigation. Naturalistic inquiry is typically thought of as interpretive and exploratory, while experimental research is normative and explanatory in nature" (Bailey, Omaggio-Hadley, Magnan, and Swaffar 94–95). Many different research modes are included under the rubric of naturalistic inquiry. In research on language education to date, the three most common are ethnographies, case studies, and diary studies.

Ethnography is "the study of people's behavior in naturally occurring, ongoing settings, with a focus on the cultural interpretation of behavior" (Watson-Gegeo 576). It is "a field of study which is concerned primarily with the description and analysis of culture" (Saville-Troike 1). As a research method, ethnography has been used most frequently in anthropology. However, it has also been productively utilized in studies of both general education and language education.

Ethnography is characterized by two key tenets: the holistic principle and the emic principle (van Lier, *Classroom*; Watson-Gegeo). As Karen Watson-Gegeo notes, the holistic principle states that "any aspect of a culture or a behavior has to be described and explained in relation to the whole system of which it is a part" (577), and the emic principle states that "every situation investigated by an ethnographer must be understood from the perspective of the participants in that situation." A distinction is made between the "emic or culturally specific framework used by the members of society/culture for interpreting and assigning meaning to experience" and the etic perspective, which is "the researcher's ontological or interpretive framework" (579). Watson-Gegeo articulates two additional principles: that "ethnography focuses on people's behavior in groups and on cultural patterns in that behavior" (577) and that data collection in ethnography "begins with a theoretical framework directing the researcher's attention to certain aspects of situations and certain kinds of research questions" (578).

An example of an ethnographic study of foreign language learning in the United States is Peter Shaw's exploration of a curricular innovation: content-based instruction. Content-based instruction was introduced at his school, the Monterey Institute of International Studies, as a substantial addition to the existing, more traditional foreign language curriculum based on skills courses, literature courses, and courses in language for specific purposes. This change meant that students could now take courses in their major disciplines (business, political science, etc.) using their various target languages (Japanese, Chinese, German, Russian, French, and Spanish). For the language faculty, it meant having to prepare new materials and, in some instances, team teaching with colleagues from the students' major disciplines.

Shaw used teachers' and students' diary entries, his observational field notes, debriefing interviews with faculty members and students, and audio and video recordings (and transcriptions of them) to study the impact of introducing content-based instruction as a curricular model. His analysis focused on four issues that he saw as related to the improvement of learning: jigsaw reading, the process approach to writing, learner training, and the use of group work. These topics emerged from the data; they were not predetermined. For each issue, Shaw discusses the problem that emerged, the data sources relevant to the problem, and the solution reached by the participants.

As Shaw's study illustrates, naturalistic inquiry uses a variety of data that are primarily qualitative in nature, and these data are often used in combination with one another. The data include, but are not limited to, observers' field notes, audio and video recordings, interviews with teachers and learners, journal entries (by language learners, teachers, or researchers), personal narratives, photographs, maps and drawings, examples of students' output (either written or spoken), and archival data.

The use of triangulation in naturalistic inquiry is based on the multiple data sources. Triangulation is "the inspection of different kinds of data, different methods, and a variety of research tools" (van Lier, *Classroom* 13). According to Norman Denzin, triangulation in naturalistic inquiry can take four forms (data triangulation, theoretical triangulation, investigator triangulation, and methodological triangulation) and is an essential quality-control procedure: "The greater the triangulation, the greater the confidence in the observed findings" (472).

Another type of naturalistic inquiry and one that has been particularly important in research on second language acquisition is the case study. When conducting a case study, "one selects an instance from the class of objects and phenomena one is investigating (for example, 'a second language learner' or 'a science classroom') and investigates the way this instance functions in context" (Nunan, *Research Methods* 75). The case may be one person or a few people, single or multiple classrooms, one school or a group of schools. There are even case studies of individual interactions, as in Allwright's study of turns, topics, and tasks in language classrooms ("Turns"). Allwright conducted a number of analyses based on data from two classes of adult ESL learners, but then he focused on one very interesting and illustrative sample of conversation in the transcribed interactions between a teacher and a single student.

In the experimental research tradition, case studies (or one-shot case studies, as they are often called) are considered to be in the preexperimental class of research designs. They are held in low regard because their lack of control over variables prohibits researchers from making strong causal claims. In the experimental research tradition, the primary value of case studies is seen as their ability to generate hypotheses. However, in the tradition of naturalistic inquiry, well-documented longitudinal case studies are held in high regard because of the illuminating insights and vivid exemplars they provide. In our field, case studies have been especially important in research on second language acquisition.

Richard Schmidt's article "Interaction, Acculturation, and the Acquisition of Communicative Competence: A Case Study of an Adult" is a classic example of the case study genre. It is particularly interesting because it challenges a widely held theory of language acquisition, the acculturation model, presented by John Schumann ("Model"). Schmidt summarizes, "The acculturation model claims that two groups of variables, social and affective, cluster into a single variable of *acculturation* which is the major causal variable in SLA, i.e., that the degree to which a learner acculturates to the target language group will control the degree to which he acquires a second language" (139). Schmidt's case study follows Wes (an adult Japanese artist who spoke virtually no English before he immigrated to Hawaii) for a three-year period as Wes acquired English without formal instruction.

Schmidt describes Wes as having "generally low social and psychological distance from target language speakers" and "steadily increasing interaction and communicative need" (139). Given such conditions, the acculturation model would predict successful second language acquisition. But Schmidt concludes, on the basis of massive amounts of convincingly presented longitudinal data, that "there are clear limits to Wes's communicative ability . . . both receptive and productive" and that "Wes's grammatical control of English has hardly improved at all over the three-year period" (144). We are also told that, "because of his inadequacies in the handling of English grammar, misunderstandings frequently arise in interaction with native speakers" (145). Schmidt's study of Wes thus poses a serious threat to the predictive power of the acculturation model.

Schmidt's study is also exemplary for its detailed treatment of the data. Commenting on case studies as research vehicles, Schmidt says:

> While it can be argued that case studies cannot be used as proof or disproof of theoretical models which have to do essentially with group tendencies, the acculturation model makes sufficiently explicit claims about the way in which diverse factors interact in the individual to make all case study material relevant for its evaluation. Particular case studies will support or detract from the model to the extent that they represent common types of learners rather than idiosyncratic exceptions. I believe that many readers will recognize similarities between Wes and other non-native speakers they have known. (173)

Regarding his interpretation of the data, Schmidt notes, "The judgments given here, as in most case studies, are . . . ultimately subjective, deriving their validity only from close personal friendship and familiarity with the subject, observations of his behavior, and discussions with him and others who know him well" (142). While researchers in the experimental tradition would see this intense involvement as posing a threat to objectivity, well-written case studies are indeed valuable because this very familiarity enables the author to convincingly portray the individual or site under investigation.

The third form of naturalistic inquiry that has frequently been used in language education is the diary study, which may be seen as a particular type of case study. According to Kathleen Bailey and Robert Ochsner,

> A diary study in second language learning, acquisition, or teaching is an account of a second language experience as recorded in a first-

person journal. The diarist may be a language teacher or a language learner—but the central characteristic of the diary studies is that they are introspective: The diarist studies his own teaching or learning. Thus he can report on affective factors, language learning strategies, and his own perceptions—facets of the language learning experience which are normally hidden or largely inaccessible to an external observer.   (189)

In other words, the diary studies are "first-person case studies—a research genre defined by the data collection procedures" (Bailey, "Diary Studies" 60–61). Typically, a language learner or teacher keeps an intensive longitudinal journal, using introspection, retrospection, and observation to make the entries. The results are analyzed by the diarist or by another researcher using the diary entries as data.

An example of a diary study on foreign language learning in the United States is Cheryl Brown's research on older and younger learners of Spanish at Brigham Young University's Mission Training Center ("Requests"). Brown used a combination of learners' journal entries and her own participant observation notes to investigate how the input needs of learners aged nineteen to twenty-one differ from those of learners aged fifty-five or older. She found that the younger learners wrote about the input they were receiving four times as often as the older learners, but over twenty-eight percent of the older learners' diary entries discussed changes they wanted in the input. The younger learners wrote about input changes less than three percent of the time.

Diary studies have been published on learners of Arabic (Rubin and Henze; F. Schumann; Schumann and Schumann), French (Bailey, "Introspective Analysis" and "Competitiveness"), German (Ellis, "Learning Styles"), Portuguese (Schmidt and Frota), Farsi (F. Schumann; Schumann and Schumann), English (Matsumoto, "Analysis"; Hilleson), and Spanish (C. Brown, "Requests"; Campbell). Wilga Rivers kept a journal of her learning of Spanish but did not analyze the results. The value of these studies lies in the fact that introspection yields insights into processes (e.g., the use of internal strategies or affective responses) that may not be available for inspection by outside observers.

Besides these three forms of naturalistic inquiry utilized in foreign language education, there are other promising avenues of naturalistic research, such as conversational analysis, which is the detailed microanalysis of such conversational features as topicalization, repair, speech acts, and turn taking. Conversational analysis is a subfield of an important area of naturalistic inquiry called ethnomethodology: "Ethnomethodologists are interested in societal members' knowledge of their ordinary affairs and their own organized enterprises, in practical reasoning and everyday accomplishments" (Richards and Schmidt 118). Examples of conversational analysis in language education are the studies of conversational repair between native and nonnative speakers (Gaskill) and between pairs of nonnative speakers (Schwartz).

Advantages and Disadvantages

People who work in the naturalistic inquiry tradition feel that it offers several advantages. It permits in-depth study of individuals, settings, or interactions. Its emphasis on developing both the emic and the etic perspectives ensures that no point of view is disregarded. Naturalistic inquiry provides many examples of language issues that are often lost in statistical analyses associated with experimental studies having large numbers of subjects.

Likewise, the analytic procedures of naturalistic inquiry are not restricted to quantifiable data; rather, a wide range of data types is admitted as evidence. Naturalistic inquiry typically yields reader-friendly results that do not require statistical training to understand, and it can provide rich interpretive accounts of linguistic and sociolinguistic phenomena.

There are also disadvantages of naturalistic inquiry. Data collection, reduction, and analysis are extremely labor-intensive and time-consuming, particularly since ethnographies, diary studies, and case studies are longitudinal by nature. There is also the problem of the absence of agreed-upon criteria for determining the significance of the outcomes. As Smith and Heshusius note, "For many inquirers, the most pressing problem now is to develop criteria and procedures that will do for qualitative inquiry what certain criteria and procedures have done for quantitative inquiry (act as a constraint on our subjective selves, allow for the possibility of certitude, etc.)" (6). Furthermore, the analytic procedures of naturalistic inquiry are not as well understood or as well codified in our field as are those of experimental research; as a result, there are few methodology texts available, although this situation is changing rapidly. There are also few naturalistic studies of foreign language education available as examples to language teachers. Indeed, as late as 1989, Charles Ferguson and Thomas Huebner wrote, "Very few classroom-centered qualitative studies of second language acquisition, and virtually none of foreign language acquisition, exist" (7).

Another concern is that some data collected in naturalistic inquiry are particularly susceptible to the "observer's paradox" pointed out by William Labov (209). This problem is inherent in observational research: We wish to record and analyze behavior (in our case, linguistic or cultural behavior) as it normally occurs, but the very act of observing may cause alterations in the behavior we wish to study. If, for example, a researcher observes a foreign language classroom to study the learners' communication strategies in the target language, the presence of the researcher may inhibit the use of the strategies to be documented. Fortunately, researchers can at least partially surmount the observer's paradox by allowing sufficient time in the field and doing careful triangulation.

Another problem that often surfaces, particularly in diary studies, is associated with introspection. There is concern that typical language learners may not be able to accurately report on the complex cognitive processes involved in language acquisition (see Seliger). This concern touches all research that elicits mentalistic data from the subjects (Chaudron, "Research"). And in cases where language learning diaries are kept by linguists who are skillful at analyzing second language acquisition processes, the results may not be applicable to more typical language learners.

Resources

There are a few published resources available for teachers who wish to learn more about naturalistic inquiry in language classrooms. Leo van Lier's *The Classroom and the Language Learner* both discusses the findings of such research and exemplifies its methodology. Another useful book is Muriel Saville-Troike's *Ethnography of Communication*: "The focus of the ethnography of communication is the speech community, the way communication within it is patterned and organized as a system of communicative events, and the ways in which these interact with all other systems of culture" (3). Examples of well-written ethnographies in language education are Ailie Cleghorn and Fred Genesee's study of a French immersion school, Patricia Duff's research on dual-language schools in Hungary, and van Lier's moving account of a Quechua-Spanish bilingual program in Peru ("Conflicting

Voices"). Donald Freeman's study of the construction of shared understandings in a high school French class provides a perfect example of a researcher developing the emic perspective, and of the research questions that emerge and evolve as a study progresses.

Two research methods books in our field—Johnson's *Approaches to Research in Second Language Learning* and Nunan's *Research Methods in Language Learning*—contain clear chapters on case studies and ethnography. A seminal article on ethnography in the field of English as a second language is Watson-Gegeo's "Ethnography in ESL." Van Lier's "Ethnography: Bandaid, Bandwagon, or Contraband?" compares ethnography with cause-and-effect research. Katharine Samway has written a short, helpful piece for teachers who wish to keep field notes. Judith Green and Cynthia Wallat edited a volume on ethnography and language in educational settings. Henry Trueba, Grace Guthrie, and Kathryn Au edited a collection of studies in classroom ethnography that includes papers about Hawaiian children, black students, and Native Americans. Bailey and Nunan have edited an anthology of qualitative research on language education issues in eleven countries.

Craig Chaudron's "Research on Metalinguistic Judgments" and Nunan's *Research Methods in Language Learning* contain excellent reviews of procedures using mentalistic data. Nunan's work also includes a chapter on introspection. Claus Færch and Gabriele Kasper edited a valuable collection of articles on introspection in second language research; the chapter by Grotjahn provides a clear description of the methodological bases of introspective research methods.

Methodological information on language learning diary studies is also available to teachers. Some ideas on how to get started are available in Allwright and Bailey's *Focus on the Classroom*. Bailey and Ochsner have addressed issues of quality in diary studies. Both Keiko Matsumoto ("Diary Studies") and John Fry have written critical reviews of studies. Cheryl Brown discusses and contrasts the contributions of two naturalistic research methods—diary studies and participant observation—in her research on older and younger learners of Spanish ("Two Windows"). Bailey compares eleven diary studies for evidence of a relation between competitiveness and anxiety ("Competitiveness") and later reviews the diary studies available in print ("Diary Studies"). Her review adopts Peter Elbow's heuristic metaphor of the "doubting game and the believing game" (148–73), first criticizing the diary studies for not fitting the experimental mold, and then accepting them for what they have to offer.

Several books on naturalistic inquiry from anthropology, sociology and general education (as opposed to language education) are potentially useful to language teachers. A classic text is Lincoln and Guba's *Naturalistic Inquiry.* Guba previously laid out the methodological rationale that underlies this approach, in *Toward a Methodology of Naturalistic Inquiry in Educational Evaluation.* Catherine Marshall and Gretchen Rossman provide guidelines for writing qualitative research proposals. James Spradley has written two very helpful books, one on the ethnographic interview and one on participant observation, which give clear examples and excellent step-by-step procedures. Well-regarded introductory texts on ethnography are by Robert Bogdan and Steven Taylor and by Martyn Hammersley and Paul Atkinson. Hammersley's subsequent volume *What's Wrong with Ethnography?* addresses serious methodological arguments.

It is highly likely that the coming decades will witness an increasing interest in naturalistic inquiry on the part of language researchers. As this interest develops, more examples of naturalistic studies and more methodological guidance will be available in published form.

ACTION RESEARCH

The third major approach to empirical research in instructional language settings is called action research. This approach is less known in the United States than the other two, but in my opinion it is very promising for teachers who wish to conduct research in language classrooms.

While experimental research is often directed at theory building, action research has a more immediate and practical focus. Its results may contribute to emerging theory, but as Allwright and Bailey point out, it is not typically theory-driven. To say that action research has a practical focus does not demean its worth. Van Lier observes, "We must never forget that it is equally important to do research on practical activities and for practical purposes, such as the improvement of aspects of language teaching and learning" ("Action Research" 31; see also van Lier, "Some Features").

The term *action research* refers to a reiterated cycle of procedures. After planning, an action (or "small-scale intervention") is taken in an attempt to improve a situation. The apparent results are systematically observed through a variety of data collection procedures (audio or video recordings, teachers' diary entries, observers' notes, etc.). The action researcher reflects on the outcome and plans a subsequent action, after which the cycle begins again.

Van Lier's *Interaction in the Language Curriculum* reports his action research project, which combined teaching a low-level ESL grammar class with teaching graduate classes in applied linguistics. The purpose was to investigate the relevance of issues important in the ESL class as input for the theoretical classes, and vice versa. The project involved videotaping and transcribing classes, obtaining feedback from observers and students, keeping a diary, designing activities in the light of practical or theoretical concerns, and other procedures. A persistent difficulty van Lier faced was the lack of active participation and interaction among the students (all of them Asian, a constituency van Lier had not worked with before). While van Lier was searching for possible solutions, the value of an approach to interaction based on Lev Vygotsky's ideas became apparent, and different options for task design and their theoretical underpinnings became available to the graduate classes. In this way, van Lier consciously used action research to relate theory and practice.

As this example illustrates, action research, like naturalistic inquiry, is conducted in naturally occurring settings rather than with groups artificially composed for the sake of an experiment. And, like naturalistic inquiry, action research often uses multiple forms of data. It is sometimes described as participatory research, because the researchers are members of the speech community under study (a clear contrast to the desired distance and objectivity of experimental research). Indeed, van Lier takes the position that "action research is a type of research which assumes that the practitioners themselves are often the best people to carry out research on their own practices, perhaps at times with help from academics who have some relevant expertise to offer" ("Action Research" 31).

The broad goals of action research are to seek local understanding and to bring about improvement in the context under study. But Louis Cohen and Lawrence Manion (cited in Nunan's "Action Research in the Language Classroom" 64) suggest that action research can be used to accomplish more specific goals:

to remedy problems in specific situations, to improve a given set of circumstances;

to provide inservice training, giving teachers new skills and greater self-awareness;

to inject additional or innovative teaching and learning approaches into a system that normally inhibits change;

to improve communications between the practicing teacher and the academic researcher;

to provide an alternative to the more subjective, impressionistic approach to problem solving in the classroom.

These five goals clearly imply a social agenda, which Steven Kemmis and Robin McTaggart describe as follows: "Action research is a form of 'self-reflective enquiry' undertaken by participants in social situations in order to improve the rationality and justice of their own social or educational practices, as well as their understanding of these practices and the situations in which these practices are carried out" ("Action Research" 2).

One example of action research in foreign language education that supports Kemmis and McTaggart's concept of self-reflective inquiry is Carolyn Szostek's introduction of cooperative learning techniques in her high school honors Spanish 2 classes. Over the research project's four-and-a-half-week period, Szostek collected data through a variety of methods: her daily teacher's journal, observations by three colleagues, and attitude questionnaires completed by the students. She repeatedly used four different cooperative learning procedures: student team learning, group investigation, think-pair-share, and the three-step interview. The data from her journal, her colleagues, and the student questionnaires all converged to indicate that students perceived the benefits of and enjoyed the cooperative learning procedures and that more Spanish was being spoken in the classroom. Szostek notes that even though her action research project was conducted without a control group, the findings were valid: "The corroboration of teacher observations by outside visitors and the congruence between these observations and the perceptions of the students, as evidenced by their responses to the final questionnaire, gives validity to those observations" (259). Such corroboration in action research, with an emphasis on the various participants' point of view, is analogous to triangulation in ethnography.

Advantages and Disadvantages

People who work in the action research tradition feel that it has several advantages. It can be conducted by teachers in their own classrooms. It does not require quantifiable data, large numbers of subjects, or artificial control over variables. By definition, it is intended to lead directly to applicable results. It involves participants in the investigating and improving of their own settings. Van Lier notes, "Ultimately, action research leads to a re-evaluation of our reality and goals as teachers, of the students' needs and aspirations, and of the contextual (social, institutional, political, etc.) constraints and resources that facilitate or inhibit our work." It is true that teachers already think about and discuss such things, but, van Lier continues, "by making them the object of systematic and sustained enquiry, we may actually have the chance to become *proactive* rather than remaining *reactive*" ("Action Research" 36). Thus conducting action research can be an empowering process for teachers. And, as Cohen and Manion point out, action research can bring about innovative practices in schools, which are typically conservative entities.

There are also disadvantages of action research. The most obvious is simply a function of its youth. Although action research was begun in the United States in the 1940s (see Lewin), for various reasons it has not enjoyed much prestige or development in this country. As a result, not many published examples are available yet in the literature on linguistics or language education, and there is still limited professional status associated with conducting action research (see, e.g., Jarvis). But there is now a new journal, *Educational Action Research,* which will no doubt promote a wider understanding of this approach among educators.

No agreed-upon criteria exist for determining the significance of the results in action research. Critics claim that, since there is only limited control over variables, no strong causal statements are possible. Because the subjects are not randomly selected from the population, the findings may not be generalized (as the term is used in experimental research) beyond the particular setting of and the people involved in the project.

Since the goals of action research are to develop local understanding and bring about improvement in one's own context, action researchers typically don't concern themselves with issues of generalizability or causality. But there are two dangers. First, if action research is conducted exclusively by participants in a given setting, the results will be limited to an entirely emic perspective. Second, if there is no concern for generalizability (and particularly if action research continues to be held in low esteem in the profession), then action researchers may not be motivated to disseminate their findings, and much useful information could be hidden in in-house discussions at the site of the study.

Another concern often raised is that conducting action research creates additional work for teachers. Van Lier describes the problem as follows:

> Many of us at times fall into unexamined routines, or rush headlong from one session to another, collapsing into the first available easy chair at the end of a long exhausting day. Clearly if action research is going to make us even more exhausted than we already are, then it will not be a very popular or successful activity. It has to enrich our professional lives, improve the success rate of our students, contribute to our understanding of language learning, and so on. If it cannot reduce our exhaustion, at least it ought to make it more bearable by reducing frustration, lack of direction and boredom.   ("Action Research" 32)

One solution to the concern about overburdening teachers is offered by Sharon Oja and Lisa Smulyan, who have written about a collaborative model of action research in which teams of teachers and outside researchers pair up to conduct action research in the teachers' setting. When van Lier discusses collaborative action research, he concludes positively, as Oja and Smulyan do, that "action research, by systematizing, documenting, and thus legitimizing our investigative activities as teachers, can make our work more purposeful, interesting, and valuable, and as such it tends to have an energizing and revitalizing effect" (33).

The possible benefits of action research have yet to be realized in the foreign language field. It will be interesting to see whether, in the next few decades, this approach to empirical research in instructional language settings will gain acceptance, momentum, and prestige.

Resources

Of the useful references available on action research, few are from foreign language education in the United States context. Nunan's *Understanding Language Classrooms* should be helpful for language teachers wishing to learn more about the topic. Two key articles about action research in language education are by Graham Crookes and by van Lier ("Action Research"). In addition to Szostek's study of her Spanish classes, there is Amy Tsui's report about action research she and her colleagues conducted on students' oral participation in English classes in Hong Kong. Marguerite Snow, John Hyland, Lia Kamhi-Stein, and Janet Yu have engaged teachers of linguistic minority children in a large-scale action research project in California. Catherine Kebir has used the action research model to investigate the communication strategies of adult language learners. And Nunan has described the use of the action research model in language education ("Action Research in Language Education"), as well as in language teacher education ("Action Research in the Language Classroom").

Information from general education on how to conduct action research is more plentiful (see Argyris, Putnam, and Smith; Carr and Kemmis; Ebbutt; Goswami and Stillman; Hustler, Cassidy and Duff; Strickland). *A Teacher's Guide to Action Research,* edited by John Nixon, provides an interesting collection of action research studies in general education, and Kemmis and McTaggart's *The Action Research Planner* is an essential guide for people who wish to begin an action research project. Given the applicability of action research to language teaching, I expect more methodological guidance will be available in the near future for language professionals interested in this approach to empirical research in instructional language settings.

The experimental approach, naturalistic inquiry, and action research in instructional language settings have been discussed in this essay as if they were completely separate—and indeed, as we have seen, their underlying philosophies and goals are quite different (Smith and Heshusius). But we should not overlook commonalities or affinities among the three approaches, particularly at the level of procedure. For example, some survey research uses both quantitative and qualitative data to assess preexisting conditions or attitudes; there is no treatment at all involved, even though survey research is typically associated with statistical analyses and the experimental tradition. Likewise, qualitative data collected in the naturalistic inquiry tradition can be coded and quantified in a variety of ways (Chaudron, "Interaction"), as we saw in discussing Cheryl Brown's statistical analyses of some of the diary data from her older and younger learners of Spanish ("Requests").

When the experimental tradition was dominant and alternative research paradigms were scorned for yielding "soft" data, one seldom saw researchers combining procedures drawn from the different traditions. Nowadays, language education researchers utilize diverse procedures to address questions of interest. For example, Susan Bacon studied low-proficiency college students listening to authentic passages in Spanish; she wanted to determine what comprehension strategies they used to process the material. Although the design of her study was clearly experimental, she collected qualitative data (transcriptions of interviews with the learners), which were then coded and tabulated. She calls her study "a descriptive analysis of an experiment" (317). In a study of a Japanese FLES (foreign language in the elementary school) program, Richard Donato, Janis Antonek, and G. Richard Tucker describe their research as a multiple perspectives analysis, because it utilized data derived from questionnaires completed by parents and learners, oral interviews, reflections from the Japanese teacher, questionnaires from other teachers at the school, and an observation scale. Statistical analyses were conducted with some of the data, and a descriptive analysis was done of the children's interviews. The authors conclude, "To understand the complexity of FLES programs requires diverse sources of evidence anchored in the classroom and connected to the wider school community. We offer this multiple perspectives analysis to illustrate the myriad of variables at play in the processes and products of a FLES program" (376). In other words, the language learning and teaching they investigated was too complex to be treated satisfactorily with a single type of data or a single analytic method.

The combining of data collection and analytic procedures from the different research approaches is not a new development, either in general educational research or in language education research. In 1979, Robert Ochsner, making a comparison of nomothetic (theory-driven) and hermeneutic (interpretive) research, urged language researchers to develop what he called a bilingual perspective. Although some authors object strongly to the blending of these traditions (see, e.g., Smith and Heshusius), Chaudron, citing the anthology edited by Thomas Cook and Charles Reichardt, explains that

> the qualitative paradigm involves naturalistic, uncontrolled, subjective, and process-oriented observation, while the quantitative paradigm is obtrusive, controlled, objective, and product oriented. [Cook and Reichardt] point out, however, that qualitative participant observation is not necessarily completely naturalistic or unobtrusive and that experimental, controlled procedures do not

necessarily elicit non-natural behaviors for measurement. The qualitative paradigm can be pursued with objectivity in the form of interobserver agreement, while the theoretical underpinnings of a quantitative approach invariably bias observation in some possibly unrecognized, subjective way.   ("Interaction" 709–10)

So while there are clear differences in goals and philosophies, these various approaches to research may not be so far apart as we first thought. Even a dyed-in-the-wool ethnographer has noted that "in practice ethnographers employ a range of techniques which lie along a continuum from non-intervention to intervention and from unstructured to structured . . . and exactly at which point ethnography stops and normative science starts is unclear" (van Lier, *Classroom* 56).

The differences and similarities among the broad approaches to research can be summarized by comparing them according to three factors: (1) the extent of control the researcher exerts over the variables (Allwright and Bailey; van Lier, *Classroom* and "Classroom Research"), (2) the a priori selection of variables and structuring of data (van Lier, *Classroom* and "Classroom Research"), and (3) the extent of intentional intervention by the researchers (Allwright and Bailey; Bailey, Omaggio-Hadley, Magnan, and Swaffar). The figure below gives this comparison in a somewhat simplified form.

A COMPARISON OF THREE APPROACHES TO RESEARCH

Experimental Research	*Naturalistic Inquiry*	*Action Research*
+ control	– control	– control
+ selection and structuring	– selection and structuring	– selection and structuring
+ intervention	– intervention	+ intervention

These three approaches to empirical research in instructional language settings have very different purposes as well as different advantages and disadvantages. None can be said, a priori and out of context, to be superior or inferior to the others. It is simply an issue of appropriateness. A researcher must choose the approach that is right for the hypotheses or research questions under investigation and appropriate to the situation, which includes the researcher's training, resources, and time constraints. But whatever the approach, as van Lier notes, "all scientists would insist on carefully motivated, explicitly documented, and skillfully implemented procedures appropriate to the investigative matter at hand" ("Forks" 333).

Arguments over which approach is best tend to overlook the multiple purposes of empirical research. Such arguments also ignore questions of personal preference. Some people are more comfortable with the necessary control of the experimental research tradition; others, finding control dehumanizing and distancing, prefer naturalistic inquiry or action research. John Schumann made this point in his eloquent discussion of art and science in second language acquisition research: "In art, perspectives are neither right nor wrong; they are simply more or less appealing to various audiences. For that reason, no perspective has to be disposed of; they all contribute to a greater or lesser degree to the history of art, but none of them has to be discredited in order to capture the ultimate truth" ("Art" 115).

Regardless of our choice of approach, it is incumbent on us as foreign language educators to be well informed about research alternatives. "The blacksmith cannot criticize the carpenter for not heating a piece of wood over a fire. However, the carpenter must demonstrate a principled control over the materials," says van Lier (*Classroom* 42). It is my hope that, in the years ahead, the potential of each approach will be more fully realized and that we can improve our work in instructional language settings, in part, through more effective research.

WORKS CITED

Allwright, Richard L. "Classroom-Centered Research on Language Teaching and Learning: A Brief Historical Overview." *TESOL Quarterly* 17 (1983): 191–204.

———. "Turns, Topics, and Tasks: Patterns of Participation in Language Learning and Teaching." Larsen-Freeman 165–87.

Allwright, Richard L., and Kathleen M. Bailey. *Focus on the Language Classroom: An Introduction to Classroom Research for Language Teachers.* Cambridge: Cambridge UP, 1991.

Argyris, Chris, Robert Putnam, and Diane McLain Smith. *Action Science: Concepts, Methods, and Skills for Research and Intervention.* San Francisco: Jossey-Bass, 1985.

Bacon, Susan M. "Phases of Listening to Authentic Input in Spanish: A Descriptive Study." *Foreign Language Annals* 25 (1992): 317–34.

Bailey, Kathleen M. "Classroom-Centered Research on Language Teaching and Learning." *Beyond Basics: Issues and Research in TESOL.* Ed. Marianne Celce-Murcia. Rowley: Newbury, 1985. 96–121.

———. "Competitiveness and Anxiety in Adult Second Language Learning: Looking *at* and *through* the Diary Studies." Seliger and Long 67–102.

————. "Diary Studies of Classroom Language Learning: The Doubting Game and the Believing Game." *Language Acquisition and the Second/Foreign Language Classroom.* Ed. Eugenius Sadtono. Singapore: SEAMEO Regional Lang. Centre, 1991. 60–102.

————. "An Introspective Analysis of an Individual's Language Learning Experience." Scarcella and Krashen 58–65.

Bailey, Kathleen M., and David Nunan, eds. *Voices from the Language Classroom: Qualitative Research on Language Education.* New York: Cambridge UP, 1996.

Bailey, Kathleen M., and Robert Ochsner. "A Methodological Review of the Diary Studies: Windmill Tilting or Social Science?" *Second Language Acquisition Studies.* Ed. Bailey, Michael H. Long, and Sabrina Peck. Rowley: Newbury, 1983. 188–98.

Bailey, Kathleen M., Alice Omaggio-Hadley, Sally S. Magnan, and Janet Swaffar. "Research in the 1990s: Focus on Theory Building, Instructional Innovation, and Collaboration." *Foreign Language Annals* 24 (1991): 89–100.

Bateson, Gregory. *Steps to an Ecology of Mind.* New York: Ballantine, 1972.

Bogdan, Robert, and Steven J. Taylor. *Introduction to Qualitative Research Methods.* Toronto: Wiley, 1975.

Brown, Cheryl. "Requests for Specific Language Input: Differences between Older and Younger Adult Language Learners." *Input in Second Language Acquisition.* Ed. Susan L. Gass and Carolyn Madden. Rowley: Newbury, 1985. 272–84.

————. "Two Windows on the Classroom World: Diary Studies and Participant Observation Differences." *On TESOL '84: Brave New World for TESOL.* Ed. Penny Larson, Elliott L. Judd, and Dorothy S. Messerschmitt. Washington: TESOL, 1985. 121-34.

Brown, James D. "Statistics as a Foreign Language—Part 1: What to Look for in Reading Statistical Language Studies." *TESOL Quarterly* 25 (1991): 569–86.

————. "Statistics as a Foreign Language—Part 2: More Things to Consider in Reading Statistical Language Studies." *TESOL Quarterly* 26 (1992): 629–64.

————. *Understanding Research in Second Language Learning: A Teacher's Guide to Statistics and Research Design.* New York: Cambridge UP, 1988.

Brumfit, Christopher, and Rosamund Mitchell, eds. *Research in the Language Classroom: ELT Documents,* 133. London: Modern English Publications and British Council, 1990.

Campbell, Cherry C. "Socializing with the Teachers and Prior Language Learning Experience: A Diary Study." Bailey and Nunan 201–23.

Campbell, Donald, and Julian C. Stanley. *Experimental and Quasi-Experimental Designs for Research.* Chicago: Rand McNally, 1966.

Carr, Wilfred, and Stephen Kemmis. *Becoming Critical: Education, Knowledge and Action Research.* London: Falmer, 1986.

Chaudron, Craig. "The Interaction of Quantitative and Qualitative Approaches to Research: A View of the Second Language Classroom." *TESOL Quarterly* 20 (1986): 709–17.

————. "Research on Metalinguistic Judgments: A Review of Theory, Methods, and Results." *Language Learning* 33 (1983): 343–77.

————. *Second Language Classrooms: Research on Teaching and Learning.* Cambridge: Cambridge UP, 1988.

Clark, John L. D. "The Pennsylvania Project and the Audiolingual vs. Traditional Question." *Modern Language Journal* 53 (1969): 388–96.

Cleghorn, Ailie, and Fred Genesee. "Languages in Contact: An Ethnographic Study of Interaction in an Immersion School." *TESOL Quarterly* 18 (1984): 595–625.

Cohen, Louis, and Lawrence Manion. *Research Methods in Education.* London: Croom Helm, 1985.

Cook, Thomas D., and Charles S. Reichardt, eds. *Qualitative and Quantitative Methods in Evaluation Research.* Beverly Hills: Sage, 1979.

Crookes, Graham. "Action Research for Second Language Teaching: Going beyond Teacher Research." *Applied Linguistics* 14 (1993): 130–42.

Denzin, Norman K. *Sociological Methods: A Source Book.* Chicago: Aldine, 1970.

Donato, Richard, Janis L. Antonek, and G. Richard Tucker. "A Multiple Perspectives Analysis of a Japanese FLES Program." *Foreign Language Annals* 27 (1994): 365–78.

Duff, Patricia A. "Different Languages, Different Practices: Socialization of Discourse Competence in Dual-Language School Classrooms in Hungary." Bailey and Nunan 407–33.

Ebbutt, David. "Educational Action Research: Some General Concerns and Specific Quibbles." *Issues in Educational Research: Qualitative Methods.* Ed. Robert G. Burgess. Lewes, Eng.: Falmer, 1985.

Edge, Julian, and Keith Richards, eds. *Teachers Develop Teachers Research: Papers on Classroom Research and Teacher Development.* Oxford: Heinemann, 1993.

Elbow, Peter. *Writing without Teachers.* New York: Oxford UP, 1973.

Ellis, Rod. "Classroom Learning Styles and Their Effect on Second Language Acquisition: A Study of Two Learners." *System* 17 (1989): 249–62.

———. *Learning through Instruction: The Study of Classroom Language Acquisition:* Oxford: Blackwell, 1990.

Færch, Claus, and Gabriele Kasper, eds. *Introspection in Second Language Research.* Clevedon Eng.: Multilingual Matters, 1987.

Ferguson, Charles R., and Thomas Huebner. *Foreign Language Instruction and Second Language Acquisition Research in the United States.* Occasional Papers 1. Washington: Natl. Foreign Lang. Center, 1989.

Freed, Barbara F., ed. *Foreign Language Acquisition Research and the Classroom.* Lexington: Heath, 1991.

Freeman, Donald. "Collaboration: Constructing Shared Understandings in a Second Language Classroom." *Collaborative Language Learning and Teaching.* Ed. David Nunan. Cambridge: Cambridge UP, 1992. 56–80.

Fry, John. "Diary Studies in Classroom SLA Research: Problems and Prospects." *JALT Journal* 9 (1988): 158–67.

Gaies, Stephen J. "The Investigation of Language Classroom Processes." *TESOL Quarterly* 17 (1983): 205–17.

Gaskill, William H. "Correction in Native Speaker–Nonnative Speaker Discourse." Larsen-Freeman 125–37.

Goswami, Dixie, and Peter R. Stillman. *Reclaiming the Classroom: Teacher Research as an Agency for Change.* Upper Montclair: Boynton, 1987.

Green, Judith, and Cynthia Wallat, eds. *Ethnography and Language in Educational Settings.* Norwood: Ablex, 1981.

Grotjahn, Rüdiger. "On the Methodological Basis of Introspective Methods." Færch and Kasper 54–81.

Guba, Egon G. *Toward a Methodology of Naturalistic Inquiry in Educational Evaluation.* CSE Monograph Ser. in Evaluation 8. Los Angeles: U of California, Los Angeles, Center for the Study of Evaluation, 1978.

Hammersley, Martyn. *What's Wrong with Ethnography?* London: Routledge, 1992.

Hammersley, Martyn, and Paul Atkinson. *Ethnography: Principles in Practice.* London: Tavistock, 1983.

Hatch, Evelyn, and Anne Lazaraton. *The Research Manual: Design and Statistics for Applied Linguistics.* New York: Newbury, 1991.

Hilleson, Mick. "'I Want to Talk to Them but I Don't Want Them to Hear': An Introspective Study of Second Language Anxiety in an English-Medium School." Bailey and Nunan 248–75.

Hustler, David, Anthony Cassidy, and E. C. Duff, eds. *Action Research in Classroom and Schools.* London: Allen 1986.

Jaeger, Richard M. *Statistics: A Spectator Sport.* Beverly Hills: Sage 1983.

Jarvis, Gilbert A. "Action Research versus Needed Research for the 1980s." *Proceeedings of the National Conference on Professional Priorities.* Hastings-on-Hudson: ACTFL, 1980. 59–63.

Johnson, Donna M. *Approaches to Research in Second Language Learning.* New York: Longman, 1992.

Kaplan, Abraham. *The Conduct of Inquiry: Methodology for Behavioral Science.* New York: Crowell, 1964.

Kebir, Catherine. "An Action Research Look at the Communication Strategies of Adult Learners." *TESOL Journal* 4 (1994): 28–31.

Kemmis, Steven, and Robin McTaggart. "Action Research." *IATEFL Newsletter* 102 (1989): 2–3.

———. *The Action Research Planner.* Victoria: Deakin Univ., 1982.

Labov, William. *Sociolinguistic Patterns.* Philadelphia: U of Pennsylvania P, 1973.

Larsen-Freeman, Diane, ed. *Discourse Analysis in Second Language Research.* Rowley: Newbury, 1980.

Lett, John A., Jr. "Research: What, Why, and for Whom?" *Practical Applications of Research in Foreign Language Teaching.* Ed. Charles James. ACTFL Foreign Lang. Educ. Ser. 14. Skokie: Natl. Textbook, 1983. 9–49.

Lewin, Kurt. "Action Research and Minority Problems." *Journal of Social Issues* 2 (1946): 34–46.

Lincoln, Yvonna S., and Egon G. Guba. *Naturalistic Inquiry.* Newbury Park: Sage, 1985.

Long, Michael H. "Inside the 'Black Box': Methodological Issues in Research on Language Teaching and Learning." *Language Learning* 30 (1980): 1–42. Rpt. in Seliger and Long 3–35.

———. "Process and Product in ESL Program Evaluation." *TESOL Quarterly* 18 (1984): 409–25.

Marshall, Catherine, and Gretchen B. Rossman. *Designing Qualitative Research.* Newbury Park: Sage, 1989.

Matsumoto, Keiko. "An Analysis of a Japanese ESL Learner's Diary: Factors Involved in the L2 Learning Process." *JALT Journal* 11 (1989): 167–92.

———. "Diary Studies of Second Language Acquisition: A Critical Overview." *JALT Journal* 9 (1987): 17–34.

Nixon, John, ed. *A Teacher's Guide to Action Research.* London: Grant McIntyre, 1981.

Nunan, David. "Action Research in Language Education." *Teachers Develop Teachers Research: Papers on Classroom Research and Teacher Development.* Ed. Julian Edge and Keith Richards. Oxford: Heinemann, 1993. 39–50.

———. "Action Research in the Language Classroom." *Second Language Teacher Education.* Ed. Jack C. Richard and Nunan. Cambridge: Cambridge UP, 1990. 62–81.

———. *Research Methods in Language Learning.* Cambridge: Cambridge UP, 1992.

———. *Understanding Language Classrooms: A Guide for Teacher-Initiated Action.* New York: Prentice, 1989.

Ochsner, Robert. "A Poetic of Second Language Acquisition." *Language Learning* 29 (1979): 53–80.

Oja, Sharon Nodie, and Lisa Smulyan. *Collaborative Action Research: A Developmental Approach.* London: Falmer, 1989.

Otto, Frank M. "The Teacher in the Pennsylvania Project." *Modern Language Journal* 53 (1969): 411–20.

Richards, Jack C., and Richard W. Schmidt. "Conversational Analysis." *Language and Communication.* Ed. Richards and Schmidt. London: Longman, 1983. 117–54.

Rivers, Wilga M. "Learning a Sixth Language: An Adult Learner's Daily Diary." *Canadian Modern Language Review* 36 (1979): 67–82. Rpt. in *Communicating Naturally in a Second Language: Theory and Practice in Language Teaching.* By Rivers. Cambridge: Cambridge UP, 1983. 169–88.

Rubin, Joan, and Rosemary Henze. "The Foreign Language Requirement: A Suggestion to Enhance Its Educational Role in Teacher Training." *TESOL Newsletter* 15 (1981): 17+.

Samimy, Keiko K., and Jennybelle P. Rardin. "Adult Language Learners' Affective Reactions to Community Language Learning." *Foreign Language Annals* 27 (1994): 379–90.

Samway, Katharine Davies. "But It's Hard to Keep Fieldnotes While Also Teaching." *TESOL Journal* 4 (1994): 47.

Saville-Troike, Muriel. *The Ethnography of Communication: An Introduction.* Baltimore: University Park, 1982.

Scarcella, Robin, and Steven Krashen, eds. *Research in Second Language Acquisition: Selected Papers of the Los Angeles Second Language Research Forum.* Rowley: Newbury, 1980.

Scherer, George A. C., and Michael Wertheimer. *A Psycholinguistic Experiment in Foreign Language Teaching.* New York: McGraw, 1964.

Schmidt, Richard W. "Interaction, Acculturation, and the Acquisition of Communicative Competence: A Case Study of an Adult." *Sociolinguistics and Language Acquisition.* Ed. Nessa Wolfson and Elliot Judd. Rowley: Newbury, 1983. 137–74.

Schmidt, Richard W., and Sylvia Nagem Frota. "Developing Basic Conversational Ability in a Second Language: A Case Study of an Adult Learner of Portuguese." *Talking to Learn: Conversation in Second Language Acquisition.* Ed. R. R. Day. Rowley: Newbury 1986. 237–326.

Schumann, Francine E. "Diary of a Language Learner: A Further Analysis." Scarcella and Krashen 51–57.

Schumann, Francine E., and John H. Schumann. "Diary of a Language Learner: An Introspective Study of Second Language Learning." Ed. H. Douglas Brown, Ruth H. Crymes, and Carlos A. Yorio. *On TESOL '77: Teaching and Learning English as a Second Language—Trends in Research and Practice.* Washington: TESOL, 1977. 241–49.

Schumann, John H. "The Acculturation Model for Second Language Acquisition." *Second Language Acquisition and Foreign Language Teaching.* Ed. Rosario C. Gingras. Arlington: Center for Applied Linguistics, 1978. 27–50.

———. "Art and Science in Second Language Acquisition Research." *On TESOL '82: Pacific Perspectives on Language Learning and Teaching.* Ed. Mark A. Clarke and Jean Handscombe. Washington: TESOL, 1983. 107–24.

Schwartz, Joan. "The Negotiation for Meaning: Repair in Conversations between Second Language Learners of English." Larsen-Freeman 138–53.

Seliger, Herbert W. "The Language Learner as Linguist: Of Metaphors and Realities." *Applied Linguistics* 4 (1983): 179–91.

Seliger, Herbert W., and Michael H. Long, eds. *Classroom Oriented Research in Second Language Acquisition.* Rowley: Newbury, 1985.

Shavelson, Richard J. *Statistical Reasoning for the Behavioral Sciences.* Boston: Allyn, 1981.

Shaw, Peter A. "Voices for Improved Learning: The Ethnographer as Co-agent of Pedagogic Changes." Bailey and Nunan 318–37.

Smith, Phillip D. *A Comparison of the Cognitive and Audiolingual Approaches to Foreign Language Instruction: The Pennsylvania Foreign Language Project.* Philadelphia: Center for Curriculum Dev., 1970.

Smith, John K., and Lois Heshusius. "Closing Down the Conversation: The End of the Quantitative-Qualitative Debate among Educational Inquirers." *Educational Researcher* 15.1 (1986): 4–12.

Snow, Marguerite Ann, John Hyland, Lia Kamhi-Stein, and Janet Harclerode Yu. "U.S. Language Minority Students: Voices from the Junior High Classroom." Bailey and Nunan 304–17.

Spradley, James P. *The Ethnographic Interview.* New York: Holt, Rinehart, 1979.

———. *Participant Observation.* New York: Holt, Rinehart, 1980.

Strickland, Dorothy S. "The Teacher as Researcher: Toward the Extended Professional." *Language Arts* 65 (1988): 754–64.

Szostek, Carolyn. "Assessing the Effects of Cooperative Learning in an Honors Foreign Language Classroom." *Foreign Language Annals* 27 (1994): 252–61.

Trueba, Henry J., Grace Pung Guthrie, and Kathryn Hu-Pei Au, eds. *Culture and the Bilingual Classroom: Studies in Classroom Ethnography.* Rowley: Newbury, 1981.

Tsui, Amy B. M. "Reticence and Anxiety in Second Language Learning." Bailey and Nunan 145–67.

Tuckman, Bruce W. *Conducting Educational Research.* 3rd ed. New York: Harcourt, 1988.

van Lier, Leo. "Action Research." *Sintagma* 6 (1994): 31–37.

———. *The Classroom and the Language Learner: Ethnography and Second Language Classroom Research.* London: Longman, 1988.

———. "Classroom Research in Second Language Acquisition." *Annual Review of Applied Linguistics* 10 (1989): 173–86.

———. "Conflicting Voices: Language, Classrooms, and Bilingual Education in Puno." Bailey and Nunan 363–87.

———. "Ethnography: Bandaid, Bandwagon, or Contraband?" Brumfit and Mitchell, 33–53.

———."Forks and Hope: Pursuing Understanding in Different Ways." *Applied Linguistics* 15 (1994): 328–46.

———. *Interaction in the Language Curriculum: Awareness, Autonomy, and Authenticity.* London: Longman, 1996.

———. "Some Features of a Theory of Practice." *TESOL Journal* 4 (1994): 6–10.

Vygotsky, Lev. *Mind in Society.* Cambridge: Harvard UP, 1978.

Watson-Gegeo, Karen A. "Ethnography in ESL: Defining the Essentials." *TESOL Quarterly* 22 (1988): 575–92.

Woods, Anthony, Paul Fletcher, and Arthur Hughes. *Statistics in Language Studies.* London: Cambridge UP, 1986.

Cognitive Characteristics of Adult Second Language Learners

Bill VanPatten

Human behavior for any given activity is describable along two dimensions: traits or patterns of behavior that are particular to one person and traits or patterns of behavior that are shared among most, if not all, persons. The former are generally referred to as individual variations or individual differences and the latter are referred to as universals. Because language acquisition (whether first or second) involves human behavior, it is no different; it exhibits both individual variation in and universal aspects of learning. This essay focuses on the universal aspects of second language acquisition.

First I describe and discuss the empirical evidence that second language acquisition is strongly constrained on a number of levels. I argue that second language learners, their individual differences notwithstanding, do not create unique and idiosyncratic versions of the second language during acquisition. I review several perspectives on the nature of the underlying processes and mechanisms that might constrain language acquisition. I argue that no single perspective can account for all universal aspects of second language acquisition and that different mechanisms and processes work together to shape the linguistic system that learners create in their minds. I conclude with a brief discussion of the tension between universals and individual differences in the literature of the field.

UNIVERSALS IN SECOND LANGUAGE ACQUISITION

It is clear to researchers and theorists that, regardless of context (i.e., whether classroom or nonclassroom), second language acquisition is strongly constrained. This conclusion is based on substantial evidence of systematicity and universality in learner development in a number of domains. I review below these pieces of empirical evidence: orders of acquisition, developmental sequences, a lack of certain kinds of errors, and the limited effects of explicit grammar instruction.

Orders of Acquisition

Research in second language acquisition has found that certain grammatical morphemes (within governing syntactic categories) are acquired in a fixed order. Over time, noun-phrase morphemes are acquired in one predictable order, verb-phrase morphemes in another, and other morphemes in yet another (VanPatten, "Morphemes"; Larsen-Freeman and Long). In English, the language about which there is perhaps the most research on second language acquisition, second language learners predictably acquire morphemes and functors in the orders displayed in figure 1. Regardless of first language background, learners acquire, for example, -*ing* first, then past tense, and finally third-person -*s*. These orders do not seem to be affected by instruction, since both classroom and nonclassroom learners exhibit the same orders.

Figure 1
ACQUISITION ORDERS FOR EIGHT ENGLISH MORPHEMES
AND FUNCTORS

Noun Phrase	*Verb Phrase*	*Auxiliary Component*
Plural -*s*	-*ing*	Contractible copula (e.g., *John's tall*)
⇓	⇓	⇓
Articles	Past tense	Contractible auxiliary (e.g., *John's eaten already*)
⇓	⇓	
Possessive -*s*	Third-person -*s*	

Source: VanPatten, "Morphemes"

Interestingly, the second language acquisition orders displayed in figure 1 are the same as those found for child first language acquisition of

English (VanPatten, "Morphemes"). Thus it would appear that there is not only systematicity or universality among different first language speakers learning English as a second language but also a degree of systematicity and universality among all learners of English, whether first or second language learners. To be sure, there has been argument over the validity of acquisition orders, especially in the late 1970s, as researchers grappled with new research methodologies in second language acquisition. But since the 1970s a great deal of evidence has emerged that acquisition orders do exist. They are now regarded as a fundamental fact of second language acquisition (see, for example, Larsen-Freeman and Long; Towell and Hawkins; Ellis).

Developmental Sequences

Developmental sequence is a term used to describe the acquisition pattern for a particular form. One might describe the developmental sequence for the acquisition of tense or aspect or for the acquisition of negation. These sequences represent the stages through which learners universally pass as they acquire the structure, form, or property in question. Developmental sequences have been documented for a variety of linguistic features: negation in English; negation in German; *wh-* questions in English; word order in German; tense and aspect in English, Spanish, and French; plural formation in English; *ser* and *estar* in Spanish. For example, learners of English (again, whether first language or second and whether in a classroom or nonclassroom context) traverse four stages in the acquisition of English negation. These stages are described in figure 2.

It goes without saying that the concept of stages is idealized; stages may overlap, features of one stage coexisting with features of the next. No learner moves clearly and neatly through the stages in acquiring any particular form. Nonetheless, the systematicity and universality of these stages are evidence of the constraints on language acquisition. No feature or structure can simply pop into the mind of the learner; the learner must in effect (re)create the linguistic property based on the linguistic input provided.

Lack of Certain Kinds of Errors

It is clear not just to researchers but also to instructors that learners make errors on their way toward nativelike ability. But what is often ignored by

Figure 2

DEVELOPMENTAL SEQUENCE FOR SECOND LANGUAGE
ACQUISITION OF NEGATION IN ENGLISH

Stage	Description	Example
1. External	The negative particle is externally attached to a declarative sentence.	No + you playing here.
2. Internal	The negative particle is found within the declarative sentence. *Don't* may appear as a variation of *no.*	Juana no have job.
3. Auxiliary + negative particle	*Not* appears and is attached to an auxiliary or modal verb. However, some *-n't* forms may be unanalyzed chunks.	I can't play this one.
4. Analyzed auxiliary	Auxiliary verbs are now part of the learner's linguistic system, and there is productive use of negation both in contracted and full forms.	He doesn't know anything.

Based on VanPatten, "Second-Language Acquisition Research" 53

instructors is that errors are restricted, that some errors are actually impossible for learners to make. Although it is clear that learners make errors based on their first language (transfer errors), certain first-language-based errors are never found in the output of learners.

In the heyday of audiolingualism, it was believed that the first language was the source of all second language learners' errors. Contrastive analysis was developed and used to predict errors that learners would make and then to offer suggestions for instruction (i.e., what needed to be drilled and practiced the most). As researchers began to examine the output of learners, it became clear that not all errors were transfer errors. Indeed, the research conducted on the quantity of transfer errors revealed that only between five percent and twenty-five percent of the total errors made by learners could be traced to the first language (Dulay, Burt, and Krashen). Instructors, of course, find this hard to believe. When learners use the indicative instead of the subjunctive in Spanish, an instructor may be quick to cite English as the problem, since English does not have an active subjunctive. But when one examines the output of first language learners of Spanish, one finds that they also do not incorporate the subjunctive until a rather late stage of development. For an error to be categorized as a transfer error, it cannot be an error that first language learners make too.

More to the point, learners often do not make transfer errors that they could make. In addition, when learners could correctly transfer from their first language to the second in order to make productive rules, they don't always do so. (A productive rule is one that forms part of the learner's evolving linguistic system.) In studies on relative clause formation, negation in French, and object pronouns in Spanish, it was found that learners often made errors that they would not have made had they simply transferred patterns from the first language. In a study conducted by Susan Gass, Romance learners of English produced what is called pronoun copy in relative clauses, even though this is not allowed in Romance languages or in English. Pronoun copy is the production of a pronoun in the relative clause that copies the function of the relative clause marker. For example, a learner of English with Italian as a first language may add an object pronoun to a direct-object relative clause:

| I saw | the man | who | I met | last week. |
| *Ho veduto* | *l'uomo* | *che* | *ho conosciuto* | *la setimanna passata.* |

Learner error: I saw the man who I met him last week.

Neither English nor Italian allows such pronouns, and in fact the two languages are virtually parallel in how they structure relative clauses. Yet Gass found that only twenty-eight percent of the direct-object relative clauses produced by the Romance speakers were well formed. The question is, of course, why these speakers do not simply transfer the structure of their relative clauses and get them correct in English. That they do not is evidence that language acquisition—in this case, first-language transfer—is constrained.

Researchers have also observed that learners do not place past-tense endings on nouns and do not split noun phrases to produce errors such as *The came man (The man came*; in linguistics, a preceding asterisk indicates an erroneous form). Learners of Spanish as a second language get data that suggest that object pronouns can "move up" in a sentence.

No puedo hacerlo.	I can't do it.
No lo puedo hacer.	
Juan me dice que no lo puedo hacer.	John tells me I can't do it.

Learners never mistakenly place the direct-object pronoun before the negative particle to produce the following error:

*Lo no puedo hacer.

And they never produce sentences in which the direct object moves from the embedded clause to the main clause:

*Juan me lo dice que no puedo hacer.

For some reason, they know that there is a limited range of movement, a limited number of positions the direct-object pronoun can occupy. It would seem, then, that errors are not produced willy-nilly, that only certain errors are possible.

The Limited Effects of Explicit Grammar Instruction

Research on acquisition orders, developmental sequences, and errors and error types has been conducted on both classroom and nonclassroom learners for the same reason that child first language acquisition has been examined: to understand the processes that guide acquisition. There is also research that focuses on the question of whether instruction in grammar makes a difference. Given that acquisition is constrained in particular ways, it makes sense to see if the explicit teaching of grammar is also constrained, that is, if instruction is somehow overridden or circumvented by what learners do naturally. Four positions have been advocated: Instruction has no effect on acquisition, is detrimental, is necessary, is beneficial.

Those who claim that instruction has no effect find strong evidence in the research that compares classroom and nonclassroom learning. It is unequivocal that instruction has no effect on acquisition orders and developmental sequences. As researchers compared and contrasted the acquisition orders and developmental sequences of learners both in and out of the classroom, only slight and usually trivial differences could be found. For example, the developmental sequence for negation described in figure 2 is not disrupted by classroom instruction. That learners from different contexts make more or less use of a particular negator at a given stage does not alter the fundamental nature of the four stages. Likewise, the acquisition orders listed in figure 1 are found both in and out of the classroom, which suggests that learners will acquire these morphemes and functors independently of when they are introduced in instruction and independently of how much practice time is devoted to any given item. In one study, Patsy Lightbown found an apparent disruption of the order for a group of classroom learners who were heavily engaged in practice and drilling of one particular morpheme. This disruption lasted for about a year; then the order of acquisition reasserted itself, the morpheme in question taking its rightful place. As Diane Larsen-Freeman and Michael Long state in their overview of the research, "Acquisition orders [and developmental sequences] may well be immutable" (307).

Those who argue that instruction may be detrimental have just several studies on which to base this claim, but the evidence in those studies is strong. Manfred Pienemann attempted to teach a rule to children who were at different developmental stages in the acquisition of German word order. His results showed that only children who were about to move to the next stage in natural acquisition could be taught the rule. A child who was several stages away from the rule regressed and went back to her previous stage of development; the instruction was cognitively too much for her. Thus instruction may be detrimental if learners are forced to acquire a structure they are not psycholinguistically ready for. The detriment would be regression, or what has been called backsliding.

The Lightbown study too addresses possible deleterious effects of instruction. Lightbown found that French-speaking learners overlearned the verbal inflection *-ing* in grade 6 in Canadian grade school only to have the correct use of the inflection decrease in frequency in grade 7 and be replaced by incorrect, uninflected forms. For example, grade 6: *He is taking the cake* grade 7: **He take the cake.* In nonclassroom learning, the reverse holds: learners begin with simple forms and build more complex ones on them. Lightbown's data suggest that the time spent overlearning *-ing* caused a delay in the natural sequence of acquisition learning and actually postponed the acquisition of *-ing* itself. Lightbown says:

> By forcing learners to repeat and overlearn forms which have no associated meaning to contrast them with any other form(s), we may be setting up barriers which have to be broken down before the learners can begin to build up their own interlanguage systems. Interlanguage systems developed in communicative language use probably reflect a number of factors in addition to frequency in the environment—salience, usefulness for communication, uniqueness of form, etc. . . . Rote learning may have to be overcome before a real system can be built.   (239)

The evidence is limited but highly suggestive: any attempt to alter a sequence of development, to force acquisition of a form before it is "scheduled" to be acquired by the learner, can result in a delay in acquisition, which is the opposite of what instruction aims to do.

A number of prominent scholars have argued that instruction is necessary. Their argument is based on the concern about ultimate attainment, about how far learners can get without instruction in grammar. They claim that without instruction, the learner's system will fossilize (Higgs and Clifford; Omaggio; Hammerly). In actuality, there is no empirical evidence reported in second language studies to support this claim. Learners fossilize regardless of instruction. What the evidence does show is that classroom learners, on the whole, do go further in acquisition than nonclassroom learners. Maria Pavesi found that nonclassroom learners of English as a second language did not acquire as many functions of the relative clause as did classroom learners. But the classroom learners did not acquire the full range of relative-clause functions and still made substantial numbers of pronoun-copy errors in relative clauses. In short, it seems that classroom learners obtain higher levels of accuracy (fossilize at a higher level) than nonclassroom learners. But this kind of research has difficulty attributing its findings to instruction per se. As Pavesi argues, classroom input tends to be different from nonclassroom input. Classroom input that is used by teachers and found in readings contains more marked structures and more syntactic complexities than nonclassroom input does. If learners acquire what they are exposed to, then classroom learners get a richer diet. Thus it may not be the instruction that makes the difference in levels of ultimate attainment but, rather, the quality of language that learners hear and see in day-to-day communicative use.

The final position, that instruction is beneficial (but not necessary), has received the widest support in the literature. Findings show that the rate of acquisition can be increased by certain kinds of instruction. Learners who receive steady exposure to communicative language use in the classroom coupled with instruction in grammar appear to acquire certain forms more quickly. But the route of acquisition orders and developmental sequences remains unaltered. The Pienemann study is widely known in the field for demonstrating that learners can be taught the next stage in their development if they are ready for it. One learner's linguistic system incorporated the next stage after several days of instruction whereas in a nonclassroom environment that might have taken several months. But again, the learner who was furthest from the targeted stage did not benefit from the instruction and in fact regressed.

Despite the encouraging finding that instruction can speed up acquisition, experiments do not indicate long-term gains. In a number of studies, gains made by instruction were short-lived (e.g., White, "Adverb Placement"; Lightbown.) Some interpret this to mean that instruction cannot circumvent any of the processes involved in language acquisition or that instruction results not in any true underlying competence but in some sort of peripheral knowledge that is available for certain kinds of performance but not for others (Krashen; Schwartz).

Instruction appears to benefit the rate of acquisition but does not have any effect on the route of development. In addition, there is no evidence that instruction is necessary and some evidence that in certain cases it can be detrimental. In short, instruction's potential for long-lasting and important effects is limited.

Language acquisition is constrained, and learners construct linguistic systems in highly systematic and universal ways. Errors are limited in range and scope, and learners are somewhat impervious to instruction. The question is, of course, What constrains language acquisition? It appears that learners themselves contribute a lot more to acquisition than scholars thought during the height of audiolingualism and behaviorism. Learners must come to the task of second language acquisition with some kind of predetermined mechanisms that allow for certain options and not others, mechanisms that guide the construction of a linguistic system.

LEARNER CONTRIBUTIONS TO SECOND LANGUAGE ACQUISITION

There are three different but not necessarily contradictory perspectives on the cognitive mechanisms that learners bring to the task of acquisition. If we view second language acquisition and use as sets of processes, at least three sets can be distinguished (fig.3). Language acquisition begins with input; learners, exposed to communicative language data, use them to construct a linguistic system. Thus the first set of processes is concerned with how learners initially perceive and receive incoming linguistic data. We will call this input processing. Input data that is processed in some way is called intake. Intake, a reduced and possibly altered version of the original input data, is held in short-term memory and may become incorporated into the developing linguistic system. If the system is ready to incorporate these data, it will make adjustments. I call this set accommodation and restructuring. When learners need to speak or write, they must tap the developing system to create output. I refer to this tapping as access. Each of the three perspectives examined below is related to a set of processes.

Figure 3
THREE SETS OF PROCESSES IN SECOND
LANGUAGE ACQUISITION AND USE

	I	*II*	*III*
input ⟶	intake ⟶	developing system ⟶	output
	I = input processing II = accommodation & restructuring III = access		

Based on VanPatten, "Cognitive Aspects"

Attention and Input Processing

Input processing is how learners attend to incoming linguistic data and how they make connections between form and meaning. The fundamental question is, What do learners pay attention to in the input and why?

In my essay "Cognitive Aspects of Input Processing in Second Language Acquisition," I developed and researched a series of hypotheses regarding learner attention during input processing.

P1. Learners process input for meaning before they process it for form.
   P1(a). Learners process content words in the input before anything else.
   P1(b). Learners prefer processing lexical items to grammatical items (e.g., morphological markings) for semantic information.
   P1(c). Learners prefer processing "more meaningful" morphology before "less or nonmeaningful morphology."
P2. For learners to process form that is not meaningful, they must be able to process informational or communicative content at no (or little) cost to attention.

The first principle, P1, addresses the relation between form and meaning and is consistent with the observations of other researchers in both first language acquisition and second language acquisition (Sharwood Smith; Peters; Klein; Færch and Kasper; Swain). P1 states that learners are driven to look for the message in the input before looking for how that message is encoded. While meaning and form are not necessarily mutually exclusive, this principle suggests that they often compete for processing time and that meaning generally wins out, especially during the early and intermediate stages of acquisition. Form, here, is defined as the surface features of language: verb endings, noun endings, particles, functors, and so forth; it does not include abstract syntax, rules of movement, or constraints on movement. Principle 1 is context-dependent: the input is communicative in nature and encodes information to which the learner must attend.

To present principle 1 more fully, I backtrack to the concept of attention and attentional capacity in cognitive psychology. It is widely accepted in current cognitive theory that learning takes place almost exclusively when the learner attends to stimuli. Attention brings stimuli (in this case, language data) into focal awareness instead of allowing them to be merely perceived (Lachman, Lachman, and Butterfield). But attention takes effort and cognitive psychologists generally agree that the capacity to deal with stimuli is limited: only so much incoming data can be attended to at a given time (Wickens).

From the perspective of second language acquisition, Richard Schmidt has provided the profession with an excellent synthesis and analysis of the literature on attention, consciousness, and learning. Arguing against any kind of subconscious or subliminal learning, he concludes that adult language learning requires attention to form in order to convert input to intake: "The existing data are compatible with a very strong hypothesis: *you can't learn a foreign language (or anything else, for that matter) through subliminal perception*" (Schmidt, "Role" 142). In short, the language learner's limited capacity processor must make decisions about how to allocate attention when processing input. When the learner's purpose is to process input for meaning, then the processor will encourage the storage and analysis of data that are most directly relevant to deriving meaning from the input.

For the beginning language learner, this means searching for and attending to *words*. For this reason, P1b suggests that learners would attend to lexical indications of tense in the input rather than morphological markings. That is, they would attend to words and phrases such as *yesterday, last week*, and *in a month* to process tense in the input and would most likely skip over inflectional markers of present, past, or future tense. Only as learners progress in their ability to process input for meaning will these other grammatical markers be attended to (P2). Capacity needs to be freed up during real-time comprehension so that the internal processors can attend to grammatical devices that were previously skipped. (For more detailed discussion of attention and processing, see VanPatten, *Input Processing*).

The acquisition of surface features of language is constrained by attentional resources. Learners are not free to process all features of language in the input they hear. Instead, they bring to the task of acquisition certain cognitive processing mechanisms that filter input data.

The Structuring and Restructuring of the System

If data are attended to in some way, what happens to them? Are they merely incorporated into the system in an add-on, linear fashion? The research on developmental sequences shows that this is clearly not the case. Therefore learners must possess some kind of cognitive mechanism that does something to the linguistic data made available to it. What might this mechanism be?

A number of scholars contend that humans are innately endowed with what is called Universal Grammar. Universal Grammar (UG) is a knowledge system and contains a set of abstract language-related principles and parameters that constrain natural languages. Children are thus not free to create completely idiosyncratic grammars in their heads as they interact with the input that surrounds them. Instead, UG limits the hypotheses that children can entertain. For example, it has been suggested that UG contains information about head position. Languages consist of phrases—noun phrases, verb phrases, prepositional phrases, and so on—each of which has a head (a noun, verb, preposition, and so on). Head position refers to the placement of the head in relation to the other elements of the phrase. For a verb phrase that consists of a verb and its object, there can be either verb-object order or object-verb order. That is, the head (verb) can either precede its complement (object) or follow it. In the first case, a language is head-initial; in the second, head-final. This information is useful to a child, since languages tend to be consistent in head position: if in language X verb phrases are verb-initial, prepositional phrases will most likely be preposition-initial, and so on. Thus a child does not have to watch for every instance of headedness to learn the syntax of phrases.

The principles of UG reduce the amount of learning that must take place. To put this in other words, if language acquisition were a simple matter of stimulus and response, child language acquisition would take inordinately long, children would make mistakes currently not documented in the child language acquisition literature, and the theory could not account for the fact that a fully formed grammar in the mind consists of more information (rules) than can be learned from simple stimulus and response. This paradox is referred to as underdetermination, since the complex and abstract linguistic knowledge that a speaker possesses is underdetermined by the input. Of the following sentences, only those without asterisks are acceptable for the typical native speaker of English:

1. John filed the letter without reading it.
2. *John filed the letter without reading.
3. Which letter did John file without reading?
4. The letter that I filed without reading was very long.
5. *The letter was filed without Bill reading.
6. *Who filed the letter without Mary reading?

From White, *Grammar*

How does the speaker of English come to know that sentences 2, 5, and 6 are not possible but that 3 and 4 are? If a speaker has never heard 3 and 4—or 1, for that matter—how does the speaker know they are good sentences? Just as important, if a person has heard 1, 3, and 4, what keeps that person from mistakenly accepting or producing sentences such as 2, 5, and 6? A learner who relies solely on distributional evidence in the input will never come to know what every speaker of English knows about the above sentences.

UG, then, is language-specific, a cognitive mechanism that processes intake to construct a linguistic system. UG interacts with incoming data to instantiate certain principles and trigger certain parameters. It structures and restructures the syntax of the language being learned as the relevant data are made available to it.

Much research and scholarship since the mid-1980s addresses the question of whether UG is still available to adult second language learners. Are the grammars of these learners guided and constrained by the knowledge contained in UG? If so, in what way? Directly? Indirectly, through their first language? The issue remains unclear. What complicates the question is that if UG aids the child in acquiring completely and implicitly the abstract syntactic properties of the first language that all native speakers come to possess, why don't second language learners show that same success? Indeed, why do second language learners show a strong tendency *not* to achieve native competence in the second language? Some researchers contend that UG is unavailable to second language learners (Bley-Vroman), while others contend that UG is available only through the first language (White, *Grammar*) and that learners transfer the already instantiated parameters of the first language. These parameters must then be reset. Both positions allow for incomplete acquisition.

As Lynn Eubank and Maria Beck point out, however, a number of methodological issues in the research on universal grammar access must be resolved before significant progress can be made regarding the role of UG in second language acquisition. One issue is the problem of measurement. Typically, UG-related studies, measuring whether learners have knowledge that is identical to that of native speakers, tend to ignore that a learner may possess a knowledge system that differs from a native speaker's yet does not violate any of the constraints imposed by UG. That is, UG may still be active in second language learning, but the result may not be a linguistic system exactly like that of a native speaker. It may appear incomplete on the surface yet still possess certain characteristics of the first language.

Whether or not universal grammar is available for the construction of a syntactic system in second language acquisition, it is clear that learners possess cognitive mechanisms that organize data processed in the input. The presence of mechanisms is evident in the developmental sequences learners pass through as they acquire a particular form or feature. A frequently cited case in both first language and second language literature is the acquisition of past-tense forms. In the developmental sequence in English (fig. 4), learners actually seem to unlearn a correct form, *went*, and replace it with **goed/*wented*, only to relearn the correct form later on. A mechanism in learners restructures the system as new data are made available, and such restructuring occurs even when the resultant rule or form is not exemplified in the input. An incorrect rule or form is driven out, because the restructuring mechanism contains some principle that governs this aspect of acquisition. According to Steven Pinker, the uniqueness principle underlies acquisition of morphology and keeps multiple forms from performing one function or encoding one meaning. This principle allows learners to overgenerate and then, as they encounter conflicting data in the input, to begin restricting the range of linguistic items on which a rule or form operates. (The uniqueness principle is involved in the learning of closed-class inflectional morphology, and attempts to extend it to syntax have not been entirely successful. See Trahey and White.)

Figure 4
THE ACQUISITION OF PAST-TENSE FORMS IN ENGLISH

Stage	Example
1. No markings on verbs	*go* (meaning *went*)
2. Strong irregulars	*went, came*
3. Regulars, with regularization of irregulars	*talked, walked* **goed/*wented*
4. Both regulars and irregulars	*talked, walked, went*

Whether through UG or some other cognitive mechanism, second language acquisition theory endows the learner with a mental device that uses data from the input to structure and restructure a system. It will be a number of years before the exact mechanism(s) can be confidently described and supported empirically. (For an excellent discussion of UG versus general cognitive mechanisms at work in second language acquisition, see Towell and Hawkins.)

Speech Processing and Access

Hypothesized in the set of processes responsible for access in language use (fig.3) are those mechanisms that determine how learners access their developing systems to make output. First, it is not clear that all aspects of the developing system are equally available during real-time speech performance. A learner's internalization of a feature of language is no guarantee that the feature can be used when the learner is pressed to communicate.

Pienemann and his associates have posited a set of speech-processing constraints on language acquisition and use. These constraints on what learners can produce at any given stage of acquisition account for certain developmental sequences evidenced in output. Two psycholinguistic principles or strategies form the core of the model proposed by Pienemann and his associates: the canonical order strategy and the initialization-finalization strategy.

The canonical order strategy constrains learners from producing utterances that do not adhere to the canonical (basic or prototypical) word order that their linguistic systems initially develop. It blocks learners from rearranging or interrupting orders in any way. If a learner has developed for example, a subject-verb-object order based on the second language input data (and possibly also through first language transfer), then the canonical order strategy will prohibit the learner from rearranging the units to produce anything other than subject-verb-object order, even if the underlying system allows the possibility of different orders.

The initialization-finalization strategy recognizes that the beginnings and ends of strings are the easiest to process and allows learners to move elements there but not to the internal parts of strings. Thus learners who initially place adverbs at the end of an utterance (*Jane plays ball today*) become able to move the adverb to the beginning (*Today Jane plays ball*).

According to Pienemann, these two cognitive mechanisms are speech-processing constraints that limit what learners can do at any given stage of development. The stages of speech production may be characterized in the following general way: first, neither strategy is violated; second, canonical order strategy is violated but not initialization-finalization strategy; third, both strategies are violated.

The stages account for a wide variety of production phenomena in second language acquisition that are related to word order and placement of particular linguistic elements. So far, this framework has been applied to English and German. Speech-processing strategies—like attentional resources, universal grammar, and whatever mechanisms are responsible for restructuring the knowledge system—are presumed to be universal and to constrain the language performance of all learners. The strategies are part of the cognitive hard-wiring that learners bring to the task of acquisition. Recently, Pienemann has attempted to account for stages of acquisition with what he calls processability theory (Pienemann and Hakansson). In this theory, strategies and the subsequent relaxing or violation of strategies are replaced with cumulative acquisition of processing mechanisms. The result is an expanded theory that accounts for a wider range of learner data.

But Pienemann's speech-processing constraints do not speak to the issue of fluency and eventual accuracy. They account only for learners' ability to produce a particular word order permutation when it first emerges in output. The mechanisms responsible for the ability to perform rapidly and accurately when producing output for communicative purposes — that is, fluency—are not addressed. A number of second language scholars have appealed to the cognitive psychological constructs of controlled and automatic processes to account for the development of fluency (Omaggio; McLaughlin). Automaticity in any kind of skill development is characterized as fast, efficient, effortless, not limited by short-term memory, not under voluntary control, difficult to modify or inhibit, and unavailable to introspection. Automaticity is normally a result of practice or, as Walter Schneider, Susan Dumais, and Richard Shiffrin put it, of consistently mapping the same thing encountered or done under the same conditions repeatedly. Whether actual focused practice is involved is a separate issue. Controlled processing is basically the opposite of automatic processing: it is relatively slow and inefficient, requires effort, is limited by short-term memory, is largely under subject control, flexible, and available for introspection. In general, controlled processing precedes automatic processing. Beginners of any skill are said to rely mostly on controlled processes in their attempt to get the skill.

Those who apply the controlled-to-automatic framework to second language acquisition claim that learners become better at using rules during output because of the opportunity to perform consistent mapping—a sort of practice-makes-perfect explanation of how fluency and accuracy develop. But appealing to the controlled-automatic distinction to account for the development of speaking as skill is based on the unstated, false assumption that language acquisition is the linear accumulation of rules and forms that are mapped directly onto output. Learning the past tense, for example, is not simply a matter of knowing regular and irregular verb forms and then being given opportunities to practice them. The knowledge that underlies second language ability does not develop in a linear fashion; it develops by restructuring. Rules evolve, and a change in one rule can affect other rules; sequences of development may be discontinuous; and so on. The move from controlled to automatic processes does not—indeed, cannot—be applied to the developmental sequence displayed in figure 2. Learners move from stage 1 of negation to stage 2 not as a result of increasing automaticity but because their underlying knowledge has changed in important ways. In short, whatever internal mechanisms promote automaticity, they cannot rely on a simple frequency-of-practice algorithm except in the most trivial way (e.g., putting the correct ending on an adjective).

An additional problem that a theory of fluency must address is the use of chunks and memorized wholes during second language speech performance. Second language acquisition has been concerned mainly with the acquisition of forms and rules. Language is seen as rule-governed. But it has been demonstrated that native speakers do not create novel utterances each time they speak. Parts of utterances and sometimes whole utterances are chunks of language stored and accessed as complete units; they are not generated anew. James Nattinger and Jeanette DeCarrico describe a number of different chunk types (they call them lexical phrases), including polywords (*step on the gas, hold your horses*); institutionalized phrases, which are related to polywords (*have a nice day, get a life*); phrasal constraints, which have slots but allow a limited number of ways to fill those slots (*see you _____ [soon/later/tomorrow], as far as I _____ [can tell/know/'m concerned]*); and sentence builders, which have slots but an infinite number of ways to fill them *(I think that _____ , My point is that _____ , It seems to me that _____)*. Nattinger and DeCarrico point out that chunks are used in everyday speech in a variety of functional contexts, allowing a speaker to generate units larger than a word, thus maximizing processing resources. Second language fluency, then, should be based in part on chunking. Learners may become fluent not just because they practice rules but also because they use chunks in addition to word-by-word generated speech.

Schmidt has reviewed a number of theories that attempt to account for fluency in native speaker language performance, including the controlled-automatic processing model of skill development and models that incorporate chunks and memorized wholes into their theories. However, it is unclear whether these theories can be used to account for second language speech performance, because of the irrelevant empirical base on which they are founded. As Schmidt states:

> It is unsettling to realize that the mechanisms made available by psychological theorizing for understanding L2 fluency derive

primarily from the study of skill in such tasks as typing, the detection of target letters in fields of distractors, judgments about digital logic gates, alphabet arithmetic, and computer simulations of the same tasks, tasks that cannot be assumed to rely necessarily on the same learning mechanisms as speaking a second language.

("Mechanisms" 378–79)

The development of second language fluency is the aspect of second language acquisition and use least thought about and least researched. Creating output is much more complex than once believed, and learners must come to the task of learning with mechanisms that help them develop procedural abilities.

Second language acquisition researchers are attempting to explain the systematic and universal aspects of acquisition by positing cognitive mechanisms that learners bring to that task. Whether these mechanisms are responsible for processing input, accommodating new data and restructuring the linguistic system, or assembling utterances during production, they operate to constrain acquisition. Long gone are the days when a learner was seen as a tabula rasa on which the new linguistic system could be written. The learner is neither an empty vessel into which knowledge can be poured nor a robot that can be programmed to learn through repetition and practice. The adult second language learner, like the child first language learner, ultimately determines in what way acquisition will proceed.

GENERAL DISCUSSION

This essay has examined some of the evidence for systematicity and universality in language acquisition. The evidence suggests that language acquisition is constrained in ways that may not be influenced by such external manipulation as instruction. The evidence has led researchers to posit and explore psycholinguistic mechanisms that cause all learners to take similar paths of acquisition. We are far from understanding these mechanisms and in some cases are not even sure that we have posited the right ones. But the need to understand these mechanisms is not just theoretical, it is also pedagogical.

In contrast to the universal and systematic aspects of language acquisition, there exists the phenomenon of individual variation. The professional literature is not short on articles and books that deal with what individuals bring to the task of language learning. Cognitive style, learning styles, motivation, aptitude, attitude, gender, affective variables, Lev Vygotsky's zone of proximal development, and other constructs have been offered as relevant to understanding classroom language learners and classroom language learning. Some scholars have described "style wars" (Oxford and Lavine) to address how learning and teaching styles clash, making for less than optimal learning environments for students. Others have addressed affective variables such as anxiety (Horwitz and Young) to understand how individual reactions to tasks and tests may impede or help learning. This line of research is clearly motivated by pedagogical concerns, since it tries to explain what makes classroom learners successful and to offer suggestions for classroom teachers.

The response of the foreign language teaching profession to these two lines of research has been different. Opinions are commonly voiced that the universal line of research is "theoretical," "irrelevant," "without classroom implications," "distant from the classroom," and, in some cases, "just another form of mental masturbation." The individual line of research, in contrast, "speaks to teachers," "has implications," "is highly relevant," "helps me understand my students better," and is "student-friendly." This difference in response is not peculiar to language teaching. Every field, every business, every human endeavor involves similar perceptions and is based on the perceived contrast between those on high and those in the trenches.

It is unfair to call the important psycholinguistic research and theorizing of the last two decades irrelevant to the language classroom. Perhaps it is the fear of having individuals lumped into groups that has led to such criticism. But the research has shown us valuable things: the role of comprehensible input in second language acquisition and how the human brain interacts with the linguistic environment. It has also shown us why certain teaching strategies are questionable and has thereby encouraged some of us to develop alternative approaches to pedagogical issues (VanPatten and Cadierno). Researching systematicity-universality and the mechanisms that underlie it should help instructors understand the limits of some of their endeavors. "Why can't they learn X, when it really isn't that difficult a structure?" is a lament too often heard. Instructors need to understand the cognitive constraints on language acquisition. The language classroom is, after all, a place where psycholinguistic processing and cognitive mechanisms are called on to work their magic. The more familiar instructors become with this magic, the less likely they will be to adopt witch-doctor solutions to language teaching and the more likely they will be to work with learners' internal mechanisms rather than against them.

WORKS CITED

Bley-Vroman, Robert. "What Is the Logical Problem of Language Learning?" *Linguistic Perspectives on Second Language Acquisition*. Ed. Susan M. Gass and Jacquelyn Schachter. Cambridge: Cambridge UP, 1989. 41–68.

Dulay, Heidi C., Marina K. Burt, and Stephen D. Krashen. *Language Two*. New York: Oxford UP, 1982.

Ellis, Rod. *The Study of Second Language Acquisition*. Oxford: Oxford UP, 1994.

Eubank, Lynn, and Maria Beck. "Generative Research on Second Language Acquisition." *Research in Language Learning*. Ed. Alice Omaggio Hadley. Lincolnwood: Natl. Textbook, 1993. 24–45.

Færch, Claus, and Gabriele Kasper. "The Role of Comprehension in Second Language Learning." *Applied Linguistics* 7 (1985): 257–74.

Gass, Susan M. "Language Transfer and Universal Grammatical Relations." *Language Transfer in Language Learning*. Ed. Gass and Larry Selinker. Rowley: Newbury, 1983. 69–82.

Hammerly, Hector. *An Integrated Theory of Language Teaching and Its Practical Consequences*. Blaine: Second Lang., 1985.

Higgs, Theodore V., and Ray Clifford. "The Push toward Communication." *Curriculum, Competence, and the Foreign Language Teacher*. Ed. Higgs. Skokie: Natl. Textbook, 1982. 57–79.

Horwitz, Elaine K., and Dolly J. Young. *Language Anxiety: From Theory and Research to Classroom Implications*. Englewood Cliffs: Prentice, 1991.

Klein, Wolfgang. *Second Language Acquisition*. Cambridge: Cambridge UP, 1986.

Krashen, Stephen D. *Principles and Practices of Second Language Acquisition*. Oxford: Pergamon, 1982.

Lachman, Roy, Janet L. Lachman, and Earl Butterfield. *Cognitive Psychology and Information Processing: An Introduction*. Hillsdale: Erlbaum, 1979.

Larsen-Freeman, Diane, and Michael H. Long. *An Introduction to Second Language Acquisition Research*. London: Longman, 1991.

Lightbown, Patsy. "Exploring Relationships between Development and Instructional Sequences in L2 Acquisition." *Classroom Oriented Research in Second Language Acquisition*. Ed. Herbert W. Seliger and Michael H. Long. Rowley: Newbury, 1983. 217–43.

McLaughlin, Barry. *Theories of Second-Language Learning*. London: Arnold, 1987.

Nattinger, James R., and Jeanette S. DeCarrico. *Lexical Phrases and Language Teaching*. Oxford: Oxford UP, 1992.

Omaggio, Alice. *Teaching Language in Context: Proficiency-Oriented Instruction*. Boston: Heinle, 1986.

Oxford, Rebecca L., and Roberta Z. Lavine. "Teacher-Student Style Wars in the Language Classroom: Research Insights and Suggestions." *ADFL Bulletin* 23.2 (1992): 38–45.

Parasuraman, Raja, and D. R. Davies, eds. *Varieties of Attention.* Orlando: Academic, 1984.

Pavesi, Maria. "Markedness, Discoursal Modes, and Relative Clause Formation in a Formal and an Informal Context." *Studies in Second Language Acquisition* 8 (1986): 38–55.

Peters, Ann. "Language Segmentation: Operating Principles for the Perception and Analysis of Language." *Theoretical Issues.* Ed. Dan I. Slobin. Hillsdale: Erlbaum, 1985. 1029–67. Vol. 2 of *The Cross-linguistic Study of Language Acquisition.*

Pienemann, Manfred. "Psychological Constraints on the Teachability of Languages." *First and Second Language Acquisition Processes.* Ed. Carol Wollman Pfaff. Cambridge: Newbury, 1987. 143–68.

Pienemann, Manfred, and Gisela Hakansson. "Towards a Theory of L2 Processability: Swedish as a Test Case." Unpublished ms. Australian Natl. U, 1996.

Pinker, Steven. *Language Learnability and Language Development.* Cambridge: Harvard UP, 1984.

Schmidt, Richard. "Psychological Mechanisms Underlying Second Language Fluency." *Studies in Second Language Acquisition* 14 (1992): 357–85.

———. "The Role of Consciousness in Second Language Learning." *Applied Linguistics* 11 (1990): 129–58.

Schneider, Walter, Susan Dumais, and Richard Shiffrin. "Automatic and Control Processing and Attention." Parasuraman and Davies 1–27.

Schwartz, Bonnie D. "On Explicit and Negative Data Effecting and Affecting Competence and Linguistic Behavior." *Studies in Second Language Acquisition* 15 (1993): 147–63.

Sharwood Smith, Michael. "Comprehension versus Acquisition: Two Ways of Processing Input." *Applied Linguistics* 7 (1986): 239–74.

Swain, Merrill. "Communicative Competence: Some Roles of Comprehensible Input and Comprehensible Output in its Development." *Input in Second Language Acquisition.* Ed. Susan M. Gass and Carolyn G. Madden. Rowley: Newbury, 1985. 235–53.

Towell, Richard, and Roger Hawkins. *Approaches to Second Language Acquisition.* Clevedon, Eng.: Multilingual Matters, 1994.

Trahey, Martha, and Lydia White. "Positive Evidence and Preemption in the Second Language Classroom." *Studies in Second Language Acquisition* 15 (1993): 181–204.

VanPatten, Bill. "Cognitive Aspects of Input Processing in Second Language Acquisition." *Festschrift in Honor of Tracy D. Terrell.* Ed. P. Hashemipour, R. Maldonado, and Margaret van Naerssen. New York: McGraw, 1994. 170–83.

———. "Communicative Value and Information Processing in Second Language Acquisition." *On TESOL '84.* Ed. Penny Larson, Elliot Judd, and Diane Messerschmitt. Washington: TESOL, 1985. 89–99.

———. "Evaluating the Role of Consciousness in Second Language Acquisition: Terms, Linguistic Features, and Methodology." Ed. Jan Hulstijn and Richard Schmidt. *AILA Review* 11 (1994): 27–36.

———. *Input Processing and Grammar Instruction: Theory and Research.* Norwood: ABLEX, 1996.

———. "Morphemes and Processing Strategies." *Universals of Second Language Acquisition.* Ed. Fred Eckman, Lawrence Bell, and Diane Nelson. Cambridge: Newbury, 1984. 88–98.

———. "Second-Language-Acquisition Research and Foreign Language Teaching, Part 1." *ADFL Bulletin* 23.2 (1992): 52–56.

VanPatten, Bill, and Teresa Cadierno. "Explicit Instruction and Input Processing." *Studies in Second Language Acquisition* 12 (1993): 25–43.

White, Lydia. "Adverb Placement in Second Language Acquisition: Some Effects of Positive and Negative Evidence in the Classroom." *Second Language Research* 7 (1991): 133–61.

———. *Universal Grammar and Second Language Acquisition.* Amsterdam: Benjamins, 1989.

Wickens, Christopher D. "Processing Resources in Attention." Parasuraman and Davies 63–102.

Acquiring Competence in a Second Language

Catherine Doughty

Form and Function

Second and foreign language teachers are facing a difficult decision: To what extent should linguistic form (aka grammar) be incorporated into language teaching? Of course, the question is not a new one. Since language comprises form and function, learners must acquire both to be fully competent in their second language. However, our contemporary perspective on the issue perhaps is different in the sense that the question can now be considered in the light of two extensive pedagogical experiences: decades (if not hundreds of years) of *traditional language teaching,* which held linguistic form to be the primary object of teaching and learning, as well as twenty years of *communicative language teaching* (CLT), which eschewed the teaching of linguistic form entirely in favor of promoting language use. Thus far, the two extremes have been tried, and neither has been found to be entirely satisfactory. Fortunately, the consideration of this decision is increasingly well informed by a rapidly expanding body of empirical second language classroom investigations into exactly this issue.

FROM "GRAMMAR IS EVERYTHING" TO THE GRAMMAR TABOO

The successes and failures of the mainstream traditional and communicative approaches have sparked and shaped a vital second language pedagogy discussion involving the efficacy of attention to form. Before 1970, much of second and foreign language teaching in the United States and throughout the world could be characterized as what is often referred to as traditional language teaching (although, by now, communicative language teaching is also, in a general sense, quite traditional). The traditional approach held two important tenets: that language is a system of linguistic forms and functions and that classroom learners, especially adults, can profit from studying these linguistic features explicitly (Richards and Rodgers). Well-known examples of traditional language teaching methods are those based on structural and functional syllabi. The common factors in these syllabi and in all types of traditional language classes are that forms or functions or other components of language are the organizing units of the syllabus, and these are to be taught explicitly, more or less in isolation. The belief is that learners, presented with a sequence of forms or functions planned in advance and presented one by one by the teacher or through materials, will eventually build up a complete linguistic repertoire.

The problems with this structure-by-structure approach have been often described and are well known. Particularly damaging criticisms have come from empirical investigations of classroom L2 learner ability. For instance, Tracy Terrell, Bernard Baycroft, and Charles Perrone have shown that knowledge of language structures demonstrated on discrete-point tests or in tests of metalinguistic knowledge does not in any way guarantee communicative ability, that is, when the measure of language knowledge is one of more spontaneous language use. In their study of the acquisition of the subjunctive in Spanish, traditional classroom instruction resulted in improvement on controlled, written tasks; but learners were largely inaccurate in less controlled, oral tasks. There is evidently a difference in knowing about a language and knowing how to use it to communicate. This state of affairs is familiar to teachers, since this finding is "replicated" daily in the foreign language classroom.

Not only do traditional learners often fail to deploy language knowledge, but they also may be amassing knowledge that is inaccurate or ultimately unnecessary in the process of second language acquisition (SLA). Studies of the acquisition of ESL have shown that some of the rules learners master in the classroom are not the rules of English but rather are pseudo-rules learners have wrongly inferred from instructional drills. Patsy Lightbown, for example, has discovered a francophone-learner-of-English rule that goes something like this: Place an -*s* morpheme or the copula *is* after every clause-initial noun ("Exploring"). This pseudorule works well for nouns that precede the copula, as in sentence 1 below, or for nouns that precede auxiliary verbs, as in sentence 2, but it does not work in other contexts, such as for nouns that precede an ordinary lexical verb, as shown in sentences 3 and 4, in which common ESL learner errors are recognizable. (A preceding asterisk indicates unacceptable usage.)

1. *She is there.*
2. *She's going there.*
3. **She's thinks.*
4. **She is think.*

Other studies that have shown that the attempt to acquire competence solely by the intensive practicing of isolated forms has four rather unproductive possible outcomes:

1. The form is never learned.
2. The form is learned but overgeneralized to the wrong contexts.
3. The use of the form declines quickly after the intensive practicing ends.
4. One learned form may disappear when another, related form is learned, almost as if the first form had never been learned, as is shown by comparison with other learners who do not undergo the intensive practicing: both groups of learners arrive at the same point.

For instance, Rod Ellis found that, overall, learners of English who drilled intensively for three hours on wh questions did not improve in the accuracy of the questions they asked during subsequent games designed to make the asking of questions spontaneous. The few students who did improve somewhat were not those who had practiced the most during the drilling session. Thus, the traditional instruction method of drilling could not be credited with efficacy in the L2 acquisition of question formation. In her study of the effects of traditional instruction on the acquisition of aspect, Lightbown found that, after drilling, francophone learners both used and overused the present progressive *-ing* ("Exploring"). In fact, *-ing* was the only inflection they used, despite their exposure to other verb forms in the input. At a later point in the curriculum, those learners who had been using and overusing the progressive verb ending as a result of drilling stopped using *-ing* and began using uninflected verb forms when they encountered instruction on present and imperative verbs. In other words, as shown in the data below (sentences 5–7), learners eventually abandoned both targetlike (matches the native standard) and overextended -*ing* in favor of a leave-all-inflections-off-verbs interlanguage rule, which was the approach taken by control, naturalistic learners who had never drilled on progressive -*ing* in the classroom.

5.	*He is taking a cake.*	(in grade 6)
6.	*He is walking to school every day.*	(in grade 6)
7.	**He take a cake.*	(same students in grade 7)

This seemingly unsuccessful outcome prompted some SLA researchers to claim that instruction is unnecessary, since natural language acquisition processes take over in the long run (Felix; Krashen). However, an outright rejection of instruction is not warranted on the basis of the failure of drilling (or of other traditional approaches to language teaching) to promote language acquisition. Instead, we must examine further the approach taken in traditional language teaching and consider whether linguistic form could be taught in a more effective manner.

Traditionally organized syllabi have language forms or functions arranged according to teachers' or materials designers' best guesses about what would be easiest to learn first and which aspects of language should be reserved for later instruction. The notion of learning complexity has always been derived from the perception of the relative difficulty of the rules of a language. The pedagogical rules utilized in traditional language teaching have generally been metalinguistic statements of linguistic regularity, and level of complexity has been determined as a function of the extent and difficulty of the metalinguistic explanation. But empirical findings from SLA studies put into question whether the kinds of rules traditionally taught are involved at all in SLA. Peter Green and Karlheinz Hecht, for example, have shown that there is little relation between the rules learners are taught and their developing knowledge of the second language. In Green and Hecht's study, both native speakers and learners were asked to make grammaticality judgments and then to state the rule that explained each judgment. Native speakers were accurate in their judgments but were unable to verbalize any linguistic rules, as the researchers had predicted. In contrast, the second language learners were less accurate, also as predicted. However, though the researchers expected that the second language learners would be better at stating the grammatical rules for the judgments they made, this was not the case. Despite having been taught the rules in the class, the learners could not verbalize them in conjunction with their intuitive judgments.

In addition to the traditional assumption that a syllabus should progress from easy to hard levels and should be based on statable rules, there is the strongly held assumption that second language development typically involves only nativelike features of the second language. Much research has revealed these assumptions to be patently false. In particular, it has been demonstrated that certain aspects of SLA cannot be altered through instruction and that intermediate, nontargetlike second language competencies, known as stages of interlanguage, characterize the progression of SLA. Studies have shown robust developmental sequences for the acquisition of negation (Schumann), of question formation (Cazden et al.), and of word order (Meisel, Clahsen, and Pienemann), each sequence involving nontargetlike production as necessary en route to the targetlike norm. Furthermore, learners cannot acquire the aspects of these subsystems of language out of sequence (Pienemann, "Psychological Constraints"; Pienemann and Johnston), and they must go through all the stages in order (even when nontargetlike language is involved), although instruction may speed up progression through a stage, allowing learners to reach the next stage sooner (Doughty, "Second Language Instruction"; Pienemann and Johnston; J. White).

The notion of rule complexity appears to have been completely misunderstood by syllabus designers. What, then, is the explanation for developmental sequences if not the complexity of stated linguistic rules? SLA researchers have suggested that developmental sequences reflect cumulative psycholinguistic processing that cannot proceed from one stage to the next until each successive type of processing is mastered. Manfred Pienemann has referred to this as the learnability of the features of the second language. In "Learnability and Syllabus Construction," Pienemann sets forth the stages of development, which are roughly exemplified in figure 1, using the case of the developmental sequence for questions.

Each successive stage involves a new kind of psycholinguistic processing that must be applied *in addition to* or *instead of* earlier learned processes. Since studies have proved that learners in stage 2 can benefit from instruction on subject-auxiliary inversion but that learners in stage 1 cannot (Pienemann, Brindley, and Johnston), developmental sequences are apparently immutable, and the developmental readiness of the learner must be

Figure 1

DEVELOPMENTAL ORDER OF THE
ACQUISITION OF ENGLISH *Wh-* QUESTIONS

TARGET QUESTION CONSTRUCTIONS

Wh- question: *What is he doing?*
Embedded *wh-* question: *I don't know what he is doing.*

Stage 1. Preserve basic word order, using only intonation to indicate the asking of a question.
Process: indicate that you are asking a question.
He is doing?

Stage 2. Preserve basic word order and use rising intonation, but place a question word at the start.
Process: front a question word.
What he is doing?

Stage 3. Manipulate word order, but only in simple clauses.
Process: invert subject and auxiliary verb.
What is he doing?

Stage 4. Preserve the question word order, even in embedded questions.
Process: embed a question into a sentence.
I don't know what is he doing?

Stage 5. Cancel the earlier-learned processes of question inversion and remove rising intonation in embedded clauses.
Process: cancel inversion.
I don't know what he is doing.

taken into account by the teacher and materials designers. In the past, approaches in traditional language teaching were not constructed in accordance with this knowledge of natural stages of language acquisition, and thus it is not surprising that early studies revealed that learning orders did not follow teaching orders.

In sum, research on traditional language teaching indicates that traditional language learners lack fluency; do not mentally represent their second language knowledge as explicit metalinguistic rules; do not learn what is taught and, if sometimes they do, later abandon the form in favor of another; and truly learn only what they are developmentally ready for. All in all, because traditional language teaching isolates linguistic form, provides no opportunities for the development of fluency, misconstrues the notion of complexity, and ignores the existence and ordering of natural acquisition processes, it has not been an effective way to promote classroom language acquisition.

Communicative approaches to language teaching have been a strong antidote to these failed pedagogies. Today, second language classes organized solely on the basis of features of grammar hopefully are few and far between, though situational-functional syllabi certainly persist. The communicative movement has been so influential that even the most traditional of language teachers make at least some attempt to "contextualize" the grammar to be learned or to "add on" a culture or literature component, and it is rare to find a teacher who does not aspire to develop communicative competence in learners.

The complete pedagogical swing from language in isolation to language as communication may have been inevitable in overcoming the constraints of the traditional environment that made the classroom perhaps the worst place to acquire competence in a second language. The traditional classroom environment ordinarily evokes the expectation of subject matter to be learned and a teacher who is in charge of directing the learning of the material. One consequence of this expectation is that the teacher talks much of the time, often in the students' native language rather than in the target language. In the foreign language classes Charlene Polio and Patricia Duff studied, teachers spoke in English fifty percent of the time, on average, which was far more than they intended to or believed they had during class. Moreover, the amount of curriculum time devoted to the traditional classroom language learning endeavor is inadequate, usually from 3 to 5 hours a week over an academic year that lasts about nine months, for an annual, maximum total of about 180 hours. In the United States, where the learning of a second language is generally not considered very important, even a highly interested student tends to study a second language for only four to six years in secondary schools and then may study for another two to four years at a university. In the best-case scenario, the grand total of hours studied over the course of ten years is 1,800. These 1,800 hours are typically spent in a room where everyone sits in chairs at desks, and any materials used must be contrived in advance and brought into the room for each class meeting. Also, the motivation for participating in second language learning, more often than not, is an amorphous desire to speak in "language X"; that is, there is no immediately specifiable need to do so. Thus the language classroom is constrained by traditional educational expectations, by the dominance of teacher talk, by less-than-immediate motivation, and, perhaps most of all, by time.

Communicative language teaching classrooms attempted to provide conditions that are closer to those of naturalistic language acquisition, such as native language acquisition by children. Of course, the acquisition setting of the child first language learner is about as different as it can possibly be from the second language classroom: children acquire their native language every waking hour from the moment they are born and reach the 1,800-hour mark somewhere around the one hundred and twelfth day of their first year of life. It takes children another 15,000 waking hours, at least, to reach the point (by about age 3) of acquiring most of the syntax and morphology, though still only a fraction of the lexicon, of their first language. The argument that children do not learn language every waking hour of the day is easily refuted. Small children need the supervision of a caregiver and thus are generally in the company of speakers of the community language most of the time. If child language learners are not directly engaged in conversation with adults or older children, they are continually in the presence of competent speakers of the language who are interacting with one another. Being spoken to or being present while others speak is characteristic of the first language acquisition experience of all children from all cultures. And those who are spoken to more learn faster (Nelson). Even if children were tuned into the language opportunities around them only half of the time, they would still be receiving language input for nearly 8,000 hours during their first three years—about four and a half times more exposure than the most dedicated classroom language learners receive over ten years!

Moreover, children have the advantage of constant pressure to communicate their needs to their caregivers, as children generally cannot take care of themselves. Children also have many supports for language learning in that they participate often in life experiences with their caregivers and thus are able to observe a variety of agents (nouns functioning as subjects), actions (verb predicates) and acted-upon entities (nouns functioning as objects), as well as many examples of causation, transformation, and all the other semantically encoded human events that speakers wish or need to talk about (Bowerman "Mapping"; Farrar, Friend, and Forbes). Caregivers tend to make sure that they and their child interlocutors are paying attention to the same events around them (Tomasello and Kruger; Tomasello and Todd) and tend to use a special, child-directed discourse register that helps the children map linguistic forms onto functions as they struggle to communicate their needs (Farrar, "Discourse" and "Evidence"; Snow). Small wonder, then, that very young children are always successful at the complete acquisition of the language of the speech community in which they live.

Older, traditionally instructed classroom language learners, in contrast, rarely acquire much competence in their second language. Traditional, structure-based language classes have embodied all the worst features of education and offered none of the advantages of experiential language learning. Communicative language teaching approaches—that is, theme-based learning, content-based learning, and immersion—have attempted to remedy this problem by giving students more of the talking time and by bringing human experience within the walls of the classroom. Depending on the particular format of the language curriculum, communicative classes have been sometimes more or sometimes less successful in fostering communicative competence in the second language. But their success is, in any case, much greater in terms of promoting fluency than that of the traditional language-as-object approaches that came before them. Two language-teaching contexts illustrate this success: the communicative language class where the aim of all the class activities is to foster interaction among the students and the immersion class where academic content is learned through the medium of the second language which is then implicitly learned as well in the process.

In the communicative language class, group work and pair work have become important task formats that facilitate the opportunities learners have for developing their ability to use the second language to express and understand messages as well as to transfer information. The pedagogical advantages of group work are summarized by Michael Long and Patricia Porter: group work "increases language practice opportunities, improves the quality of student talk, helps individualize instruction, . . . promotes a positive affective climate, . . . [and] motivates learners" (208). The interactionist SLA approach says that increased opportunity for practice during activities in which learners must effectively communicate and comprehend information by negotiating meaning with interlocutors will promote language acquisition. Several studies have substantiated this (Gass and Varonis; Pica, Doughty, and Young; Pica, Young, and Doughty). It has also been shown that learners modify their own language production such that interlanguage development may be observed, at least in the short term. Two examples of that development, taken from Pica (217–18), are given in figure 2. Though these conditions seem favorable for language acquisition, it must be admitted that there is, as yet, no direct evidence that group work contributes to sustained interlanguage development.

Figure 2
LANGUAGE SELF-MODIFICATION THROUGH INTERACTION

	Native Speaker	Nonnative Speaker
Morphological modification		there is three building, right?
	huh?	
		there is three—there are three
	right, right, I've only described one so far	
	Native Speaker	Nonnative Speaker
Lexical modification		so there's a cross in the center
	what do you mean by cross?	
		traffic cross
	oh, where people can cross, or a traffic light	
		yes

The extensive findings of programmatic evaluations of French and English immersion in Canada contribute to the claim that communicative language teaching is beneficial. These evaluations were generally made by comparing immersion students with counterpart students whose L1 academic program included a handful of hours per week of traditional second language instruction. The evaluation measures were of academic achievement, literacy skills, and second language interpersonal communication.[1] In academic achievement and literacy, immersion students at first lag behind their peers in the comparison group. But they quickly catch up and, by the end of secondary education, reach the level of their peers. Of greatest interest here is the finding that the L2 skills of immersion students become much better than those of the traditionally instructed students (see Genesee for a review of this research). Studies of anglophone learners of French indicate that immersion students develop nativelike levels of ability in second language oral and written comprehension and adequate ability in second language oral and written production (Swain and Lapkin, "Immersion"). Although highly formal comparisons have not been made, it is evident that the second language abilities of immersion students are far superior to the second language abilities of any students in once-a-day foreign language classes.

The communicative language teaching revolution has taught the profession an important lesson: Communication must be the primary goal of instruction if comprehensible input and output as well as fluency in the second language are the goals. But, does this mean that grammar should *not* be taught?

THE EMERGENCE OF THE FOCUS-ON-FORM DEBATE

Exciting language learning successes in group work and immersion have led to a virtual taboo on grammar teaching among communicatively trained and oriented second language teachers. If what is meant by "grammar" is the traditional teaching of language in isolation, then such an aversion is welcome. Teacher training of the past twenty years has emphasized the insights of functional linguists who stress that learners are "surrounded by language, but not in the form of grammars and dictionaries, or of randomly chosen words and sentences; what [they] encounter is 'text,' or language in use" (Halliday 20). Furthermore, it has come to be understood that learners must develop a communicative competence that includes "the rules of use without which the rules of grammar would be useless" (Hymes 278). Some SLA researchers have argued that the best the classroom teacher can hope to do is provide conditions conducive to experiential language learning and that any attention to linguistic form will only hinder this endeavor (Krashen). But a complete lack of attention to form may not be in the best interest of the learners. Researchers in Canada who investigated the long-term benefits of immersion programs began to notice weaknesses in the purely communicative approach. Lightbown claims that students in communicative classrooms have trouble getting what she calls "quality input" and suggests that the reason for this difficulty comes about because they sometimes cannot distinguish in the varied input available in the classroom what *is* and what is *not* quality input to interlanguage development ("Getting"). She suggests that, in immersion classrooms, linguistic form is virtually ignored by teachers, to the detriment of learners.

Canadian empirical studies support Lightbown's claim that the purely communicative approach does not serve language learners well enough. Children and adolescents in Canadian immersion programs attend classes from kindergarten through high school, and all the instruction they receive during the initial years and much of the instruction in the later years is delivered in the target language. According to Stephen Krashen's theory of comprehensible input, these students should achieve high fluency and comprehension of the target language, because they have received large doses of native language input in a communicative setting over an extended period of time. But long-term studies of the programs have shown that the communicative approach is not sufficient to give learners the competence they need to produce targetlike forms in the second language, even after many years of study (see Davidson and Snow; Day and Shapson; Hammerly; Harley and Swain, "Interlanguage"; Swain and Lapkin, "Canadian Immersion"). These recent studies suggest that Lightbown may be correct in her claim. Even in these richest of contexts for language learning, full nativelike ability is not ultimately acquired. In fact, studies of French immersion programs conducted by Merrill Swain ("Competence" and "Manipulating") and others reveal what has come to be called a classroom register or even a classroom pidgin.

Such a classification overstates the classroom learners' linguistic shortcomings since, after seven to ten years of immersion during primary and secondary education, anglophone immersion learners speak French far better than counterpart students who have studied French more traditionally, perhaps for one hour a day. The interesting finding is that a number of features of immersion learners' French are not targetlike and appear to have systematized in a classroom form. These students seem to settle for functional communication and consequently to stabilize in their second language production (Hammerly). One example of a stabilized interlanguage system is that of nominal gender: apparently, perhaps because there is no communicative pressure, immersion students do not bother to mark the gender of nouns with the appropriate determiner. Another example is that, even after using French all the time for many years in school, immersion learners fail to achieve a targetlike range of tense and aspect marking. Birgit Harley and Swain report that after years of French immersion classes, students' language was still plagued by error; with certain types of verb morphology (e.g., the conditional tense), their performance was less than fifty percent accurate ("Analysis"). Students in the classroom can communicate what they need to say without much variety in verb inflection (Harley).

Swain notes that purely content-based instructional design may be inadequate in part because the input learners receive often does not include the full range of functional uses of certain forms. For example, the use of French *vous* as a formal singular pronoun almost never occurs in classroom discourse and consequently does not develop in the second language French of immersion students ("Manipulating"). Furthermore, error correction is essentially nonexistent in immersion classes: in an immersion history class, students frequently used the present tense to discuss past events, and the teacher did not correct them. Swain claims that a focus only on meaning provides insufficient input of certain forms and no way to encourage practice of others. Overall, Harley and Swain show that the resulting interlanguage systems of immersion learners are less complex, less redundant, less idiomatic, and less accurate than the second language target although the learners are functionally adequate in the classroom and receive the same academic grades as their native-speaking counterparts ("Interlanguage"). Since complexity, redundancy, idiomaticity, and accuracy are all necessary for fully nativelike communication outside the classroom, special steps may have to be taken to provide more practice of neglected features. Swain, like Lightbown, suggests that perhaps these pidginized features of language can evolve into nativelike accuracy in the classroom only if they are explicitly attended to by teachers.

The dilemma that classroom second language learners and their teachers now face may be stated thus: Putting sole emphasis on forms is unsuccessful, since this approach results in learners who know about the second language but cannot use it. Putting sole emphasis on function and communication, while a far better approach in terms of the high degree of fluency attained by learners, nonetheless places a taboo on attention to form that prevents them from becoming *accurate* and *precise* speakers. So two problems of language teaching remain to be solved: expanding the register range and improving accuracy. Gabriele Kasper's essay in this volume addresses the first issue; we turn now to the second issue, examining research on attention to form in communicative language teaching. Starting with a context in which accuracy is considered an important learning goal, I discuss not *whether* to "teach grammar" but rather *how* and *when*.

PROMOTING ACCURACY WITHOUT
COMPROMISING FLUENCY

In the light of the still inadequate outcomes of immersion, researchers are now asking how language teaching can facilitate the acquisition of those linguistic forms that go unnoticed by and seem unnecessary to the learner during communicative interaction. To avoid the overly prescriptive and wholly inadequate assumptions of the traditional language teaching model, we should begin looking for the answer to this question by considering how SLA processes work. Since, in the past, structural, functional, and communicative approaches all lacked a theoretical foundation for language acquisition, SLA researchers have emphasized the need for a model of second language learning to serve as the basis for making decisions about pedagogy. A learning model that has motivated much seminal SLA research is the well-known concept of interlanguage development (Selinker). Since the introduction of this notion, SLA researchers have consistently recognized that the language second language learners are acquiring is neither an imperfect version of the target language nor unduly influenced by the first language. Instead, learners actively construct a new language that is characterized by a series of intermediary systems, each system overall roughly and successively a closer approximation to the target language (Nemser). How this interlanguage develops has been the central focus of all but the most rigidly nativist SLA research.

The interlanguage model proposes that learners mentally formulate and test hypotheses about what is and what is not possible in the target language and test those hypotheses through interaction with speakers of the target language.[2] The input, interaction, and informational and social outcomes of that interaction provide both the data and the testing ground for such data in support of or against learners' interlanguage hypotheses. Learners are thought to be equipped with significant psycholinguistic mechanisms that assist in the language-construction and hypothesis-testing processes of SLA. They appear to have a propensity to look for labels for agents and entities (nouns) and actions (verbs) that can encode the events of human experience. Another important ability is the process of noticing the rule-governed nature of language yet somehow overcoming the inevitable overgeneralizations that the language acquisition mechanism makes (Bowerman, "No Negative Evidence"). And, there may be specific cognitive processing mechanisms that help learners interpret the form-function relations in the surrounding linguistic data (Bates and MacWhinney; Slobin). The psycholinguistic mechanisms include attention, comparison, mapping, noticing differences, noticing frequencies, and storage in memory of complexes (e.g., chunks or phrases) for later processing. Learners use these mechanisms to analyze how the target language works.

Specifically, utterances that learners hear before speaking provide information about what *is* possible in the second language.[3] Such information is sometimes called positive evidence; information about what is not possible is called negative evidence. Positive evidence comes in several forms in the language classroom: it can be authentic, that is, completely unmodified; or it can be modified for the benefit of learners, even if no learning problem has been detected. Such modifications typically involve simplification or elaboration by interlocutors (fig. 3). But input serving as positive evidence is likely to be available and useful to language learners only in the most general way, since each and every utterance encountered contains a complex of phonological, semantic, morphosyntactic, and pragmatic information. Learners could not possibly attend to all that information during rapid modeling by competent speakers. To benefit from the input evidence, learners

Figure 3
EVIDENCE FOR LEARNER DEVELOPMENT OF HYPOTHESES

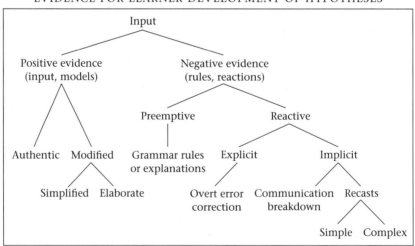

From Long, *Teaching*

need some reason to pay attention to a specific feature in the mass of available data.

A further problem is that learners may formulate hypotheses based on their L1 but may never encounter positive evidence in the data to confirm them. For example, francophone learners of English have trouble with adverb placement (White et al.). In English, an adverb cannot be placed between a verb and its object or complement, though such word order is fine in French (as are the equivalent sentences with the adverb placed before the verb):

* I like always to go.
* I drink every day coffee.

That adverb ordering is freer in French than in English causes an evidence problem for francophone learners of English who often formulate an overly general L1-based hypothesis. Learners are left wondering whether their hypothesis is wrong or whether they simply need more opportunity for positive evidence to confirm that an adverb may be placed between a verb and its complement. As a result of this kind of waiting strategy, learners sometimes seem to stabilize in a classroom register. In this instance, negative evidence, information about what is *not* possible in the second language, is probably needed to disconfirm the interlanguage hypothesis for English adverb placement. Positive evidence alone is not sufficient for learners to develop fully the target language, so the lack of negative evidence in the communicative language classroom may be a source of inaccurate learner language. In other words, communicative language teaching has not given learners the means to assess what is and what is not possible in the second language as they formulate and test out their interlanguage hypotheses.

Although the value (and even the existence) of negative evidence has been questioned in theories of child language acquisition, it seems indisputable that negative evidence exists in language classrooms and that under the right circumstances it is useful to learners (Schachter). Some applied linguists advocate complementing purely communicative instruction with a component designed to improve formal accuracy by bringing particularly unnoticeable features to the attention of learners and by providing learners with needed negative evidence (Doughty and Williams). While the suggested techniques are varied, there is a common rejection of the claim that all that is necessary for second language acquisition is exposure to comprehensible input (contra Krashen), accompanied by the belief that learners must attend to formal aspects of the target language input if they are to make the necessary adjustments to their own interlanguage system (Sharwood Smith, "Input Enhancement"; VanPatten). Long has introduced the term *focus on form* to describe phenomena that induce learners to attend to linguistic form in a meaningful context ("Focus on Form: A Design Feature"; Long and Robinson). He contrasts the notion of focus on form with traditional grammar instruction, which teaches forms exclusively or in isolation:

> Whereas the content of lessons with a focus on *forms* is the *forms* themselves, a syllabus with a focus on *form* teaches something else—biology, mathematics, workshop practice, automobile repair, the geography of a country where the foreign language is spoken, the cultures of its speakers, and so on—and overtly draws students' attention to linguistic elements as they arise incidentally in lessons whose overriding focus is on meaning, or communication.
>
> ("Focus on Form: A Design Feature" 45–46)

This nearly operational definition suggests an implicit approach to drawing learners' attention to form. Nonetheless, some SLA researchers advocate more-explicit means of focus-on-form instruction (Kowal and Swain; Swain, "Manipulating"). The danger of an explicit approach is the potential for a return to the traditional teaching of forms in isolation. The balance is so delicate that many communicatively trained language teachers are unwilling to consider even implicit attention to linguistic form. To remedy this, researchers are investigating how acquisition is affected by explicit or implicit focus on a language form—usually, but not limited to, an aspect of syntax or morphology—generally within a communicative setting that requires meaningful interaction. A key distinction of the focus-on-form approach is that learners attend to form; and teachers, materials designers, or researchers can only set up the conditions for this to happen (Leeman, Arteagoitia, Fridman, and Doughty).

There is as yet no theoretical consensus on what causes some forms to be more noticed than others, but empirical studies suggest factors: limits on learners' processing capacity (VanPatten; VanPatten and Sanz), the communicative value of the forms (VanPatten; VanPatten and Sanz) or importance for accessing meaning (Hulstijn; Schmidt and Frota), perceptual saliency (Doughty, "Second Language Instruction"), and learners' developmental readiness (Pienemann, "Learnability"). Whatever the constraints, it is potentially the role of instruction to utilize them. There are various methods to encourage classroom learners to focus on form, but it remains to be seen which are most efficacious. Michael Sharwood Smith proposes a whole range of types of enhanced input that may focus learners' otherwise wandering attention: explicit discussion of the form, metalinguistic description of the form, implicit error correction through the use of special patterns of stress or intonation or through the use of gestures or facial expressions, and textual enhancement ("Input Enhancement"). An additional technique on the implicit end of the range is input "flooding," which provides learners with many and frequent instances of positive evidence (J. White). See figure 4.

Figure 4
RANGE OF FOCUS-ON-FORM TECHNIQUES

EXPLICIT ◄——————————► IMPLICIT					
Brief rule presentation	Brief metalinguistic comment	Dictagloss	Repetition of error with intonation or gesture focus	Recast	Input flooding

Many of these techniques are now being investigated because immersion studies have revealed that, when second language learning is entirely experiential or communicative, some linguistic features do not ultimately develop to targetlike levels. It has been specifically claimed that focus on form is needed to push learners beyond communicatively effective language toward targetlike second language ability. Several effects-of-instruction studies have already demonstrated that focus on form in meaningful contexts can improve the accuracy of second language output (Day and Shapson; Doughty, "Second Language Instruction"; Kowal and Swain; Swain and Lapkin, "Problems"). Elaine Day and Stan Shapson developed an interdisciplinary unit requiring students to design a space colony. The tasks in this unit flooded the input with the conditional tense and opportunities for producing conditional forms without explicit instruction. Students in the experimental group were directed to take note each time the conditional tense was used. Day and Shapson found, in general, that "the improvement of immersion students' oral and written grammatical skills can be achieved through curricular intervention that integrates formal, analytical [approaches] with functional, communicative approaches to language teaching" (55). I used enhanced reading materials to compare how explicit rule instruction, implicit meaning-oriented instruction, and exposure without instruction affected the acquisition of English relative clauses ("Second Language Instruction"). I found that explicit and implicit instruction were equally beneficial for subjects' performance on oral and written production tasks but that the group that received implicit instruction (as well as the exposure-only group) outperformed the explicit-instruction group on comprehension tasks. Reexamining the computer-delivered materials, I discovered that both the implicit and explicit approaches provided the same kind of visual enhancements of the input. Those enhancements rather than the rules and examples that had been incorporated into the reading lesson may have been what the learners actually processed during the instructional treatment. It has been argued that opportunities for comprehensible output are essential for developing targetlike production skills in a second language (Swain and Lapkin, "Problems"). Maria Kowal and Swain demonstrated that metalinguistic discussion can be a useful technique for drawing learners' attention to form in the context of reconstructing a text. In a procedure called dictagloss, learners listen to a short text and then try to reconstruct it from memory, working in pairs. Transcripts show that they discuss and adjust the accuracy of their reconstructed language. Where such discussion involves features of language that are notoriously nontargetlike in immersion students' interlanguage (e.g., gender and tense), Kowal and Swain argue that this explicit attention to form is vital.

Thus a major component of focus on form can be seen as one of initially attracting or directing learners to attend to features of the second language. Although many SLA researchers agree that some kind of attentional process is required for input to become intake, opinions vary on the amount, type, and duration of attention necessary for SLA (Hulstijn; Rutherford and Sharwood Smith; Schmidt, "Awareness," "Consciousness," "Role of Consciousness"; Sharwood Smith, "Input Enhancement," "Speaking"; Tomlin and Villa). Richard Schmidt argues that "noticing is the necessary and sufficient condition for the conversion of input to intake for learning" ("Consciousness" 17), where noticing is operationalized as availability for self-report at or immediately after the experience. Noticing, therefore, for Schmidt, entails conscious registration of the contents of focal attention. Russell Tomlin and

Victor Villa, however, hold that conscious registration is not a necessary component of attentional processes in second language learning. Instead, detection is proposed as the minimally necessary process of acquisition and is the process "by which particular exemplars are registered in memory" (193). Detected information is available for further cognitive processing, such as hypothesis formation and testing, but detection itself does not require awareness. Sharwood Smith has raised the issue of learner noticing in terms of the degree of explicitness recommended for focus-on-form techniques. In figure 4, the focus continuum ranges from explicit techniques, such as metalinguistic discussion or presentation of a grammar rule, to implicit techniques, such as input flooding and textual enhancements (use of highlighting and color). Regardless of differences in the factors suggested and the differences concerning the degree of explicitness needed to secure attention to formal aspects of the target language, there is a consensus that increased focus of some kind is beneficial to learners.

It follows that if the input can be manipulated or enhanced to draw learners' attention to specific forms, or to form in general, learning will be facilitated. However, Sharwood Smith cautions we should not assume that external manipulation of input alone will increase learners' attention and stresses that artificially induced noticing might not result in the incorporation of target forms into the developing interlanguage. In other words, forms may be noticed perceptually but not linguistically. Sharwood Smith writes, "Although learners may notice the signals, the input may nevertheless be nonsalient to their learning mechanisms" ("Speaking" 121). The determination of the range of effective means and the degree to which explicit attention is needed or should be avoided during focus on form have emerged as an important question in SLA research.

Studies have demonstrated the usefulness of various types of input enhancement but are unable to shed light on the relative value of the different techniques. There is no clear empirical support for one enhancement type over another. Nonetheless, it may be worthwhile to classify and evaluate the techniques according to whether they integrate attention to form with attention to meaning or treat attention to form as a separate component (Leeman, Arteagoitia, Fridman, and Doughty). Because humans have a limited attentional capacity, performance on an attention-demanding task often declines when subjects are simultaneously required to perform a second independent task (VanPattern). But performance on the first task is not adversely affected when the two tasks are "somehow compatible" (Tomlin and Villa 189). Thus tasks or enhancements designed to integrate attention to form with attention to meaning should divert learners' attentional resources less. Moreover, if SLA generally consists of acquiring new form-meaning mappings, it follows that the most efficient type of attention to form takes place in a meaningful context rather than as an isolated grammar component. Long stresses that communicative interaction should remain the priority at all times and should be interrupted only briefly, if at all. ("Focus on Form and Implicit Negative Feedback"). What makes rule presentation and metalinguistic discussion undesirable is not that they are explicit but rather that they separate form from meaning instead of integrating the focus on form within the focus on meaning.

Researchers have experimentally increased attention to form while attempting to remain within an overall focus on meaning. Jan Hulstijn exposed subjects to target sentences and assigned them tasks designed to require focus either on meaning or on formal properties of the input. Administering cued recalls and repetition tasks to all subjects, he found that not only did the meaning group score better than the form group on the recalls but they also were not at a disadvantage on at least some of the production tasks. Similarly, Nina Spada and Lightbown found that meaning-based instruction was improved by focus on forms consisting of various techniques, including teacher correction. Although Spada and Lightbown originally set out to compare a communicatively taught group (the control group) with one that was communicative but with added focus on forms, they suggest that the unplanned "context-embedded focus on form" that occurred unexpectedly in their control group caused the controls to outperform the subjects in the experimental group (Lightbown, "Getting"; Spada and Lightbown, "Instruction"). These findings exemplify how a combination of enhancement techniques, all integrated within an overall focus on meaning, can be beneficial.

In the light of the suggestion that, even if both are carried out, independent form and meaning tasks are at best ineffective, and at worst detrimental to language learning, the central pedagogical question stemming from focus-on-form studies is how to develop linguistic accuracy in classroom learners without compromising the concurrent development of communicative fluency. Learners whose classroom experience has stressed accuracy and metalinguistic knowledge to the exclusion of communication often have difficulty comprehending and producing natural speech. In contrast, learners whose classroom experience has centered only on the communication of meaning are often inaccurate and seemingly stabilized. Striking a balance between emphasizing accurate production of second language forms and promoting meaningful communication in real contexts has become a vital concern. Doughty and Jessica Williams list these key questions for detailed, classroom-relevant focus-on-form research:

Forms to focus on. Which forms are amenable to focus on form? Are some forms resistant to focus on form? Are forms that are persistent learning problems those best targeted for focus on form?

Tasks and procedures that promote focus on form. Can tasks and procedures be designed such that problematic forms are likely to arise, thereby providing an opportunity for focus on form? How intensive should focus on form be? Should an entire segment of a curriculum be designed to highlight a particular form or set of related forms? Should focus on form be implicit or explicit?

Timing of focus on form. When should focus on form occur in the overall curriculum? Should it occur initially, continuously, or only after the communicative ability of second language learners has been well developed? When should focus on form occur in individual classrooms? Should it be planned a priori by the teacher or provided only when needed? How long should focus on form continue in order to be effective?

While these questions clearly raise a range of complex issues the discussion of which would be beyond the scope of this essay, several examples may serve to indicate the direction of current classroom research into how to increase learner accuracy through focus on form (see Doughty and Williams for an expanded discussion). The effectiveness of instruction may differ depending on which forms are selected for special attention in the classroom. The complexity of the forms, their prototypicality, or their status in learners' interlanguages may influence effectiveness (Harley). Treatment of forms that have not yet emerged in the interlanguage should not necessarily be the same as treatment of forms that have. Williams and Jacqueline Evans demonstrated this in a study of instructional attention comparing participial adjectives that had emerged in interlanguage form (sentence 1) with a feature of English that had not yet been attested in the classroom discourse, the passive voice (sentence 2):

1. *I am very interesting in your work.
2. *The work was done by everyone.*

Learners whose attention was drawn to the errors in their participial adjectives were able to improve the accuracy of their interlanguage production. But the passive voice, which had not yet emerged in the subjects' interlanguage, remained resistant to instruction.

With regard to how teachers can select and develop techniques and design classroom activities that are consistent with a variety of pedagogical goals, certain activities may be best suited to specific learner needs. For instance, textual enhancement may be an effective way of drawing learner attention to form without disturbing ongoing communication. It is a relatively implicit technique that works well when a lesson's emphasis is on meaning. In one study, all input pertaining to Spanish preterite and imperfect verb forms was enhanced: all written texts included salient highlighting, and all learner errors (of the preterite and imperfect only) were responded to with corrective feedback (Leeman, Arteagoitia, Fridman, and Doughty). These enhancements were accomplished in a content-based second language Spanish history unit whose central curricular aim was the transmission of information about the Spanish civil war. Results showed that the students who were given implicit, enhanced input showed more specific interlanguage development in their tense-aspect system than did the control subjects. Whether it was any one enhancement or all the enhancements in combination that prompted learners to notice and restructure the necessary morphology remains to be investigated.

The question of when to focus on form is related to the issue of developmental stages in language acquisition. There is also the question of whether to focus on form in advance of learner errors or in response to them. Because preemptive focus on form may inhibit communication as well as errors, researchers are investigating reactive feedback. The effectiveness of providing learners with corrective feedback, or "negative input enhancement" (Sharwood Smith, "Input Enhancement" 177), has been examined under conditions that, in essence, set learners up to make a mistake. For example, Michael Tomasello and Carol Herron compared two groups of second language French learners who received different types of input combined with explicit grammar instruction on a variety of structures. The first group received positive input, or modeling, of exceptions to rules; the second group was encouraged to overgeneralize. The subjects of the second group, after they received feedback on the errors they had been led to commit, performed better than the subjects of the first group on a sentence translation task. In a similar fashion, Susanne Carroll, Swain, and Yves Roberge found feedback to be beneficial in their experimental study of two rules of French suffixation, though subjects were unable to generalize their newly acquired knowledge to novel items. But in a study of the acquisition of the English dative alternation, Carroll and Swain found that subjects in four different feedback conditions were able to generalize to novel items.

It is likely that reactive feedback is effective, because it draws learners' attention not only to the relevant aspects of the input but also to the specific problems of their own output. Doughty and Elizabeth Varela investigated whether corrective feedback could be incorporated into a content-based science ESL class without interrupting the information flow of the science lesson. Past and past conditional, two known learning problems, were targeted in advance, and two kinds of implicit feedback were provided to students, as needed, as they engaged in science experiments. In the oral feedback mode, errors in past and past conditional were repeated by the teacher with rising intonation and were recast in targetlike fashion. No further comment was made by the teacher, and no other type of learner error was given feedback. The written focus on form was similar to the oral: the learner errors were circled and the target forms supplied without further comment. The overriding focus of the lessons was on the completion and reporting of science experiments, and the attention to form was incidental to that focus. The learners in the implicit feedback group improved both in their number of attempts to use past and past conditional as well as in their accuracy, particularly of the past tense, which had already begun to emerge in their interlanguage. The control group did not improve in either fashion. Thus it was shown that attention to form that is almost completely incidental to the content lesson can be effective.

All the studies mentioned above on promoting accuracy without compromising fluency lead to the tentative conclusion that attention to form should be contingent on rather than anticipatory of language learning problems (for more discussion of the timing issue, see Lightbown, "Timing").

The accumulating findings that focus on form during meaningful communication is successful in implementing interlanguage change suggest that some of the intractable problems of both traditional language teaching and communicative language teaching can be resolved by attending simultaneously to natural form and function relations in the second language classroom. Though no really long-term studies have yet been conducted, focus on form does not seem to prevent the development of communicative fluency, since it is easily integrated into content lessons. At the same time, such attention to form appears to improve learners' accuracy during communication. It remains to be seen whether such incidentally achieved instructional effects are enduring, but the research so far is promising.

If it can be assumed that the integration of attention to form into a communicative classroom includes the benefit of the communicative language teaching approach—the development of fluency—then the focus-on-form approach will have the great advantage of being *efficient*. Efficiency of language instruction continues to be important, given that the time constraint discussed above is one of the most daunting obstacles to language learning success.

NOTES

The issues raised in this paper were developed from discussions with foreign and second language teachers at two conferences (see Doughty, "Finetuning" and "Focus").
1. These evaluations also assessed the maintenance of the learners' L1 ability. This issue lies outside the scope of my essay, but it is interesting to note that L1 maintenance enhances rather than detracts from SLA (Genesee).
2. These natural psycholinguistic processes, in the L1 model, occur automatically and without conscious attention.
3. In the "no negative evidence" debate in the child language acquisition literature, it is claimed that children face a "logical problem of language acquisition" (Baker). The information they receive about what is possible in the adult language is not sufficient, because they learn far more language than they hear. Furthermore, it is argued that children do not receive negative evidence (e.g., correction). The debate currently centers on whether or not explicit correction is negative evidence for children. Some believe that in the absence of correction, children must be innately constrained not to formulate hypotheses that need negative evidence to be reigned in. If negative evidence comes to children in more implicit forms (e.g., recasts), then innate constraints are not needed. It is important to note that learners in classroom SLA can and do encounter negative evidence. The question is, Can they make use of it?

WORKS CITED

Baker, C. "Syntactic Theory and the Projection Problems." *Linguistic Inquiry* 10 (1979): 533–81.

Bates, Elizabeth, and Brian MacWhinney. "Competition, Variation, and Language Learning." *Mechanisms of Language Acquisition*. Ed. MacWhinney. Hillsdale: Erlbaum, 1987.

Bowerman, Melissa. "Mapping Thematic Roles onto Syntactic Functions: Are Children Helped by Innate Linking Rules?" *Linguistics* 28 (1990): 1253-89.

———. "The 'No Negative Evidence' Problem: How Do Children Avoid Constructing an Overly General Grammar?" *Explaining Language Universals.* Ed. J. Hawkins. Oxford: Blackwell, 1988. 73–101.

Carroll, Susanne, and Merrill Swain. "Explicit and Implicit Negative Feedback. An Empirical Study of the Learning of Linguistic Generalization." *Studies in Second Language Acquisition* 15 (1993): 357–86.

Carroll, Susanne, Merrill Swain, and Yves Roberge. "The Role of Feedback in Adult Second Language Acquisition: Error Correction and Morphological Generalization." *Applied Psycholinguistics* 13 (1992): 173–89.

Cazden, Courtney, et al. *Second Language Acquisition Sequences in Children, Adolescents, and Adults.* Washington: United States Dept. of Health, Educ., and Welfare, 1975.

Davidson, Rosalind G., and Catherine E. Snow. "The Linguistic Environment of Early Readers." *Journal of Research in Childhood Education* 10.1 (1995): 5–21.

Day, Elaine, and Stan Shapson. "Integrating Formal and Functional Approaches in Language Teaching in French Immersion: An Experimental Study." *Language Learning* 41 (1991): 25–58.

Doughty, Catherine. "Finetuning as Focus on Form." Focus on Form: What Is It? McGill and Concordia Universities symposium. Montreal. Oct. 1994.

———. "Focus on Form: Research and Pedagogical Issues." Focus on Form: What Is It? Georgetown University Round Table on Languages and Linguistics Presession. Washington. Mar. 1992.

———. "Second Language Instruction Does Make a Difference: Evidence from an Empirical Study of SL Relativization." *Studies in Second Language Acquisition* 13 (1991): 431–69.

Doughty, Catherine, and Elizabeth Verela. "Communicative Focus on Form." Doughty and Williams, *Focus.*

Doughty, Catherine, and Jessica Williams, eds. *Focus on Form in Classroom Second Language Acquisition.* Cambridge Series on Applied Linguistics. Cambridge: Cambridge UP, 1998.

Ellis, Rod. "Can Syntax Be Taught? A Study of the Effects of Formal Instruction on the Acquisition of Wh Questions by Children." *Applied Linguistics* 5 (1984): 138–55.

Farrar, Michael. "Discourse and the Acquisition of Grammatical Morphemes." *Journal of Child Language* 17 (1990): 607–24

———. "Negative Evidence and Grammatical Morpheme Acquisition." *Developmental Psychology* 121 (1992): 62–75.

Farrar, Michael, Margaret Friend, and James Forbes. "Event Knowledge and Early Language Acquisition." *Journal of Child Language* 20 (1993): 591–606.

Felix, Sasha. "The Effect of Formal Instruction on Second Language Acquisition." *Language Learning* 31 (1981): 87–112.

Gass, Susan, and Evangeline Varonis. "Input, Interaction, and Second Language Production." *Studies in Second Language Acquisition* 16 (1994): 283–302.

Genesee, Fred. *Learning through Two Languages.* New York: Newbury, 1987.

Green, Peter, and Karlheinz Hecht. "Implicit and Explicit Grammar: An Empirical Study." *Applied Linguistics* 13 (1992) : 385–407.

Halliday, M. A. K. *Learning How to Mean: Explorations in the Development of Language.* New York: Elsevier, 1975.

Hammerly, Hector. "The Immersion Program: Litmus Test of Second Language Acquisition through Language Communication." *Modern Language Journal* 71 (1987): 395–401.

Harley, Birgit. "Instructional Strategies and SLA in Early French Immersion." *Studies in Second Language Acquisition* 15 (1993): 245–60.

Harley, Birgit, and Merrill Swain. "An Analysis of the Verb System by Young Learners of French." *Interlanguage Studies Bulletin* 3.1 (1978): 35–79.

———. "The Interlanguage of Immersion Students and Its Implications for Second Language Teaching." *Interlanguage*. Ed. Alan Davies, C. Criper, and A. Howatt. Edinburgh: Edinburgh UP, 1984. 291–311.

Hulstijn, Jan. "Implicit and Incidental Language Learning: Experiments in the Processing of Natural and Partly Artificial Input." *Interlingual Processing*. Ed. Hans Dechert and Manfred Raupach. Tübingen: Narr, 1989. 49–73.

Hymes, Dell. "On Communicative Competence." *Sociolinguistics: Selected Readings*. Ed. J. B. Pride and Janet Holmes. Baltimore: Penguin, 1972. 269–83.

Kowal, Maria, and Merrill Swain. "Using Collaborative Language Production Tasks to Promote Students' Language Awareness." *Language Awareness* 3 (1994): 73–93.

Krashen, Stephen. *The Input Hypothesis: Issues and Implications*. London: Longman, 1985.

Leeman, Jennifer, Igone Arteagoitia, Boris Fridman, and Catherine Doughty. "Integrating Attention to Form with Meaning: Focus on Form in Content-Based Spanish Instruction." *Attention and Awareness in Foreign Language Learning and Teaching*. Technical Report 9. Ed. Richard Schmidt. Honolulu: U of Hawaii P, 1995. 217–58.

Lightbown, Patsy. "Exploring Relationships between Developmental and Instructional Sequences in L2 Acquisition." *Classroom-Oriented Research in Second Language Acquisition*. Ed. Herbert W. Seliger and Michael H. Long. Rowley: Newbury, 1983. 217–43.

———. "Getting Quality in the Second and Foreign Language Classroom." Kramsch and McConnell-Ginet 187–97.

———. "Timing and Focus on Form." Doughty and Williams, *Focus*.

Long, Michael. "Focus on Form: A Design Feature in Language Teaching Methodology." *Foreign Language Research in Cross-Cultural Perspective*. Ed. Kees de Bot, Claire Kramsch, and Ralph Ginsberg. Amsterdam: Benjamins, 1991. 39–52.

———. "Focus on Form and Implicit Negative Feedback." Focus on Form: What Is It? McGill and Concordia Universities symposium. Montreal. Oct. 1994.

———. *Task-Based Language Teaching*. Oxford: Blackwell, forthcoming.

Long, Michael, and Patricia Porter. "Groupwork, Interlanguage Talk, and Second Language Acquisition." *TESOL Quarterly* 19 (1986): 207–28.

Long, Michael, and Peter Robinson. "Focus on Form: Theory, Research, and Practice." Doughty and Williams 15–40.

Meisel, Jürgen, Harald Clahsen, and Manfred Pienemann. "On Determining Developmental Stages in Natural Second Language Acquisition." *Studies in Second Language Acquisition* 3 (1981): 109–35.

Nelson, Keith. "Toward a Rare-Event Cognitive Comparison Theory of Syntax Acquisition." *Child Language: An International Perspective*. Ed. P. Dale and David Ingram. Baltimore: University Park, 1981. 229–40.

Nemser, William. "Approximative Systems of Foreign Language Learners." *International Review of Applied Linguistics in Language Teaching* 9 (1971): 115–24.

Pica, Teresa. "The Textual Outcomes of Native Speaker–Non-native Speaker Negotiation: What Do They Reveal about Second Language Learning?" Kramsch and McConnell-Ginet 198–237.

Pica, Teresa, Catherine Doughty, and Richard Young. "Making Input Comprehensible: Do Interactional Modifications Help?" *International Review of Applied Linguistics in Language Teaching* 72 (1986): 1–25.

Pica, Teresa, Richard Young, and Catherine Doughty. "The Impact of Interaction on Comprehension." *TESOL Quarterly* 21 (1987): 737–58.

Pienemann, Manfred. "Learnability and Syllabus Construction." *Modelling and Assessing Second Language Acquisition*. Ed. Kenneth Hyltenstam and Pienemann. Clevedon, Eng.: Multilingual Matters, 1985. 23–76.

———. "Psychological Constraints on the Teachability of Languages." *Studies in Second Language Acquisition* 6 (1984): 186–214.

Pienemann, Manfred, Geoffrey Brindley, and Malcolm Johnston. "Constructing an Acquisition-Based Procedure for Second Language Assessment." *Studies in Second Language Acquisition* 10 (1988): 217–43.

Pienemann, Manfred, and Malcolm Johnston. "Factors Influencing the Development of Language Proficiency." *Applying Second Language Research*. Ed. David Nunan. Adelaide: Natl. Curriculum Resource Centre, 1987. 46–141.

Polio, Charlene, and Patricia Duff. "Teachers' Language Use in University Foreign Language Classrooms: A Qualitative Analysis of English and Target Language Alternation." *Modern Language Journal* 78 (1994): 313–26.

Richards, Jack C., and Theodore Rodgers. *Approaches and Methods in Language Teaching*. Cambridge: Cambridge UP, 1986.

Rutherford, William, and Michael Sharwood Smith. "Consciousness-Raising and Universal Grammar." *Applied Linguistics* 6 (1985): 274–82.

Schachter, Jacquelyn. "Corrective Feedback in Historical Perspective." *Second Language Research* 7 (1991): 89–102.

Schmidt, Richard. "Awareness and Second Language Acquisition." *Annual Review of Applied Linguistics* 13 (1993): 206–26.

———. "Consciousness and SLA: Cognitive Perspectives on Intention, Attention, Awareness, and Control." Amer. Assn. for Applied Linguistics meeting. Baltimore. Mar. 1994.

———. "The Role of Consciousness in Second Language Learning." *Applied Linguistics* 11 (1990): 17–46.

Schmidt, Richard, and Sylvia Frota. "Developing Basic Conversational Ability in a Second Language." *Talking to Learn*. Ed. Richard Day. Rowley: Newbury, 1986. 237–326.

Schumann, John. "The Acquisition of English Negation by Speakers of Spanish: A Review of the Literature." *The Acquisition and Use of Spanish and English as First and Second Languages*. Ed. Roger Andersen. Washington: TESOL, 1979. 1–32.

Selinker, Larry. "Interlanguage." *International Review of Applied Linguistics in Language Teaching* 10 (1972): 209–31.

Sharwood Smith, Michael. "Input Enhancement in Instructed SLA: Theoretical Bases." *Studies in Second Language Acquisition* 15 (1993): 165–79.

———. "Speaking to Many Minds: On the Relevance of Different Types of Language Information." *Second Language Research* 7 (1991): 118–32.

Slobin, Dan I., ed. *Theoretical Issues*. Hillsdale: Erlbaum, 1985. Vol. 2 of *The Crosslinguistic Study of Language Acquisition*. Ed. Slobin.

Snow, Catherine. "Understanding Social Interaction in Language Acquisition: Sentences Are Not Enough." *Interaction in Human Development*. Ed. Marc Bornstein and Jerome Bruner. Hillsdale: Erlbaum, 1987. 83–103.

Spada, Nina, and Patsy Lightbown. "Instruction and the Development of Questions in the L2 Classroom." *Studies in Second Language Acquisition* 15 (1993): 205–21.

Swain, Merrill. "Communicative Competence: Some Roles of Comprehensible Input and Comprehensible Output in Its Development." *Input in Second Language Acquisition*. Ed. Susan M. Gass and Carolyn G. Madden. Rowley: Newbury, 1985. 235–53.

———. "Manipulating and Complementing Content Teaching to Maximize Learning." *Foreign/Second Language Pedagogy Research*. Ed. Eric Kellerman et al. Clevedon, Eng.: Multilingual Matters, 1992. 234–50.

Swain, Merrill, and Sharon Lapkin. "Canadian Immersion and Adult Second Language Teaching: What's the Connection?" *Modern Language Journal* 73 (1989): 105–59.
———. "Problems in Output and the Cognitive Processes They Generate: A Step towards Second Language Learning." *Applied Linguistics* 16 (1995): 370–91.
Terrell, Tracy, Bernard Baycroft, and Charles Perrone. "The Subjunctive in Spanish Interlanguage: Accuracy and Comprehensibility." *Foreign Language Learning: A Research Perspective.* Ed. Trisha R. Dvorak, James F. Lee, and Bill VanPatten. New York: Newbury, 1987.
Tomasello, Michael, and Carol Herron. "Down the Garden Path: Inducing and Correcting Overgeneralization Errors in the Foreign Language Classroom." *Applied Psycholinguistics* 9 (1988): 237–46.
Tomasello, Michael, and Ann Kruger. "Joint Attention on Action Verbs: Acquiring Verbs in Ostensive and Non-ostensive Contexts." *Journal of Child Language* 19 (1992): 311–33.
Tomasello, Michael, and Jody Todd. "Joint Attention and Lexical Acquisition Style." *First Language* 4 (1993): 197–212.
Tomlin, Russell S., and Victor Villa. "Attention in Cognitive Science and Second Language Acquisition." *Studies in Second Language Acquisition* 16 (1994): 183–203.
VanPatten, Bill. "Can Learners Attend to Form and Content While Processing Input?" *Hispania* 72 (1989): 409–17.
VanPatten, Bill, and Cristina Sanz. "From Input to Output: Processing Instruction and Communicative Tasks." Unpublished essay, 1994.
White, Joanna. "Getting the Learners' Attention: A Typographical Enhancement Study." AAAL Colloquium on Focus on Form (1995).
White, Lydia, et al. "Input Enhancement and L2 Question Formation." *Applied Linguistics* 12 (1993): 416–32.
Williams, Jessica, and Jacqueline Evans. "Which Form to FonF?" Doughty and Williams, *Focus.*

Constraints and Resources in Classroom Talk

Leo van Lier

Issues of Equality and Symmetry

Most current views of language education are based on the assumption that social interaction plays a central role in learning processes, as a quick glance at the dominant terminology shows. "Communication," "negotiation of meaning," "coconstruction," "cooperative learning," "responsive teaching," and many other terms like them testify to a fundamental shift from conditioning, association, and other laboratory-based notions of learning to human learning as it is situated in the everyday social world of the learner.

This shift to the social context (and construction) of language learning does not make the investigation of learning processes any easier. On the contrary. The security of isolating variables and defining them operationally, a security obtained by laboratory-like experiments and statistical inferences, is largely lost, as the researcher is forced to look for determinants of learning in the fluid dynamics of real-time learning contexts.

Traditionally we have thought of scientific research as a matter of looking into causes and effects, and the benefits have been cast in the shape of generalizations from a sample to a population and of accurate predictions of future occurrences. This research scenario, while adequate for simple physical processes and laboratory-controlled behaviors, will no longer work once we venture forth into the real world of complexity, in which many people and circumstances act and interact. Here there are no simple causes, and predictability must yield to contingency. Research must be aimed at increasing our understanding, both holistically and in the smallest details, of the social setting as a complex adaptive system. Increased understanding allows us not to generalize but to particularize, that is, to adapt our skills, ideas, and strategies to the changing circumstances and the multifarious influences of the contexts in which the investigated processes occur.

It is of the utmost importance to realize how different the job of researching language learning becomes once we decide that the social context is central. To continue looking for operationally defined, discretely measured, statistically manipulated, and causally predictive variables would be to approach one job with tools that belong to another. It would be like going to an archaeological site with a combine harvester or like shining shoes with a nail file.

In this essay I examine social interaction in language-learning settings from the point of view that such settings are complex systems in which both attention to detail and global understanding are necessary. There are many different kinds of interaction that may occur in these settings, but I group them into two broad types: teacher-learner interaction and learner-learner interaction. Both have been the subject of considerable research, and their potential to facilitate (or hinder) language learning has been much debated. I look at transcribed examples of learning talk to try to understand how social interaction facilitates learning.

The first example is an extract from a teacher-learner interaction; the second, an extract from a learner-learner interaction. (In the transcriptions that follow, *x*'s in parentheses indicate an unintelligible, brief exclamation or word; a left square bracket indicates overlap; colons indicate lengthening of the previous sound; the equals sign indicates that the turn continues below at the next equals sign; and three ellipsis dots indicate a pause of about one second. These transcription conventions can be found in van Lier, *Classroom*; Atkinson and Heritage.)

> Teacher: *Put the umbrella . . .*
> Student: *Put the umbrella on the floor . . .*
> Teacher: *On the floor . . .*
> Student: *. . . between . . .*
> Teacher: *. . . between . . .*
> Student: *. . . the bookshelf and the TV.*
> Teacher: *Very good.*

In this example of interaction in an ESL classroom, it is easy to distinguish teacher from student. The teacher prompts and gives feedback, while the student produces language as part of a task (here, placing objects in a picture as a way of practicing prepositions).

That such classroom interaction is easily recognizable is often taken as evidence of its artificiality. The characteristic pattern has the teacher doing most of the talking while the students act as rather passive responders and followers of directions. As Anthony Edwards and David Westgate put it, classroom talk seems to run along "deep grooves," even in settings that aim to break new ground (27). Students "have only very restricted opportunities to participate in the language of the classroom," as John Sinclair and David Brazil note (3).

What makes classroom talk the way it is? How does it differ from inter-action in other settings, and how can it be brought in line with present-day critical and constructivist goals for education?

> Learner 1: *Here I—sometimes go to the beach* (xxxxxx)
> Learner 2: *Pebble Beach?*
> Learner 1: *Not Pebble Beach. My* (xxxxxx)
> Learner 2:   *[They near— Oh, yeah.*
> Learner 1:   *[Uhuh*
> Learner 2: *Wow. Is it good?*
> Learner 1: *Yeah, I think so.*
> Learner 2: *But I think here the beach not beautiful*
> Learner 1: *O:h, re::ally?*
> Learner 2: *Yes. It's not white. The sand is not white.*
> Learner 1:   *[Uhuh*
> Learner 2: *And the water—you cannot swim.*
> Learner 1: *I see because yeah! We can swim but=*
> Learner 2: *[This water is—*
> Learner 1: *[=the water is cold.*

In this conversation between two ESL learners, in contrast to the teacher-student interaction above, no one dominates or is in control: both learners contribute fairly equally to the talk. The learners understand each other per-fectly and are able to express viewpoints and advance arguments. They do not, at least not in this extract, infect each other with linguistic errors or cre-ate some form of interlingual pidgin, as teachers sometimes fear learners might do when left to their own devices.

But what kinds of opportunities do learners have to learn new language when they talk to each other in this way? Are the blind leading the blind here, or can such learner-learner conversation become a sort of interactional bootstrapping, where participants assemble learning material or contribute learning material to each other in the natural course of their talk?

The effectiveness of teacher talk and of learner talk as input for learning has been extensively discussed and researched (Chaudron; Pica, "Outcomes"; Ellis). Teacher talk has been lauded for being comprehensible and criticized for being inauthentic and not attuned to student needs. Learner talk has been lauded for providing opportunities for negotiating meaning and criticized for being a defective model, riddled with inaccuracies. On the whole, research has been supportive of learner-learner interaction more than of teacher talk, but the learner-learner talk studied has usually been interactional (e.g., as group work; see Long and Porter), and the teacher talk has tended to be monologic (e.g., in the form of lectures or instructions; see Parker and Chaudron). We therefore do not know if it is the nature of the talk or the nature of the interlocutor or a combination of both that makes the difference.

CONSTRAINTS AND RESOURCES

The British sociologist Anthony Giddens describes the structure of social systems in terms of rules that both enable and constrain characteristics. Just as in a game, and I include the special sense that Ludwig Wittgenstein attaches to "language game," the social world is governed by rules that allow certain moves to be made while disallowing (or disfavoring) others.[1] In a game like chess, these rules and moves are clear and circumscribed, but in social settings the rules are often tacit and ambiguous, and their precise interpretation or definition may have to be negotiated in interaction.

In the social setting of the classroom, interaction among participants takes place against a backdrop of constraints and resources that are in some ways different, in some ways similar, to those that characterize other settings. The classroom thus can be seen to constitute a speech exchange system (Sacks, Schegloff, and Jefferson 729) that has its own rules for turn taking and gives its participants certain rights and duties. The classroom is the primary setting in which talk-for-language-learning (learning talk) is carried out, and as such the classroom demonstrates the norms for proper behavior (what is called "fixity" by Giddens [118] or "habitus" by Bourdieu [57]) that underlie the institutional task of language teaching.

People in language classrooms, engaged in the official business of language learning, tend to behave and talk in ways that ratify that business, in other words, they behave and talk "appropriately" (see Fairclough for an incisive discussion of this problematic term). Elements of appropriateness, most prominent inside the classroom, may remain visible also outside the classroom, whenever learning talk is carried out in nondesignated places and at nonscheduled times (in cafeterias, around picnic tables, and so on), as when two students in the extract of learner-learner interaction given above agree to engage in a conversation at the request of a researcher. But time and place may make a difference in the way talk is conducted, and learning talk inside lessons may differ structurally from learning talk outside lessons. This possibility needs to be taken into account when learners' and teachers' interactions are analyzed.

There are practical consequences of this constraints-resources view of language learning contexts. In an article entitled "No Talking in Class," J. H. Lii depicts the traditional role of teacher as one of lecturing and that of students as "mostly listening passively in class." Indeed, a student is quoted as saying that he used to have "trouble concentrating because he was so bored by lectures." These comments fit the known stereotypes of teaching well enough. The interesting twist here is that in the innovative class described (which has twenty-five students), the problem is solved not by the teacher's changing his way of speaking and interacting with the students but by the placing of a computer between the teacher and the taught. Thanks to the insertion of the computer, students "now have the opportunity to interact with teachers and receive instant feedback." A skeptical person might ask, Why do interaction and feedback require an artificial interface? Why can't professors interact with their students without a computer?

Pierre Bourdieu and Jean-Claude Passeron, in their work on cultural reproduction, suggest that the institution equips the teacher with certain distancing techniques; the most efficient technique is "magisterial discourse," which condemns the teacher to "theatrical monologue." So powerful is this institutional control over the teacher's language use, according to Bourdieu and Passeron, that "efforts to set up dialogue immediately turn into fiction or farce" (109). The possibility that computer use may be able to circumvent these institutional constraints is intriguing.[2]

This characterization of teacher-student interaction may seem overdrawn and unrepresentative of today's classrooms, many of which are more dynamic and democratic. But there is no doubt that in various subtle or overt ways the institutional setting constrains the types of talk that can occur within its domain, and it is an open question whether a teacher is free to ignore such constraints in the interests of pedagogical action. Bourdieu and Passeron are clearly skeptical about the possibility of that freedom, though perhaps transformation-minded educators may want to see how far they can go, and to what effect.

The institutional setting, of course, offers resources and facilitates their deployment in the tangible form of budgets, materials, equipment, and the like, but also in the form, less palpable though perhaps more important, of authority and power: the authority to set the agenda, the power to judge (and grade, test, pass, fail); the authority to speak, the power to control and evaluate the speech of others. This authority and this power have traditionally defined the teacher and the work of teaching, but they are increasingly viewed as no longer appropriate in today's learning environments. John Merrow reports the story of a teacher's not knowing how to continue with a multimedia project after a specialized instructor was laid off. It had not occurred to this teacher that she could ask the students to teach her; asking them did not fit her concept of the teacher's role. As Merrow suggests, "teachers won't survive, and school will become increasingly irrelevant, if teachers don't change their style of teaching," a style he refers to as "the bank deposit approach" (52).

It is within the structure of institutional constraints and resources that the teacher's interaction with learners must take place. When teacher talk and teacher-learner interaction are examined, particularly when recommendations for changes are made, these structuring forces must be kept in mind. If interaction is as important for language learning as current theories claim it is, then the kinds of interaction the classroom permits and the changes the teacher can realistically make to those kinds of interaction are of great importance to research.

Taking a closer look at teacher-learner interaction in the language classroom, I ignore such common types of teacher talk as the lecture, the story, and various forms of explanation and instruction, since my focus is on social interaction. But I do not deny the importance and potential value for learning of these more monologic forms.

THE INITIATION-RESPONSE-FEEDBACK EXCHANGE

Teacher: *What is this called?*
Learner: *Plastic.*
Teacher: *You called it plastic. Good! It's plastic. But it's got another name*
              too . . .   . . . a transparency.

This exchange between a teacher and a learner is unmistakably classroom talk. It contains the following steps:

1. The teacher, holding up an overhead transparency, asks a question to which the teacher already knows the answer.
2. The teacher wishes to see if the learner has some particular piece of knowledge and can display this knowledge.
3. The learner responds effectively and efficiently, but also elliptically, using just one word.
4. The teacher evaluates the learner's response, approving of it, but then suggests that there might be another, more felicitous, answer.

This particular form of classroom interaction, the teaching exchange, is considered among the most frequently occurring types of teacher-student talk in the classroom (Sinclair and Coulthard; Mehan; van Lier, *Classroom;* Wells) and is usually called an IRF exchange, since it consists of these three parts (or moves): initiation, response, feedback.

In the IRF format, a number of different things can be accomplished. At the most mechanical, rote-learning end of IRF, the teacher's questions require the students merely to recite previously learned items. IRF may also be used by the teacher to see if students know a certain word or linguistic item. IRF can demand more, challenging students to think, reason, and make connections. At the most demanding end of IRF, students must be articulate and precise; they are pushed by successive probing questions, to clarify, substantiate, or illustrate some point that they made previously.

Teacher-learner interaction in the three-turn format of IRF therefore occupies a continuum between mechanical and demanding, as shown in the figure below.

IRF CONTINUUM

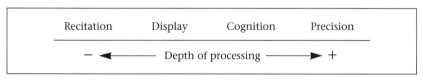

Given the variety of pedagogical work that the IRF format permits, it would be a mistake to dismiss it altogether as bad practice. Every case must be examined on its merits. As a rule of thumb, the precise nature of the IRF being employed in a particular instance is revealed in the third turn,[3] since this is where the teacher typically reveals the purpose of the question or sequence of questions. After the following question-answer pair

> Teacher: *What's the difference between "water is heating" and "water is heated"?*
> Learner: *Water is heating, it— it's the one who's heating.*

a variety of third turns are possible. In each case, a different type of task is revealed to be in progress:

> Teacher: *Good. Say the whole sentence: Water is heating the radiators.*
> (recitation)

> Teacher: *Good. What do we call that construction?*
> (display)

> Teacher: *And can you think of some things that it might be heating?*
> (cognition)

> Teacher: *Aha, can you explain that in a little more detail?*
> (precision)

Adapted from van Lier, Interaction 154

This example shows that the IRF structure cannot be regarded as a single type of pedagogical activity. All four IRF types of teacher-learner interaction given above can be used to evaluate or control or to invite participation. Knowing the purpose of a particular IRF exercise, though this may not always be easy, is crucial in determining its pedagogical value. But there are some things that all IRF sequences have in common, and these common features must be examined before IRF can be assessed as a pedagogical tool.

LEARNING AS COCONSTRUCTION: THE LIMITS OF IRF

The central feature of IRF is that the teacher is unequivocally in charge. This being in charge manifests itself in a number of ways.

Every IRF exchange is a step in an overall plan designed by the teacher.

The plan may be to check what the students know (as in recitation or display), to construct knowledge or an argument, perhaps along Socratic lines, or to push the students toward clarity of expression. It is important to note that the plan is not coconstructed. To varying degrees, students may be aware of the nature of the plan and aware of the direction in which the discourse is moving, but usually these matters are revealed only gradually and incidentally.

The teacher does all the initiating and closing (in other words, takes all the first and third turns), and the students' work is done exclusively in the response slot. The IRF format therefore discourages student initiation and student repair work. As Denis Newman, Peg Griffin, and Michael Cole note, "the three-part unit has a built-in repair procedure in the teacher's last turn so that incorrect information can be replaced with the right answers" (127). It is extremely hard, if not impossible, in the IRF format, for the student to ask questions, to disagree, to self-correct, and so on. Indeed, I found that such student utterances overwhelmingly occur as private turns, side sequences, or in other ways outside the IRF format. Often they are whispered comments to a fellow learner or questions written down in a notebook. The IRF format discourages interruption (or disruption) and can therefore be called a closed rather than open discourse format, in that it structurally and functionally controls what takes place (*Classroom*). It is like a discursive guided bus tour, but the itinerary is often unknown to the students.

Students' opportunities to exercise initiative (see van Lier, *Classroom*; Kinginger) or to develop a sense of control and self-regulation (a sense of ownership of the discourse, a sense of being empowered) are extremely restricted in the IRF format. Not only are student utterances often highly elliptical and syntactically reduced, occurring only in the response slot, sandwiched between two teacher turns (van Lier, *Interaction*), they also prevent the student from doing turn taking, topic development, and activity structuring work. They do not allow, to any significant extent, negotiation of the direction of instruction.

Given these basic features, how does IRF relate to current recommendations of coconstruction, responsive teaching (Bowers and Flinders; Shuy), or the instructional conversation (Tharp and Gallimore), especially if such recommendations are discussed from the perspective of critical pedagogy (Darder; Shor)? I explore this question from three different though related angles.

Vygotsky's Zone of Proximal Development and the Notion of Pedagogical Scaffolding

Lev Vygotsky discusses the range of activities a learner can accomplish with the assistance of a more capable person, such as a teacher. At any point in a learner's development, some activities (skills, operations, etc.) are within the learner's competence (this might be called the area of self-regulation), others can be accomplished only with special guidance, and yet others lie entirely outside the learner's scope. The middle band of activity, which is naturally the focus of pedagogical action, is referred to by Vygotsky as the zone of proximal development (84–91). Working within this zone (the "construction zone" in Newman, Griffin, and Cole), a teacher develops strategies for assisting the learner. The various kinds of assistance, which guide a learner into an activity that initially is too complex, are often called scaffolding (Bruner, 60).

The initiation-response-feedback exchange, at least when it moves beyond mere recitation and display, can be regarded as a way of scaffolding instruction, a way of developing cognitive structures in the zone of proximal development, or a way of assisting learners to express themselves with maximum clarity. IRF is frequently used to draw on students' prior experiences and current background knowledge to activate mental schemata and to establish a platform of shared knowledge that will facilitate the introduction and integration of new knowledge. IRF, used in several steps in a lesson or during one activity among other activities (see Wells), contributes to the attainment of a larger goal. Once it has served its purpose, it yields to other ways of structuring participation.

Scaffolding, to be of true pedagogical benefit, must be temporary. The scaffold must be gradually dismantled as the learner shows signs of being capable of handling more of the task in question. This process is called handover (Bruner 60), and without it scaffolding would simply breed dependence and helplessness. It is unclear whether IRF has in its structure the flexibility to effect handover. I suspect that, for handover to be possible, IRF must be abandoned at some point to make place for autonomous learner discourse. This switch from IRF to more open discourse structures may be a crucial pedagogical decision point, and research should focus on it closely.

Intrinsic Motivation and Learner Autonomy

Intrinsic motivation can be defined as the human response to innate needs for competence, relatedness, and autonomy (Deci and Ryan, "Initiation"; Deci, Vallerand, Pelletier, and Ryan). It expresses itself as a here-and-now interest in conducting an activity for its own sake, for the pleasure, stimulation, or challenge the activity provides. Intrinsic motivation is closely related to the perception of being able to choose and of being somehow in control of one's actions. Actions that are perceived as being externally controlled have a tendency to reduce intrinsic motivation, as do extrinsic rewards and praise or criticism (see Deci and Ryan, *Motivation*, "Initiation," for examples and summaries of research into intrinsic motivation; see van Lier, *Interaction*).

Since IRF is clearly other-controlled (from the learner's perspective) and since the rewards (in the form of teacher approval or praise in the third turn) are extrinsic, prolonged use of the IRF format may have a negative effect on intrinsic motivation and cause a decrease in levels of attention and involvement. IRF exchanges are like discoursal training wheels. In bicycle riding the training wheels must eventually come off, and likewise in interaction IRF must be replaced by free social interaction.

According to proponents of intrinsic motivation (see van Lier, *Interaction*), pedagogical action must be oriented toward increasing levels of intrinsic motivation and hence toward increasing self-regulation and autonomy. IRF must break its lockstep and yield to other participation patterns, ones that allow student initiative and choice to develop.

Transformation; or, Changing Educational Reality through Interaction

Critical pedagogy seeks to transform existing structures of control and inequality (Young; Darder) and to allow students to find voices of their own and become critical and autonomous learners (Wertsch). This emancipatory process requires true dialogue, which, according to Paulo Freire, can flourish only in a climate of equality among participants. Freire maintains that dialogue is indispensable for education: "Without dialogue there is no communication, and without communication there can be no true education" (81).

Characterized by one-sided control, IRF is only minimally dialogic, and the students' participation in its construction (and in the progression toward the overall goal) is largely passive. Therefore IRF cannot not be regarded as fostering equality or contributing to a transformation of educational reality; it embodies the status quo. Yet, as indicated above, it may be used as a preparatory step toward more emancipatory forms of discourse; it may be valuable not for what it is but, rather, for what it potentially leads to. For that potential to be realized, discourse must move from the patterns Robert Young aptly calls WDPK (What do pupils know?) and GWTT (Guess what teacher thinks; 106) to more discursive patterns marked by shared inquiry. It thus becomes important to investigate how IRF itself can be transformed and how transitions from IRF to other discourse forms can be effected.

EQUALITY AND SYMMETRY

The IRF structure is clearly a significant advance over the ritual magisterial performances Bourdieu and Passeron referred to as "theatrical monologue" (see above), since at least it involves students and asks them to contribute, albeit within someone else's agenda. However, in terms of communication, control, initiative, meaning creation and negotiation, message elaboration, and a number of other features characteristic of social interaction, the learner's side of the IRF interaction is seriously curtailed.

It is therefore useful to consider other forms of interaction, including conversational (such as learner-learner interactions) and see what characteristics they have that might be relevant to language learning. For a general examination of interaction, I suggest that there are two main groups of issues:

Issues of equality and inequality, including control and power. In this context, one thinks primarily of teacher talk, but more generally the question of equality may play a role in any interaction between native and nonnative speakers or between a more proficient and a less proficient nonnative speaker (van Lier and Matsuo).

Issues of negotiation and the joint construction of talk. This relates to shared rights and duties of participation, that is, interactional symmetry. Such symmetry, most clearly visible in conversation among equals, may be more difficult to achieve for less proficient speakers. But, as the conversation between two ESL students quoted above demonstrates, it is by no means impossible.

The phenomena relating to, on the one hand, control, power, and equality and, on the other, conversational symmetry and negotiation of meaning are connected: unequal participants tend to have asymmetrical interactions. But a distinction must be made between interactions that are oriented toward achieving symmetry and those that are not (IRF, lectures, instructions, and other common teacher talk belong to the second category).

An orientation toward symmetry does not necessarily involve an assumption of equality or some sort of abdication of authority. A separation between symmetry and equality is crucial for the possibility of fruitful communication between teachers and learners and, indeed, between native speakers and nonnative speakers. If true communication were possible only between equals, then teachers and learners (and even parents and their children) would be forever condemned to pseudocommunication. This is obviously not so.

Having postulated that communication, whether between equals or unequals, requires an orientation toward interactional symmetry, I now show, first, how such an orientation may be visible and, second, what benefits it might have for language learning.

In what ways can utterances be oriented toward symmetry? Basically, the orientation expresses itself in relations of contingency between an utterance and other entities—primarily other utterances (preceding, concurrent, and following), shared knowledge, and relevant features in the world (Gibson calls them affordances [559]; see further below).

CONTINGENCY

The term *contingency* refers to two distinct characteristics of interaction: first, the signaling of relations between a current utterance and previous utterances, either directly (utterance to utterance) or through shared knowledge or shared affordances in the environment; second, the raising of expectations and the crafting of deliberate ambiguities so that future utterances can find a conversational home (see van Lier, "Not," "Language Awareness," and *Interaction*). The first characteristic has been well studied under the heading of contextualization by John Gumperz. The ways in which utterances are linked to one another have also been studied extensively by ethnomethodologists, who have used related concepts such as conditional relevance and reflexive tying (Garfinkel; Sacks, Schegloff, and Jefferson).

My preoccupation with contingency originates in the belief that speakers, by using language contingently, unite structure and function in the most fundamental way possible (unite the given and the new, the topic and the comment, the foregrounded and the backgrounded). Contingent language use encourages, justifies, and motivates grammaticalization. Noncontingent language use—or, rather, less contingent, since the quality of contingency exists on a continuum—proceeds more statically and encourages a treatment of language as either form or function instead of as an organic whole.

Contingent features are most visible in the kind of talk usually referred to as conversational. Of all forms of talk, conversation is perhaps the hardest to define. It is, in a sense , a catchall concept that can contain other kinds of talk—such as instructions, requests, stories, business deals. A complication is that other kinds of talk can have conversation embedded in them. Interviews, lessons, or sales transactions may suddenly become chatty, then after a while switch back to business. So neat boundaries cannot be drawn around the phenomenon of conversation. Yet we usually know when a conversation is taking place.

In conversation, every utterance is connected by many links—some of them overt, many more of them covert—to previous utterances and through them to the shared (or to-be-shared) world of the participants. Every utterance sets up expectations for what will be said next. Utterances in conversation are thus, at the same time, predicted and predicting; in this way the interactants' mutual engagement (what Rommetveit calls intersubjectivity) is achieved and maintained.

When talk is contingent, utterances are constructed on the spot rather than planned in advance. In addition, there is symmetry, that is, equal rights and duties of participation, at least ideally.[4] I say "ideally," since it often happens that one person monopolizes the conversation and does not let the others get a word in edgewise. But the orientation toward symmetry still holds, since the participants will note that the conversation was one-sided, that so-and-so monopolized it, and that it was therefore not a "good" conversation.

To illustrate what makes an interaction conversational, I quote two extracts from nonnative speaker interactions. In the first there is a high level of contingency; in the second, a much lower level:

Speaker 1: *From my room I can see the ocean view*
Speaker 2: *Wow*
Speaker 1: *And—*
Speaker 2:   *[And how many room do you have?*
Speaker 1: *Two bedroom two full bathroom*
Speaker 2: *What what what*
Speaker 1: *Two bedroom=*
Speaker 2:   *[Two bedroom*
Speaker 1: *=and two full bathroom*

Speaker 1: *I never asked you, what did you do in Japan before you came here?*
Speaker 2: *Uhm—after finish high school*
Speaker 1: *Uhuh*
Speaker 2: *I work—for . . . . three years*
Speaker 1: *Hmm*
Speaker 2: *And—*
Speaker 1:   *[Where did you work?*
Speaker 2: *It—this is very—difficult for explain*
Speaker 1: *Try*
Speaker 2: *I use . . . the computer*
Speaker 1: *Uhuh*

Speaker 2, an ESL learner, is the same person in both interactions, but in the first her interlocutor is of roughly equal proficiency and in the second her interlocutor is a nativelike bilingual speaker. The first extract illustrates symmetry, and all utterances exhibit a high degree of contingency. The second extract is more like an interview in which speaker 1 encourages speaker 2 to speak. Relations of contingency are weaker, and symmetry is reduced. If contingency could be visualized as bundles of strings connecting utterances, then the strings would be thicker and more numerous in the first conversation and more sparse and spindly in the second.

Many sorts of devices can be used to create contingency: empathy markers (*"Wow!"*), repetitions of parts of each other's utterances (*"two bedroom— two bedroom"*), intonation patterns, gestures, and so on. The devices come from a stock of resources similar to Gumperz's "contextualization cues" (231; indeed, as I suggested above, the creation of contingencies overlaps significantly with the process of contextualization), though any interactional marker that can be used to make a contingent link can also be used for other purposes, and this makes tabulating and quantifying contingency impossible.

CONTINGENCY, NEGOTIATION, AND LANGUAGE LEARNING

The dynamics of interaction have been studied in most detail by Teresa Pica and her colleagues (Pica, "Second Language Acquisition," "Outcomes"; Pica and Doughty; Pica, Young, and Doughty). This research, which focuses on opportunities for learners to carry out repair strategies following communicative problems, has revealed various conditions that favor or disfavor such interactional modification and has shown how it benefits comprehension. According to Pica, "What enables learners to move beyond their current interlanguage receptive and expressive capacities when they need to understand unfamiliar linguistic input or when required to produce a comprehensible message are opportunities to modify and restructure their interaction with their interlocutor until mutual comprehension is reached" ("Second Language Acquisition" 8).

By resolving communicative problems through the use of interactional modifications (requests for clarification or confirmation, comprehension checks, recasts, and other such repairing moves), the learner obtains comprehensible input or makes new input available for learning. Research has shown how learners actively work on the language to increase their knowledge and proficiency.

The following observations, based on these analyses of repair in interlanguage talk, might help to place repairing in the overall context of interactional language use.

First, as Guy Aston has pointed out, repair work and adjustments of various kinds can be used to express convergence of perspectives among participants or to "seek closure on a problem" (Rudduck 73), not necessarily to make something comprehensible. George Yule found that more-proficient interlocutors sometimes simply decide to give up on certain problematic items in a task and move on. Therefore repair may have results other than increased comprehension, though increased comprehension can reasonably be regarded as its chief aim.

Second, the preponderance of repair (in the highly visible form of interactional modifications) may be the result of the type of discourse investigated. In much of the work of Pica and associates (Pica, Young, and Doughty; Pica, "Outcomes"), the activity types in question are communication tasks in which participants (often a native speaker and a nonnative speaker) need to exchange information. This need leads to interaction that is usually both asymmetrical and unequal, an environment in which explicit repair, with imbalances of the kind illustrated by Yule, tends to be salient. A similar focus on repair can be seen in the analysis by Michael Moerman of interaction among native speakers of Thai. He concludes that "repair is of central importance to the organization of conversation" (51). Moerman's discussion of repair, however, is based on transcripts of testimony in Thai court cases, where the status of overt repair is probably different from that in general conversation. Indeed, ethnomethodological analyses of repair and related matters in conversation (Schegloff, Jefferson, and Sacks; Heritage; Pomerantz) indicate a strong preference for self-repair and an avoidance of overt reactive repair, that is, repair that follows communication problems.

Third, and related to the second observation, the interactional activity of repairing must be placed in its social context. Repairing, an attempt to achieve mutual understanding in the face of problems, is one set of actions among many that manifest orientation toward mutual engagement (intersubjectivity) and symmetry. Repairing occurs in response to the perception of those troubles. But since troubles should be avoided in the first place, it makes sense to focus attention also on other mechanisms for achieving mutual understanding and intersubjectivity. It makes no sense, from a discourse-analytical or a pedagogical perspective, to assign special status to an activity that is undertaken only when other, more-preferred activities have been unsuccessful. To use an analogy, ice skaters are judged more on how they skate than on how they pick themselves up after falling on the ice.

Success in interaction—that is, the achievement of mutual understanding, contingency, and intersubjectivity—is dependent on the skillful use of all relevant social and linguistic resources, including those described by Gumperz as contextualization cues and those that create contingency. These resources can be divided into three categories, as follows (see Atkinson and Heritage; Duncan; Kasper; van Lier and Matsuo for additional examples):

Proactive (planning, predicting)
    Opening sequences   (*By the way; Do you know what?*)
    Cataphora   (*Now; Listen to this*)
    Grounders and preparers   (*OK, three points I wanna make*)
    Strategic moves   (*Let me give you an example*)

Concurrent (making signals during one's own or another person's turn)
    Back channels   (*Uhuh; Hm*)
    Gaze   (eye contact, looking away)
    Turnover signals   (*Let me finish; What do you think?*)
    Empathy markers   (*Oh; Wow; Really?*)

Reactive (summarizing, rephrasing, wrapping up)
    Repair and correction   (*Do you mean* x*?; Actually, it's* y)
    Demonstrations of under-
        standing   (*Oh; I see*)
    Gists and upshots   (*So; In a nutshell; What you're saying is*)

The relations between interaction and learning are not explained by this list or, indeed, by any other that might be devised. But at the very least the analysis shows that the concept of negotiation may need to be expanded from Pica's definition: "When a listener signals to a speaker that the speaker's message is not clear, and listener and speaker work interactively to resolve this impasse" ("Outcomes" 200). Negotiation includes the proactive and concurrent resources for utterance design, as well as reactive resources other than repair. Repair is thus only one among many forms of negotiation of meaning.

A fourth and final consideration goes to the very foundations of learning and its relation to the environment. Almost all the work in applied linguistics that addresses the role of input and interaction (see Ellis for an overview) assumes an input-output model of communication and learning. This model is based on a view of language use as the transfer of linguistic matter from one person to another and largely ignores issues of reciprocity and contingency. Being basically a transmission model (as words like *input* and *output* indicate), it does not address learning as transformation and language learning as grammaticalization (the development of grammatical complexity in the organic sense, outlined, e.g., by Rutherford). It is likely that the true role of interaction in learning and the true sense of what Vygotsky meant by the zone of proximal development can be revealed only through an organic or ecological approach (see Gibson; Bowers and

Flinders). In such an approach, notions like contingency and symmetry will be central, and overt acts of repairing will be epiphenomenal (Marcus and Zajonc; Graumann; Platt and Brooks). Linguistic matter in the environment, to the extent that the learner has access to it (see van Lier, *Interaction,* for a detailed discussion of access), provides affordances to the active and perceptive learner (Gibson; Deci and Ryan, "Initiation").[5] Whether or not such affordances are packaged as repair sequences is likely to be a minor issue.

A THEORETICAL CONCLUSION

I have discussed two different types of interaction in language learning, teacher-learner interaction in the IRF mode and learner-learner interaction, to illustrate equality and symmetry. I have suggested that interaction is particularly beneficial for learning when it is contingent. Symmetrical interaction is naturally contingent in a variety of ways, but asymmetrical interaction is deficient in contingency. Unequal discourse partners tend to find it more difficult to orient their interaction toward symmetry; as a result their interactions often look like IRF sequences or interviews where one of the partners takes a controlling role.

Two questions remain: What are some ways in which unequal discourse partners—such as teachers and learners or native speakers and nonnative speakers—can engage in symmetrical and contingent interaction, and how would that engagement benefit learning? What are the pedagogical benefits of various forms of asymmetrical discourse, such as lectures and IRF exchanges?

Language learning depends on the access learners have to relevant language material (affordances) in the environment and on internal conditions like motivation. Social interaction is the prime external condition to ensure access and learners' active engagement. Contingent interaction provides an "intrinsic motivation for listening" (Sacks, Schegloff, and Jefferson 727). Learners' natural learning processes, through the desire to understand and be understood, synchronize with efficient perception and focusing. Learners will be vigilant toward linguistic features and will make an effort to be pragmatically precise yet ambiguous where ambiguity is needed. Grammaticalization is thus a natural by-product of contingent interaction. To put this idea in the strongest possible (though of course hypothetical) terms: the organic, self-regulating process of contingent interaction is a necessary and sufficient condition for language development to occur. In the absence of appropriate research, this is of course a speculative hypothesis.

But that is only one side of the coin. To the extent that the target of language learning is a standardized, official code (a set of cultural habits) to which the learner has to or wants to conform, linguistic affordances marked as appropriate and desirable must be presented in the environment, and access to these affordances must be facilitated. Here organic language development and external language demands (socioculturally and institutionally mandated) meet each other halfway, and Vygotsky's zone of proximal development is the space wherein internal and external realms (inner resources and outer constraints) of language are mediated.

This mediation takes place under the guidance of parents, teachers, and other competent persons, and the different ways they do this can be captured by terms such as Bruner's *scaffolding*. (*Teaching, didactics, instruction, training, drilling,* and so on are of course also terms that have traditionally been used for such expert-novice activities.)

If this view of the relations between language learning and social interaction has merit, then the dynamic connections between more didactic (asymmetrical, less contingent) and more conversational (symmetrical, more contingent) forms of interaction are of central importance in the language learning enterprise.

A PRACTICAL CONCLUSION

In a book on talented teenagers, Mihaly Csikszentmihalyi, Kevin Rathunde, and Samuel Whalen compare current teaching with the traditional role of the master in an apprentice system. They observe that the teacher, instead of being a practitioner in a domain, is now a transmitter of information and thus discourages the development of extended and transforming relationships such as those between master and apprentice. Relationships between teachers and students are depersonalized and "kept highly specialized, programmatic, and brief" (178). Technical terms such as "instructional delivery systems" and detailed specifications of instructional objectives corroborate this tendency. Things can only get worse when, as is currently happening in many parts of the Western world, class sizes and school sizes keep increasing, as do teachers' workloads.

There are thus physical and institutional constraints that tend to minimize the possibilities for meaningful interaction between teachers and students. In Giddens's structuration theory, constraints ideally direct and guide, facilitating the deployment of resources. But in a defective institution (definable as one in which constraints and resources are out of balance), constraints may obstruct the very purposes for which they were brought into being. Against constraints of this second type, the teacher must marshal all the resources, meager though they often appear to be, that are available to provide learning opportunities to students. As the history of educational reform movements shows, large-scale reforms tend to achieve little transformation of the status quo. But grassroots, bottom-up innovations, usually based on individual initiative, can produce dramatic results, albeit at the local level only.

Marshaling available resources to promote rich and varied interaction with and among students must be the individual responsibility of every teacher. For teacher development this responsibility means the promotion of what Max van Manen calls "pedagogical thoughtfulness" or "tact," a mindful, understanding orientation in dealings with students and an ability to act wisely. Many teachers have responded to calls for more interactive and responsive ways of teaching by reducing their teacher-fronted activities and increasing learner-learner interaction through cooperative learning and task-based learning. In current jargon, they have become a "guide on the side" instead of a "sage on the stage."

However, before we swing the pendulum from teacher-centered entirely to teacher-peripheral, it may be worth reflecting on what the optimal roles of a teacher should be. Learners need, in addition to peer interaction, direct interaction with the teacher, provided it is quality interaction. If we ask learners, many will say that they want lectures, explanations and other forms of explicit teacher guidance. And we should never neglect the universal power of stories (Egan).

The answer to a disproportionate amount of highly controlling and depersonalized teacher talk is not to minimize all teacher talk per se but to find ways to modify it in more-contingent directions. In addition, teacher-learner interaction, such as the IRF, that is designed for scaffolding learners' language use (cognitively or socially) must contain within it the seeds of handover (Bruner), that is, the teacher must continually be on the lookout for signs that learners are ready to be more autonomous language users.

The classroom must regularly provide learners with opportunities to engage in symmetrical interactions, since such interactions immerse learners in contextualized and contingent talk, and since these interactions are intrinsically motivating and attention focusing. Symmetrical interactions are most easily achieved when interlocutors are equal in status and proficiency, but equality is not always essential. Research by Yule suggests that inequality in proficiency can be counterbalanced by having the less proficient speaker carry the main burden of information transfer.

Teachers can also experiment with ways of counterbalancing the inherent inequality of their talk with learners (though in most institutional and cultural settings it would be absurd for them to pretend that status differences between them and their learners do not exist). In a documentary video, classes in various British schools set up links with classes in far-flung places like Finland, Greece, and Portugal (Twitchin). At one point, a fax came in from a class in Greece; it contained drawings and descriptions of weaving techniques, with labels and expressions in Greek. The teacher and learners were naturally at the same level with respect to this text, and interaction among them became symmetrical and exploratory. When a parent who knew Greek was found and invited to class to explain the text, the teacher and his students were all learners.

Taking guidance from these and other examples, the thoughtful teacher-researcher looks for ways to make classroom interaction varied and multidimensional. In the world of language, we all embody different voices on different occasions (Bakhtin; Wertsch; Maybin). It is useful for learners to find that their teachers have various voices and that the learners themselves can experiment with multiple voices in the target language. Such experimentation is crucial if they are to find their own voice, and this is the true purpose of language education.

NOTES

I thank Kathi Bailey for insightful comments on an earlier draft.

1. I realize I gloss over the problems that are inherent in the concept of rule and that have been highlighted in much of the work of Wittgenstein, for example, *Philosophical Investigations*.
2. While the problem of poor teacher-student communication cannot be solved by just any computer work, there is certainly evidence that innovative use of computers can enhance interaction, for example, through interactive writing programs and collaborative project work (for extensive discussion, see Blake in this volume; Crook; van Lier, "Social Interaction").

3. Wells distinguishes between third turns that evaluate or provide follow-up (29–30). See also Barnes.
4. Symmetry and contingency are closely related but not synonymous. Symmetry is a structural discourse term, the result of interactional work by participants. Contingency is a cognitive quality. They usually occur together, but this does not mean that they are identical. As an analogy, light and heat often occur together, for example, in flames, sunlight, and light bulbs, but they are not the same.
5. Gibson describes *affordance* as follows: "The affordances of the environment are what it offers the animal, what it provides or furnishes, either for good or ill . . . something that refers both to the environment and the animal. . . . It implies the complementarity of the animal and the environment" (127). The term *affordance* specifically refers to those aspects of the linguistic environment that become perceivable by the learner as a result of meaningful activity. Affordance is neither the external language nor the learner's internalization of it. It refers to the relations among the engaged learner, meaningful signs, and relevant properties of the real world.

WORKS CITED

Aston, Guy. "Trouble-shooting in Interaction with Learners: The More the Merrier?" *Applied Linguistics* 7 (1986): 123–43.

Atkinson, J. Maxwell, and John Heritage, eds. *Structures of Social Action: Studies in Conversation Analysis.* Cambridge: Cambridge UP, 1984.

Bakhtin, Mikhail M. *The Dialogic Imagination.* Austin: U of Texas P, 1981.

Barnes, Douglas. *From Communication to Curriculum.* Harmondsworth, Eng.: Penguin, 1976.

Bourdieu, Pierre. *The Logic of Practice.* Stanford: Stanford UP, 1990.

Bourdieu, Pierre, and Jean-Claude Passeron. *Reproduction in Education, Society and Culture.* London: Sage, 1977.

Bowers, C. A., and David J. Flinders. *Responsive Teaching: An Ecological Approach to Classroom Patterns of Language, Culture, and Thought.* New York: Teachers Coll. P, 1990.

Bruner, Jerome. *Child's Talk: Learning to Use Language.* New York: Norton, 1983.

Chaudron, Craig. *Second Language Classrooms: Research on Teaching and Learning.* Cambridge: Cambridge UP, 1988.

Crook, Charles. *Computers and the Collaborative Experience of Learning.* London: Routledge, 1994.

Csikszentmihalyi, Mihaly, Kevin Rathunde, and Samuel Whalen. *Talented Teenagers: The Roots of Success and Failure.* Cambridge: Cambridge UP, 1993.

Darder, Antonia. *Culture and Power in the Classroom: A Critical Foundation for Bicultural Education.* New York: Bergin, 1991.

Deci, Edward L., and Richard M. Ryan. "The Initiation and Regulation of Intrinsically Motivated Learning and Achievement." *Achievement and Motivation: A Social-Development Perspective.* Ed. Ann K. Boggiano and Thane S. Pittman. Cambridge: Cambridge UP, 1992. 9–36.

———. *Intrinsic Motivation and Self-Determination in Human Behavior.* New York: Plenum, 1985.

Deci, Edward L., Robert J. Vallerand, Luc G. Pelletier, and Richard M. Ryan. "Motivation and Education: The Self-Determination Perspective." *Educational Psychologist* 26 (1991): 325–46.

Duncan, Starkey. "Some Signals and Rules for Taking Speaking Turns in Conversation." *Journal of Personality and Social Psychology* 23 (1972): 283–92.

Edwards, Anthony D., and David P. G. Westgate. *Investigating Classroom Talk*. London: Falmer, 1987.

Egan, Kieran. *Teaching as Storytelling*. Chicago: U of Chicago P, 1986.

Ellis, Rod. *The Study of Second Language Acquisition*. Oxford: Oxford UP, 1994.

Fairclough, Norman. "The Appropriacy of 'Appropriateness.'" *Critical Language Awareness*. Ed. Norman Fairclough. London: Longman, 1992. 33–56.

Freire, Paulo. *Pedagogy of the Oppressed*. New York: Herder, 1972.

Garfinkel, Harold. *Studies in Ethnomethodology*. Englewood Cliffs: Prentice, 1967.

Gass, Susan M., and Carolyn G. Madden. *Input in Second Language Acquisition*. Rowley: Newbury, 1985.

Gibson, James J. *The Ecological Approach to Visual Perception*. Boston: Houghton, 1979.

Giddens, Anthony. *The Constitution of Society*. Berkeley: U of California P, 1984.

Graumann, Carl F. "Perspectival Structure and Dynamics in Dialogue." *The Dynamics of Dialogue*. Ed. Ivana Marková and Klaus Foppa. New York: Harvester, 1990. 105–26.

Gumperz, John J. "Contextualization and Understanding." *Rethinking Context: Language as an Interactive Phenomenon*. Ed. Alessandro Duranti and Charles Goodwin. Cambridge: Cambridge UP, 1992. 229–52.

Heritage, John. "A Change-of-State Token and Aspects of Its Sequential Placement." Atkinson and Heritage 299–345.

Kasper, Gabriele. "Variation in Speech Act Realization." *Variation in Second Language Acquisition*. Ed. Susan Gass, Carolyn Madden, Dennis Preston, and Larry Selinker. Clevedon, Eng.: Multilingual Matters, 1989.

Kinginger, Celeste. "Learner Initiative in Conversation Management: An Application of Van Lier's Pilot Coding Scheme." *Modern Language Journal* 78 (1994): 29–40.

Lii, J. H. "No Talking in Class." *New York Times* 10 Apr. 1994, educ. supp. 7.

Long, Michael, and Patricia Porter. "Group Work, Interlanguage Talk, and Second Language Acquisition." *TESOL Quarterly* 19 (1985): 207–28.

Marcus, H., and R. B. Zajonc. "The Cognitive Perspective in Social Psychology." *Theory and Method*. Ed. Gardner Lindzey and Elliott Aronson. New York: Random, 1985. 137–230. Vol. 1 of *Handbook of Social Psychology*. 3rd ed.

Maybin, Janet. "Children's Voices: Talk, Knowledge, and Identity." *Researching Language and Literacy in Social Context*. Ed. David Graddol, Maybin, and Barry Stierer. Clevedon, Eng: Multilingual Matters, 1994. 131–50.

Mehan, Hugh. *Learning Lessons: Social Organization in the Classroom*. Cambridge: Harvard UP, 1979.

Merrow, John. "Four Million Computers Can Be Wrong!" *Education Week* 29 Mar. 1995: 52+.

Moerman, Michael. *Talking Culture: Ethnography and Conversation Analysis*. Philadelphia: U of Pennsylvania P, 1988.

Newman, Denis, Peg Griffin, and Michael Cole. *The Construction Zone: Working for Cognitive Change in School*. Cambridge: Cambridge UP, 1989.

Parker, Kate, and Craig Chaudron. "The Effect of Linguistic Simplifications and Elaborative Modifications on L2 Comprehension." *University of Hawaii Working Papers in English as a Second Language* 6.2 (1987): 107–33.

Pica, Teresa. "Second Language Acquisition, Social Interaction, and the Classroom." *Applied Linguistics* 7 (1987): 125.

———. "The Textual Outcomes of Native Speaker–Non-native Speaker Negotiation: What Do They Reveal about Second Language Learning?" *Text and Context: Cross-*

Disciplinary Perspectives on Language Study. Ed. Claire Kramsch and Sally McConnell-Ginet. Lexington: Heath, 1992. 198–237.

Pica, Teresa, and Catherine Doughty. "Non-native Speaker Interaction in the ESL Classroom." *Input in Second Language Acquisition.* Ed. Susan Gass and Carolyn Madden. Rowley: Newbury, 1985. 115–32.

Pica, Teresa, Richard Young, and Catherine Doughty. "The Impact of Interaction on Comprehension." *TESOL Quarterly* 21 (1987): 737–58.

Platt, Elizabeth, and Frank B. Brooks. "The 'Acquisition-Rich Environment' Revisited." *Modern Language Journal* 78 (1994): 497–511.

Pomerantz, Anita. "Pursuing a Response." Atkinson and Heritage 152–63.

Rommetveit, Ragnar. *On Message Structure.* New York: Wiley, 1974.

Rudduck, Jean. *Innovation and Change: Developing Involvement and Understanding.* Milton Keynes: Open U, 1991.

Rutherford, William. *Second Language Grammar: Learning and Teaching.* London: Longman, 1987.

Sacks, Harvey, Emanuel Schegloff, and Gail Jefferson. "A Simplest Systematics for the Organization of Turn Taking in Conversation." *Language* 50 (1974): 696–735.

Schegloff, Emanuel A., Gail Jefferson, and Harvey Sacks. "The Preference for Self-Correction in the Organization of Repair in Conversation." *Language* 53 (1977): 361–82.

Shor, Ira. *Empowering Education: Critical Teaching for Social Change.* Chicago: U of Chicago P, 1992.

Shuy, Roger. "Secretary Bennett's Teaching: An Argument for Responsive Teaching." *The Enlightened Eye: Qualitative Inquiry and the Enhancement of Educational Practice.* Ed. Elliott Eisner. New York: Macmillan, 1991. 135–49.

Sinclair, John M., and David Brazil. *Teacher Talk.* Oxford: Oxford UP, 1982.

Sinclair, John M., and Malcolm Coulthard. *Towards an Analysis of Discourse.* Oxford: Oxford UP, 1975.

Tharp, Roland, and Ronald Gallimore. *Rousing Minds to Life.* Cambridge: Cambridge UP, 1988.

Twitchin, John. *European Awareness in Primary Schools.* Mosaic Films. Central Bureau for Educ. Visits and Exchanges, 1993.

van Lier, Leo. *The Classroom and the Language Learner: Ethnography and Second-Language Classroom Research.* London: Longman, 1988.

———. *Interaction in the Language Curriculum: Awareness, Autonomy and Authenticity.* London: Longman, 1996.

———. "Language Awareness, Contingency, and Interaction." *Consciousness in Second Language Learning.* Ed. Jan Hulstijn and Richard Schmidt. *AILA Review* 11 (1994): 69–82.

———. "Not the Nine O'clock Linguistics Class: Investigating Contingency Grammar." *Language Awareness* 1.2 (1992): 91–108.

———. "Social Interaction and Cooperative Learning at, around, with, and through Computers." Eleventh World Congress of Applied Linguistics (AILA 96). U of Jyväskylä, Finland. 5 Aug. 1996.

van Lier, Leo, and Naoko Matsuo. "Varieties of Conversational Experience." Unpublished essay. Monterey Inst. of Intl. Studies, 1995.

van Manen, Max. *The Tact of Teaching: The Meaning of Pedagogical Thoughtfulness.* Albany: State U of New York P, 1991.

Vygotsky, Lev S. *Mind in Society.* Cambridge: Harvard UP, 1978.

Wells, Gordon. "Reevaluating the IRF Sequence: A Proposal for the Articulation of

Theories of Activity and Discourse for the Analysis of Teaching and Learning in the Classroom." *Linguistics and Education* 5 (1993): 1–37.

Wertsch, James V. *Voices of the Mind: A Sociocultural Approach to Mediated Action.* Cambridge: Harvard UP, 1991.

Wittgenstein, Ludwig. *Philosophical Investigations.* Oxford: Blackwell, 1958.

Young, Robert. *Critical Theory and Classroom Talk.* Clevedon, Eng: Multilingual Matters, 1992.

Yule, George. "Interactive Conflict Resolution in English." *World Englishes* 9 (1990): 53–62.

Interlanguage Pragmatics

Gabriele Kasper

This essay sets out by delineating the field of interlanguage pragmatics and defining some basic concepts. It then reviews the research on pragmatic comprehension, production of linguistic action, development of pragmatic competence, and pragmatic transfer. After discussing the relation of pragmatic divergence and communicative effect and the problems in establishing pragmatic norms for language teaching and research, studies examining the effect of instruction on the development of pragmatic competence are considered. The essay concludes with a brief account of the research methods that have been used in ILP and with some suggestions for further reading.

DEFINITION AND SCOPE

Interlanguage pragmatics (ILP) represents an intersection of pragmatics and the study of second language acquisition. According to a recent definition proposed by Jacob Mey, pragmatics is "the societally necessary and consciously interactive dimension of the study of language" (315). This perspective on language is particularly useful for such applied linguistic concerns as language teaching. Indeed, a pragmatic view of language is highly compatible with the notion that has been the guiding construct of Anglo-European second and foreign language instruction for the past two decades: communicative competence. In one of its original formulations, communicative competence comprises the knowledge "as to when to speak, when not, and as to what to talk about with whom, what, where, and in what manner" and the ability "to accomplish a repertoire of speech acts, to take part in speech events, and to evaluate their accomplishment by others" (Hymes 277).

In Lyle Bachman's model of communicative language ability in language teaching and testing, pragmatic competence is one of two major components of language competence, including the ability to carry out linguistic action and to assess the appropriateness of utterances in different contexts (89). Organizational competence, the other main component in Bachman's model, comprises knowledge of linguistic material and the ability to sequence it into sentences and texts. There is considerable overlap between these components: for instance, knowing the semantic and syntactic properties of formal markers of tense, mood, and modality in French is part of a speaker's organizational knowledge; knowing how these forms index linguistic acts and social meanings is a matter of pragmatic competence.

Interlanguage (IL), a central construct in second language acquisition research, refers to second language learners' developing knowledge of a target language (L2) (Selinker). As knowledge under construction, interlanguages are partly instable and transient. They typically include features from L2, from learners' first language (L1) or other languages learners may know (Ln), and autonomous features that can be found neither in L1/n or L2. Interlanguage theory was first formulated with a view to describing and explaining learners' formal linguistic knowledge. When the first interlanguage pragmatics studies appeared in 1979, interlanguage syntax, morphology, and phonology were already well-established areas of investigation.

By putting the two components of ILP together, then, ILP can be defined as the study of nonnative speakers' comprehension, production, and acquisition of linguistic action in L2, or, put briefly, ILP investigates "how to do things with words" (Austin) in a second language. In authentic language use, linguistic action is always situationally and textually embedded; in many discourse types—conversation is the prototypical example—action is *inter*actionally constituted, that is, not only are utterances designed with a view to one interlocutor or more (and perhaps also for the benefit of overhearers, bystanders, etc.), but utterance meaning itself is jointly constructed. While these assumptions are fundamental to pragmatic theory and well substantiated empirically, much of the ILP research has adopted a reductionist approach, abstracting from the dynamics of ongoing interaction and reducing context to a few controlled and independent variables. To a large extent, such reductions follow from ILP's commitment to the comparative methodology recommended by Larry Selinker for interlanguage research, that is, to the comparison of parallel sets of IL, L1, and L2 data. The comparative approach links ILP strongly to cross-cultural pragmatics (see Blum-Kulka, House, and Kasper for an example), and it is from this field that most of ILP's research topics, theories, and methods of data collection and analysis have been borrowed. Another feature that aligns ILP research more with cross-cultural pragmatics than with interlanguage studies at large is ILP's focus on second language *use* rather than *development.*

In ILP studies, a distinction is frequently made between pragmalinguistic and sociopragmatic aspects of linguistic action, as proposed by the British pragmaticists Jenny Thomas and Geoffrey Leech. In Leech's and Thomas's original definition, *pragmalinguistic* refers only to "the particular resources which a given language provides for conveying particular illocutions" (Leech 11). For instance, the utterance (locution) "I'm sorry" is conventionalized in English to express the illocution of apology. However, in performing a particular linguistic act, interlocutors choose from a variety of strategies and forms that convey the same illocution but vary in their relational meaning. The utterances "Oops — sorry" and "I'm terribly sorry, I had no idea what I was doing. Are you all right? Can I do anything to help?" can both convey the illocution of apology, but they would not normally be used in the same context. Therefore, the notion of pragmalinguistics has to be expanded to include the resources that express relational meaning. Directness and indirectness and a multitude of lexical, syntactic, and prosodic means used to mitigate or aggravate illocutionary force have been identified cross-linguistically as relational or politeness markers (e.g., Fraser, "Mitigation"; House and Kasper, "Markers"; Brown and Levinson; Held; Blum-Kulka, House, and Kasper).

Sociopragmatics was described by Leech as "the sociological interface of pragmatics," referring to the social perceptions underlying participants' performance and interpretation of linguistic action (10). Speech communities differ in their assessment of a speaker's and a hearer's social distance and social power, rights and obligations, and degree of imposition involved in linguistic acts (Takahashi and Beebe; Blum-Kulka and House; Olshtain, "Apologies"). The values of context factors can change through the dynamics of conversational interaction, as shown by interactional sociolinguists (e.g., Gumperz, *Strategies;* Erickson and Shultz), and are captured in Bruce Fraser's notion of the conversational contract ("Perspectives").

Because sociopragmatic knowledge is closely related to people's cultural and personal beliefs and values, it has been argued that this knowledge is less amenable to language instruction than pragmalinguistic knowledge (Thomas). Indeed, it makes immediate sense that learners will be less personally invested in learning and using pragmalinguistic aspects of the target language—for example, what linguistic forms can be used to apologize, complain, or compliment and how one can apologize, complain, or compliment more or less politely. Although even advanced learners often have trouble choosing appropriate strategies and linguistic means to do things with words in their second or foreign language (e.g., Kasper and Blum-Kulka, *Pragmatics;* Bardovi-Harlig and Hartford, "Congruence," "Learning"), it stands to reason that most pragmalinguistic difficulties are cognitive and processing difficulties — knowing which L2 resources can be used to express particular pragmatic meanings and being able to access the required linguistic material fast and efficiently.

PRAGMATIC COMPREHENSION

Studies of pragmatic comprehension address both pragmalinguistic and sociopragmatic issues. Pragmalinguistic studies examine how learners understand the propositional content and illocutionary force of nonliteral utterances and how learners assess the politeness value of conventions of means and form. Sociopragmatic studies investigate how learners perceive variables in the social context and in the linguistic act itself.

Comprehension of Nonliteral Utterances

Even though adult nonnative listeners or readers possess fully developed cognitive strategies to infer indirectly conveyed meaning, they do not always make full use of their inferencing ability (Carrell, "Indirect Speech Acts"). One problem is that learners as readers or conversationalists often rely more on linguistic than on contextual cues in message comprehension (Carrell, "Difficulty"). In a large study on advanced ESL learners' ability to understand indirect responses, Lawrence Bouton found that both the type of indirect utterance and learners' cultural and linguistic background influenced the success of learners' comprehension activity (Bouton, "Cross-Cultural Study"). A prominent research issue in studies of utterance comprehension by native speakers is whether the indirectly conveyed pragmatic meaning is understood immediately and without the literal utterance meaning, concurrently with the literal meaning, or only after the literal meaning. Advanced ESL learners seem to adopt the same comprehension process as native speakers (Takahashi and Roitblat). But whether less proficient learners will take a different route remains unknown (see Takahashi, "Exploring," for a review of studies on nonliteral utterance comprehension).

Assessment of Politeness

Nonnative listeners or readers distinguish different degrees of politeness in conventions of means and form but not always in the same way as native speakers. For instance, Japanese learners of English and English native speakers perceived modification of requests through modal verbs, tense, negation, and supportive moves differently. American judges rated strategies by which native speakers of English express solidarity with the hearer (positive politeness) as more polite than strategies that emphasize respectful distance (negative politeness), whereas Japanese judges did not (Kitao). Learners' assessments of politeness values may be influenced by such factors as transfer from their first language (Takahashi, "Pragmatic Transferability") or social characteristics of the message receiver, for instance, age and gender (Rintell). Nonnative speakers' convergence to L2 sociopragmatic norms tends to increase with the time spent in the target community: learners of Hebrew, who initially based their politeness assessments of requests and apologies on L1, became more tolerant of directness and positive politeness the longer they lived in Israel (Olshtain and Blum-Kulka). Quality and quantity of exposure to the target language can account for the different politeness ratings given by foreign language learners (i.e., classroom learners of a language that is not a regular means of communication in their community) and second language learners (i.e., residents of the target community). In one study, Japanese learners of English as a second language in the United States gave more nativelike politeness ratings to various request strategies than did learners of English as a foreign language in Japan (Kitao).

Sociopragmatic Assessment

Nonnative speakers' assessment of whether or not a linguistic act is appropriate in a particular social context may differ according to the linguistic and cultural environment. Japanese female learners of English felt that refusing a request or offer was less acceptable in English than in Japanese (Robinson). Native speakers of English expressed a greater need to apologize for an offense when they spoke English than when they spoke Hebrew, while Russian learners of Hebrew felt that the type of offense, not the language, determined whether an apology was called for (Olshtain, "Competence"). For German learners of English, the severity of offenses warranting apology was greater than for native speakers of British English (House, "Oh"). Thai learners of English differed most strongly from native speakers of American English on the obligation to apologize (Bergman and Kasper). Learners may also differ from native speakers in their assessment of participant factors. For instance, compared with American informants, Japanese learners of English demonstrated more status differentiation (Beebe and Takahashi, "Do You Have," "Variation") but less differentiation of social distance (Fukushima).

PRODUCTION OF LINGUISTIC ACTION

Most data-based studies in ILP examine how learners perform a particular speech act in L2 (see Kasper and Blum-Kulka, "Pragmatics," for review). Speech acts studied thus far include requests, apologies, refusals, compliments, suggestions, expressions of gratitude, invitations, rejections, expressions of disagreement, corrections, and complaints; of these, requests and apologies have been investigated the most thoroughly. Adult learners have an implicit knowledge of the strategies by which such speech acts can be realized, but they do not always make full use of this knowledge (Blum-Kulka, "Pragmatics"). Intervening factors may be learners' limited linguistic proficiency (Blum-Kulka, "Learning"), negative pragmatic transfer from L1, stereotypical assumptions about what is pragmatically appropriate in target language contexts (Tanaka; Robinson), or cultural resistance, that is, more or less deliberate deviations from L2 norms, by which nonnative speakers can mark themselves as distinct from the target community (Blum-Kulka, "Pragmatics").

One recurring observation is that learners differ in the directness with which they realize a linguistic act. According to most studies, learners opt for strategies more direct than those of native speakers in comparable contexts, for instance, in refusing (Robinson) and in making suggestions to an interlocutor of higher status (Bardovi-Harlig and Hartford, "Congruence"). But the opposite is noted as well: nonnative speakers of Hebrew expressed requests (Blum-Kulka, "Learning") and complaints (Olshtain and Weinbach) less directly than native speakers, and Japanese learners of English used more indirect request strategies than American native speakers (Takahashi and DuFon). Whether learners prefer more direct or more indirect strategies than native speakers do may reflect the relative preference for directness or indirectness in L1 and L2, but that preference can be overridden by the factors listed above.

Learners may differ from native speakers not only in their preference for specific strategies but also in their overall politeness approach. Japanese (Takahashi and Beebe) and Taiwanese learners of English (Fiksdal) and Athabaskans (Scollon and Scollon) favored a negative politeness style in contexts where native speakers of American English preferred a positive politeness approach; conversely, learners of English with Venezuelan Spanish as L1 relied on positive politeness in apologizing where native speakers of American English were negatively polite (García).

In sum, learners have access to the same range of conventions of means as target language speakers, but they often make different choices from "speech act sets" (Olshtain and Cohen). The conventions of form used by nonnative speakers, however, are typically more restricted than those available to native speakers; and even if forms such as tense, aspect, modal verbs, and modal particles are part of learners' linguistic competence, learners may not fully control the pragmalinguistic functions of this material (Færch and Kasper; Eisenstein and Bodman). Among the conventions of form that seem particularly difficult to acquire are routine formulas (Coulmas), that is, prefabricated patterns used for specialized functions in recurrent situations. Although learning a set of highly frequent routines is not difficult in itself, since such routines are learned and stored as lexical items, matching them with their pragmalinguistic functions and sociopragmatic context constraints is often only partially achieved even by highly proficient nonnative speakers (House, "Developing").

A number of studies find that intermediate to fairly advanced learners tend to produce longer, more verbose utterances than native speakers do.

This interlanguage feature has been related to learners' either lacking or not having sufficient control over routine formulas (Edmondson and House). But Thai learners of English both used appropriate routine formulas in apologizing and overused nonroutinized apology strategies (Bergman and Kasper). While there is some indication that verbosity, whether compensatory or additive, may occur in written production only, one study reports prolixity also in conversational data (Nyyssönen).

The function and communicative effect of overproduction remains a topic for debate. Although with respect to native speaker norms, verbosity is a violation of H. Paul Grice's maxims of quantity and manner, native standards are often not appropriate to assess nonnative linguistic action. Nonnative speakers frequently have to make their intentions, motivations, and reasoning explicit because they cannot take for granted shared experiences and assumptions; therefore they have to establish common ground with speakers of the target language or with other nonnative speakers.

DEVELOPMENT OF PRAGMATIC COMPETENCE

Compared with the large number of studies on various aspects of pragmatic performance by nonnative speakers, the body of literature on pragmatic development is small. Most developmental studies are based on a cross-sectional design, few on longitudinal data, and only a few theoretical proposals have been offered to date to account for the acquisition of pragmatic competence by adult nonnative speakers (see Kasper and Schmidt).

Cross-Sectional Studies

Cross-sectional studies compare how samples of L2 learners at different levels of proficiency understand or produce linguistic action. Most of these studies show that learners can use the same pragmatic strategies as native speakers regardless of proficiency level. Studies on apologizing have consistently found that learners can produce the full range of apology strategies: using an illocutionary force indicator or apologetic formula (*I'm sorry*), assuming responsibility for the offense (*I deleted your file*), downgrading responsibility (*There must be a virus in your software*) or the severity of the offense (*Fortunately you have a hard copy*), offering repair (*I'll ask Tom to retrieve it for you*) or other forms of redress such as expressing concern for the offended party (*I hope the file wasn't important*), trying to appease the listener (*I'll install your new software for you*), or promising forbearance (*I'll be more careful the next time*). These studies also showed effects of proficiency on the linguistic forms by which apologies are implemented (Trosborg, "Strategies") and on the contextual distribution of meaning and form conventions (Maeshiba, Yoshinaga, Kasper, and Ross). A problem of the cross-sectional studies is that the most frequently employed data collection techniques, written questionnaires and roleplays, are too taxing for beginning L2 learners; hence studies usually include only intermediate and advanced learners. The absence of proficiency effects on the use of conventions of means may thus be a design artifact.

Longitudinal Studies

The few longitudinal studies on pragmatic development confirm that L2 proficiency is a powerful constraint on beginning learners' linguistic action. Studies reporting on individuals or groups of learners from the early stages on show that, consistent with naturalistic second language acquisition generally, learners initially rely on a few prepackaged routines, which are later analyzed into rules and elements that become available for productive use (Schmidt, "Interaction"; Ellis; Sawyer). For instance, conventionally indirect requests may be realized at an early stage through sentence frames such as *Can I have* or *Can you*, modifications through tense and modal adverbs (*Could you perhaps*) appearing only later. While analyzed use of linguistic material in various pragmatic functions is a more advanced achievement, it also requires a fair level of proficiency to be able to chunk linguistic forms into pragmatic routines and have such chunks available for fluent access (Schmidt, "Psychological Mechanisms").

Theoretical Accounts

Theoretical accounts of pragmatic development, based on cognitive and anthropological theory and research, have first been conceptualized as models of second language acquisition at large and then extended to the acquisition of pragmatic competence. One such proposal is Richard Schmidt's theory of the role of consciousness in pragmatic development ("Consciousness"). Distinguishing between *acquiring* and *using* pragmatic information, Schmidt suggests that performing linguistic action often happens without conscious awareness, since much pragmatic knowledge is routinized and therefore requires little attentional capacity in proficient language users. To acquire pragmatic information in the first place, however, learners need to focus attention on relevant forms, their pragmalinguistic functions, and the sociopragmatic constraints under which they occur. *Noticing* relevant input features is required in order to make the information available for further processing and storage. A second theoretical proposal is Ellen Bialystok's two-dimensional model of language use and proficiency. This model views language learning as developing in two orthogonal dimensions, analysis of knowledge and control of processing. Bialystok contends that children's primary learning task in pragmatics is to develop analytic representations of pragmalinguistic and sociopragmatic knowledge, whereas adult L2 learners mainly have to acquire processing control over already existing representations. The two proposals are compatible in that they address different stages of pragmatic learning: Schmidt is concerned with the conditions of initial intake, whereas Bialystok considers how acquired pragmatic information is represented and restructured. Both proposals await empirical testing in future studies.

From Lev Vygotsky's theory of cognitive development, the construct of a zone of proximal development has been adapted to ILP and connected to the input and practice opportunities afforded by different participation structures (Shea). This construct also lends itself to examine interaction formats in L2 classrooms, such as teacher-fronted formats, pair work, and different types of small-group interaction. Other Vygotskyan concepts, such as inner speech and activity type, may prove useful for the study of pragmatic development in L2 but have not yet been extended to ILP (see Lantolf and Appel). As a social-psychological approach, communicative accommodation theory (Giles, Coupland, and Coupland) explains the relation of interactional dynamics and attitudinal factors. In the framework of that approach, the conversational practices of learners and their interlocutors can be examined as pragmatic convergence and divergence and related to the learning opportunities provided in different kinds of encounters. Finally, language socialization theory (Schieffelin and Ochs) has a particularly rich potential to explain ILP development, since it locates L2 acquisition in its sociocultural context and connects it with participants' social values, practices, and identity construction (Poole).

PRAGMATIC TRANSFER

Definition

Pragmatic transfer has been defined as the influence exerted by learners' pragmatic knowledge of other languages and cultures on their comprehension, production, and acquisition of L2 pragmatic information (Kasper, "Pragmatic Transfer," which also contains a review of the research). Learners' and bilingual speakers' linguistic action patterns regularly show some evidence of transfer, but the conditions of cross-cultural and crosslinguistic pragmatic influence are far from clearly understood. It is well established, however, that transfer in interlanguage pragmatics, just as in second language acquisition and use generally, cannot be entirely predicted or explained by a contrastive analysis of L1 and L2 pragmatics, although contrastive relations (on the assumption they are equivalent to learners' cognitive representations) do factor into the presence or absence of pragmatic transfer.

Positive Transfer

Outcomes of transfer can be distinguished according to their relation to the target language. When learners' production of a pragmatic feature is the same (structurally, functionally, distributionally) as a feature used by target language speakers in the same context and when this feature is paralleled by a feature in learners' L1, the converging pattern is referred to as positive transfer. Empirically, positive transfer is often difficult to distinguish from the manifestation of pragmatic universals, but sometimes the distinction is clear. For instance, in all languages examined so far, requests can be performed directly (e.g., using an imperative, as in *Water the plants!*), conventionally indirectly (using illocutionary force indicators such as routinized sentence frames, as in *Would you mind watering the plants?*), or indirectly (hinting at the intended illocutionary or propositional act, as in *These plants look pretty dry*). When learners use any of these strategic options, they are therefore likely to be relying on universal pragmatic knowledge of request realization. But when learners' interlanguage use features particular pragmalinguistic means that occur in their L1 and L2 but are not universal, positive transfer is likely. For example, learners transferred the Danish past tense of the modal verb *at kunne* as in *Kunne du låne mig dine noter?* and the German subjunctive of the modal verb *können* as in *Könntest Du mir Deine Vorlesungsmitschrift leihen?* to the corresponding modal past form of English *can* as in *Could you lend me your notes?* (House and Kasper, "Interlanguage Pragmatics"; Færch and Kasper).

Negative Transfer

Despite the obviously important role of positive pragmatic transfer in L2 learners' linguistic action, ILP research has paid much more attention to negative pragmatic transfer, which is observable when a pragmatic feature in the interlanguage is (structurally, functionally, distributionally) the same as in L1 but different from L2. For instance, Japanese learners of English may express gratitude by saying *I'm sorry*, a negative transfer from the Japanese routine formula *Sumimasen*. In Japanese, apologetic expressions are often used in conveying gratitude when the speaker's emphasis is on the incurred debt, especially if the benefactor is a person of higher status (Ikoma). Danish learners frequently transfer the syntactic request strategy of modal verb + interrogative + negation to English, as in *Can't you clean the kitchen* (from Danish *Kan du ikke rydde op i køkkenet*), apparently not realizing that the negation carries an overtone of exasperation in English, whereas in Danish it mitigates the request (Færch and Kasper). Strategies of speech act realization are particularly prone to negative transfer. Japanese learners of English may use statements of principle (*I never yield to temptations*) as refusal strategies (Beebe, Takahashi, and Uliss-Weltz), or information questions as disagreements, rejections, warnings, or requests for action (Beebe and Takahashi, "Do You Have," "Variation"; Bardovi-Harlig and Hartford, "Congruence"). German learners of English tend to extract themselves from conversation by referring to some specific obligation of their own, following the German convention (*I must pick up Veronica from kindergarten*), while native speakers of English prefer vague routines that refer to the other person's needs (*I mustn't keep you any longer*) (Kasper, *Pragmatische Aspekte*; House, "Developing"). Studies of Chinese-English discourse have shown that pragmalinguistic transfer operates not only at the act or turn level but also in the sequential organization of discourse (Shi and Yeh).

In addition to negative transfer of pragmalinguistic knowledge, the sociopragmatics of L1 may be transferred to L2 communication. Whether or not learners perform a particular linguistic act may be influenced by L1 preference patterns. Japanese learners of English expressed reluctance about refusal in an American context, because in Japanese they would comply (Robinson). Nonnative speakers of English with a Chinese language background tend to reject compliments, based on Chinese cultural norms. Sociopragmatic assessments of interlocutor relationships are also prone to cross-cultural transfer. Japanese learners of English modeled their perceptions of status in unequal power relations on Japanese norms (Takahashi and Beebe). Particularly interesting from a pedagogical perspective is the negative transfer of pragmatic norms in institutional settings such as language classrooms. In studies on classroom participation by students of different ethnic backgrounds, Asian students were outperformed by non-Asians (Sato), Japanese by non-Japanese (McLean), Japanese Americans by Caucasians (Doi), and Japanese by Chinese (Shimura). Even though no baseline data on Japanese classroom interaction were available in any of the studies, there is a strong likelihood, worthy of investigation, that the Japanese students were following their L1 participation patterns. Even the Japanese American students in Hawai'i, although members of the English language community, seemed to adhere to the traditional receptive participation style of Japanese college classrooms. This observation supports the notion of an *intercultural style* as a stable sociolinguistic variety in the pragmatics of immigrant populations (Blum-Kulka, "Interlanguage Pragmatics").

Transferability

While the phenomenon of pragmatic transfer is well attested, the conditions of transfer and especially the interaction of different factors in it are less clearly understood. In interlanguage studies of morphosyntax and phonology, structural properties of L1 and L2—both objective features and their subjective perception by native and nonnative speakers—have been identified as predictors of transferability. In ILP, so far only one study has been carried out that explicitly focuses on transferability. Satomi Takahashi reports that Japanese learners of English found several indirect request strategies transferable to different degrees and that transferability perceptions interacted with the degree of imposition implied by the goal of the request ("Pragmatic Transferability"). Since transferability perceptions were often not consistent with English native speakers' judgments of contextual appropriateness and since learners' proficiency had little effect on transferability, it seems likely that these college students received insufficient pragmalinguistic and sociopragmatic input in their English classrooms to develop more targetlike pragmatic competence.

Transfer and L2 Proficiency

In addition to structural factors, nonstructural factors influence pragmatic transfer. Even though Takahashi has found little effect of L2 proficiency on transferability, actual transfer is often related to learners' proficiency level. There is evidence that pragmatic transfer may correlate negatively or positively with proficiency. Each of the following four options has some empirical support:

Low proficiency learners may transfer L1 conventions of means or form to L2 without realizing the pragmalinguistic meaning of these structures. An example is Japanese learners of English using *I'm sorry* to express gratitude (Eisenstein and Bodman).

Low proficiency learners may not transfer L1 conventions of means or form because such transfer overtaxes their linguistic competence in L2. In one study, learners of Hebrew did not transfer English indirectness strategies because their Hebrew interlanguage did not yet include the necessary complex structures (Blum-Kulka, "Learning").

Advanced learners may transfer conventions of means and form because their L2 linguistic competence enables them to do so, but they may lack the pragmalinguistic and sociopragmatic knowledge to assess correctly the functional and contextual equivalence relations between L1 and L2. Examples are transfers into English of the more speaker-oriented, explicit, and specific strategies of linguistic action by German learners (Kasper, *Pragmatische Aspekte*; House, "Developing") and the more ritualistic, vague, and implicit strategies used by Japanese nonnative speakers (Takahashi and Beebe).

Advanced learners may not transfer L1 conventions of means even though they have the required linguistic L2 competence, because they believe that such transfer would not be pragmalinguistically or sociopragmatically successful according to L2 pragmatic norms. An example is Japanese learners of English opting for refusal strategies that are less polite than those in Japanese because they believed that refusing is more socially acceptable in English and therefore requires less mitigation (Robinson).

Current research on pragmatic transfer has concentrated on whether and where transfer occurs. Future study will have to focus on the structural and nonstructural factors that promote or depress crosslinguistic and cross-cultural influence on learners' linguistic action.

COMMUNICATIVE EFFECT

It is important to distinguish negative pragmatic transfer from miscommunication or pragmatic failure. Positive and negative transfer describes the outcomes of putative cognitive processes, operationalized according to the structural, functional, and contextual relations among pragmatic features in L1, L2, and interlanguage. Positive transfer is a converging relation, negative transfer a relation in which interlanguage and L1 converge and L1 and L2 diverge. While it is true that negative pragmatic transfer *can* cause miscommunication, there is no logical or empirical reason that it has to. Just as the equation "L1-L2 divergence = negative transfer" does not hold up, because for a variety of reasons learners may opt against transfer, neither does the analogous equation "negative transfer = pragmatic failure." Whether induced by negative transfer or other causes, the divergence of nonnative speakers' communicative style or pragmatic strategies from those of the target community is not in and of itself a source of miscommunication. But there is abundant evidence that divergence *can* cause pragmatic failure, from small misunderstandings that can easily be ignored or repaired to major communication breakdowns with disastrous consequences for participants, especially those in the less powerful position. In high-stake interactions such as gatekeeping encounters, insufficient coordination of knowledge and action between participants may be both the cause and the result of pragmatic failure, as documented in studies of job interviews (Gumperz, *Strategies*), counseling sessions (Fiksdal), academic advising sessions (Bardovi-Harlig and Hartford, "Congruence"; Gumperz, "Contextualizaiton"), medical interviews (Rehbein), pretrial interviews (Scollon and Scollon), and language proficiency interviews (Ross). When, as in the studies cited, nonnative speakers are positioned at the powerless end of an unequal power encounter, they have few opportunities to control the discourse and initiate repair if something goes wrong. At the same time, pragmatic failure in such encounters can be consequential for the client's personal and professional life. An interesting type of intercultural institutional discourse where nonnativeness does not coincide with powerlessness is interactions between international teaching assistants and their students. In such encounters, the power relationship is one of mutual dependency: the students depend on the international teaching assistant for grades, the international teaching assistant on the students for teaching evaluations, which are the basis for contract renewal (Madden and Myers; Tyler). It is not clear at this point how the differences in international teaching assistant–student relationships and less complex asymmetric types of institutional discourse are reflected in pragmatic success and failure.

Whether or not pragmatic divergence leads to miscommunication and, if it does, how disruptive the miscommunication is, depends on a variety of factors. One factor is whether the divergent behavior occurs at the pragmalinguistic or sociopragmatic level. Jenny Thomas has suggested that pragmalinguistic divergence (discrepancies in the use of linguistic material for illocutionary and politeness functions that are conventionalized differently in L2) is less serious than sociopragmatic divergence (discrepancies in the assessment of context factors, especially those relating to power and solidarity), because interlocutors tend to regard the first as a linguistic problem and the second as indicative of the speaker's poor manners and questionable moral character. But the distinction is not always easy to maintain, because pragmalinguistic choices carry sociopragmatic information. Heidi Byrnes has shown how conflicting interactional styles in encounters between American and German students resulted in mutual negative social perceptions. The difference between the more transactional, self-oriented style of the German conversationalists and the more interpersonal, other-oriented style displayed by the American interlocutors agrees well with contrastive-pragmatic studies on conversational organization and strategies of linguistic action and politeness in German-British interpersonal discourse (House, "Opening and Closing"; Watts).

But pragmatic divergence in itself is not problematic if the social values indexed by the divergent behavior are acceptable or perhaps even appreciated by the recipient. For instance, in a study on students' attitudes to teachers' styles in courses on English as a foreign language and Japanese as a second language, Sayoko Yamashita and Ted Miller found that Japanese college students welcomed the more egalitarian, positive politeness style practiced by their gaijin teachers, because it offered them an enjoyable and productive alternative to the hierarchical participation structure of the traditional Japanese college classroom. As long as interlocutors experience pragmatic divergence as complementary rather than conflicting, it may be regarded as just another way of doing things—perhaps even a way that participants prefer. A shared communicative style does facilitate successful communication, but miscommunication among competent adult members of the same speech community is a regular fact of everyday life (Coupland, Giles, and Wiemann) rather than a particular hazard of intercultural communication. Intercultural communication is more vulnerable to pragmatic failure than intracultural communication only when *relevant* knowledge and practices are not shared. But such lack of common ground cannot generally be assumed, as successful interpersonal and professional interaction between members of different speech communities amply demonstrates.

Recent studies have therefore emphasized that context, identity, and interpersonal relationships are negotiated by participants in situ and that conversational process and outcomes are seen more appropriately as locally emerging, constructive enterprises than as simply reflecting participants' culture-specific frames of reference. While participants partly rely on L1-based strategies and interpretive frameworks, intracultural pragmatic knowledge is modified or suspended to meet the relational and transactional demands of intercultural encounters (see Janney and Arndt for a theoretical proposal and Piirainen-Marsh for a literature review and a key study).

Pragmatic Norms

The effect of linguistic action on participants is closely related to the issue of pragmatic norms in research and teaching. Since the dominant research model in interlanguage studies is comparative, a yardstick is needed to measure L2 learners' pragmatic knowledge and behavior. Likewise, the communicative abilities students are expected to develop have to be specified in the curricula for second or foreign language courses. In both cases, the more or less implicit assumption is that native speakers of the target language are the relevant population to serve as a model for nonnative speakers. In ILP research, this assumption is particularly obvious because, as noted above, most studies compare learners' linguistic action patterns against those of L2 native speakers.

But a native speaker norm in ILP is problematic for several reasons.

Determining such a norm is difficult because of the sociolinguistic variability in native speaker behavior. Selecting the variety or varieties most relevant for a particular learner population in a principled manner is not a straightforward task for any target language; it is a particularly daunting task with respect to English, the language most studied and taught worldwide. Sociolinguistic variation in the English language community extends to pragmatics, including conversational styles (Tannen) and strategies of speech act realization (Michaelis).

It is unrealistic to posit an ideal communicatively competent native speaker as a target for L2 learners since communication among native speakers is often partial, ambiguous, and fraught with potential and manifest misunderstanding (Coupland, Giles, and Wiemann).

Little is known about adult L2 learners' ability to attain native proficiency in pragmatics. Although it seems unlikely that a construct parallel to an innate language acquisition device will be proposed for pragmatic competence, early and sustained contact with the target language and culture may be required to attain native pragmatic knowledge and skill, as is suggested by the many studies documenting the nonnative pragmatic behavior of advanced learners. If early and sustained contact was indeed a precondition for native pragmatic competence, positing a native speaker norm for language teaching to adult L2 learners would be futile, although such a norm would provide a meaningful baseline for ILP research.

Learners may not aspire to L2 native speaker pragmatics as their target. Foreign language learners may not feel that the effort is worth their while, since they do not intend to become part of the L2 community; second language learners such as immigrants may opt for partial divergence from the pragmatic norms of the target community as a strategy of identity maintenance (Blum-Kulka and Sheffer).

L2 native speakers may perceive nonnative speakers' total convergence as intrusive and inconsistent with the nonnative speakers' role as outsiders in the L2 community. Some measure of divergence as a disclaimer to membership may be appreciated.

The communicative style developed by nonnative speakers in interaction with L2 native speakers or other nonnative speakers may differ significantly from that of L2 native speakers, and that style may persist over generations as a particular ethnic style in immigrant communities (Clyne, Ball, and Neil).

Since L2 learners are by definition bilingual or multilingual speakers, the only reasonable norm for them is a bilingual or multilingual rather than a monolingual L2 norm (Grosjean; Kasper, "Wessen Pragmatik?" and "Bilingual Perspective"). Establishing such a norm for language teaching and testing purposes is obviously a highly complex undertaking, requiring as input not only studies that examine pragmatic failure but also research on divergent but successful nonnative speaker communication.

LANGUAGE TEACHING

Little research examines the effect of language instruction on pragmatic development, but the few studies to date are encouraging. Research on teaching compliments (Billmyer), on pragmatic routines (Wildner-Bassett; House, "Developing"), and on comprehension of indirect responses (Bouton, "Cross-Cultural Study") has demonstrated that adult learners respond well to a combination of consciousness-raising activities and communicative practice. Such a combination appears to be beneficial for learners' pragmatic comprehension and production and helps them establish metapragmatic information about sociopragmatic and pragmalinguistic target language norms. In fact, it seems doubtful whether children or adults can acquire pragmatic competence without some direct teaching and assistance in noticing relevant information in the input. The literature on language socialization and developmental pragmatics suggests that children are taught about politeness, form-function mappings, and contextual appropriateness of conventions of means and form (see DuFon for a review of research). Adult L2 learners in a second language environment are in a better position to acquire relevant pragmatic information than foreign language learners because second language learners have access to richer and more frequent input. However, teaching can be facilitative or even necessary, depending on L1 background, for learners to notice pragmatic information (Bouton, "Conversational Implicature"). Foreign language learners are at a double disadvantage: first, they have less exposure to the target language, and second, since traditional classroom interaction differs markedly in action patterns and discourse structure from ordinary conversation, language classrooms provide little opportunity for learners to obtain relevant input to produce the variety of linguistic action and politeness functions required for communication outside the classroom (Lörscher and Schulze; Kasper, "Interactive Procedures"). These drawbacks can be compensated to some extent through pragmatically focused curricula, student-centered classroom activities, and teaching materials that provide pragmatic information (House, "Developing"). The potential of audiovisual and electronic media for pragmatic consciousness-raising and communicative activities is particularly rich and still awaits full exploration (see Rose for a proposal).

RESEARCH METHODS

Because most studies are based on a comparative design, the predominant data type in ILP is some form of elicited data (see Kasper and Dahl, for a literature review). For comprehension, the most frequently used instrument is questionnaires including multiple choice and ranking or rating tasks. Production of linguistic action has been assessed mainly by written production questionnaires; fewer studies have employed some form of simulation or open roleplay. Multimethod approaches are common, often combining sociopragmatic assessment and pragmalinguistic comprehension or production data. A sequential design for a study on speech act realization by native and nonnative speakers may include the following data types: observation of authentic interaction; metapragmatic assessment of sociopragmatic factors; production, elicited through roleplays or written production questionnaires; informants' verbal reports on the production task; metapragmatic assessment of the production data by native and nonnative raters. A study that closely approximates this design is Miriam Eisenstein and Jean Bodman's research on expressions of gratitude.

Fewer studies are based on authentic discourse. These studies are typically not comparative or only partially comparative, and they report mostly on interaction in institutional settings (see references in this essay in the section "Communicative Effect"). Two key studies examine graduate advising sessions (Bardovi-Harlig and Hartford, "Congruence") and fine-art tutorials (Turner, Hiraga, and Fujii). Because the student populations in these academic speech events comprise native and nonnative speakers of English, an L2 baseline is an authentic design feature of these studies. The joint management of transactional and interpersonal goals in intercultural encounters is only just beginning to be examined. Future research will have to provide microanalyses of such encounters in a variety of institutional and noninstitutional settings, especially of interactions conducted in a language other than English.

FURTHER READING

Larsen-Freeman, Diane, ed. *Discourse Analysis and Second Language Acquisition*. Rowley: Newbury, 1980.

Wolfson, Nessa, and Elliot Judd, eds. *Sociolinguistics and Language Acquisition*. Rowley: Newbury, 1983.
Although labeled "discourse analysis" and "sociolinguistics," these volumes include some important early cross-cultural and interlanguage pragmatics studies.

Kasper, Gabriele, and Shoshana Blum-Kulka, eds. *Interlanguage Pragmatics*. New York: Oxford UP, 1993.
This collection offers studies of L2 learners' speech acts and discourse and two theoretical proposals to account for nonnative speakers' learning of L2 pragmatics.

Studies in Second Language Acquisition: The Development of Pragmatic Competence 18.2 (1996).
This special issue examines several central aspects in the development of pragmatic ability by adult nonnative speakers, such as the input opportunities afforded by different institutional settings, the transferability and teachability of pragmatic information, and the production strategies learners use to engage in speech act performance.

Hudson, Thom, Emily Detmer, and J. D. Brown. *Developing Prototypic Measures of Cross-Cultural Pragmatics*. Technical Report 7. Honolulu: U of Hawai'i at Mānoa, Second Lang. Teaching and Curriculum Center, 1995.

Yamashita, Sayoko Okada. *Six Measures of JSL Pragmatics*. Technical Report 14. Honolulu: U of Hawai'i at Mānoa, Second Lang. Teaching and Curriculum Center, 1996.
Hudson, Detmer, and Brown present a multitrait multimethod approach designed to provide valid, reliable, and effective measurements of nonnative speakers' pragmatic competence. Yamashita applied Hudson, Detmer, and Brown's framework to the assessment of pragmatic competence in learners of Japanese as a second or foreign language.

Kasper, Gabriele, and Kenneth R. Rose. *Methods for Research on Pragmatics*. Mahwah: Erlbaum, forthcoming.
This book reviews the methods of data collection commonly used in pragmatics. Each approach is illustrated by examples from the published research, discussed in its theoretical and empirical context and evaluated with respect to its potential for answering different research questions in cross-cultural and interlanguage pragmatics.

WORKS CITED

Austin, John L. *How to Do Things with Words*. Oxford: Oxford UP, 1962.

Bachman, Lyle F. *Fundamental Considerations in Language Testing*. Oxford: Oxford UP, 1990.

Bardovi-Harlig, Kathleen, and Beverly S. Hartford. "Congruence in Native and Nonnative Conversations: Status Balance in the Academic Advising Session." *Language Learning* 40 (1990): 467–501.

———. "Learning the Rules of Academic Talk: A Longitudinal Study of Pragmatic Development." *Studies in Second Language Acquisition* 15 (1993): 279–304.

Beebe, Leslie M., and Tomoko Takahashi. "'Do You Have a Bag?' Social Status and Patterned Variation in Second Language Acquisition." *Variation in Second Language Acquisition: Discourse and Pragmatics*. Ed. Susan Gass, Carolyn Madden, Dennis Preston, and Larry Selinker. Clevedon, Eng.: Multilingual Matters, 1989. 103–25.

———. "Sociolinguistic Variation in Face-Threatening Speech Acts." *The Dynamic Interlanguage*. Ed. Miriam R. Eisenstein. New York: Plenum, 1989. 199–218.

Beebe, Leslie M., Tomoko Takahashi, and Robin Uliss-Weltz. "Pragmatic Transfer in ESL Refusals." *On the Development of Communicative Competence in a Second Language*. Ed. Stephen D. Krashen, Robin Scarcella, and Elaine Andersen. Cambridge: Newbury, 1990. 55–73.

Bergman, Marc L., and Gabriele Kasper. "Perception and Performance in Native and Nonnative Apology." Kasper and Blum-Kulka 82–107.

Bialystok, Ellen. "Symbolic Representation and Attentional Control in Pragmatic Competence." Kasper and Blum-Kulka 43–59.

Billmyer, Kristine. "'I Really Like Your Lifestyle': ESL Learners Learning How to Compliment." *Penn Working Papers in Educational Linguistics* 6.2 (1990): 31–48.

Blum-Kulka, Shoshana. "Interlanguage Pragmatics: The Case of Requests." Phillipson, Kellerman, Selinker, Sharwood Smith, and Swain 255–72.

———. "Learning How to Say What You Mean in a Second Language: A Study of Speech Act Performance of Learners of Hebrew as a Second Language." *Applied Linguistics* 3 (1982): 29–59.

Blum-Kulka, Shoshana, and Juliane House. "Cross-Cultural and Situational Variation in Requestive Behavior." Blum-Kulka, House, and Kasper 123–54.

Blum-Kulka, Shoshana, Juliane House, and Gabriele Kasper, eds. *Cross-Cultural Pragmatics*. Norwood: Ablex, 1989.

Blum-Kulka, Shoshana, and Hadass Sheffer. "The Metapragmatic Discourse of American-Israeli Families at Dinner." Kasper and Blum-Kulka 196–223.

Bouton, Lawrence F. "Conversational Implicature in the Second Language: Learned Slowly When Not Deliberately Taught." *Journal of Pragmatics* 22 (1994): 157–67.

———. "A Cross-Cultural Study of Ability to Interpret Implicatures in English." *World Englishes* 7 (1988): 183–96.

Brown, Penelope, and Stephen D. Levinson. *Politeness: Some Universals in Language Usage*. Cambridge: Cambridge UP, 1987.

Byrnes, Heidi. "Interactional Style in German and American Conversations." *Text* 6 (1986): 189–206.

Carrell, Patricia L. "Indirect Speech Acts in ESL: Indirect Answers." *On TESOL '79*. Ed. Carlos A. Yorio, Kyle Perkins, and Jacquelyn Schachter. Washington: TESOL, 1979. 297–307.

———. "Relative Difficulty of Request Forms in L1/L2 Comprehension." *On TESOL '81* Ed. Mary Hines and William Rutherford. Washington: TESOL, 1982. 141–52.

Clyne, Michael, Martin Ball, and Deborah Neil. "Intercultural Communication at

Work in Australia: Complaints and Apologies in Turns." *Multilingua* 10 (1991): 251–73.

Coulmas, Florian, ed. *Conversational Routine.* The Hague: Mouton, 1981.

Coupland, Nikolas, Howard Giles, and John M. Wiemann, eds. *"Miscommunication" and Problematic Talk.* Newbury Park: Sage, 1991.

Doi, Toshiyuki. "An Ethnographic Study of a Japanese as a Foreign Language Class in Hawai'i: Analyses and Retrospective Notes." Second Lang. Research Forum. Honolulu, U of Hawai'i at Mānoa. Feb. 1988.

DuFon, Margaret Ann. "Input and Interaction in the Acquisition of L1 Pragmatic Routines: Implications for SLA." *University of Hawai'i Working Papers in ESL* 12.2 (1994): 39–79.

Edmondson, Willis, and Juliane House. "Do Learners Talk Too Much? The Waffle Phenomenon in Interlanguage Pragmatics." Phillipson, Kellerman, Selinker, Sharwood Smith, and Swain 273–86.

Eisenstein, Miriam, and Jean Bodman. "Expressing Gratitude in American English." Kasper and Blum-Kulka 64–81.

Ellis, Rod. "Learning to Communicate in the Classroom: A Study of Two Language Learners' Requests." *Studies in Second Language Acquisition* 14 (1992): 1–23.

Erickson, Frederick, and Jeffrey Shultz. *The Counselor as Gatekeeper: Social Interaction in Interviews.* New York: Academic, 1982.

Færch, Claus, and Gabriele Kasper. "Internal and External Modification in Interlanguage Request Realization." Blum-Kulka, House, and Kasper 221–47.

Fiksdal, Susan. *The Right Time and Pace: A Microanalysis of Cross-Cultural Gatekeeping Interviews.* Norwood: Ablex, 1990.

Fraser, Bruce. "Conversational Mitigation." *Journal of Pragmatics* 4 (1980): 341–50.

———. "Perspectives on Politeness." *Journal of Pragmatics* 14 (1990): 219–36.

Fukushima, Saeko. "Offers and Requests: Performance by Japanese Learners of English." *World Englishes* 9 (1990): 317–25.

García, Carmen. "Apologizing in English: Politeness Strategies Used by Native and Non-native Speakers." *Multilingua* 8 (1989): 3–20.

Giles, Howard, Justine Coupland, and Nikolas Coupland, eds. *Contexts of Accommodation.* Cambridge: Cambridge UP, 1991.

Grice, H. Paul. "Logic and Conversation." *Syntax and Semantics.* Vol. 3. Ed. Peter Cole and Jerry Morgan. New York: Academic, 1975. 41–58.

Grosjean, François. "The Bilingual as a Competent but Specific Speaker-Hearer." *Journal of Multilingual and Multicultural Development* 6 (1985): 467–77.

Gumperz, John J. "Contextualization and Understanding." *Rethinking Context.* Ed. Alessandro Duranti and Charles Goodwin. Cambridge: Cambridge UP, 1992. 229–52.

———. *Discourse Strategies.* Cambridge: Cambridge UP, 1982.

Held, Gudrun. "On the Role of Maximization in Verbal Politeness." *Multilingua* 8 (1989): 167–206.

House, Juliane. "Developing Pragmatic Fluency in English as a Foreign Language: Routines and Metapragmatic Awareness." *Studies in Second Language Acquisition* 18 (1996): 225–52.

———. " 'Oh Excuse Me Please . . .': Apologizing in a Foreign Language." *Englisch als Zweitsprache.* Ed. Bernhard Kettemann, Peter Bierbaumer, Alwin Fill, and Annemarie Karpf. Tübingen: Narr, 1988. 303–27.

———. "Opening and Closing Phases in English and German Dialogues." *Grazer Linguistische Studien* 16 (1982): 52–83.

House, Juliane, and Gabriele Kasper. "Interlanguage Pragmatics: Requesting in a Foreign Language." *Perspectives on Language in Performance: Festschrift für Werner Hüllen.* Ed. Wolfgang Lörscher and Rainer Schulze. Tübingen: Narr, 1987. 1250–88.

———. "Politeness Markers in English and German." Coulmas 157–85.

Hymes, Dell H. "On Communicative Competence." *Sociolinguistics.* Ed. John B. Pride and Janet Holmes. Harmondsworth, Eng.: Penguin, 1972. 269–93.

Ikoma, Tomoko. "'Sorry for Giving Me a Ride': The Use of Apologetic Expressions to Show Gratitude in Japanese." Master's thesis. U of Hawai'i at Mānoa, 1993.

Janney, Richard W., and Horst Arndt. "Intracultural Tact versus Intercultural Tact." *Politeness in Language: Studies in Its History, Theory, and Practice.* Ed. Richard J. Watts, Sachiko Ide, and Konrad Ehlich. Berlin: Mouton de Gruyter, 1992. 21–41.

Kasper, Gabriele. "A Bilingual Perspective on Interlanguage Pragmatics." *The Language of Leadership.* Literary Studies East and West 15. Honolulu: U of Hawai'i at Mānoa, and East-West Center, forthcoming.

———. "Interactive Procedures in Interlanguage Discourse." *Contrastive Pragmatics.* Ed. Wieslaw Oleksy. Amsterdam: Benjamins, 1989. 189–229.

———. "Pragmatic Transfer." *Second Language Research* 8 (1992): 203–31.

———, ed. *Pragmatics of Japanese as Native and Target Language.* Second Lang. Teaching and Curriculum Center Technical Rept. 3. Honolulu: U of Hawai'i P, 1992.

———. *Pragmatische Aspekte in der Interimsprache.* Tübingen: Narr, 1981.

———. "Wessen Pragmatik? Für eine Neubestimmung sprachlicher Handlungskompetenz." *Zeitschrift für Fremdsprachenforschung* 6 (1995): 1–25.

Kasper, Gabriele, and Shoshana Blum-Kulka, eds. *Interlanguage Pragmatics.* New York: Oxford UP, 1993.

———. "Interlanguage Pragmatics: An Introduction." Kasper and Blum-Kulka, *Pragmatics* 3–17.

Kasper, Gabriele, and Merete Dahl. "Research Methods in Interlanguage Pragmatics." *Studies in Second Language Acquisition* 13 (1991): 215–47.

Kasper, Gabriele, and Richard Schmidt. "Developmental Issues in Interlanguage Pragmatics." *Studies in Second Language Acquisition* 18 (1996): 149–69.

Kitao, Kenji. "A Study of Japanese and American Perceptions of Politeness in Requests." *Doshisha Studies in English* 50 (1990): 178–210.

Lantolf, James P., and Gabriela Appel, eds. *Vygotskyan Approaches to Second Language Research.* Norwood: Ablex, 1994.

Leech, Geoffrey. *Principles of Pragmatics.* London: Longman, 1983.

Lörscher, Wolfgang, and Rainer Schulze. "On Polite Speaking and Foreign Language Classroom Discourse." *International Review of Applied Linguistics in Language Teaching* 26 (1988): 183–99.

Madden, Carolyn G., and Cynthia L. Myers, eds. *Discourse and Performance of International Teaching Assistants.* Alexandria: TESOL, 1994.

Maeshiba, Naoka, Naoka Yoshinaga, Gabriele Kasper, and Steven Ross. "Transfer and Proficiency in Interlanguage Apologizing." *Speech Acts across Cultures.* Ed. Susan Gass and Joyce Neu. Berlin: Mouton de Gruyter, 1996. 155–87.

McLean, K. P. "Japanese/Non-Japanese Differences in Classroom Discourse Turn-Taking." *Selected Papers in TESOL.* Ed. C. Ward and D. Wren. Monterey: Monterey Inst. for Intl. Studies, 1983.

Mey, Jacob L. *Pragmatics: An Introduction.* Oxford: Blackwell, 1993.

Michaelis, Kathleen. "National and Regional Target Language Variation in English Requests." Unpublished scholarly paper. U of Hawai'i at Mānoa, 1992.

Nyyssönen, H. The Oulu Project. *Proceedings from the Second Finnish Seminar on Dis-*

course Analysis (1988). Ed. Nyyssönen, L. Kuure, E. Kärkkäinen, and P. Raudaskoski. Oulu: U of Oulu, 1990. 7–26.

Olshtain, Elite. "Apologies across Languages." Blum-Kulka, House, and Kasper 155–73.

———. "Sociocultural Competence and Language Transfer: The Case of Apology." *Language Transfer in Language Learning.* Ed. Susan Gass and Larry Selinker. Rowley: Newbury, 1983. 232–49.

Olshtain, Elite, and Shoshana Blum-Kulka. "Degree of Approximation: Nonnative Reactions to Native Speech Act Behavior." *Input in Second Language Acquisition.* Ed. Susan M. Gass and Carolyn G. Madden. Rowley: Newbury, 1985. 303–25.

Olshtain, Elite, and Andrew Cohen. "Apology: A Speech Act Set." Wolfson and Judd 18–35.

Olshtain, Elite, and Liora Weinbach. "Interlanguage Features of the Speech Act of Complaining." Kasper and Blum-Kulka 108–22.

Phillipson, Robert, Eric Kellerman, Larry Selinker, Michael Sharwood Smith, and Merrill Swain, eds. *Foreign/Second Language Pedagogy Research.* Clevedon, Eng.: Multilingual Matters, 1991.

Piirainen-Marsh, Arja. *Face in Second Language Conversation.* Studia Philologica Jyväskyläensia 37. Jyväskylä: U of Jyväskylä, 1995.

Poole, Deborah. "Language Socialization in the Second Language Classroom. *Language Learning* 42 (1992): 593–616.

Rehbein, Jochen. "Institutioneller Ablauf und interkulturelle Missverständnisse in der Allgemeinpraxis." *Curare* 9 (1986): 297–328.

Rintell, Ellen. "Sociolinguistic Variation and Pragmatic Ability: A Look at Learners." *International Journal of the Sociology of Language* 27 (1981): 11–34.

Robinson, Mary Ann. "Introspective Methodology in Interlanguage Pragmatics Research." Kasper, *Pragmatics* 27–82.

Rose, Kenneth R. "Pragmatics Consciousness-Raising in an EFL Context." *Pragmatics and Language Learning Monograph Series.* Vol. 5. Ed. Lawrence F. Bouton and Yamuna Kachru. Urbana: U of Illinois at Urbana-Champaign Div. of English as an Intl. Lang. Intensive English Inst., 1994. 52–63.

Ross, Steven. "Accommodation in Oral Proficiency Interviews." Diss. U of Hawai'i at Mānoa, 1995.

Sato, Charlene J. "Ethnic Styles in Classroom Discourse." *On TESOL '81.* Ed. Mary Hines and William Rutherford. Washington: TESOL, 1982. 11–24.

Sawyer, Mark. "The Development of Pragmatics in Japanese as a Second Language: The Sentence-Final Particle 'ne.'" Kasper, *Pragmatics* 85–127.

Schieffelin, Bambi B., and Elinor Ochs. "Language Socialization." *Annual Review of Anthropology* 15 (1986): 163–91.

Schmidt, Richard. "Consciousness, Learning, and Interlanguage Pragmatics." Kasper and Blum-Kulka 21–42.

———. "Psychological Mechanisms Underlying Second Language Fluency." *Studies in Second Language Acquisition* 14 (1992): 357–85.

———. "Interaction, Acculturation, and the Acquisition of Communicative Competence." Wolfson and Judd 137–74.

Scollon, Ron, and Suzanne B. K. Scollon. "Face in Interethnic Communication." *Language and Communication.* Ed. Jack C. Richards and Richard W. Schmidt. London: Longman, 1983.

Selinker, Larry. "Interlanguage." *International Review of Applied Linguistics in Language Teaching* 10 (1972): 209–30.

Shea, David P. "Perspective and Production: Structuring Conversational Participation across Cultural Borders." *Pragmatics* 4 (1994): 357–90.

Shi, Austina Yi-Peng, and Jody Yeh. "A Study of Pragmatic Transfer in Taiwan English Learners' Interlanguage Discourse Behavior." Unpublished scholarly paper. U of Hawai'i at Mānoa, 1993.

Shimura, Akihiko. "The Effect of Chinese-Japanese Differences on Turn-Taking in an ESL Classroom." *University of Hawai'i Working Papers in ESL* 7.2 (1988): 99–115.

Takahashi, Satomi. "Exploring Comprehension Processes of Nonliteral Utterances and Some Implications for Automaticity." *University of Hawai'i Working Papers in ESL* 9.2 (1990): 67–97.

———. "Pragmatic Transferability." *Studies in Second Language Acquisition* 18 (1996): 189–223.

Takahashi, Satomi, and Margaret Ann DuFon. *Cross-linguistic Influence in Indirectness: The Case of English Directives Performed by Native Japanese Speakers.* ERIC, 1989. ED370439.

Takahashi, Satomi, and Herbert Roitblat. "Comprehension Process of Second Language Indirect Requests." *Applied Psycholinguistics* 15 (1994): 475–506.

Takahashi, Tomoko, and Leslie M. Beebe. "Cross-linguistic Influence in the Speech Act of Correction." Kasper and Blum-Kulka 138–57.

Tanaka, Noriko. "Politeness: Some Problems for Japanese Speakers of English." *JALT Journal* 9 (1988): 81–102.

Tannen, Deborah. "The Machine-Gun Question: An Example of Conversational Style." *Journal of Pragmatics* 5 (1981): 383–97.

Thomas, Jenny. "Cross-Culturral Pragmatic Failure." *Applied Linguistics* 4 (1983): 91–112.

Trosborg, Anna. "Apology Strategies in Natives/Non-natives." *Journal of Pragmatics* 11 (1987): 147–67.

———. *Interlanguage Pragmatics.* Berlin: Mouton de Gruyter, 1995.

Turner, Joan M., Masako K. Hiraga, and Yoko Fujii. "Pragmatics in Academic Discourse: A Case Study of Tutorials in Britain." Unpublished essay, 1994.

Tyler, Andrea. "The Co-construction of Cross-Cultural Miscommunication: Conflicts in Perception, Negotiation, and Enactment of Participant Role and Status." *Studies in Second Language Acquisition* 17 (1995): 129–52.

Vygotsky, Lev Semyonovich. *Thought and Language.* Cambridge: MIT P, 1965.

Watts, Richard J. "Relevance and Relational Work: Linguistic Politeness as Politic Behavior." *Multilingua* 8 (1989): 131–66.

Wildner-Bassett, Mary. *Improving Pragmatic Aspects of Learners' Interlanguage.* Tübingen: Narr, 1984.

Wolfson, Nessa, and Elliot Judd, eds. *Sociolinguistics and Language Acquisition.* Rowley: Newbury, 1983.

Yamashita, Sayoko, and Ted Miller. "Japanese and American Students' Attitudes toward Classroom Interaction." *ICU Language Research Bulletin* 9 (1994): 51–73.

The Role of Technology in Second Language Learning

Robert J. Blake

The call to use technology in second language learning evokes a wide range of responses from members of our profession — some positive, many not. Negative reaction is not entirely unexpected if one remembers that the profession's first wholesale introduction to technology was the audiolingual language lab of the 1960s. At that time, many promises were made that could not realistically be fulfilled. Dashed expectations set the stage for language teachers' reluctance to plunge into the implementation of new technologies in the face of few demonstrable results (Roblyer) and even fewer tangible career paybacks (Quinn 300).[1]

But the social and technical infrastructures have changed drastically since the 1960s. To begin with, the current round of technological innovations has not been heralded with exaggerated claims of pedagogical superiority. One advantage of the new computer-centered technology is its inherent lack of a methodological stance (González-Edfelt 175), in sharp contrast to the heavy burden of behaviorism that accompanied the introduction of audiolingual lab of the 1960s (Bickes and Scott). The computer is simply a tool that can be used to strengthen whatever language learning is being fostered in the classroom. Software, however, involves an instructional design or interface and will therefore reflect, like any other textual teaching materials, the pedagogical biases of its creator.

More important, the venue of technology is no longer limited to the physical space defined by the language lab. With the advent of microcomputers, networking, and computer-assisted programs, technology is ever-present in the lab, the home, the classroom, and even in faraway places that coexist with the learner through the guise of the virtual (i.e., electronic) university.

But why should the language teacher be interested in incorporating technology into the language curriculum in the first place? Will technology end up replacing the teacher? A rational response to this last question might be that technology will not replace teachers in the future but that teachers who use technology will probably replace teachers who do not. Without a doubt the curricular ideal, in human terms, would still be for us to take each and every one of our students abroad for total immersion in the target language. Since this ideal is impractical—most colleges are fortunate if they send even one percent of their students abroad—the great majority of second language learners must tackle learning a new language in the traditional framework defined by seat time: three to five hours a week for one to two years, at best.

Technology can play an important role in fostering second language acquisition by electronically increasing learners' contact with a wide array of authentic materials; technology can also provide additional opportunities for negotiated language use with instructors and classmates alike—both in and out of the classroom. Susan Gass and Evangeline Varonis have shown the profession how important oral negotiation of meaning is for the second language classroom. Why wouldn't the same pedagogical principle hold true for the electronically enhanced classroom? Far from eliminating the central role of the teacher, the electronic classroom challenges the teacher to take advantage of new materials and tools to increase interconnections and language enrichment. We need teachers to tell us what works, and how it works, in the new electronic classroom. But technology is not a monolithic concept; it includes Web-based materials, CD-ROMs, CALL (computer-assisted language learning) programs, and network-based communication. Network-based communication has the potential to open up the traditional classroom to learners from remote sites around the nation and the world, a prospect that should be explored and exploited by language professionals. Language teaching, assisted by technology, is entering a new paradigm. Humanities teachers must all learn to adapt their curricula to take advantage of a community classroom that has resources much richer than before.

Finally, today's students are much more technologically oriented than they were in past generations. For them technology is a welcome environment, and in it we can convey our basic professional message: Learn languages and cultures. Students' openness to technology allows teachers to harness useful techniques to make the task of second language learning less arduous and time-intensive.

This essay gives an overall assessment of the role of technology in second language learning and attempts to help language teachers recognize the potential of adding a technological component to the present foreign language curriculum; make more informed hardware and software choices when modernizing existing, outdated lab facilities; perceive the benefits of using the computer to design research projects in second language acquisition (SLA); and evaluate the work of colleagues involved in CALL research and development.

BACKGROUND

Computer-centered technology for learning languages has undergone three important paradigmatic shifts in the last thirty years: in the hardware base, in the role of the learner, and in the interface, or presentation format. Other researchers have chronicled these changes (Ahmad, Corbett, Rogers, and Sussex; Davies; Dunkel; Hainline; W. Smith, *Media*; Stevens, Sussex, and Tuman; Swann; Underwood, *Linguistics*; Wyat), but a short summary is in order here.

The Hardware Base

Second language learning through the computer has its roots in the 1960s. But computing in the 1960s meant mainframe computing. Students accessed powerful IBM, Digital, or VAX machines located in some cool and inaccessible place on campus through a hard-wired (i.e., directly connected) terminal in a public area. The best-known mainframe project is PLATO (Programmed Logic for Automated Teaching Operations) at the University of Illinois, Urbana. The PLATO project began by offering drill-and-practice exercises in Russian; later, in the 1970s, it added lessons for all the principal languages being taught (Ahmad, Corbett, Rogers, and Sussex 30–31). Stanford University had a similar program for Russian (Suppes; Van Campen). For the elementary programming required to provide drill-and-practice routines or word processing, the dedication of a mainframe computer was overkill—and an uneconomical way to proceed, because PLATO was available only through expensive remote links. In the early 1980s, high costs and the increased mobility offered by microcomputers conveniently located in dorms or offices finally put an end to the use of mainframes as a delivery tool for language software.

The Role of the Learner

Throughout the 1960s, 1970s, and early 1980s computer practitioners talked about creating computer-assisted instruction (CAI) for foreign languages. The focus was more on the program than on the learner. CAI programs typically guided learners through a series of tutorials with exercises, tutorials embellished by branching routines that responded to the students' success or difficulty with the lesson. But the basic design of CAI materials was linear and teacher-driven (Garrett, "Perspective" 170). Students had to follow a predetermined program, a path that, even with the branching routines, they did not choose. Developers were preoccupied with what Nina Garrett has described as machine-driven concerns: limits on machine memory, the ability to produce foreign language accents and fonts, and varied methods of providing feedback (170). This learning paradigm seemed to work for the hard sciences, where CAI programs were used extensively, but it did not translate well to the study of languages, where old content (e.g., workbooks) was merely dressed in new technological clothes.[2]

In the 1980s, a greater emphasis on the role of the language learner caused software developers to cede some presentational control to the learner. As a consequence, linear programming architecture ceased to dominate courseware design. This change, signaled by a new generation of software programs now bearing the acronym CALL, reflected a more learner-driven and communicative approach (Garrett, "Perspective" 170).

Interface

The third shift, which is still under way, involves the overall flexibility of the user interface. Most mainframe and CAI-CALL software has had a tendency to be textually oriented. The current trend is to produce software with a multimedia interface that combines text, digitized sound, digitized video or laserdisc video, and graphics in nonlinear ways. The main menu of today's CALL lesson may conceivably consist of icons or miniaturized digitized pictures, accompanied by just a few textual directions. This new conceptualization of the interface is possible because the computer is no longer a stand-alone device but the main component in a workstation offering the learner a myriad of multimedia options (Quinn 301).

The term *interactive* is typically used to describe this multimedia interface, but there remains much discussion about what constitutes true interactiveness. Often interactive means nothing more than immediate error correction and record keeping. But such an application, as Dorothy Chun and Klaus Brandl recognize, "does not foster negotiating or communicating beyond purely linguistic matters" (255–56). The term *hypermedia* is often used instead of *multimedia* to refer to lessons that approximate more communicative and creative uses of language through the computer.[3]

Perhaps the greatest excitement of the hypermedia approach comes from its potential to bring authentic materials into the classroom, home, and lab. Authentic dialogues by themselves are very effective, but authentic dialogues with video are even better, because learners can see the cultural and pragmatic context right on screen. That today's students respond well to the medium of images, especially video, makes hypermedia particularly important in the context of the proficiency classroom (Brown and Jahn). The need to present authentic materials, optimize classroom hours, accomplish preproficiency tasks (e.g., practice complex morphological systems), and address disparate levels in student abilities all make hypermedia a crucial asset to the modern language curriculum.

LEARNING PARADIGMS AND TYPOLOGIES
FOR CALL LESSONS

Despite the rosy prospects painted here for hypermedia, technology should not be expected to provide a panacea for all the concerns of the second language learner. The computer supports some language activities quite well, but others are completely unsuited to this medium. The computer is particularly good at providing the linguistic and cultural support needed to tackle the challenge of reading authentic materials without direct assistance from the teacher. John Underwood found that texts accompanied by video rich in culturally authentic images appeal to students' visual memory; that is, students better remember the language associated with the images ("Edge" 78). In addition, these benefits can be exploited in either a collaborative or personalized (i.e., self-paced) learning environment.

But the computer, as of yet, "cannot effectively conduct an 'open-ended' dialogue with the student," nor is it good at handling linguistic ambiguities (Ahmad, Corbett, Rogers, and Sussex 8). While the computer clearly has a powerfully enriching role to play for the classroom and a critical role in fostering second language learning at a distance, it does not represent a fully autonomous alternative to exposure to language through human contact. To use a favorite analogy of Terry Winograd and Fernando Flores, well-known computer scientists and program designers, expecting a computer to replace human contact is a bit like asking pigs to fly (104–06). In genetic evolution it might be possible for pigs to develop wings, but would they then still be called pigs? Clearly, computers cannot now and may never use language as humans do (Hendricks).

How, then, can the computer effectively assist second language learning? John Higgins and Tim Johns have summarized the possible learning paradigms for CALL software into four groups: instructional, revelatory, conjectural, and emancipatory (18–19). The instructional paradigm is the one most closely associated with tutorials (i.e., the presentation of new information) and drill-and-practice exercises. Much has been written that argues against the overuse of such exercises, derogatorily referred to as "drill and kill," especially if the lessons are conceived in isolation from meaningful language contexts. But highly inflected languages, like Russian, impose a heavy morphological burden on students that tutorial-based software might alleviate, at least in part. There is no reason why the language curriculum cannot be supported by a variety of educational materials, including some with a clear form focus. Instructional CALL software does not have to be merely an electronic workbook. If interesting feedback, meaningful contexts, online dictionaries, and grammar support are provided as well, a CALL lesson becomes a qualitatively different entity from the traditional pen-and-paper workbook.

Revelatory software requires students to instantiate some discovery procedure or vicarious learning experience. Most adventure games and simulations fall into this category. Typically, students must answer appropriately to get in and out of a series of imagined or real-life situations. CALL programs of this type frequently involve extensive use of graphics and animation.

Underwood's *Juegos Communicativos* for Spanish and Chun and Brandl's *Communicative Gap Software* for German (Brandl) are good examples of early successes with this kind of software development.

When hypothesis testing and substantial data manipulation are also involved, revelatory CALL overlaps with Higgins and Johns's third category: conjectural computer-assisted language learning. Conjectural CALL obviously involves a higher degree of metalinguistic awareness and therefore features a more advanced level of simulation, such as the type advocated by the Athena Project (MIT) and illustrated by the program *A la rencontre de Philippe*. This courseware group has tried to produce computer-based dialogues for the second language learner, as if the computer were an imaginary interlocutor (Murray 2; Murray, Morgenstern, and Furstenberg). Such software invites learners to explore authentic video materials and to solve information puzzles by asking and answering pertinent questions and exercising their own observational powers (Murray, Morgenstern, and Furstenberg 111–12). Learners become fully engaged in a narrative and have the ability to influence its events at various critical junctures.

In Higgins and Johns's final software grouping, the emancipatory students perform their own, authentic labor. Authentic labor is the most engaging use of CALL programs and translates into "valued learning" (19). Bernd Ruschoff has a similar concept, referring to "utility software," tools that address students' needs and engage them to look at materials in new ways. The true role of computer technology is to provide an environment where language materials — text, sound, graphics, and video — are handled in ways that are unique to the medium and that respond in concert to the learners' self-directed need to fill information gaps. The computer acts as a companion or pedagogue (from the Greek *paidagōgos* 'a boy's teacher'), facilitating and even anticipating students' needs. This role is the basic idea behind intelligent tutoring systems (given the acronym ITS).

Specialists in the field generally agree that a well-designed CALL lesson should provide appropriate feedback (not just "Wrong, try again"), foster a communicative environment, offer branching, treat the subject matter in context, and follow problem-solving or discovery procedures. Somewhat harder to tease out is the question of student autonomy or control. As Gé Stoks observes, an environment that allows totally free browsing is a poor substitute for the lack of an instructional strategy (86). Margaret Roblyer also finds in her study of CALL effectiveness that unstructured computer-assisted instruction proved ineffective in teaching general thinking and problem-solving skills. Joan Jamieson and Carol Chapelle suggest that a CALL lesson begin with an authoritative strategy and gradually progress to more student-controlled strategies (154).

A pedagogy for CALL is still unfolding, and those in CALL software implementation are learning the art of using this new medium and gaining experience. Considering the incipient state of second language learning research itself (Garrett, "Technology" 77), my observations emphasize the importance of continuing to seek out the best conditions for using computer technology and of directing greater attention to CALL assessment and research.

IMPLEMENTATION OF CALL MATERIALS: HARDWARE

Today's multimedia language lab can do everything the audiolingual lab of the past did and much more. Multimedia materials combine text, digitized or laserdisc video, graphics, digitized images, digitized photographs, and digitized sound files. What hardware platform allows the language student to take advantage of this array of functionality? What hardware platform permits the CALL developer to develop? The two most widely used operating systems or hardware platforms for creating and using CALL lessons are Macintosh and DOS (identified with IBM or IBM compatibles). For the most part, software produced in one of these two formats has been incompatible with the other. But the choice of system is becoming less traumatic, because for each platform excellent software tools exist that coordinate text, sound, and images of all types and varieties. Some authoring systems are already platform-independent, that is, CALL lessons produced with them will run on both Macs and IBM compatibles.

The ideal language lab would house a bank of computers networked to one computer or server with a large storage capacity, where much of the CALL software could be stored (see *Foreign Language Studies* in the appendix, which lists resources). Such a local area network permits the sharing of data and mail among all its machines. A single computer or an entire network can be further connected, either by Ethernet wiring or a modem, to mainframe machines and other national-international networks such as the Internet. Each computer in this network would possess sufficient memory to run today's software (at least sixteen megabytes, but more is always better) and sufficient hard-disk space to function effectively as a stand-alone workstation (230 megabytes is adequate to begin with).

Technical change occurs rapidly in this field. A few years ago, hard disks were a novelty, but now all computers come packaged with them. Likewise, many new computers are being sold with an internal CD-ROM drive that will accept any type of compact disk containing up to 650 megabytes of digitized music, photos, digitized video, documents, and programs. Compact disks that use digitized sound and video offer quick random access to information and superior sound-image quality. More and more, publishers and CALL developers are packaging their materials, especially space-intensive digitalized sound and video, on compact disk rather than on laserdiscs.

Laserdiscs are a technology similar to but older than CD-ROM. With the appropriate driver, a computer can easily talk to a laserdisc player in the same way that a remote-control device executes commands. Although trends are always hard to predict, the smaller and more convenient size of the compact disk, along with the computer industry's decision to include CD-ROM drives as standard equipment, seems to be tipping the balance away from the laserdisc. Nevertheless, an impressive list of images and full-length movies continues to be marketed on laserdisc (Rubin, Ediger, Coffin, Van Handle, and Whiskeyman).[4]

Another standard feature of the current generation of computers is a built-in microphone or an external microphone plug to record digital sound. Numerous software programs, for both Mac or DOS platforms, allow developers and learners to digitize sound as they go. In a CALL lesson, then, students can hear a model dialogue, record their response, and subsequently compare the two, as in the old audiolingual lab but in much less time. Feedback messages can also be digitized. Synthesized sound can be produced on most computers, but the quality is not acceptable for the purposes of language teaching.

Finally, for the serious CALL developer, a digital scanner may be useful, not only to capture illustrations but also, using optical character recognition (OCR) software, to convert printed text into machine-readable characters. Photos and slides can be digitized in a more straightforward manner. Kodak will press a compact disk for up to one hundred photos or slides. These images can then be accessed from the CD-ROM or transferred to a hard disk, providing learners with authentic visual stimuli free from any copyright restrictions.[5] Better still, with a digital camera, the developer can make images on the spot and directly transfer them to a hard disk.

Undoubtedly, the next years will bring wave after wave of technical innovations, further simplifying the task of producing CALL lessons. But it is not the state of technology that has limited the incorporation of CALL into the second language learning curriculum. The real bottleneck in the expansion of CALL has been the dearth of good software programs and the development of appropriate CALL pedagogies.

IMPLEMENTATION OF CALL MATERIALS: SOFTWARE

Teachers will not find an abundance of well-designed CALL lessons in either the commercial market or in-house educational products. Although the pedagogical and programming demands for good CALL lessons are indeed heavy, the pitfalls are many and pedagogical guides for CALL do not exist (Quinn 305). The implementation of new technologies tends to follow what Marshall McLuhan has termed the rearview-mirror effect (74–75). Thus new CALL developers start off by producing electronic workbooks or booklike programs that duplicate the functionality found in the printed medium — clearly a waste of time. Furthermore, as Robert Quinn reminds us, the necessity of linking CALL materials to textbooks can inhibit the production of innovative software (300) or, worse, lead to the repetition of mistakes contained in a mediocre textbook.

Must all CALL developers be programmers? If an institution has the good fortune and resources to be able to create a courseware group where programmers are dedicated to working with faculty members, CALL production can proceed smoothly and effectively. Teachers and creators, no longer needing to worry about the details of computer programming, can concentrate on what they want their programs to do, while listening carefully to the programmers' suggestions. But even there, the better the teacher understands the computer medium, the better the team of teacher and programmer can function.

This type of resource pooling, however, is rare in universities, colleges, and schools. In its absence the teacher, short of embarking on a second career as a programmer, should seriously consider using an authoring language (also called "authoring template" or "authoring shell") to create CALL lessons. An authoring language allows the developer to create CALL lessons rapidly and with minimal or no knowledge of the computer and programming. The authoring language constructs the necessary machine code or instructions to run the program. The principal disadvantage to using an authoring language is its inherent inflexibility: easy to use means less power to implement routines not supported by the template. There are clear trade-offs, and the CALL developer will have to evaluate them separately with each project.

Two successful and reasonably priced authoring languages for the Mac and DOS platforms are, respectively, *HyperCard* and *Toolbook*. Other well-known authoring systems are *SuperCard, MacroMind Director, Course of Action, Authorware, Course Builder, Digital Chisel,* and *Apple Media Kit* (a cross-platform media tool). These tools are erector sets for developing software for any purpose or discipline. Authoring tools allow the CALL developer to make links to digital sound files, digitized video, laserdisc video, and CD-ROM materials. Other templates that specifically target hypermedia CALL are *Calis, Libra, HyperMedia Shells,* and *SuperMacLang.*[6] Another software-development issue concerns the level of "intelligence" a CALL program can have. The intelligence of a CALL program is measured by the extent and nature of the feedback given to the learner.

For reasons other than the obvious pedagogical and technical ones, teachers should be wary of entering into software creation. The profession has only recently begun to recognize the effort that goes into any high-quality materials development. Some institutions are now considering text-book writing as a basis for faculty promotion. But creating good CALL lessons, although it takes even more time than writing textbooks, is still less recognized at promotion time; faculty members therefore have less incentive for engaging in such work. The guidelines adopted by the MLA Committee on Computers and Emerging Technologies in Teaching and Research represent a first step toward recognizing the academic and professional worth of work done in this area.

Teachers should also be aware that good video—digitized or videodisc materials—is expensive to produce and that securing copyright permissions for its use is difficult. Yet our students, sophisticated consumers of visual images, are accustomed to seeing and will accept only the best-quality video. If CALL lessons are to include large amounts of video, these problems must be faced and the trade-offs evaluated.

"INTELLIGENT" CALL: NOW AND IN THE FUTURE

What does computer intelligence mean? Winograd and Flores write, "In framing the question [i.e., Is the computer intelligent?] in mental terms, we have already committed ourselves to an orientation toward the computer as an autonomous agent" (105). But the computer is not a responsible being; it cannot enter into commitments as human beings do (106). How can it be expected, then, to use language as human beings do? By definition, the computer will never achieve the type of communicative competence that humans enjoy. A computer's affirmation of a given proposition will never be backed by the communicative understanding that "yes" means a commitment to undertake a possible action.

Both Christine Neuwirth and John Underwood ("Edge") assert that the computer should serve as a tutor or protector that watches over the students, monitoring the learning process, refining learners' interactions, and giving advice when advice is warranted. A system that performs such a role is referred to as an intelligent tutoring system (see Holland, Kaplan, and Sams). Ideally, the computer would give instructions during problem-solving or discovery activities, and of course it would supply appropriate feedback to the learners' answers and inquiries. To give this type of feedback, however, the computer must be capable of parsing the structure of a sentence: the agent, verb, theme or direct object, recipient, and so on. It must also assign some type of semantic interpretation to that particular lexical and overall syntactic structure and exercise limited judgments about the communicative appropriateness of its response. The entire endeavor is often called natural language processing. At present, only mainframe systems have the processing power to do natural language processing successfully (Murray).[7]

Some success has been achieved in developing an intelligent tutoring system for writing programs that prompt and shape the student's composition. But the goal of implementing a fully operational intelligent tutoring system has not been reached in either the mainframe or micro environment (see Holland, Maisano, Alderks, and Martin for a report on a recent attempt; see Underwood, "Edge," for an extrapolation of where intelligent tutoring systems might lead CALL). Greater success results when programmers create a microworld, a special space that gives the student a partner "to converse with" about a highly delineated topic in a restricted semantic domain (Chapelle 61–62). In a microworld, it is possible to make communication between the user and the computer seem like a natural process (see Underwood, "Edge" 77).

How "smart" can we expect CALL programs to be in the microcomputer environment and what is the concomitant programming cost of that quality? Most CALL practitioners agree that the computer should render, at the bare minimum, contextually appropriate feedback for the learner's answers. The most straightforward computer procedure for evaluating student responses is to match strings. String matching compares the student's utterance, or string, such as *abce,* with the correct one, *abc*d.* In this example, the computer would detect two errors: the use of *e* instead of *d* at the end of the student's string and a missing asterisk after the third character in that string. But a string-matching strategy would soon be overwhelmed by the sheer number of possibilities generated by the open-ended questions that are so frequent in everyday human speech—for example, *What did you think of the movie?* Many of the communicatively appropriate responses possible do not share structural features: *I've never seen his work before*; *It stunk*; *Why doesn't he hire a real screenwriter?* A small semblance of control can be achieved by steering clear of open-ended questions and by limiting the discourse domain, as is done in microworlds.

But if a sentence parser is not available, then the programmer will have to provide the proper feedback on a case-by-case basis, for each anticipated error for each question. Trying to provide contextualized error analyses can quickly subvert the promised benefits of an authoring language, because detailed feedback requires the intervention of a programmer and many hours of programming. From the student's point of view, however, nothing is more frustrating than having a communicatively competent answer summarily rejected for lack of punctuation or for lexical-syntactic choices not allowed by the program's microworld. CALL developers should structure questions carefully so as not to exceed these present limitations of the microcomputer environment. With each program, CALL developers must weigh the benefits and disadvantages of providing extensive amounts of contextualized error analysis. In short, while a template system can easily locate, with a string-matching strategy, where errors begin and end, individualized error analysis requires extensive and expensive amounts of programming. Still, the more feedback, the better.

HYPERMEDIA EXEMPLARS

Just as there are few guides available for developing CALL lessons, software evaluation too has recourse to few signposts along the way. Jamieson and

Chapelle explain the difficulty of few signposts as the problem of matching "two entities which are not well understood: SLA and courseware use" (151). Michael Ephratt states emphatically that "the essence of CALL is the 'how' " and that the "what," or means for arriving at the "how," should remain in the background (251). In other words, students should use CALL materials that instruct by doing. But how does this advice translate into a practical checklist for recognizing good CALL products? Rather than provide here a long litany of software reviews, I single out a few exemplars striking for their contributions to hypermedia CALL.[8]

MIT's Athena Project was mentioned above in the context of fostering communicative dialogue through simulation. Originally the project was developed in a mainframe environment that included extensive natural language processing routines designed to allow for maximal tolerance of errors and minimal tolerance of ambiguity (Murray, Morgenstern, and Furstenberg 98). The Macintosh versions of the Athena Project, *A la rencontre de Philippe* and *No recuerdo,* had to eliminate these parsing systems, given the lesser space and power of the microcomputer environment. Both programs were rewritten in *SuperCard* for third-semester students and currently run on the Macintosh with videodisc player, although *No recuerdo* has not been released as of this writing.[9]

The present version of *No recuerdo* makes students adopt the role of a cub reporter in Bogotá, Colombia, interviewing people on the street and communicating with newspaper editors by fax. Reading and extensive writing are added to the listening-comprehension and cultural-awareness objectives (Morgenstern). An imaginary editor returns the faxed newspaper copy to the reporter with corrections and comments that are generated by an error-analysis routine. In *A la recontre de Philippe,* students help Philippe, a young journalist, through a difficult day that includes romantic problems and apartment hunting.

In either the French or Spanish program, students interact with characters of various social levels and linguistic registers. More important, that the learners' choices and responses affect the eventual outcome of the simulation creates for learners a vested interest in studying these language materials. Culture is an integral component of the entire presentation. Reviews of the microcomputer versions of these programs will undoubtedly confirm the effectiveness of the programs' basic pedagogical premise: students become highly engaged in language learning through meaningful discovery activities set in the milieu of the target culture. *A la rencontre de Philippe* and *No recuerdo* have enjoyed the best of all possible worlds in their development phases: in-house (and therefore customized) video production (with no subsequent copyright problems), prolonged professional programming assistance, and motivated faculty and staff members rewarded for their participation.

Two other interesting hypermedia programs are tied to textbooks: *Discovering French Interactive* is tied to Jean Paul Valette and Rebecca Valette's *Discovering French,* and *Dime* is tied to Fabián Samaniego et al.'s *Dime.* The strongest point of these programs resides in the authenticity and quality of their digitized video images. Many cultural notes and exercises accompany the video clips. Overall, the interface, programmed in *MacroMind Director,* is aesthetically pleasing and well designed. One exercise uses a visual mind-bubble metaphor to invite the students to create their own digitized dialogues or sound scripts for stick characters that can be moved in and out of still-image video background.

The Learning Company's *Learn to Speak Spanish* offers a stand-alone hypermedia program functionally based on fifteen scenarios: arriving at an airport, changing money, getting a taxi, checking into a hotel, making a long-distance phone call, making a local phone call, eating at a restaurant, asking for directions, finding an address, greeting people, attending a party, making an appointment, going to a pharmacy, going to a doctor's office, using a laundry. The story line utilizes short digitized video clips with vocabulary help and a variety of exercises: fill-in-the-blank, drag-and-match, word-jumble (i.e., scrambled-sentence) exercises, and translations (called "communication skills"). Despite the menu of everyday events, much of the video footage appears to have been shot in a studio with a neutral background and gives the appearance of talking heads devoid of cultural and pragmatic authenticity. The interface, however, again designed with *MacroMind Director,* is visually intuitive, attractive, and easy to use. The listening exercises allow students to record their voices and compare their utterances with the sound in the video clips. The error-analysis routines are based on a string-matching strategy that admits only one correct answer and tends to break down in the translation exercises, which solicit a variety of appropriate responses.

Système-D for French and *Atajo* for Spanish, programs that can be used by either IBM or Macintosh computers, focus exclusively on writing. They provide students with an online dictionary, thesaurus, grammar help, and the conjugated forms of verbs in any tense. This writing environment provides linguistic support on demand to assist students in expressing themselves.

The products reviewed above are not necessarily the best CALL products; rather, they represent some of the first hypermedia and writing programs currently available.[10] Potential CALL developers should study how these programs employ hypermedia materials and then should choose the best features from each for incorporation in future CALL projects. For instance, the video in *A la rencontre de Philippe* is of very high quality and culturally authentic, but the multiple-choice format does not allow students to type in or use real language to push the action forward. In an effort to achieve more interactivity, *No recuerdo* demands more writing, and the program keys into correctly used nouns and adjectives in the students' responses to provide feedback. But it would be possible to fax a news copy to an editor without verbs and still receive praise. *Discovering French Interactive* also provides high-quality video but follows the textbook closely, reflecting all the positive and negative features. Programs like *Système-D* or *Atajo* do not guide the students to better writing but, rather, place a collection of online writing manuals and tools conveniently at hand. Hypermedia programs of the future should take aspects of all these programs to create a new generation of CALL materials for the foreign language curriculum. CALL must be an evolving art form, its evolution driven by teachers joining in the process as users, critics and, in some cases, CALL developers.

THE VIRTUAL CLASSROOM

Current thinking about second language learning tends to play down the formal teaching of structure, to favor more communicative activities, and to relegate drill and practice to the language lab or home environment.[11] In this context, CALL will undoubtedly play an increasingly significant supplementary role in the second language learning curriculum of the future.

But the proliferation of local area networks and electronic mail is opening up another frontier for the classroom not previously imagined by the profession (Lunde, Warschauer). Margaret Beauvois has described the advantages of using a local area network for synchronous real-time collaborative writing and discussions. John Barson envisages e-mail's providing a pretext for "piping to students information-rich, comprehensible context at various appropriate levels of discourse, language structure, and usage, thus providing a new and ample avenue for potentially very productive teacher talk." He cites lack of interruption as a principal benefit of e-mail discourse. E-mail writing constitutes a special, off-the-cuff, written discourse that could almost be spoken (367). The structure of e-mail writing is qualitatively different from that of formal writing. In this light, the computer could become an instrument central to producing both planned and spontaneous discourse, in either an individual or collaborative format. The collaborative modality of e-mail provides considerable benefits: increased insights into the act of writing; involvement in and out of class in meaningful, authentic activities; and collaborations with peers (371).[12] One such collaborative program, *De orilla a orilla*, enjoys great success in connecting Spanish speakers in the United States with participants in Latin America (De Villar).

Teachers will increasingly set up or make their students join existing electronic discussion groups or bulletin boards where the registered participants can freely discuss and share their expertise and interests in synchronous or deferred-time settings.[13] But the Internet can be used for much more than e-mail, collaborative writing, or discussion groups. With a viewing program like *Mosaic* or *Netscape*, students can connect to hypertext information located on any World Wide Web server found throughout the world. By navigating through (surfing) the Web, students and teachers alike can retrieve information on a wide variety of subjects: Peruvian science projects, course syllabi from different universities, the latest update on Russian business, to name only a few. Web viewer programs provide hypertext links to other documents, graphics, digitized sounds, images, and video.

These new technical possibilities give rise to a new form of electronic, or virtual, classroom. In the very near future, students will electronically connect to a classroom full of users from all over the nation or the world. Teachers will no longer dominate the learning agenda but serve instead as living models or consultants in this communication network. Textbooks and CALL materials will also become more available for downloading or transfer to the student's individual workstation.[14]

The concept of teacher will cease to be defined locally; it will refer to a number of experts accessible through the Internet at various remote locations. Richard Walters, a computer scientist at the University of California, Davis, and I are developing a platform-independent, public-domain software program called *Remote Technical Assistance*. The program, running on the Internet, allows students and teachers in remote locations to interact with one another in either a synchronous (chat) or asynchronous (messaging) mode.[15] Language students will be able to share their computer screen with an expert or other classmates at remote locations in one-on-one or group-chat sessions. Participants can share images of text, photos, or graphics as whiteboards and then exchange comments in written or spoken form. "Office hours" will take on a completely new meaning, one that increases students' engagement with language-culture study.

Language students will also be asked to join electronic discussion groups on the Internet (Feustle; *Athelstan*). Middlebury College Language Schools, a recognized leader in second language teaching, recently implemented a Mellon-sponsored foreign language network called FlanNet for a consortium for northeast colleges and universities. (FlanNet is a client-server architecture networked communications system that supports electronic messaging through several nontraditional input methods using the *WorldScript* language extensions for writing Chinese, Japanese, Arabic, or any other language.) With this network, messages can be sent to individual users or to conferences (i.e., computer discussion groups) that several users have access to, and issues of second language learning can be freely aired. The system also supports uploading and downloading of files and attachments, such as new shareware products.[16] At present, instructors from nine participating institutions use FlanNet to exchange ideas, databases, and software innovations.

Similar networks targeting students rather than teachers are sure to appear soon. FlanNet itself, as it evolves, could conceivably be expanded to invite students from different institutions to join language-specific conferences. What a novel concept, to have so many human resources and language experiences at the touch of a keyboard! But how will a language profession oriented toward oral proficiency respond to this new possibility? Will students get credit for language courses conducted completely or partially through an electronic medium? How will the profession integrate such a language network into the mainstream curriculum? No one has answers for these questions yet — the concepts are too novel for the profession to have developed an appropriate pedagogy. But if universities, colleges, and schools fail to shape this new medium, it seems clear that private telecommunication companies will determine the medium's form, content, and use. Already companies such as America Online, Compuserve, and Prodigy are testing the waters in response to the growing popularity of telecommunications as a way of delivering education.

PEDAGOGY FOR THE NEW LANGUAGE CLASSROOM

What will the teacher provide, then, for Johnny and Joan on Monday in this new technologically assisted classroom? If the topic for the week is, say, Machu Picchu, the Peruvian Incan ruins, or, more generally, Peru as a Latin American country, the teacher may begin by brainstorming, using communicative activities that ask students what they know about Peru, the Andes, the Incas, and Machu Picchu. The teacher gradually shifts to the specific text and video the students will discuss in class the next day. Some of the brainstorming, prereading, or previewing activities may include sending the students to the lab to browse the Web for more information about Machu Picchu. If the classroom facilities allow it, interesting materials garnered by the students can be shown and discussed in class through large-screen projection.

That night, students read the target text or view the target video at home. If the text-video is included in the textbook as part of a comprehensive package from a publishing house, students will be able to insert a CD-ROM disk into their home computer and receive further online assistance with the reading-viewing task. For more in-depth work or to satisfy their curiosity, they might want to connect to the Internet from home by modem or by Ethernet from the lab and locate a remote tutor, using software similar to Walters's *Remote Technical Assistance* program.

The next day, the teacher confronts a highly motivated and well-prepared group of students and leads them in a discussion of the materials studied. No doubt interesting grammatical points will surface in the course of discussion: for example, the use of the preterite to describe travelogue actions and historical events. Communicative exercises carried out in class can be later underscored by CALL lessons done at home or in the lab. Computerized dictation lessons that focus on specific grammatical contrasts can be efficiently created on the computer using authentic CD musical recordings of Peruvian folk songs — for instance, "El condor pasa" — available at local record shops in the international section.[17] Undoubtedly, more general questions about Peru will arise: its government, ethnic makeup, and cultural traditions. These questions could stimulate the students to contact some

Peruvians directly through electronic mail on the Internet, perhaps through a news service like *NewsNet News*. After all, citizens of any country are generally eager to talk about their native land.

As the students move into the composition stage of the lesson, collaborative writing programs such as *InterChange* are incorporated. Again, the teacher becomes an expert facilitator rather than the prime actor in the language curriculum. In the course of several revisions, students may again resort to a distance-learning strategy to receive timely advice on how to polish their final composition.

This example by no means exhausts the ways in which technology stands to assist teachers and students in the delivery of modern language instruction. Furthermore, it should be clear by now that technology does not offer the teacher a single pedagogical avenue to present the curriculum but, rather, opens the door to a myriad of possibilities, most of them student-driven.

CALL RESEARCH: ISSUES IN SLA AND ASSESSMENT

The computer provides a private medium where students can experiment with the target language and make errors freely, without pressure from peers in the classroom and without public embarrassment. Consequently, both the individual workstation and e-mail can gather data that accurately reflect different stages of learners' interlanguage. James Noblitt and Susan Bland have described the computer as an ideal window for tracking students' information-processing styles with foreign language materials (120–21). This type of data can be used not only to improve the CALL curriculum but also to help investigate the nature of cognitive processing in second language learning, as Garrett has argued ("Perspective"). CALL programs can easily be designed to test such specific theoretical issues in SLA as: Does correction affect performance? Do good second language readers look up words in a passage less frequently than poor readers do? How is the learner lexicon organized at each stage of development, and when are the different parts of speech and their morphologies incorporated into the learner's grammar?

On a more practical and pedagogical level, CALL data can help answer such questions as: Do prereading exercises reduce compulsive lexical look-ups and improve reading skills? Do learners know best how to direct their learning activities, or are authoritative CALL programs that direct those activities more effective? What strategies do learners follow when they are in control? What types of feedback do they prefer? What are the linguistic characteristics of e-mail discourse and what can it contribute, if anything, to the development of overall language proficiency?

Despite the obvious advantages of computer-based data collection, surprisingly little CALL research exists to date. CALL research on the lexicon of learners presents a particularly rewarding avenue of research (Blake). Second language learners begin the task of lexicon building with what Noblitt and Bland have called the naive linguistic hypothesis, the belief that there exists a one-to-one translation in L1 for L2 (121). Learners seem to expect that a morphologically complex word will still map directly from L2 to L1 and vice versa. Bland, Noblitt, Armington, and Gay identify a developmental scale of learner strategies: first token matching (the naive linguistic hypothesis), then type matching, and finally relexification. The pedagogical implications are obvious: teachers need to change students' expectations of L1-L2 isomorphism and help students use information in the dictionary more effectively, showing them that lexical representations are intimately connected with the L2 grammar (448).

Susan Knight has shown how important having an online dictionary can be for L2 learners reading authentic materials. In her study, subjects with access to an online dictionary "not only learned more words but also achieved higher reading comprehension scores than those who guessed from context" (295). This effect was especially robust for students of lower verbal ability. Knight believes that these findings call for a reexamination of the common practice of encouraging all students to guess word meaning from context. That students of low verbal ability are often unable to perform this guessing task makes an online dictionary a suitable tool for promoting vocabulary expansion and better reading performance.[18]

With respect to learners' strategies, Klaus Brandl has found that low-verbal-ability students are less willing to engage in correction of their errors than high-verbal-ability students are. While high-verbal-ability students readily take advantage of feedback cues, low-verbal-ability students prefer to be given the correct answer after they make a mistake, a strategy Brandl characterizes as the least amount of effort to get the job done (207). Students' lack of grammatical or lexical knowledge limits their motivation to solve the linguistic problems at hand and to process more elaborate feed-back messages. Brandl suggests that CALL programs should offer and en-courage L2 students to use a number of predesigned and prestructured learning strategies that allow students to develop a meaningful learning process in a self-instructional environment.

Carol Chapelle and Suesue Mizuno have examined learners' strategies in using CALL materials but in the more general context of resourcing, practice, self-monitoring, self-management, and self-evaluation. Chapelle and Mizuno wanted to find out whether or not students would use these five essential strategies while they worked on learner-controlled CALL materials. The re-sults were mixed, and the conclusion was that "students are often doing something different from what instructors believe they are doing" (42).

But do such studies tell us what effect, if any, CALL programs might have on the development of L2 proficiency?

It is difficult to assess the effectiveness of CALL software. Both Garrett ("Problems" 76) and Jamieson and Chapelle (152) point out the perils of as-sessment in an area where there are many uncontrolled learner and design variables. Given this obstacle, how can a researcher provide statistical evi-dence that a group of students using CALL performs better than a control group? Jamieson and Chapelle stress five learner variables that should be worked into the research design when the effectiveness of CALL is evalu-ated: age, degree of control over the lesson, aptitude for learning languages, cognitive styles of processing information, and attitudes toward second lan-guage learning.

Margaret Roblyer found, in her aggregate study of CALL programs, that in all disciplines CALL was more effective at the college level than at the el-ementary level but that learner attitudes toward work and achievement were not affected by CALL. Basing her results on only three studies with English, she found that ESL CALL was ineffective. Her line of inquiry illustrates pre-cisely the assessment difficulties caused by uncontrolled learner and design variables, difficulties that can be addressed only if professionals become in-volved with CALL research.

One last research consideration: How should a profession dominated by the concept of oral proficiency view the use of a technology that is predom-inantly a text-based medium? Karen Smith's research into the effects of collaborative writing on the development of language proficiency points to a provocative answer. In her study, students using a computer conferencing program to sustain online conversations performed better both in reading and formation of written ideas than control-group students who had no computer access. At the same time, the computer group made the same progress in conversational skills and written accuracy as the control group. In overall language progress, the computer group ranked significantly higher. Smith concludes that communication practice in the target language that uses a computer increases not only written skills but also conversational ones, because it increases time on task and promotes creativity as well as accuracy. Obviously, more research is needed to confirm the trends reported here, but the initial findings should stimulate the profession's interest in the impact of technology on the classroom.

Until the profession as a whole overcomes its fear of technology, CALL will not progress, despite the most favorable technical advances. CALL practitioners need to distinguish between those language learning activities where technology can help accomplish substantive goals and others where traditional methods would suffice. Department chairs, with the support of the administration, should encourage their faculty members to experiment with CALL; significant development efforts should be rewarded with appropriate career incentives. Technology workshops at both local and national levels should complement regular institutional support.

On the individual level, language teachers interested in using or developing CALL lessons must first look to securing the appropriate hardware base. Working with outdated equipment and programs may not be better than nothing. Outdated equipment will not run the types of sophisticated programs and interfaces our students have come to expect. In making textbook requests from publishers, then, teachers should inquire what CALL programs are available, textbook-specific or otherwise, to send a clear message that CALL is an integral part of the curriculum. Teachers should also consider carefully how the computer can make classroom activities more learner-centered and more responsive to students' individual levels of proficiency. Collaborative work with the computer is another valuable way of maximizing the strengths found in today's linguistically and culturally diverse classrooms.

Above all, teachers should not be afraid to become students again. The CALL field is changing so rapidly, especially with respect to technical advances and the general understanding of how to write and use CALL lessons, that no one person can pretend to be master of this approach. Teachers must learn to share ideas and software with colleagues not only in their own institutions but also at other institutions, by e-mail. Ideally, bulletin boards should become software clearinghouses where teachers can patch in to access software programs on a variety of subjects: grammar, culture, history, literature. Inexpensive technology already exists and is obtainable on the Internet to support this type of extended communication among members of our profession. Teachers must rise to the challenge to integrate these new technologies into their curriculum. The integration will empower their students to communicate with other students and teachers from other institutions in the United States and abroad, though such empowerment means that teachers must surrender their sovereignty over the direction of the classroom. Teachers must learn to permit the students themselves to download materials from outside the established classroom curriculum. My comments do not allude to any future technological impasse; rather, they call teachers to change their attitudes toward second language learning and embrace a new social infrastructure that takes full advantage of new technology.

With respect to CALL research, the profession must escape the chicken-versus-egg dilemma: namely, no research is possible without good software, and software should not be developed without more research. CALL researchers will have to become software developers too, and vice versa. Only then will theory translate into practice and practice into theory. The call for CALL is over; it's time to start producing and testing.

The alternative to this scenario is to leave software development and information management entirely in the hands of publishing houses and private industry. The attractions of CALL and distance learning for today's students are certainly not lost on the private sector. But the profession can ill afford to abdicate its role as an educational leader and leave the development of the CALL curriculum to those whose primary motivation is financial.

NOTES

1. Masayoshi Sugiura of Nagoya University reports that in Japan language professors engaged in research and development of technology receive higher salaries and enjoy better promotion opportunities than their literature counterparts. The situation is the opposite in the United States, where language professionals often jeopardize their careers by working in computer-assisted language learning.
2. Margaret Roblyer's research has shown that CAI has been most effective with sciences, math, and the higher-order cognitive skills.

3. Jules Finkel has likened interactivity to solving a mystery instead of just watching it.
4. PICS (Project for International Communication Studies) offers videodiscs for language learning that use authentic materials.
5. The cost for this service is approximately $50.
6. See González-Edfelt for a more extensive review of authoring languages and templates (180–90).
7. For extensive references on intelligent CALL, see Matthews; Bailin et al.
8. Journals like *CALICO Journal, Computers and the Humanities,* and *Hispania* are excellent sources for CALL reviews. Chris Higgins provides a short summary for the beginner.
9. For information on these projects, write Janet H. Murray, Director, Laboratory for Advanced Technology in the Humanities (LATH), MIT, Bldg. 20B-231, 18 Vassar St., Cambridge, MA 02139, or e-mail jhmurray@athena.mit.edu.
10. See Gale for a report on *Montevidisco,* the first CALL attempt at creating a simulation-based hypermedia program. Other programs of interest are *Exito,* an intensive Spanish hypermedia course, and the product line from VideoLinguist.
11. But see Garrett, "Problems," for a more positive attitude toward teaching grammar processing.
12. See Karen Smith's article for an assessment of the effect of collaborative writing on the development of oral proficiency.
13. Examples of synchronous settings are MUDs (multiuser domains) and MOOs (multiuser domains, object-oriented); examples of deferred-time settings are listservs and bulletin boards.
14. In a recent network advertisement for the Virtual Online University, Guy Wilson, vice president for academic affairs (guyw@delphi.com), invited full- and part-time faculty members to apply for jobs in proposing and designing courseware.
15. See Walter's *Remote Technical Assistance* home page on the Internet: http://escsher.cs.ucdavis.edu:1024/. The departments of Spanish, Japanese, and Russian at the Davis and Berkeley campuses of the University of California will soon be using this program to share access to online tutors for students from both institutions.
16. Robert Lagerman of the Language Schools at Middlebury College provided me with this description of FlanNet. The FlanNet home page is http://www.middlbury.edu/~ls/technology/flannet/index.html.
17. David Harren's *CDictation* is an excellent authoring shell for creating dictation exercises linked to CD recordings of the target culture. See http://www.middlebury.edu/~ls/technology/herren/index.html.
18. See Pederson for another study centered around online reading.

APPENDIX: COMPUTER PROGRAMS AND OTHER RESOURCES

A la rencontre de Philippe. Yale UP.

Apple Media Kit Apple Computer, Inc., 20525 Mariani Ave., Cupertino, CA 95014-6299; 408 966-1010.

Atajo. Heinle and Heinle Publishers, Inc., 20 Park Plaza, Boston, MA 02166.

Authorware. Macromedia, Inc. 600 Townsend St., San Francisco, CA 94103.

Calis. DUCALL, Humanities Computing Facility, 014 Language Bldg., Duke Univ., Durham, NC 27706.

Centre of Information on Language Teaching and Research (CILT). Regent's Coll., Inner Circle, Regent's Park, London NW1 4NS, UK.

Course Builder. TeleRobotics Intl., Inc., Knoxville, TN.

Course of Action. Minneapolis, MN.

Digital Chisel 1.2. Pierian Spring Software, 5200 SW Macadam Ave., Suite 250, Portland, OR 97201; 800 472-8578.

Dime: pasaporte al mundo 21. D. C. Heath and Co., 125 Spring St., Lexington, MA 02173.

Discovering French Interactive. D. C. Heath and Co., 125 Spring St., Lexington, MA 02173.

Exito. Analysys Corp., 1615 L St., NW, Suite 1250, Washington, DC 20036; 202 429-5653.

Foreign Language Studies and Technology. Ed. Gary Dauphin. Shared database of CALL programs available on diskette (dauphin.g@applelink.apple.com). 1994.

HyperCard 2.2. Apple Computer, Inc., 20525 Mariani Ave., Cupertino, CA 95014-6299; 408 966-1010.

HyperMedia Shells. Contact: David Herren, Green Mountain Mac, Box 342, Middlebury, VT 05753.

InterChange. Deadalus Group, Inc., 1106 Clayton Lane, Suite 250W, Austin, TX 78723.

Learn to Speak Spanish. Learning Co., Foreign Lang. Div., 6493 Kaiser Dr., Fremont, CA 94555; 800 852-2255.

Libra. Contact: Michael Farris, Director, Media Services, Southwest Texas State Univ., San Marcos 78666.

MacroMind Director. MacroMedia, 600 Townsend St., San Francisco, CA 94103; 800 288-4797.

No recuerdo. MIT Technology Licensing Office, 28 Carlton St., Room E32-300, Cambridge, MA 02139.

PICS (Project for International Communication Studies). 270 International Center, Univ. of Iowa, Iowa City 52242; 800 373-7427; home page http://www.uiowa.edu/~pics/.

QuickTime 1.6.2. 800 7690-2775, ext. 6596.

SCOLA (Satellite Communications for Learning). PO Box 1619, McClelland, IA 51548-0619; 712 566-2202; scola@creighton.edu.

SuperCard. Silicon Beach Software, Inc., PO Box 261430, San Diego, CA 92126; 619 695-956.

SuperMacLang. Contact: Judith Frommer, Lang. Lab, Harvard Univ., Dept. of Romance Lang. and Lit., Boylston Hall, Room 206, Cambridge, MA 02138.

Système-D. Heinle and Heinle Publishers, Inc., 20 Park Plaza, Boston, MA 02166.

Toolbook. Asymetrix Corp., Educ. Programs, PO Box 40419, Belleview, WA 98004-1419; 800 624-8999.

VideoLinguist: French and Spanish. Cubic Media, Inc., 729 Benjamin Fox Pavilion, Jankintown, PA 19046; 800 23-CUBIC.

WORKS CITED

Ahmad, Khurshid, Greville Corbett, Margaret Rogers, and Roland Sussex, eds. *Computers, Language Learning, and Language Teaching.* Cambridge: Cambridge UP, 1985.

Athelstan Newsletter 5.4 (1993): 13–15.

Bailin, Alan, et al. "Bibliography of Intelligent Computer-Assisted Language Instruction." *Computers and the Humanities* 23 (1989): 85–90.

Beauvois, Margaret Healy. "Computer-Assisted Classroom Discussion in the Foreign Language Classroom: Conversation in Slow Motion." *Foreign Language Annals* 25 (1992): 455–63.

Bickes, Gerhard, and Andrew Scott. "On the Computer as a Medium for Language Teaching." *CALICO Journal* 6.3 (1989): 21–32.

Blake, Robert J. "Second-Language Reading on the Computer." *ADFL Bulletin* 24.1 (1992): 17–22.

Bland, Susan, James Noblitt, Susan Armington, and Geri Gay. "The Naive Lexical Hypothesis: Evidence from Computer-Assisted Language Learning." *Modern Language Journal* 74 (1990): 440–50.

Brandl, Klaus K. "Strong and Weak Students' Preferences for Error Feedback Options and Responses." *Modern Language Journal* 79 (1995): 194–211.

Brown, James, and Gary R. Jahn. "The Role of Computer-Assisted Learning in a Proficiency-Based Language Curriculum." *Computers and the Humanities* 24 (1990): 93–103.

Chapelle, Carol. "Using Intelligent Computer-Assisted Language Learning." *Computers and the Humanities* 23 (1989): 59–70.

Chapelle, Carol, and Suesue Mizuno. "Student Strategies with Learner-Controlled CALL." *CALICO Journal* 7.2 (1989): 25–47.

Chun, Dorothy, and Klaus K. Brandl. "Beyond Form-Based Drill and Practice: Meaning-Enhanced CALL on the Macintosh." *Foreign Language Annals* 25 (1992): 255–67.

Davies, Graham. *Computers, Language and Language Learning.* London: Centre for Information on Lang. Teaching, 1982.

DeVillar, Robert A. "Second Language Use within the Non-traditional Classroom: Computers, Cooperative Learning, and Bilingualism." *Language Distribution Issues in Bilingual Schooling.* Ed. Rodolfo Jacobson and Christian Faltis. Clevedon, Eng.: Multilingual Matters, 1990. 133–59.

Dunkel, Patricia, ed. *Computer-Assisted Language Learning and Testing.* New York: Newbury, 1991 .

Ephratt, Michael. "Developing and Evaluating Language Courseware." *Computers and the Humanities* 26 (1992): 249–59.

Feustle, Joseph A., Jr. "Instructions for Using the A.A.T.S. Electronic Bulletin Board." *Hispania* 703 (1987): 689–700

Finkel, Jules. "Word Abuse." *CUE Newsletter* 12.5 (1990): 7.

Freed, Barbara F., ed. *Foreign Language Acquisition Research and the Classroom.* Lexington: Heath, 1991.

Gale, Larrie E. *"Macario, Montevidisco, and Interactive Digame*: Developing Interactive Video for Language Instruction." Smith, *Technology* 235–48.

Garrett, Nina. "A Psycholinguistic Perspective on Grammar and CALL." Smith, *Media* 169–96.

———. "Technology in the Service of Language Learning: Trends and Issues." *Modern Language Journal* 75 (1991): Freed 74–101.

———. "Theoretical and Pedagogical Problems of Separating 'Grammar' from 'Communication.'" Freed 74–87.

Gass, Susan, and Evangeline Varonis. "Input, Interaction, and Second Language Production." *Studies in Second Language Acquisition* 16 (1994): 283–302.

González-Edfelt, Nidia. "An Introduction to Computer-Assisted Spanish Language Learning." Merino, Trueba, and Samaniego 171–99.

Hainline, Douglas, ed. *New Developments in Computer-Assisted Language Learning.* London: Croom Helm, 1987.

Hendricks, Harold. "Models of Interactive Videodisc Development." *CALICO Journal* 11.1 (1993): 53–67.

Higgins, Chris. "Computer-Assisted Language Learning: Current Programs and Projects." *ERIC Digest,* 1993. ED 355835.

Higgins, John, and Tim Johns. *Computers in Language Learning.* Boston: Addison, 1984.

Holland, V. Melissa, Jonathan D. Kaplan, and Michelle R. Sams, eds. *Intelligent Language Tutors: Theory Shaping Technology.* Mahwah: Erlbaum, 1995.

Holland, V. Melissa, Richard Maisano, Cathy Alderks, and Jeffery Martin. "Parsers in Tutors: What Are They Good For?" *CALICO Journal* 11.1 (1993): 28–46.

Jamieson, Joan, and Carol Chapelle. "Using CALL Effectively: What Do We Need to Know about Students?" *System* 16.2 (1988): 151–62.

Knight, Susan. "Dictionary Use While Reading: The Effects on Comprehension and Vocabulary Acquisition for Students of Different Verbal Abilities." *Modern Language Journal* 78 (1994): 285–99.

Lunde, Ken R. "Using Electronic Mail as a Medium for Foreign Language Study and Instruction." *CALICO Journal* 7.3 (1990): 68–78.

Matthews, Clive. "Grammar Frameworks in Intelligent CALL." *CALICO Journal* 11.1 (1993): 5–27.

McLuhan, Marshall. *Understanding Media: The Extensions of Man.* New York: Signet, 1964.

MLA Committee on Computers and Emerging Technologies in Teaching and Research. "Guidelines for Evaluating Computer-Related Work in the Modern Languages." *ADFL Bulletin* 28.3 (1997): 50–51.

Morgenstern, Douglas. E-mail to the author. Summer, 1994.

Murray, Janet H. "Anatomy of a New Medium: Literary and Pedagogic Uses of Advanced Linguistic Computer Science." *Computers and the Humanities* 25 (1991): 1–14.

Murray, Janet H., Douglas Morgenstern, and Gilberte Furstenberg. "The Athena Language-Learning Project: Design Issues for the Next Generation of Computer-Based Language-Learning Tools." Smith, *Technology* 97–118.

Neuwirth, Christine. "Intelligent Tutoring Systems: Exploring Issues in Learning and Teaching Writing." *Computers and the Humanities* 23 (1989): 45–57.

Noblitt, James S., and Susan K. Bland. "Tracking the Learner in Computer-Aided Language Learning." Freed 120–32.

Pederson, Kathleen Marshall. "An Experiment in Computer-Assisted Second-Language Reading." *Modern Language Journal* 70 (1986): 36–41.

Quinn, Robert. "Our Progress in Integrating Modern Methods and Computer-Controlled Learning for Successful Language Study." *Hispania* 73 (1990): 297–311.

Roblyer, Margaret D. "The Effectiveness of Microcomputers in Education: A Review of Research from 1980–87." *T.H.E. Journal* 16.2 (1988): 85–89.

Roblyer, Margaret D., W. H. Castine, and F. J. King. *Assessing the Impact of Computer Applications for Instruction: A Review and Synthesis of Recent Research Findings.* New York: Haworth, 1988.

Rubin, Joan, Anne Ediger, Edna Coffin, Donna Van Handle, and Ann Whiskeyman. "Survey of Interactive Language Discs." *CALICO Journal* 7.3 (1990): 31–56.

Ruschoff, Bernd. "Language Learning and Information Technology: State of the Art." *CALICO Journal* 10.3 (1993): 5–17.

Smith, Karen. "Collaborative and Interactive Writing for Increasing Communications Skills." *Hispania* 73 (1990): 77–87.

Smith, William Flint, ed. *Modern Media in Foreign Language Education: Theory and Implementation.* Lincolnwood: Natl. Textbook and ACTFL, 1987.

———. *Modern Technology in Foreign Language Education: Applications and Projects.* Lincolnwood: Natl. Textbook and ACTFL, 1989.

Stevens, Vance, Roland Sussex, and Walter Vladimir Tuman. *A Bibliography of Computer-Aided Language Learning.* New York: AMS, 1986.

Stoks, Gé, "Integrating New Technologies into the Modern Language Curriculum." *CALICO Journal* 11.1 (1993): 76–93.

Sugiura, Masayoshi. Conversation with the author. 1994.

Suppes, Patrick, ed. *University-Level Computer-Assisted Instruction at Stanford: 1968–1980*. Stanford: Stanford U Inst. for Mathematical Studies in the Social Sciences, 1981.

Swann, Philip Howard. "Theory and Practice of Computer-Assisted Language Learning." Diss. U of Michigan, Ann Arbor, 1992.

Underwood, John. *Juegos Comunicativos: Spanish Games for Communicative Practice*. New York: Random, 1986.

———. *Linguistics, Computers, and the Language Teacher*. Rowley: Newbury, 1984.

———. "On the Edge: Intelligent CALL in the 1990s." *Computers and the Humanities* 23 (1989): 71–85.

Valette, Jean Paul, and Rebecca M. Valette. *Discovering French*. Lexington: Heath, 1993.

Van Campen, Joseph. "Project for the Application of Mathematical Learning Theory to Second Language Acquisition with Particular Reference to Russian (Final Report)." Washington: US Dept. of Health, Educ., and Welfare, 1968. (ERIC ED026934).

Warschauer, Mark, ed. *Virtual Connections: Online Activities and Projects for Networking Language Learners*. Manoa: Second Lang. Teaching and Curriculum Center, U of Hawaii, Manoa, 1995.

Winograd, Terry, and Fernando Flores. *Understanding Computers and Cognition*. Norwood: Ablex, 1986.

Wyatt, David. *Computer-Assisted Learning in ESL*. Oxford: Pergamon, 1984.

Evaluation of Learning Outcomes in Second Language Acquisition

Elana Shohamy | A Multiplism Perspective

Language testing is concerned with the measurement of language outcomes. Thus it focuses on their definition — what it means to know a language — and on the appropriate procedures for measuring them. This essay argues that a valid assessment of language outcomes requires a broader perspective of both the definition of language outcomes and the procedures for measuring them.

The concept of multiplism (Cook) is an underlying principle for the making of that broader perspective of assessment. Multiplism refers to situations when several options are available, when it is not clear what the correct option is, when the selection of an option depends on a variety of factors, and when one selected option often confirms others.

CONNECTING LANGUAGE KNOWLEDGE
WITH ASSESSMENT

Language testers have devoted much time and effort to defining what it means to know a language. As Bernard Spolsky reminds us, "Fundamental to the preparation of valid tests of language proficiency is the theoretical question of what does it mean to know a language?" (79). Clear descriptions of the structure of language enable testers to design procedures that will match them. In turn, the match between testing procedures and descriptions will directly improve the validity of language tests.

By matching the how of testing with the what of language, one can identify a number of periods in the development of language testing, each period having different definitions of language knowledge and the specific measurement procedures to go with them. Discrete-point testing viewed language as consisting of lexical and structural items; not surprisingly, language tests then consisted of isolated items that utilized objective testing procedures. In an integrative era, language tests tapped the integrated and discoursal nature of language. During the communicative period, tests were expected to replicate actual interaction among language users and utilize authentic oral and written texts and tasks. In the current performance-testing era, in which language is viewed in a contextualized manner, the language user is expected to perform tasks in well-defined and real-life contexts, often on the job. And in an alternative-assessment era, language knowledge is exemplified in a variety of contexts, and different types of assessment procedures try to capture those different aspects.

Discrete-Point Testing

In the discrete-point era, language tests assessed isolated items, mostly those of grammar and lexicon, following structural linguistic principles of the time. Objective tests, such as multiple-choice and true-false, focused on single and independent items like verb conjugations and lexicon identification in a decontextualized way. All language skills—reading, writing, listening, and speaking—were tested as discrete aspects of language. Even a productive skill such as writing was tested in a way (e.g., multiple-choice testing) that asked learners to identify sentences containing errors rather than to produce actual written language samples.

Integrative Language Testing

In the integrative era, language tests were viewed in a holistic and more contextualized manner, and they focused on global language samples, complete paragraphs, and full texts. Testing tasks included writing letters and comprehension of whole texts with minimal reference to isolated elements. Special attention was given to the cloze test, in which words were deleted from longer texts and the learner was expected to fill in the missing slots. John Oller, who promoted the cloze test, claimed that it tapped integrative language, a concept in line with a unitary notion of language based on the learner's pragmatic grammar of expectancy, which was presumed to underlie the learner's language knowledge. Oller contended that this knowledge constituted a psychological representation of the learner's ability to map utterances onto contexts ("Evidence" and *Tests*). While integrative tests such as the cloze were widely used and accepted by many language testers, critics noted that there was no evidence the tests had validity and questioned whether the tests in fact tapped the integrative nature of language. In any case, it became apparent that language tests needed to address discourse and not just isolated sentences, words, and structures.

Communicative Testing

The communicative era that followed reflected a view of language that is situated in discoursal and sociocultural contexts. The view arose from developments in linguistics and language teaching. In linguistics, it related to the introduction of the notions of communicative competence and communicative performance by Dell Hymes; in language teaching, it was associated with the shift from the teaching of isolated language elements to communicative language. Michael Canale and Merrill Swain refined Hymes's terms and listed the components of communicative competence to be linguistic competence, sociolinguistic competence, discourse competence, and strategic competence.

In that period we also find a growing emphasis on the notion of language proficiency, defined as the knowledge needed for a specific future situation and differentiated from achievement, which was associated with language knowledge learned in a given course, usually in the past.

The new definitions resulted in criticism of traditional noncommunicative language tests, which were believed to elicit artificial language. Instead, tests were demanded that would require test takers to produce real language as it was used among real people. John Clark called for direct tests, whose format duplicated as closely as possible the setting and operation of the real-life situations in which proficiency was normally demonstrated; such tests would provide information about the test takers' functional ability. Keith Morrow described direct tests as offering the opportunity for spontaneous operation of the language in authentic settings, in activities that learners would recognize as relevant and useful. Since direct tests had higher face validity, they were also believed to have a positive effect on learning and teaching, in contrast with indirect tests, which discouraged students from using actual writing and speaking language samples.

Performance Testing

More recently, language has been viewed as performance-based, a notion that recognizes that language knowledge interacts with a specific content area and context. Thus performance tests require test takers to perform language that is anchored in a specific context, to employ authentic tasks in that well-defined context (e.g., school, the workplace), and to integrate linguistic, situational, cultural, and affective aspects (Wesche). Timothy McNamara differentiates between strong and weak hypotheses of performance testing in terms of the interaction between language knowledge and the content area (*Measuring*). In the strong hypothesis, knowledge of the language is a necessary but not sufficient condition for success; success is measured, rather, in terms of performance on the given task. In the weak hypothesis, knowledge of the language is the main factor relevant for success.

Performance tests are most appropriate for a clientele with certain shared second language needs. The first step in constructing a performance test is to conduct a needs analysis to specify the context of the second language use; the type of interactions foreseen; the role, discourse types, and language functions to be performed; and the criteria on which successful fulfillment of the second language tasks is to be judged. These specifying statements can then be translated into test tasks and overall test design. The learners' performances are judged over a range of tasks that need to be sampled with a variety of instruments and procedures. Performance tests are generally assessed with the aid of rating scales that describe what a person can do in the language in a specific situation and context.

Alternative Assessment

The most recent trend in language testing, alternative assessment, is based on the realization that language knowledge is a complex phenomenon made up of different language types and that mastering one type is no guarantee of mastering others. Since no single procedure can capture this complex construct, multiple assessment procedures need to be devised that incorporate different instruments capable of seeing and capturing different aspects of various language domains. Examples of such instruments are the portfolio, peer assessment, observation, exhibition, and self-assessment.

Alternative assessment is often referred to as complementary assessment, since each instrument adds information that the other instruments cannot provide. This approach enables testers to elicit varied and multiple language samples in a variety of contexts and thus to obtain more valid evidence of the leaner's language ability.

MULTIPLISM

The periods in approaches to testing just surveyed should be viewed not as replacive but, rather, as cumulative and additive. Today's view of assessment is broad, encompassing both new features and features from earlier periods.

The resulting multiplism means that in each of the assessment phases it is possible to select features from a variety of options. It means that there are multiple purposes of language assessment, multiple definitions of language knowledge, multiple procedures for measuring that knowledge, multiple criteria for determining what good language is, and multiple ways of interpreting and reporting assessment results. In addition, there are multiple ways of designing items and tasks, administering assessment, determining the quality of procedures, reporting, and using the assessment results.

Thus the notion of multiplism provides a broad concept of language testing. It incorporates both achievement and proficiency, linguistic and communicative competence, competence and performance, tests and other procedures, objective testing and open tasks, communicative and performance tests, and a variety of assessment procedures that involve scoring and rating, holistic and analytic rating, description and judgment, profiles and scores, formative and summative assessment, one-shot as well as continued assessment, linguistic and extralinguistic factors.

THE PROCESS OF LANGUAGE ASSESSMENT

Assessment is a complex process that has many phases: deciding on the purpose of the assessment, defining language knowledge, selecting assessment procedures, designing test items and tasks, administering the tests, determining the criteria for the quality of the language, assessing the assessment procedures, interpreting the results, and evaluating and reporting. Applying multiplism to the process of testing implies that in each phase there are alternatives to choose from. The choices made are determined primarily by the purpose of the assessment.

Multiple Purposes of Assessment

Determining the purpose of an assessment is the most fundamental phase in the assessment process, because it is directly related to the definition of what it means to know a language. There are different purposes for assessing and different ways to classify them. Tests can be used to predict whether a person can perform a certain job in a future context or has mastered certain material learned in a course in the past. The two most common purposes are to improve learning, usually in a classroom context, and to make classification decisions (acceptance, placement, etc.) outside the classroom. But in each purpose there are a number of other purposes. In classroom achievement testing, one also wants to provide ongoing feedback that will affect improvement (formative assessment) and evaluate language skills at the end of a course (summative assessment). In addition to testing proficiency one might want to predict future performance in a specific context or place candidates at levels of ability (placement tests). One might also want to establish how students are doing after they enroll in a particular program or accept a particular job. Tests can be used for accountability when agencies such as ministries of education follow the effectiveness of the programs they support. Tests can be used for research purposes. Tests can create motivation, establish discipline, or exercise power (Shohamy, "Use"). Occasionally the declared purposes differ from the real ones.

In summary, assessment can be used to predict, to place, to categorize, to accept or reject, to provide feedback, to follow progress, to motivate, to discipline, to exercise power, to hold accountable, and to conduct research.

Multiple Ways of Defining Language Knowledge and Outcomes

Defining language knowledge determines the content and procedures that will be used in an assessment and in fact provides the theoretical and conceptual foundation of the assessment. In turn, it is dependent on assessment's purpose. For example, when the purpose is to learn how much knowledge students acquired in a given course, then the definition of that knowledge will be based on what the students are expected to master. When the purpose is to learn whether students can function in the workplace with the knowledge they have, the definition of that knowledge will be based on what is needed for the job.

The various approaches to defining language knowledge in the past were determined mostly by linguistic developments. Current definitions encompass features of the different periods: language viewed as isolated linguistic and structural elements; as performance-based and therefore interacting with specific domains, such as a course or a workplace; as a construct made up of a number of different domains.

The various definitions from the different periods have led to multiple classifications and competing theories of language knowledge. Oller defined language knowledge as a unitary competence based on the learner's pragmatic grammar of expectancy.

Hymes introduced the notion of communicative competence as referring to linguistic and communicative competence and pointing to the relation and interaction between grammatical and sociolinguistic competence and performance. Canale and Swain's perspective refined Hymes's idea to include linguistic competence, sociolinguistic competence, discourse competence, and strategic competence. A later model of language structure, developed by Lyle Bachman and by Bachman and Adrian Palmer, concentrates language ability around organizational competence, which consists of grammatical and textual subcompetencies, and pragmatic competence, which consists of sociolinguistic competencies. Bachman claims that textual competence is separate from grammatical competence; it includes knowledge of the conventions for joining utterances together to form a text, which is essentially a unit of language — spoken or written — consisting of two or more utterances or sentences connected according to rules of cohesion and rhetorical organization. Bachman's model consists of both competence and the capacity for implementing or executing that competence in appropriate contextualized communicative language.

There has been a growing emphasis by testers on the achievement component of language knowledge (Shohamy, "Modes"; Lynch and Davidson; Hancock; Liskin-Gasparro). Allan Collins, J. S. Brown, and S. E. Newman note that in the real world tasks are not necessarily the same as problems in school, which typically are structured to teach a particular skill, more or less in isolation from other skills. If procedures that learners need to master to use language in real-life communicative situations (reading strategies, vocabulary, grammar, and sociolinguistic rules) are taught in separate units, learners may not have them available for use in a given context. Language in real life is strongly dependent on context. But although proficiency is ideally the end goal of foreign language learning, it is not possible to reach proficiency without a series of carefully structured steps that are made in the achievement part of knowing a language. Thus both achievement and proficiency are essential components, and school learning provides important preparation.

Rating scales are another way of defining language knowledge. Based on hierarchical and functional descriptions, they usually range from zero to five. Different types of rating scales were developed according to the purpose of the assessment. Holistic scales, which define various degrees of language knowledge in global terms, are used mostly for summative purposes, like placement and proficiency testing. Analytic rating scales give hierarchies of language knowledge in terms of specific aspects (grammar, lexicon, fluency, pragmatics). The most well known rating scales are those developed in the United States by ACTFL and, in Australia, the Australian Second Language Proficiency Ratings. Although rating scales were developed originally as criteria for determining the quality of language samples on communicative tests, they often became the de facto definitions of language knowledge and today are widely used in secondary schools and colleges and for adult immigrants.

Because of the multiple ways of defining language knowledge, testers often turn to task-oriented approaches, as is done in performance testing. Once a specific context is defined, a sample of a performance behavior occurring in it is chosen, a task that elicits the performance is determined, the task is performed by a test taker in a simulated situation, a language sample is obtained, and the language sample is assessed by a rating scale that hierarchically describes what it means to know a language. For example, learners who can order a meal may be novices (1), learners who can conduct a casual conversation on a familiar topic with a boss may be advanced (2), and learners who can read a professional brochure in a business office may be advanced-high or superior-level (3).

Multiple Procedures for Assessment

Over the years the most commonly used procedures for assessing language were tests. But beginning in the 1960s United States government agencies, in need of more-authentic assessment procedures, experimented with oral interviews and self-assessment. In the oral interview, usually two examiners asked a person questions, using a variety of elicitation techniques; the interview was employed mostly to assess speaking ability. In the performance era, a variety of performance-based assessment procedures were used; more recently, there is a growing use of alternative procedures.

Because performance tests are often used to predict performance in the workplace (Wesche; McNamara; Sajavaara), they assess language ability by creating tasks that replicate real-life tasks. The tasks are direct and contextualized and feature simulative techniques such as roleplays (Jones; Bailey; Bachman). In this respect performance testing borrows from the field of vocational testing, where test takers are expected to carry out realistic tasks in actual or simulated settings (Carroll and Hall).

Randall Jones distinguishes among three types of performance tests by the degree to which the tasks require actual performances. In a direct-assessment type the test takers are placed in the actual target context, and assessment is made of how second language performance responds to the naturally evolving situation. In the work-sample type, tasks set in the target context enable control of elicitation and enable a comparison of the performance of different test takers, while contextual realism is retained. In the simulation type, settings and tasks are contrived to represent pertinent aspects of the real-life context. Role playing is frequently used as a simulation technique, with both examiner and examinee assuming roles. The oral interview is considered a performance test, since test takers are required to perform their language in a face-to-face interaction, often in a government or corporate context.

A work-related, semidirect performance test, in which test takers speak into a tape recorder in response to communicative tasks, was developed by the Center of Applied Linguistics in a number of languages (Stansfield and Kenyon). This test can be used for candidate teachers who will need to use a second language.

One procedure that has been popular since the 1970s is self-assessment. It is being increasingly used in determining language proficiency (Oscarson), although typically in a fashion that supplements others tests. In self-assessment, language learners judge their own language ability. Marjorie Wesche describes a performance test that is part of the instructional process and includes a self-assessment instrument based on a description of learners' performance for initial placement. Rating themselves on a series of descriptions of everyday situations that require listening or reading comprehension, students indicate skill levels on a five-point scale that ranges from "I cannot do this at all" to "I can do this all the time."

Recently there has been a growing use of a range of procedures: test, portfolio, observation, reflection, peer assessment, informal assessment, interview, project, simulation, exhibition, role play, diary, homework, dialogue journal, self-assessment. Instead of relying on single tests and procedures, testers choose from among a variety. Because language ability exemplified through one procedure cannot be guaranteed to emerge with another procedure, alternative assessment should be seen as complementary or supplementary: each procedure adds information that the other instruments did not provide.

Selection of specific assessment procedures depends not only on the purpose of the assessment and the definition of language knowledge but also on practicality factors such as cost, time, the availability of experts trained in developing and using the procedures, and the extent to which students have practice in using the procedures.

Multiple Ways of Designing Items and Tasks

After assessment procedures have been selected, the next step is to construct items and tasks that will elicit and assess the language ability. It is important to distinguish between items and tasks. Items are test questions or statements, such as multiple-choice or true-false, while tasks elicit more directly, telling the test takers what to do to produce language or responses to language. Items are used mostly for measuring comprehension (listening and reading), and tasks are used mostly for measuring production (speaking and writing).

The assessment of production takes place directly, because production is an observed skill. By contrast the act of comprehension cannot be observed; consequently there is a need to elicit it through a variety of stimulations. The test taker's responses are supposed to indicate whether comprehension has occurred.

Over the years language testers have developed a variety of items and tasks to obtain information about comprehension and production. These include multiple-choice, true-false, open-ended, summary, cloze, main-points, simulations, roleplay, and telephone. It is a well-documented phenomenon that both items and tasks affect the score and ratings that testers obtain, because some test takers do better in one procedure than in another. (Shohamy, "Does the Testing Method"; Gordon). Dan Douglas and Larry Selinker demonstrated how performance can vary when different topics are covered (e.g., a specialized professional topic vs. an everyday subject). Douglas and Selinker found that test takers' familiarity with the content of what is being communicated affects language proficiency and thinking and as a result the nature and fluency of what test takers communicate. Therefore generalizations from one discourse domain to another on language tests may not be justified. Gillian Brown showed the effect the title of a text had on scores, and I found significant differences among the scores of oral tests that represented different discourse styles and genres—for example, an interview, a reporting task ("Stability"). Ofra Inbar and I observed significant differences among scores on listening comprehension tests, depending on the genre (Shohamy and Inbar), and Charles Fillmore showed that procedures for processing discourse types differ from those that learners normally use in nontesting reading situations. Researching the effect of the test mode on scores, I found that although correlation between a direct and a semidirect test was high (Stansfield and Kenyon; Shohamy and Stansfield), qualitative analyses revealed that in fact different speech genres had emerged on the two tests (Shohamy, "Validity"). Smadar Donitsa-Schmidt, Ronit Waizar, and I examined the discourse obtained from five different elicitation procedures and found that it differed in a number of features (Shohamy, Donitsa-Schmidt, and Waizer). The language obtained from the machine-induced procedures (telephone, video recorder, and tape recorder) was more direct and did not involve pragmatic devices; the language elicited from the human interactions was more elaborated and indirect and involved a large number of pragmatic and social devices.

Research on the effect of items and tasks is being done by a variety of qualitative procedures as well. Ann Lazaraton and Heidi Riggenbach showed that interviewers routinely modify their question prompts for nonnative interlocutors in response to some perceived trouble. Using conversational analysis, Lazaraton and Riggenbach described a number of the question-turn modifications that occurred in interview data, and they showed that these modifications differed in a variety of testing situations as well as in ordinary conversations. Differences in conversational style among test takers of different proficiency levels were examined by Richard Young; he studied the amount of talk and rate of speaking (advanced learners talked more and faster than intermediate learners), the extent of context dependence (advanced learners elaborated more in answers to questions), and the ability to construct and sustain narratives (advanced learners could, intermediate learners could not).

Since each item, task, and assessment procedure affects performance, testers should select a variety and not rely on one.

Multiple Ways of Administering

In the past, standardized tests were administered, and all test takers were exposed to identical conditions of time, questions, and the use of pencil and paper; in recent years, more options in administration have allowed greater flexibility of conditions. Tests now can be administered to individuals or groups, in and out of the classroom, using computers, paper and pencil, audio and video recorders, or telephone. They can be administered by humans or machines, by external or internal assessors, by teachers or representatives of agencies and other institutions. They can be administered on various occasions: at the beginning, middle, or end of a program, or even after learners have been placed in a course or are already engaged in a program where the language is being followed, such as in the workplace. For any of these occasions assessment may be one-shot, continual after the fact, or it may have multiple durations. And tests can be administered informally as well as formally.

Multiple Criteria for Determining Language Quality

Once the test has been administered and the language sample obtained, the sample needs to be evaluated, that is, its quality needs to be determined by the application of certain criteria. The choice of criteria depends on decisions made in the earlier phases of the testing process—decisions about the purpose of the test, the definition of language knowledge, the type of items and tasks to be designed—and on a variety of practical considerations.

The criteria for determining the quality of the language may be categorized as follows:

Objective criteria are applied mostly to items for which there is only one correct answer, such as the correct choice in a multiple-choice item or the correct answer to a true-false item.

Diagnostic criteria are those used by the tester to focus on specific aspects in greater detail. They are applied to pedagogical and learning strategies that lead to improvement.

Impressionistic criteria are applied generally; no specific area is chosen as the focus of the evaluation.

Rating-scale criteria are the most common basis for assessing language quality. Specific descriptions define a priori what good language is, in hierarchical and functional levels usually ranging from zero to five, beginner to advanced. Different types of rating scales have been developed according to the purpose of the assessment. Holistic scales assess global language, giving the raters' impression of the entire oral or written samples produced; these scales are used mainly for summative evaluation purposes, such as placement and proficiency testing.[1]

Analytic scales assess specific features in language, such as grammar, lexicon, fluency, or pragmatics. They are suited for classroom situations, because they provide students and teachers with feedback opportunities about specific aspects of language. Primary-trait scoring ascertains whether a language sample exhibits characteristics crucial to the specific rhetorical task that the written or oral language sample was intended to accomplish.

Problems arise from the use of rating-scales criteria. Using the native speaker as the norm, as most rating scales do, may not be appropriate. Although ACTFL specifies top-quality language to be that of an educated native speaker, it is debatable that such a norm exists, given the great variance among native speakers. Paulette Marisi shows that in one language different communities speak differently. This complicates the concept of a correct or ideal language.

The language-testing literature for many years has debated the wisdom of taking the native speaker as the measure against which performance is to be assessed (Bachman; Alderson). Jan Hamilton, Marilyn Lopes, Timothy McNamara, and Eileen Sheridan claim that performance on a test involves factors other than second language proficiency. In any case, using the native speaker as the measure is not appropriate when the purpose of the assessment is to find out whether students have mastered what has been learned in a particular foreign language class, because it may be a long time before they can remotely be compared with native speakers.

Multiple Ways of Assessing Assessment Procedures

After the assessment procedures have been administered and rated or scored, their quality needs to be examined. In large-scale, high-stakes testing this phase takes place before the actual administration of the test, through a pilot study. In most other situations this examination occurs after the test has been administered and scored but before scores are reported. The understanding is that, even if the test is found to be less than satisfactory, there will be other opportunities to evaluate the learners. When the quality of the assessment procedures has been examined, they are revised and the scores are reported. The quality of the procedures, too, is largely determined by the purpose of the assessment.

Most of the work of examining the quality of assessment procedures occurs in an external testing context, although these procedures will be used in classroom situations. There is therefore doubt about their appropriateness for the classroom. By contrast, not many criteria have been developed for examining the quality of assessment procedures used as part of classroom teaching and learning. Similarly, few criteria have been developed for examining the quality of procedures that are not tests (e.g., portfolios, self-assessment). There is an ongoing debate whether such alternative procedures need to apply existing procedures or may develop totally new ones to match better the new paradigm in assessment (Moss; Delanshere and Pertosky; Messick).

The quality of assessment procedures can be examined in a number of ways. Multiplism here implies the need to select the most appropriate ways.

Examination occurs on two interrelated levels: the assessment procedure as a whole and the specific items and tasks contained in it. Two main criteria are essential: reliability and validity. Reliability provides information on how accurate the procedures are; validity provides information on the extent to which the procedures measure what they are intended to measure. Again, it is the purpose of the assessment that leads to anticipation of where instability or unreliability will occur. That determination influences the precise form of reliability that an assessment designer will examine. To determine the extent to which a procedure's items and tasks measure the same things, internal-consistency reliability is examined; to establish agreement on the quality of language obtained from open-ended tasks, interrater reliability is examined; to ascertain whether the procedure elicits results that are consistent over time, test-retest reliability is examined; and to ensure that two versions of the same procedure elicit similar information, parallel-form reliability is examined.

The validity of assessment procedures also depends on their purpose. If future behavior is to be predicted, for example, on an entrance or placement test, then predictive validity will be examined; if one test is intended to replace another, then concurrent validity will be examined; if specific learning content is to be sampled, then content validity must be established; and if there is a need to determine whether what is being assessed is actually based on a specific theory of the field, then construct validity must be established.

Two other criteria for assessing assessment procedures are often used: the difficulty level of the procedures, which is reflected by the score that a group of learners obtained on the procedure, and the variance that through determination of the standard deviations provides information on whether the group is homogeneous or heterogeneous.

Procedures vary according to how difficult or easy their items and tasks are and to the extent that the items and tasks differentiate among different proficiency levels of learners. Numerous techniques related to item response theory can ensure that the analysis is performed in a way that keeps the data free of the specific sample being assessed.

The above criteria are applicable to most procedures, not only to tests. Thus it is possible to determine the average score of all the learners who submitted portfolios, to determine what the variance was, whether the different raters who examined the portfolio agreed about its quality, whether the portfolio sampled the appropriate context, and whether the portfolio provided a good predictor for future behavior. Determining what an acceptable level of performance is depends on a variety of factors: on whether the test is norm-referenced (aimed at differentiating among learners) or criterion-referenced (aimed at assessment according to specific criteria), or even on whether agreement among assessors is expected.

Multiple Ways of Interpreting Results

Recently testers have begun to realize that reporting test scores is not enough: there is a need to interpret them. Interpretation contextualizes a score, that is, it identifies the factors that led to the score. For example, a score of a test must be interpreted according to the length of the course that preceded it, the quality of the teaching, the structure of the curriculum, and the effort the test taker put into the test. Whether the score an immigrant language learner obtained on a language test is good or bad depends on the context: on how long the person has been in the country, on what type of program the person was exposed to, on how much effort the person invested in learning.

There are a number of ways to interpret results. David Nevo discusses the concept of a dialogue between internal and external evaluators to arrive at an understanding. I have introduced the concept of a conference where all those involved in the assessment take an active part in judging the information—the test taker, the language teacher, the classroom teacher, and often a parent ("Language Testing"). The interpretation phase is especially important in situations where a variety of different assessment procedures are used, each providing unique information. There is a need for an interpretation session that contextualizes the information obtained from them. In this constructivist view of assessment, the total does not equal the sum of all the parts.

Multiple Ways of Reporting Results

Once the information from the different procedures is obtained, contextualized, and discussed, it needs to be reported to different audiences who have different interests in the assessment results. The audience, also, will vary depending on the purpose of the assessment. The audience may include the learners themselves, the language teacher, the language program director, the municipality, the ministry of education, and the school. The type of information disseminated will need to match the needs of the audience.

For example, learners may be interested in obtaining detailed and diagnostic information so that they can improve their performance; a teacher may be interested in aspects that will provide information about specific pedagogical strategies; a program director may seek information that shows how many students are above or below a pass level; a national assessment audience may want to know how many learners belong to specific categories.

AN EXAMPLE OF MULTIPLISM IN ASSESSMENT

Although the main purpose of assessment is to focus on language knowledge, assessment can include other factors that are known to affect language learning: the level of L1 proficiency and learners' attitudes toward the language program, toward language learning in general, toward the textbook, and toward the strategy used in language learning. Here is an example of an assessment procedure that demonstrates, for each of the nine phases discussed above, how multiplism can be applied to a specific assessment system (Shohamy, "Language Testing"):

Multiple Purposes of Assessment The context of this assessment is the need to assess the learning of Hebrew as a second language among immigrant children (grades 2 to 12) in Israel. The purpose of the assessment is to identify the language areas (in reading and writing) that are problematic for these children so that pedagogical treatments to help them can be designed. Another purpose is to determine whether students have passed the threshold level to participate in regular classes.

Four principles underly the assessment: a precise definition is needed of proficient reading and writing in L2 for the children in the different age levels, different procedures need to be employed to tap language knowledge in the variety of situations where it is used, the information obtained from the different procedures must be interpreted and contextualized, and the information must lead to pedagogical and instructional strategies.

MULTIPLE WAYS OF DEFINING LANGUAGE KNOWLEDGE The assessment model based on the multiplism principle (see fig.) asks for a knowledge of reading and writing that includes a basic, threshold ability (the mastery of the elementary features of the language); an academic ability (language needed for each school subject); a "life" ability (language needed for use out of school contexts); and the ability to use learning aids, such as the dictionary and the library.

These areas of language knowledge were arrived at through extensive discussions with educational experts: subject matter teachers, Hebrew-as-a-second-language teachers, curriculum planners, and second language experts. The areas were then converted into tables of specifications for each of the four age levels (low elementary, grades 2–4; high elementary, grades 5–6; middle school, grades 7–9; and senior high, grades 10–12).

MULTIPLE PROCEDURES FOR ASSESSMENT　The rationale for using alternative procedures in this context was that language proficiency of immigrant

ASSESSMENT MODEL BASED ON THE MULTIPLISM PRINCIPLE: THE COMPONENTS OF THE EVALUATION

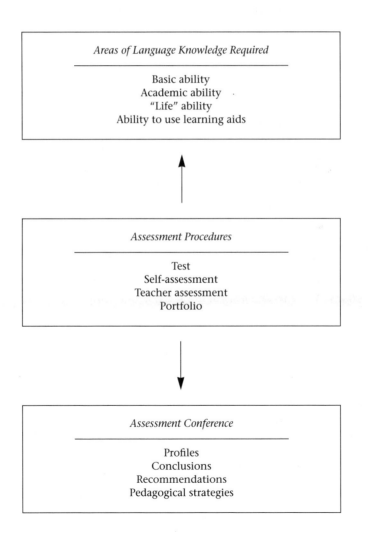

Areas of Language Knowledge Required

Basic ability
Academic ability
"Life" ability
Ability to use learning aids

Assessment Procedures

Test
Self-assessment
Teacher assessment
Portfolio

Assessment Conference

Profiles
Conclusions
Recommendations
Pedagogical strategies

children was exemplified in a variety of contexts and that therefore meaningful insights into the children's language could be obtained by sampling that variety. Thus instruments that tapped different aspects of the language were used, and each instrument contributed unique information. Through the use of multiple instruments a comprehensive picture of the achievement and proficiency of the immigrant children was obtained. The information from the varied sources was then contextualized and interpreted in a dialogue among the different assessment participants; the children, the second language teacher, the subject matter teacher, and parents.

As can be seen in the figure, four procedures were selected for the assessment: a test; self-assessment; observations by two teachers, one a humanities teacher and the other a science teacher; and a portfolio, in which students selected language samples of reading and writing from a set list. An assessment conference, in which the language teacher, the student's home teacher, and often a parent of the student met with the student to discuss and interpret the results, followed the administration of all four procedures. The assessment conference led to profiles, conclusions, recommendations, and pedagogical strategies.

MULTIPLE WAYS OF DESIGNING ITEMS AND TASKS In the different procedures, various types of items and tasks were used: multiple-choice, completion, matching, cloze, and open-ended questions. The written part of the test included specific tasks that defined the purpose, the function, and the audience of the writing. The portfolio was accompanied by a Likert-scale questionnaire, as was the self-assessment. The teacher observations included questionnaires that were accompanied by a series of open-ended, essay-type questions. All items and tasks addressed the four components of knowledge: basic ability, academic ability, "life" ability, and the ability to use learning aids.

MULTIPLE WAYS OF ADMINISTERING The test was performed by students in their own time and in any place—in the library, at home. Likewise, the self-assessment had no fixed venue. The portfolio was administered throughout the three-month semester. The teacher observation was often done by the teacher after class.

MULTIPLE CRITERIA FOR DETERMINING LANGUAGE QUALITY The test questions were rated mostly as right or wrong, to point to specific problem areas. Scales were used to rate the writing, and it was possible to summarize the different performances to arrive at individual profiles for each student in each of the areas defined.

MULTIPLE WAYS OF ASSESSING ASSESSMENT PROCEDURES Examination of the psychometric properties of the assessment battery analyzed the correlations among the four procedures and studied the contribution of each instrument to the general profile, the interrater reliability, the relation among the scores of the Hebrew-as-a-second-language assessment procedures, and the use of the instruments by teachers, which was expressed by the conclusions and recommendations the teachers made as a result of the conference.

Results indicated that rater reliability for the four instruments was high but that the correlation between observations of the humanities teacher and the science teacher was low. This low correlation shows that each teacher's assessment can be regarded as a unique source of information, because the students behaved differently in the different classes and because the different subjects required different degrees of reliance on language texts. Results showed that the test explained the variance of the general profile best; next came teacher assessment, then self-assessment, then the portfolio, which added little information. Yet all four instruments together explained eighty-seven percent of the variance in the students' general profiles. It was also found that the recommendations were not elaborated and specific enough: teachers had difficulties synthesizing and summarizing the information from the different assessment sources and translating it into instructional strategies. The assessment conference did indeed help contextualize the information, but too often it turned out to be the only source of contextualization. Steps are being taken now to improve the assessment system in these areas, especially in training teachers to consider all the procedures; to synthesize, summarize, and contextualize the information; and to connect that information with pedagogical recommendations. This final step in particular would indicate clearly that a shift toward alternative assessment requires different types of skills and intensive training.

MULTIPLE WAYS OF INTERPRETING RESULTS In the conference held with the student, the classroom teacher, the language teacher, and often the student's parent, the documents obtained from the different sources were reviewed and interpreted in the context of time on task, background of student, length of stay in the new country, conditions under which the student lived, and the student's motivation in the different subjects.

MULTIPLE WAYS OF REPORTING RESULTS Results were mostly reported in individual profiles, and pedagogical strategies and decisions were based on those profiles.

When multiple assessment is introduced, its users must be specially trained to relate the results obtained from the different instruments and, more important, to synthesize, summarize, and contextualize information so that the entire assessment process may lead to meaningful recommendations that can be used by language teachers for making pedagogical decisions. Without such training, the whole advantage of using multiple assessment is easily defeated. To reap the undeniable benefits of multiple assessment also requires asking new questions about the quality of the instruments and attending to new components of the assessment process.

Testing is a complex process that involves a number of phases, and each phase allows a number of options. It is therefore difficult and even inappropriate to prescribe formulas of assessment. Rather, a familiarity with all the options is a precondition for making decisions about which criteria should apply to the specific context of assessment. Thus making assessment choices requires extensive knowledge and consideration of a range of aspects in the process of language teaching and learning. Such knowledge is essential for creating appropriate assessment procedures, because assessment is not just writing tests; it involves a host of factors that affect the learning of languages. Assessment is shaped by its specific context, its purpose, the type of knowledge it addresses, the procedures it selects, by the different criteria for determining success, by different interpretations and different ways of reporting results. This multiplicity may seem overwhelming at first, but it opens new avenues for matching assessment to contexts and for making quality choices that are likely to have greater benefits for learners and teachers precisely because assessment and learning are seen not as separate activities but as intimately related to each other.

Over the years, language testing has been a highly productive discipline in theory and practice, a discipline whose various approaches have been developed depending on the definitions of language knowledge at the time. As a discipline closely allied to applied linguistics and drawing on a number of theories of language acquisition and learning, language testing could proceed in varied directions. But language testing has done more than attempt to relate assessment procedures to language knowledge; it has also incorporated into itself developments in general education measurement. Applying the approach of multiplism continues this beneficial tradition.

NOTE

1. Global and holistic rating scales were also developed (in Australia and the US) as yardsticks and standards of hierarchical functional proficiency of performance in the four language skills ("ACTFL Proficiency Guidelines 1986") and are widely used today in secondary schools, colleges, and for adult immigrants.

WORKS CITED

"ACTFL Proficiency Guidelines 1986." *Defining and Developing Proficiency: Guidelines, Implementations, and Concepts.* Ed. Heidi Byrnes and Michael Canale. Lincolnwood: Natl. Textbook, 1987. 15–24.

Alderson, Charles. "Native and Non-native Speaker Performance on Cloze Tests." *Language Learning* 30 (1980): 59–76.

Bachman, Lyle. *Fundamental Considerations in Language Testing.* Oxford: Oxford UP, 1990.

Bachman, Lyle, and Adrian S. Palmer. *Language Testing in Practice.* Oxford: Oxford UP, 1996.

Bailey, Kathleen M. "If I Had Known Then What I Know Now: Performance Testing of Foreign Teaching Assistants." Hauptman, LeBlanc, and Wesche 153–80.

Brown, Gillian. "Making Sense: The Interaction of Linguistic Expression and Contextual Information." *Applied Linguistics* 10 (1989): 97–108.

Canale, Michael, and Merrill Swain. "Theoretical Bases of Communicative Approaches to Second Language Teaching and Testing." *Applied Linguistics* 1 (1980): 1–47.

Carroll, Brendan J., and Patrick J. Hall. *Make Your Own Language Tests.* Oxford: Pergamon, 1985.

Clark, John L. D. *Direct Testing of Speaking Proficiency: Theory and Practice.* Princeton: ETS, 1975.

Collins, Allan, J. S. Brown, and S. E. Newman. "Cognitive Apprenticeship: Teaching the Crafts of Reading, Writing, and Mathematics." *Knowing, Learning, and Instruction: Essays in Honor of Robert Glaser.* Ed. Lauren B. Resnick. Hillsdale: Erlbaum, 1989. 459–94.

Cook, Thomas. "Postpositivist Critical Multiplism." *Social Science and Social Policy.* Ed. R. Lance Shotland and Melvin M. Mark. Beverly Hills: Sage, 1985. 21–62.

Delanshere, Ginette, and Anthony Pertosky. "Capturing Teachers' Knowledge: Performance Assessment a) and Post-structuralist Epistemology, b) from a Post-structuralist Perspective, c) and Post-structuralism, d) None of the Above." *Educational Researcher* 23.5 (1994): 5–10.

Douglas, Dan, and Larry Selinker. "Performance on a General vs. a Field-Specific Test of Speaking Proficiency by International Teaching Assistants." Twelfth Language Testing Research Colloquium, San Francisco. 1990.

Fillmore, Charles J. "Ideal Readers and Real Readers." *Analyzing Discourse: Text and Talk.* Ed. Deborah Tannen. Georgetown Univ. Round Table on Langs. and Linguistics, 1981. Washington: Georgetown UP, 1981. 248–70.

Gordon, Claire. "The Effect of Testing Method on Achievement in Reading Comprehension Tests in English as a Foreign Language." MA thesis, Tel Aviv U, 1987.

Hamilton, Jan, Marilyn Lopez, Timothy F. McNamara, and Eileen Sheridan. "Rating Scales and Native Speaker Performance on a Communicatively Oriented EAP Test." *Melbourne Papers in Applied Linguistics* 2 (1993): 1–24.

Hancock, Charles, ed. *Teaching, Testing, and Assessing: Making the Connection.* Lincolnwood: Natl. Textbook, 1994.

Hauptman, Philip C., Raymond LeBlanc, and Marjorie B. Wesche, eds. *Second Language Performance Testing.* Ottawa: U of Ottawa P, 1985.

Hymes, Dell. "On Communicative Competence." *Sociolinguistics: Selected Readings.* Ed. John B. Pride and Janet Holmes. Harmondsworth, Eng.: Penguin, 1972. 269–83.

Jones, Randall. "Second Language Performance Testing: An Overview." Hauptman, LeBlanc, and Wesche 15–24.

Lazaraton, Ann, and Heidi Riggenbach. "Oral Skills Testing. A Rhetorical Task Approach." *Applied Linguistics* 1 (1990): 196–217.

Liskin-Gasparro, Judith E. "Practical Approaches to Outcomes Assessment. The Undergraduate Major in Foreign Languages and Literature." *ADFL Bulletin* 26.2 (1995): 21–27.

Lynch, Brian K., and Fred G. Davidson. "Criterion-Referenced Language Test Development: Linking Curricula, Teachers, and Tests." *TESOL Quarterly* 28 (1994): 727–43.

Marisi, Paulette. "Questions of Regionalism in Native Speaker OPI Performance: The French-Canadian Experience." *Foreign Language Annals* 27 (1994): 505–21.

McNamara, Timothy F. *Measuring Second Language Performance: A New Era in Language Testing.* London: Longman, 1996.

Messick, Samuel. "The Interplay of Evidence and Consequences in the Validation of Performance Assessments." *Educational Researcher* 23.2 (1994): 13–23.

Morrow, Keith E. *Techniques of Evaluation for a Notional Syllabus.* Reading: Centre for Applied Lang. Studies, U of Reading, 1977.

Moss, Pamela. "Can There Be Validity without Reliability?" *Educational Researcher* 23.2 (1994): 5–11.

Nevo, David. "Utilization of Evaluation as a Basis for a Dialogue between Internal and External Decision Makers." Shohamy and Walton 43–49.

Oller John. "Evidence for a General Language Proficiency Factor: An Expectancy Grammar." *Die neueren Sprachen* 2 (1975): 165–74.

———. *Language Tests in School.* London: Longman, 1979.

Oscarson, Mats. "Self-Assessment of Language Proficiency: Rationale and Applications." *Language Testing* 6 (1989): 1–13.

Sajavaara, Kari. "Designing Tests to Match the Needs of the Workplace." Shohamy and Walton 123–44.

Shohamy, Elana. "Does the Testing Method Make a Difference? The Case of Reading Comprehension." *Language Testing* 1 (1984): 147–70.

———. "Language Testing: Matching Assessment Procedures with Language Knowledge." *Alternatives in Assessment of Achievements, Learning Processes, and Prior Knowledge.* Ed. Menucha Birenbaum and Filip J. R. C. Dochy. Boston: Kluwer, 1996.

———. "New Modes of Assessment: The Connection between Testing and Learning." Shohamy and Walton 7–28.

———. "The Stability of the Oral Proficiency Trait on the Oral Interview Speaking Test." *Language Learning* 33 (1983): 527–39.

———. "The Use of Language Tests for Power and Control." *Educational Linguistics, Crosscultural Communication, and Global Interdependence.* Ed. James E. Alatis. Georgetown Univ. Round Table on Langs. and Linguistics, 1994. Washington: Georgetown UP, 1994. 57–72.

———. "The Validity of Direct versus Semi-direct Oral Tests." *Language Testing* 11 (1994): 99–124.

Shohamy, Elana, Smadar Donitsa-Schmidt, and Ronit Waizer. "The Effects of the Elicitation Mode on the Language Samples Obtained on Oral Tests." Lang. Testing Research Colloquium. Cambridge, UK. Aug. 1993.

Shohamy, Elana, and Ofra Inbar. "Validation of Listening Comprehension Tests: The Effect of Text and Question Type." *Language Testing* 8 (1991): 23–40.

Shohamy, Elana, and Charles Stansfield. "The Hebrew Speaking Test: An Example of International Cooperation in Test Development and Validation." *AILA Review* 7 (1991): 83–95.

Shohamy, Elana, and A. Ronald Walton, eds. *Language Assessment for Feedback: Testing and Other Strategies*. Dubuque: Kendall, 1992.

Spolsky, Bernard. "Preliminary Studies in the Development of Techniques for Testing Overall Second Language Proficiency." *Language Learning* 3 (1968): 79–101.

Stansfield, Charles W., and Dorrie M. Kenyon. "Development of the Portuguese Speaking Test: Year One Project Report on Development of Semi-direct Tests of Oral Proficiency in Hausa, Hebrew, Indonesian, and Portuguese." Alexandria: ERIC, 1988. ED 296586.

Wesche, Marjorie Bingham. "Performance Testing for Work-Related Second Language Assessment." Shohamy and Walton 103–22.

Young, Richard. "Conversational Styles in Language Proficiency Interviews." *Language Learning* 45 (1995): 3–42.

Constructing Curricula in Collegiate Foreign Language Departments

Heidi Byrnes

The preceding essays of this volume have provided an overview of research and scholarship in the field of second language acquisition. My essay investigates the contributions SLA research might be able to make to the life of language and literature departments in terms of their curricula. I do not discuss foreign language curricula in the customary sense but instead argue that SLA research has already produced a body of knowledge that can enrich curricular thinking in foreign language departments, and I outline the implications this research has for the construction of future curricula.

Accumulated SLA research results provide an intellectual foundation that can help foreign language departments achieve a comprehensiveness and coherence for their entire undergraduate program that has eluded them thus far; a substantive answer to the question of whether foreign language instruction in the customary sense belongs in colleges at all; an overarching curricular concept that harnesses the increasingly powerful centrifugal forces departments experience when language becomes only a tool for a host of disciplinary and professional interests across the academic spectrum; and a bridging of the deep discontinuities among the diverse scholarly interests held by faculty members in foreign language departments. This is the same intellectual foundation that is the goal of collegiate foreign language instruction as expressed by the term *multiple literacies*.

In the past, the achievement of that goal seemed inhibited by theoretical stances and empirical insights prevailing in SLA research itself or, to put it more precisely, by the perceived or real distance of that research and its subsequent practice from literary scholarship. Now, however, the chances of reaching the goal depend more on the ability and willingness of faculty members to create the kind of cooperative departmental culture that is required for all curriculum construction.

Given the generally impoverished curricular thinking among foreign language faculty members and given the formidable negative forces throughout the academy, to create an encompassing and coherent curriculum will require vision and competent and steady leadership from the department's head, along with broad institutional support and uncommon cooperation, knowledge, and wisdom on the part of all faculty members. As my introduction to this volume shows in sketching the current tension in foreign language departments, the challenges are great. But if these challenges are met, the benefits for departments and, more important, for students' learning, are also great.

THE CHANGING FOCI OF SLA RESEARCH

It is by no means a foregone conclusion that SLA research should have produced a body of knowledge that can be expected to inform curricular work. The following historical overview explains this possibly surprising statement.

The field reached the current state of rich information about adult instructed learning of a foreign language only after exploring a number of other areas, for example, naturalistic second language acquisition by children or adults; naturalistic second language acquisition by learners, often immigrants, in an environment where that language is both spoken and instructed (ESL learning is the best-researched instance of this kind of L2 learning); and acquisition of both foreign and second languages by learners in diverse bilingual and immersion programs, often at the precollegiate level (Brinton, Snow, and Wesche; Harley, Allen, Cummins, and Swain). One can easily imagine many permutations of these major second language learning situations. In fact, the very definition of what second and foreign languages are, whether or not they are learned in an instructed environment, is by no means as clear-cut as those terms would seem to suggest (Valdés).

Though many insights were gained from studies in these areas, the remarkable growth in SLA research during the last twenty years or so is due to a shift that began to accelerate in the 1960s, a shift from the teaching and methodology side of the teaching-learning dyad to the learning or acquisition side. This focus on learners and the processes they engage in now characterizes the SLA field, as the essays of this volume have reported on the field's aspects: the distinct research methodology; the different kinds of data analyses (e.g., contrastive, error performance, discourse); the central construct of interlanguage with its key notions of systematic variation, common acquisition orders, and developmental sequences; the investigation of different linguistic environments, with particular attention to similarities and differences between first and second language acquisition, notably in the nature of the input; the attempts to explain differential success among second language learners by age, aptitude, social-psychological factors, cognitive style, and learning strategies; and, finally, the field's theories. (See Larsen-Freeman and Long for a comprehensive overview.)

But even that shift did not in and of itself make the teaching and learning of a foreign language in an instructed setting an important research focus of SLA. A nativist theoretical stance regarding second language learning dominated the agenda for a long time, and there was more interest in investigating the similarities of all second language learning, regardless of the setting, than in investigating the differences between naturalistic and instructed learning. Only recently has the classroom, with its unique characteristics regarding the effects of instruction, become a researchable learning environment in its own right. As a result, generalizations about the processes learners engage in, including adult instructed foreign language learners, are now available. These generalizations can become part of a critique of current curricular practice and inform future directions for curricular development.

THEORY AND PRACTICE OF CURRICULUM DEVELOPMENT IN FOREIGN LANGUAGE DEPARTMENTS

In general, foreign language departments have not adopted the kind of comprehensive viewpoint that should be at the heart of curriculum construction. Few curricula are the result of an agreed-on framework, of a set of understandings according to which instructional approaches, individual courses, and materials cohere (but see Grandin, Einbeck, and Reinhart for a curriculum for a highly targeted population; Allen; Lange, "Curricular Crisis" and "Sketching"; Swaffar, "Using"; and see Yalden for conceptualizations of comprehensive general language curricula).

Faculty members commonly characterize curricular planning in foreign language departments as one of the most vexing tasks they face, despite the importance of such cooperative planning for the life of a department and the welfare of its faculty members. This work is impeded, all but stifled, by the poorly established notion of curriculum itself and therefore the limited expertise faculty members have in curricular practice; by the substantive and institutional obstacles to curricular change, which are particularly strong in the foreign language field; by the well-known bifurcation of programs into language and content courses; and by the changing contexts of higher education that deeply affect programs.

The Notion of Curriculum and Its Manifestation in the Foreign Language Field

GENERAL CONSIDERATIONS REGARDING CURRICULUM

In the term's most basic sense, *curriculum* means the attempt to devise a sequence of educational opportunities for learners that builds on internal interrelations and continuities among the major units of instruction (at the college level, a course is the traditional unit) to enhance learning. Critical considerations are the selection of content and its sequencing—the what of the curriculum—and its delivery in both the larger educational environment and the particular instructional setting—the how of the curriculum.

This characterization of curriculum seems straightforward enough, but the development of curricula, no matter what the discipline or field, is much contested, as anyone engaged in core curriculum construction knows. The reason is that a curriculum is essentially a policy decision about the purpose and nature of education. Like all policy decisions, it has deep ideological roots. In a revealing discussion of syllabi in the British educational system, Christopher Candlin differentiates between two kinds of syllabi, each representing a different ideology: "One [form] requires learners, in Freire's (1975) critique, to bank received knowledge as a collection of 'communiques' or states of knowing, and the other. . . . in Dewey's (1910) sense, encourages learners to explore ways of knowing, to interpret knowledge and to engage in dialogue with it and with themselves. A negotiation, if you like, both of knowledge and of the procedures for engaging that knowledge" (30). As Henry Widdowson notes, "Formal education is of its nature a superposed second order culture which consists of schemes of conceptual organization and behaviour designed to supplement the first order processes of primary socialization. . . . The whole set of such schemes constitutes the curriculum" (23). In other words, far from being "natural" to a subject, a curriculum is a critical act of defining what the subject is, and that definition directly relates to goals of educating students.

For example, the goal of education might be to cultivate in men and women intellectual, moral, and imaginative qualities that enable them to become competent, visionary, and wise persons who can lead flourishing and rewarding lives as they respond with compassion and commitment to the demands for just societies around the world. In that case, foreign language learning should be conceptualized so that it contributes to that goal, preferably by making its contribution explicit, in theory and in practice, and also unique.

A curriculum is also a critical act of defining the role of the learner and, by extension, the act of learning. In the past, discussion was dominated by philosophical, moral, psychological, and sociopolitical perspectives that were expressed primarily in a normative, prescriptive, and overly individualistic fashion. Increasingly, however, the role of the learner and the act of learning are seen as variable, creative, and socioculturally grounded, and therefore critically dependent on the learner's being engaged—in both the active and passive meaning of *engaged*—even within the confines of an educational institution. Thus the extent to which the new learning paradigm is being followed can be ascertained by looking at the institutional context.

Learning and the learner should be at the heart of the academic enterprise, but an analysis of academic structures and procedures reveals that this is by no means the case. Robert Barr and John Tagg characterize the prevailing situation in American higher education in the following fashion: "The paradigm that has governed our colleges is this: A college is an institution that exists *to provide instruction*. Subtly but profoundly we are shifting to a new paradigm: A college is an institution that exists *to produce learning*" (13). The provider-customer-producer terminology may not be to everyone's liking; it is uncomfortably reminiscent of the management approach to education and learning. Be that as it may, the authors' eye-opening conclusion is that higher education will have to rethink itself to the core in order to undergo the shift from static to engaged learning. The mission of higher education, its criteria for success, teaching and learning structures, conceptualizations of learning, productivity and funding, and roles and rewards— all will have to change dramatically for the engaged learner and learning to be central.

The implications of shifting the focus to engaged learning are particularly far-reaching in the area of curriculum. As it stands, a college education is usually "the sum of the student's experience of a series of discrete, largely unrelated, three-credit classes" (Barr and Tagg 19). In response to a range of educational problems, the instructional paradigm continually generates additional, atomized, discrete instructional units: the individual courses. Departments, the key units of the academy, protect their interests by protecting courses, since faculty positions and courses, in a mutually dependent fashion, are what justify funding levels.

In contrast, a learning paradigm, framing learning holistically and recognizing that the chief agents of learning are the learners, requires thinking of curricula as value-laden choices that present particular beliefs or ideologies, to use current terminology. The relation the learner is given or encouraged to have with the content of a curriculum is critically different, both in the kind of knowledge that is selected and in how that knowledge is acquired and ultimately made available for use. Candlin writes:

> A syllabus of the former type [the syllabus of received knowledge] is extrinsic, idealistic and presents a picture of static "reality"; the latter type [a syllabus that explores ways of knowing] is personal, intrinsic and is one of "reality" in process . . . [and] acts to engage and challenge this world-view, through a praxis of action and reflection by all the participants to question its content and organization. (30)

CURRICULUM IN THE FOREIGN LANGUAGES

In the foreign language field, too, the notion of curriculum has been explicated in terms of complex interrelations. Jack Richards locates curriculum in a larger "matrix," which is "a metaphor for an interactive and multidimensional view of language teaching seen to result from interactions among the curriculum, teachers, students, methodology, and instructional materials. In particular, three factors are singled out as central to effective teaching: the curriculum, methodology, and instructional materials" (vii). Any curriculum discussion must at the very least address objectives, content, and sequential arrangement—in American educational parlance, the scope and sequence of a curriculum.

Since language learning in and of itself is a major concern in foreign language departments, a comprehensive understanding of the notion of curriculum requires departments, first of all, to face inherent ideological choices about the nature of language and about the nature of the learning process in the specific instance of instructed second language learning. It is a well-known fact that departments have not confronted those choices comprehensively, either from the various disciplinary vantage points that they represent or with an understanding of critical educational issues as those issues arise in curriculum construction. As a consequence, departments have been unable to address satisfactorily two central goals of a foreign language curriculum: ensuring that their students learn the foreign language in a nontrivial way and that they are educated and formed — the German words *gebildet* and *Bildung* come to mind—on the basis of that learning experience as it extends throughout their undergraduate experience and into graduate study.

J. P. B. Allen attempts to capture the relevant issues in four major approaches in general curriculum theory, approaches that influence foreign language curricula (63–64):

The academic approach, with its concern for encouraging the understanding of a discipline, has in the past fostered such directions in language teaching as grammar translation or the cognitive code approach, which favored abstract linguistic structures. Current manifestations of such an approach can be expected to emphasize the performance aspect of language in use as a basis for curriculum construction.

The technological approach, with its empirical emphasis on manipulated, measured, and observed outcomes, found a synergy with structuralism and behaviorism that resulted in the dominance of the audiolingual approach. Though that methodology has been largely discredited in the communicative era, it is still very much alive in prevailing approaches to assessment.

The humanist approach, with its concern for personal growth of the individual, has tried to promote self-realization of the learner in the foreign language classroom. It therefore prefers what it considers natural as contrasted with prescriptive (usually formalist-normative) approaches and emphasizes cooperative interaction in the classroom. The social-reformist approach focuses on issues that pertain to society. Its most prominent manifestations in the language teaching community are in the wealth of programs for immigrants and in efforts for language maintenance and bilingualism (see Valdés on Spanish heritage speakers in the United States), efforts for language planning (e.g., the Canadian immersion programs), and efforts, more diffuse, aimed at creating a multicultural and multilingual citizenry or, to use moral terms, a just society.

As foreign language departments make critical choices in their curricular discourse, they might begin their deliberations with these four approaches. But they would soon discover that these restrictive categories continue to make language learning—its processes, content, and instructional strategies —more unidimensional than is necessary, appropriate, or even advisable in the current institutional and intellectual environment. Before faculty members can reach this expanded view, however, they will have to face some troubling realities in departments' curricular practice.

Curriculum by Default, Curriculum by Design

Foreign language curricula can be described either as the result of a default position or as the product of a conscious and iterative design process.

The default end of this spectrum is a curriculum whose primary intellectual motivation and force reside at the level of the individual course, which is taught by a single faculty member and evaluated by students as a separate and independent entity. If intellectual rigor and vitality characterize most courses, students will reap the larger educational benefits of an entire program from course adjacencies or proximities. But there are obstacles. First, it is up to students to uncover deeper linkages, and all too few seem able to do this, because their academic abilities are insufficiently honed, because their general educational development is still ongoing (Egan), or because courses inherently present disparate entries into a field of inquiry. Second, courses can accomplish less singly than if they are connected to a larger whole; singly they can even lead to an incorrect understanding of the field. As a result, a quality total educational experience for students often remains an accidental outcome.

At the opposite end of the spectrum, curriculum by design, all teaching faculty members of a department engage deliberately in building a consensus about what constitutes knowledge in the foreign language field, about what the large educational outcomes should be, and about how individual courses can provide interrelated avenues for students to gain that knowledge. Such consensus building is both intellectual disciplinary work and deeply humanistic work. It requires faculty members to conceptualize anew the what of their field and to reassess their individual and specialized contributions to it. It demands as well careful consideration of how faculty members will ensure that students succeed in gaining entry into the field and acquiring its discourse, how students will become learners in the field, and, finally, how such an engaged practice helps them become competent lifelong learners. Faculty members must also clarify to themselves the nature and quality of the students' learning outcomes in order to arrive at two important judgments: about the extent to which their curriculum building and their teaching constitutes intellectual work that merits recognition in their work as faculty members and, more important, about what the criteria are that establish the quality of the learning work of their students (see MLA Commission on Professional Service).

By the above description, most collegiate curricula are closer to the default than to the design end of the continuum. At best, only the foreign language component of a department's total offerings might count as a curriculum in the real sense of that term. But such division raises serious questions. Separating the so-called content courses from the language sequence and stripping the language classes of any content other than the metalinguistic content obtained from form-focused language study deprive both language and content classes of the unique quality that justifies their presence in a college or university setting in the first place. The issue is not simply that the foreign language program needs to be revamped to justify its presence (a frequent recommendation). From a comprehensive curricular standpoint, the issue is just as much whether the literature component of a foreign language department has a sufficient academic and educational justification when it is unconnected to, even divorced from, its language base.

Departments and entire institutions provide a range of clues about where they stand on the issue of this separation. All too often they do not commit the necessary resources, quite broadly understood, to their language component; they place language under a different administrative unit; they increasingly teach their literature in translation; in their engagement with a national literature, they tip the balance in favor of formalized theorizing about literature in general; competing with English departments in their desire to teach their national literature in English, they do not provide their students with a rich offering of the decidedly different experience foreign language speakers have when they encounter that literature in its original language.

The dire consequences of this literature-language separation are well known and have been commented on extensively from a variety of perspectives (see particularly James; Swaffar, "Articulating," "Curricular Issues," and "Using"; also Byrnes, "Addressing" and "Issues"; Crawford-Lange; Henning; Hoffman and James; Lambert; Lange, "Curricular Crisis" and "Sketching"; Parsons; Redfield; Silber; Snow; Stern; Wesche). I focus on two particularly far-reaching repercussions: the substitution of the textbook or of methodology for curricular decision making.

The Language Curriculum and Its Substitutes

THE TEXTBOOK AS CURRICULUM

In most foreign language departments the periodic ritual of selecting textbooks for the language classes has almost completely replaced larger curricular deliberations. Answers to the question "What textbook(s) do you use?" substitute for principles by which a program would facilitate students' total learning experience in the foreign language department. Within their narrow course domains, foreign language textbooks can fulfill that purpose because they do contain aspects of a curricular discussion. They state goals, explicitly as well as implicitly; they have selected in great detail what is to be taught; and they specify how it is to be taught. Indeed, given faculty members' unsophisticated knowledge base in language learning and teaching and given the transient staffing of language courses, textbooks may offer the only way the enterprise can function.

But there are major differences between the kinds of discussions that generally accompany the selection of textbooks and the essential features of curriculum deliberation. Even within the restricted scope of the language program, choosing a particular textbook requires independently stated criteria for selection and sequencing of materials, an issue that is far from uncontroversial, as the three major approaches to the problem illustrate.

The structural-analytic approach to materials development gives priority to formal grammatical criteria, as linguists, usually structural linguists, have identified them. For the major European languages an almost immutable canon focused on grammatical structures has developed. Since use orientation has only recently raised an awareness that students are overwhelmed by grammatical rules (i.e., what is taught does not equal what is available for communicative use), the inventory of rules of form has been either reduced or stretched out over longer instruction time (see Omaggio Hadley; Tschirner). But the basic premise holds: instructed second language learning is effectively facilitated by — or, more strongly, instructed second language learning is — a form-focused, rule-governed activity: selection, focus, subdivision, and sequencing all follow that premise, though they go through many permutations and deviations. In other words, the selection criteria that underlie the curriculum derive not from the act of learning but from the language system, which is expressed in structuralist terms.

The functional or, in the British context, functional-notional approach to materials creation sees the basis for a curriculum in variously derived units of language use as contrasted with language form. This approach would seem to provide for communicative teaching; but often it does not. In fact, guidelines for the British creation of functional-notional curricula and syllabi (see Munby) and most current American materials aimed at promoting communicative competence or proficiency maintain an analytic approach (e.g., the essays in Byrnes and Canale and in Higgs; Johnson; Medley). Even though such work must now capture the considerably more complex and contextually varied issues of language use, it tends to persist in the kind of prescriptivism inherent in the structuralist stance. But it should be pointed out in defense of curriculum (and textbook) designers that they assume that a selection of data is unavoidable, if for no other reason than efficiency. The implied and much stronger claim, of course, is that analytic rules, whether they are focused on form or use, can indeed transfer effectively into situationally varied language use. That transfer is a very demanding and at the same time the crucial test that must be met.

It is not surprising, then, that the third approach essentially gives up on the claim (or hope) of the communicative use of analytic rules and takes the opposite stance. Experiential and, in contrast with the two previous approaches, nonanalytic, "the natural growth hypothesis . . . appears to constitute the most serious challenge to traditional concepts of syllabus planning" (Allen 65; see also Long). Indeed, to the adherents of the natural approach, "it is not the grammatical syllabus in particular but the whole concept of a preselected inventory of items which is wrong" (Allen 65). In this approach, which is most closely associated with Stephen Krashen and Tracy Terrell, "comprehensible input," a concept with only post hoc explanatory power, becomes central to what is called the natural process of acquisition and is set against the conscious process of learning, thereby effectively discrediting a fundamental aspect of instruction and the classroom. Given the enormous complexity of linguistic rules of form — transformational-generative grammar certainly drove home that point better than any previous grammar ever had — and, even more, given the daunting complexity of rules of use, it is easy to understand why the natural approach has intuitive appeal.

Faculty members, by failing to address central aspects of language and language learning in advance, must deal with them at the point when they are least able to do so: in the act of choosing textbooks. The result is a process many loathe for the sometimes not-so-subtle questioning of colleagues' teaching competence, for the wrangling over petty matters alongside attempts to solve major issues, and, finally, for the cynical view that in any case teachers will do as they please in the privacy of their classrooms (see Shulman for the implications of a privatized understanding of the act of teaching).

METHODOLOGY AS CURRICULUM

The second powerful substitute for coherent curricular decision making is methodology. Methodology, like the textbook, addresses important aspects of a curriculum discussion: the how of teaching is presumed to ensure attainment of the envisioned learning goals. But, also like the textbook, methodology is a poor answer to the problem of curricular consensus building, as demonstrated by the many pendulum swings of the last three decades. Among the more familiar methodologies are the grammar-translation method; the direct method; audiolingual methodology; Total Physical Response, which appeals to students' kinesthetic-sensory system and emphasizes listening comprehension before production; and the Natural Approach. Less prominent are Community Language Learning, which stresses the affective domain to promote cognitive learning; the Silent Way, a cognitivist approach that focuses on building up the learners' independence, autonomy, and responsibility; and Suggestopedia, which gives prominence to relaxation techniques and concentration in order to tap students' subconscious powers of memory (see the first edition of Omaggio Hadley for a good summary).

Despite considerable excitement, even fervor, at a particular time, these methodologies do not—cannot—possess the level of completeness and systematicness required for curriculum building (Kumaravadivelu offers a recent, brief, and accessible discussion).

Methodological purism is not viable for another reason. Janet Swaffar, Katherine Arens, and Martha Morgan discovered long ago that syllabus designers, textbook writers, and, ultimately, teachers do not adhere to a particular method in their practice, presumably because they know intuitively that the complexity of language learning and of language teaching goes far beyond what any one methodology can address. But without criteria to guide instruction it is but a small step from being liberated from methodological dictates to succumbing to methodological anarchy. Instead of motivated pedagogical decision making we find random eclecticism, a bag of tricks, on-location how-tos that make successful foreign language teaching neither an art nor a science as claimed by the big methodologies, but an amateurish practice that, for good measure, requires a pleasant personality.

Thus classroom teaching seems to be caught in a bind between unprincipled eclecticism and a fixed methodology with the claim of scientific rigor. As Diane Larsen-Freeman and Michael Long observe, the difficulty with methodologies is that they tend to assume "that a programme with . . . the necessary and sufficient characteristics for successful language learning is automatically the most efficient/effective programme possible" (303). After further specifying the nondirect relations among SLA theory, SLA research, and teaching, they say, "In other words, while identifying the simplest, least powerful, theory is the goal of SLA research, that theory (alone) will not necessarily constitute the soundest basis for SL teaching, precisely because it is the simplest *minimal* solution" (304; see the entire concluding chapter of Larsen-Freeman and Long for an excellent summary of the issues). For this reason, SLA researchers (e.g., Pica, "Questions") have increasingly been seeking valid connections between research and the classroom, an approach that is far removed from the unwarranted claims both of theoretical constructs and of set methodologies.

Foreign Language Faculty Members as Curriculum Designers

Why do questionable curricular practices persist? One reason is that collegiate faculty members only infrequently engage in extensive reflection of educational and pedagogical issues. Such issues are often seen as concerns unbecoming to someone in a rigorous academic environment (but see the efforts of the Amer. Assn. for Higher Educ. to connect the disciplines with teaching [*AAHE Teaching Initiative*]). Another reason is that disciplinary preparation has by and large not developed in faculty members the rich culture of collaboration necessary for addressing larger professional issues (but see Arens).

Most important, education in a special area in the foreign language field has not provided faculty members with a firm general, not to mention an extensive specific, knowledge base in SLA. This lack becomes a major problem: the United States educational system is unusual in that critical elements of students' second language learning can be addressed only at the college level. In other words, with regard to developing a coherent curriculum, the existing larger educational system demands knowledge of the whole field of language from all faculty members, no matter what their disciplinary specialty (e.g., linguistics, the national literature, comparative literature, cultural studies). The dearth of comprehensive curricular planning is therefore quite understandable.

Contextual Obstacles to Curriculum Development

United States higher education as an enterprise sets up major roadblocks to curriculum construction in foreign languages. The two discussed below convey the complexity of the matter.

DECENTRALIZED EDUCATION AND THE CURRICULAR
POSITION OF FOREIGN LANGUAGES

Unlike most industrialized countries, the United States has a decentralized educational system. Known for its enviable flexibility and responsiveness, that system also makes troubling demands and is plagued by uncertainties and discontinuities. The situation is particularly grave for postsecondary school foreign language curriculum development and instruction.

Many uncertainties arise from the simple fact that languages do not have a secure role in the core of the American curriculum at any educational level. For example, until quite recently, the profession found it impossible to produce a comprehensive statement about the outcomes standards that should be expected at the end of the K–12 sequence. In order to be able to do so, the creators of the document *National Standards in Foreign Language Education,* in a bold futuristic vision, presumed that foreign languages did in fact hold a firm presence at the heart of American education throughout all grades.

The issue of *articulation,* a term that most frequently refers to curricular continuity between high schools and colleges, owes its stubborn life to the noncentrality of foreign languages. The multiplicity of language learning experiences students have during their K–12 education and the resultant utter nonpredictability of their language competence present additional burdens for college language departments attempting to create coherent curricular sequences out of great complexity (Phillips, "If Not Consensus").

THE CULTURE OF THE ACADEMY AND INSTITUTIONAL FACTORS

In the academy powerful institutional and intellectual habits and prejudices (e.g., practices of governance, resource allocation, financing, and personnel decision making) have had the far-reaching consequence of bifurcating the work of foreign language departments into language instruction versus content instruction — or, to put it even more strongly, language versus literature, skills versus humanistic learning. Unfortunately that split has essentially been naturalized, and this state of affairs requires, as a first order of business, a clearheaded and unflinching untangling of what is in a department's ability to change from what seems beyond a department's reach.

One powerful feature of academic culture is that faculty members identify more and more with their disciplines, less and less with their institutions. That is the deeper meaning of the opposition between some faculty members' commitment to teaching and some faculty members' commitment to research and of the low esteem in which professional service is held (but see the recent reconsideration of this issue in the report of the MLA Commission on Professional Service). Research, particularly in the humanities, rarely requires institutional grounding. Teaching and service, however, take place in a specific institution and are part of a specific program for specific students. Foreign language departments are caught in the middle of this tension. As programmatic entities they are concerned with language teaching, because their enrollments are in language teaching. Their faculty members, however, focus on the disciplinary affiliation that determines rewards: it is the disciplines, after all, that provide important judgments regarding the quality of scholarship and open up diverse professional opportunities.

Departments and faculty members seek to minimize or cover up the contradiction in various ways. They subscribe to and administratively enact an understanding of the teaching (and learning) of language that limits it to the barest of commitments, generally to between two and four semesters. They thus separate the teaching of language from the remainder of the curriculum, which, despite significantly lower student enrollments and for reasons of academic prestige, becomes the center of resource allocations. Departments create numerous layers of teaching staff (graduate students and full-time and part-time adjunct teachers versus regular faculty members) and find ways of outsourcing language teaching into different departments or centers. Ultimately, departments resort to avoidance behavior, best exemplified in the nearly complete absence of comprehensive curricular discussion (Byrnes, "Addressing" and "Issues").

Beyond these primarily administrative separations known to most disciplines, foreign language departments face unique intellectual obstacles to coherent curriculum construction. No obstacle is more powerful than the enormous divide between, on one side, the received interpretation and doctrinal construction of language learning and teaching along formalist lines and, on the other side, the humanistic academic heart of a foreign language department, its literary enterprise.

On the language teaching side of this divide, the synergism between a normative American structuralism and behaviorism allowed audiolingual methodology to become practically synonymous with all foreign language learning and teaching. Even when the Chomskyan revolution replaced the structuralist approach with a cognitivist approach, no major shift occurred, precisely because the nativist focus on competence instead of on performance was of no interest in the classroom in the first place. Thus, even with this major reorientation in linguistic theory, language and language learning and teaching continued to be divorced from a sociocultural context of use and from the cultural content language conveys—a curious separation, considering the simultaneous demand of nativelike behavior from learners on the purely procedural level.

On the literature side of the divide, too, native speaker competence and performance are taken for granted. Only the erroneous assumption of nativelike, socioculturally anchored linguistic competence of readers can explain the almost total absence of an intellectually rich pedagogy of foreign language literatures that truly considers the nonnative learner of a language as a reader of literary texts. (The latest example of the absence of such consideration is a special issue of *PMLA, The Teaching of Literature*). Instead, the profession can draw on only sporadic reflections regarding the unique needs of foreign language learners and learning — reflections on how to engage young adults who are second language learners and how to measure the progress of their developing ability to see the other and be the other, as they become multiply literate. As long as there is no deep reflection on the value of foreign language study in a collegiate context and no thought given to the complex task of translating that reflection into curricula and pedagogies, repeated affirmations that the encounter with foreign languages and literatures helps learners perform the humanist act of discovering themselves by stepping out of themselves will be viewed with serious skepticism (for discussion of various aspects of this issue see Berman; Kramsch; Lange, "Sketching"; and particularly Swaffar, Arens, and Byrnes). As Jeffrey Peck observes about foreign language and literature departments, "they have not made enough of the 'foreign' and its anthropological and ethnographic revelance for the work that they have always been doing" (15). Claire Kramsch and Thomas Nolden call "for a new type of literacy, centered more on the learner, based more on crosscultural awareness and critical reflection" (28).

To frame such reflections, I have suggested the concept of multiple literacies. It links foreign languages to the larger intellectual enterprise of literacy as it is currently being considered in L1 research and also in conjunction with bilingual education, though both fields tend to focus on learners in grades K–12. As a consequence L1 literacy would not be excluded from the consideration of L2 literacy and conceptualized as separate from and nonconcurrent with L2 literacy. Instead, the foreign language classroom would become one of numerous environments in which multiple literacies can emerge and develop along a continuum of contingent language use, L1 and L2.

The concept of L1 literacy, too, is being reconsidered. A particularly comprehensive proposal is made by a group of scholars from the United States, the United Kingdom, and Australia (known as the New London Group, from their meeting place in Connecticut) who want to lift the restriction of past literacy pedagogy to "formalized, monolingual, monocultural, and rule-governed forms of language" (61). To them what increasingly globalized societies need is a populace that can negotiate a multiplicity of text forms and discourses in a number of cultures. The term *multiliteracy*, then, refers to the fact that the multiplicity of communications channels and increasing cultural and linguistic diversity in the world today call for a much broader view of literacy than portrayed by traditional language-based approaches. Multiliteracies . . . [overcome] the limitations of traditional approaches by emphasizing how negotiating the multiple linguistic and cultural differences in our society is central to the pragmatics of the working, civic, and private lives of students.   (60)

My proposal for multiple literacies, by comparison with the New London Group's proposal, maintains a central role for language. While I agree with the stance that an overreliance on linguistic channels can restrict — and in the past often has restricted — our approaches to language learning, I also believe that, in the specific contexts of foreign language learning, language itself can become a powerful entrée to students' realization of multiple ways of being.

By extending the theoretical framework for bilingualism proposed by Nancy Hornberger, the foreign language department and its curriculum would gain important strategic advantages. The department would gain an overarching concept for all its programmatic concerns, from foreign language acquisition to literary interpretation to language for special purposes. The department would also be able to link itself to and benefit from the emerging efforts in research and theory that see literacy as a set of social or cultural practices and its participants as a community of practice. As Stephen Reder states, "as a set of socially patterned activities, literacy develops and spreads through a process of socialization, the means of which may include but are not necessarily limited to formal instruction. . . . Indeed, these formal instructional activities are seen as just another — albeit often highly valued — set of literacy practices themselves" (33–34). The foreign language classroom is one such locus.

Kramsch and Nolden have alerted us to the limitations of current practice in the teaching of foreign language literature and culture by pointing out that "the problems of the practice are the deficiencies of the theory" (29). Information-processing theories of reading, reader-response theories, and reception theory in their own ways all ignore the individual nonnative reader who does not belong to the discourse community in which the native text was produced and for which it was intended. A multiple-literacies approach allows an expansion of theory, allows language learning to arise in diverse discourse communities, oral and written, that comprise "multiple genres, or practices, each of which has distinct characteristics located at different points of linguistic and interactional continua" (Reder 37). Reder says, "There is significant overlap among the functions and features of speech and writing across a much wider range of cultural activities than was once believed; and ... many culturally patterned communicative practices draw *jointly* on speech and writing in their routine accomplishment" (38). This comprehensive understanding of language, language use, and language acquisition is now at the forefront of SLA research, thereby making possible linkages among heretofore disparate components of the foreign language department, particularly for the purpose of curriculum development, linkages that enhance students' ability to become multiliterate in conjunction with becoming literate in a second language.

In the task to further multiple literacies, two interrelated phenomena must be addressed: the incomplete development of the foreign language field's position in the American academy as distinct from its manifestations in the home culture and a strong intellectual tradition that constructs literacy in a unidimensional fashion (see Cummins). Both kinds of deficiency may be related to the fact that a significant proportion of faculty members were native-speaking immigrants during the peak growth time of American higher education after World War II. The task is made more difficult by the current divisive debates that draw connections among the concept of nationhood, presumed good governance, and the use of language(s) and in the process continues practices of identity formation, for nations and individuals, that are in need of serious reconsideration (for discussion of various aspects of this issue, see Peck).

When these formidable obstacles in the foreign language department are compounded by the more general trend in the academy that William Massy, Andrea Wilger, and Carol Colbeck have called "hollowed collegiality" because of the academy's desire to avoid complex issues and preserve a semblance of harmony, comprehensive curriculum discussion becomes extraordinarily difficult to initiate and maintain.

External Challenges Demanding a Redesigning of Curricula

The challenges for the foreign language department have, by and large, not been met successfully, either from an intellectual or from an institutional, administrative standpoint. The shape of foreign language curricula provides primary evidence of that failure. Meanwhile, more demands are being made more forcefully in the near future, demands that the foreign language department become more expansive and more inclusive even as it is asked to become more sharply defined as a scholarly unit.

GENERAL SOCIETAL CHANGES

Developments in society at large are creating a mandate for greater inclusiveness. These developments include the arrival of new immigrant groups to this country and a greater awareness of the cultural and linguistic heritage in long-established immigrant groups (e.g., Spanish-speaking or Japanese-speaking); an end to the dominance of native-speaking faculty members in the profession, which makes possible a redefinition of the field and of departments by an American-educated faculty; the increasing demand for communicative abilities as the outcome of instruction, which puts pressure on colleges that do not wish to be supplanted by commercial language instruction; incidents of dwindling enrollments and fiscal constraints that lead to program closings; a tightness in the academic job market, which requires greater flexibility in graduate programs to ensure employment opportunities for students; increasing preprofessionalization of undergraduate college curricula, which leaves less room for electives, including languages; escalating tuition costs, which encourage a narrowly utilitarian cost-benefit analysis that, despite the globalization of our lives, has not resulted in students' giving consistent priority to language study as they select their electives; the growing dominance of English on the international scene (particularly in markets but also in the sciences, entertainment, and the arts), which suggests less need of or less economic return for foreign language learning; the increasing demand from academic programs (e.g., business, the health sciences, environmental professions, law, engineering) for language for specific purposes (Wesche) or advanced language and culture competence.

THE FOREIGN LANGUAGE DEPARTMENT'S CHANGING STUDENTS

These societal changes are best observed in changes in the student body. One fundamental issue arising from these changes is that collegiate foreign language departments must decide the extent to which the formal, analytic, accuracy- and mastery-focused approach they have traditionally favored will be satisfactory in the future. It will be increasingly difficult to persist in offering curricula based on the replication of an idealized norm, when the process of language acquisition yields performance that depends on specific tasks (Valdman). And, from a purely administrative standpoint, past practice allowed departments to force students who did not fit their conception of tidy additive language acquisition into their beginning or intermediate classes, but in the future such a policy may not be accepted by the public, students, university administrators, and overseeing authorities.

Among the students who will demand totally different curricula are those who are now graduating from secondary schools with curricula that follow a communicative approach, according to national standards that are communicatively oriented. With its focus on communication, cultures, connections, comparisons, and communities, the experiential (as opposed to analytic) learning these students have had cannot readily be fitted into or reduced to the form-focused language teaching that dominates in colleges. Totally different curricula will need to be conceptualized if foreign language departments wish to serve this very important student group.

The problem of articulation has been seen primarily in terms of inappropriate assessment instruments and procedures, but a deeper reason why colleges have made so few contributions to articulation is that articulation necessitates curriculum discussion, and such discussion is more difficult for colleges than launching a new assessment program (but see Mosher; *Articulation*; and esp. Welles). Departments will see the diverse experiential learners who are now entering colleges (e.g., heritage speakers, students with diverse international experiences, immigrants) only if those learners decide that departmental offerings match their language learning profile and are relevant to their interests. Departments therefore must judge such students' interlanguage characteristics no longer as deficits but as accomplishments that need further improvement and elaboration (Shohamy). And the students' learning goals, which will span everything from academic to professional environments, must be taken seriously in academic terms. Public and professional performance is at the heart of what we call advanced language ability: a specialized use of language from sociolinguistic, sociopragmatic, discoursal, and formal perspectives, taken seriously whether it occurs in the academy, the public setting, business, law, engineering, or the health sciences.

Whatever their goals or institutional realizations, efforts like "language for specific purposes" (Grandin, Einbeck, and Reinhart; Grosse and Voght) and "language across the curriculum" or "language and content" (Jurasek and Jurasek; Jurasek; Krueger and Ryan; Met; Snow, Met, and Genesee) are ways to begin to overcome the limited, entrenched curricula that currently exist in foreign language departments. But these efforts also run the risk of remaining a limited answer. Not only are multiple-literacy issues rarely a focal point; it is not even clear whether, how, and under what circumstances programs that implement them enhance language acquisition. Indeed, in a number of cases in the United States, the primary motivation for introducing a language-across-the-curriculum program was not language acquisition. Instead, programs were created to give a department visibility in the larger academic community, because visibility has become identified as vital for a department's continued existence on campus. Although visibility is certainly a worthy goal, unless the program is designed to meet the challenges listed above, the program runs the risk of creating the very situation that nobody wishes to contemplate—namely, the reduction of the foreign language department to a service arrangement and of its faculty members to dilettantes. In addition, such programs are known to be complex, resource-intensive, and difficult to coordinate and administer. A thorough rethinking of curricular options that sees, from the beginning, language and content instruction as united by the concept of multiple literacies would avoid these risks and problems; such a rethinking would allow a department to reap and keep all the gains of this approach for all its students, not just a select few, and for all its faculty members.

Foreign language departments must learn to play a crucial role in enhancing students' literacy, students' ability to interpret and produce texts, orally and in writing, in a fashion that shows a rich awareness of the relation among the sociocultural contexts of use, meaning, and significance. If the claim that a humanistic education is incomplete, perhaps even impossible, without the deep knowledge of more than one language and culture is to be convincing, faculty members must be able to draw on a deeply humanistic but also richly informed pedagogy of and for multiple literacies, a knowledge base that SLA research is increasingly able to provide. Russell Berman identifies the crucial question that foreign language departments face as "why we think language, literature, and culture ought to be taught at all and whether they belong together for other than merely conventional reasons" (11).

Without a doubt, curricular deliberations and curricular planning are the ideal context in which to attempt an answer to that question in theory and in practice. The only response to the challenges that is neither patch-work nor quick-fix, neither a panicked abandonment of our mission nor a shirking of responsibilities to the point of stubborn retrenchment, is a dual strategy: comprehensive, intelligent curricular planning combined with long-term and carefully mentored faculty development so that the delivery of such curricula will become a reality.

SLA RESEARCH AND FUTURE CURRICULUM DEVELOPMENT

Through historical overview, presentation of major theoretical positions, or critique, the above discussion has introduced important positions that SLA research takes. The discussion has also entered areas that SLA research has not yet devoted much attention to but that are fruitful extensions of SLA's current focus. I now turn the perspective around: starting with SLA research, I suggest implications for curriculum development of the future.

A few caveats: my focus on curriculum has determined the choice of SLA issues to be dealt with, but SLA researchers might well consider other approaches more significant; my notion of curriculum deals primarily with instructional issues, with content and aspects of sequencing; for lack of space and because the emphasis is on insights that could lead to innovative curricular projects, I have said little about research that validates existing practice; and the nature of curricular practice dictates that my discussion of SLA work be limited to major issues that are largely beyond dispute.

General Observations

The relation between second language research and the classroom is increasingly not indirect or incidental; the relation is deliberately sought to enhance students' learning. In 1985 Teresa Pica conceded the possibility that "teachers and curriculum developers, who often have different perspectives from researchers regarding the language learner's task, may find little to abstract from second language acquisition research which is relevant to their concerns for language syllabus design" ("Simplicity" 149). Less than ten years later, she observed:

> So urgent and important is the need for our collaboration that we can no longer complain as teachers that there is nothing to apply from the research we hear or read about, nor as researchers, that

tests of validity and reliability take precedence over practical class-room issues and applicability. . . . Much of this work has been car-ried out by language researchers who are deeply interested in teaching practice because many of them were teachers at one time.

("Questions" 49–50)

SLA Research and the Nature of Language

The understanding of language that is central to classroom-based SLA re-search is captured in the term "communicative competence." It signals the shift from a systems-and-norms focus to a use-and-performance orientation. The term refers to both underlying knowledge about language and the abil-ity to use that knowledge in actual communication (Hymes). Michael Canale and Merrill Swain suggested that the four major components of commu-nicative competence are grammatical competence, sociolinguistic compe-tence, discourse competence, and strategic competence. While there is some dispute about the extent to which the shift has dislodged the normative model that contrasted competence and performance (e.g., Candlin; Lange, "Sketching"; Lantolf), all the essays in this volume provide evidence of a vastly expanded theoretical construct for SLA research. The emphasis is on dynamic, creative, interpersonal, context-embedded, synchronically and diachronically variable aspects of language, attributes that Sandra Savignon summarizes in the term *negotiation* (8–9).

Another way to describe the shift would be to say that it focuses on process instead of on a product. But such a characterization applies only if one recognizes that process and product are no longer seen as in opposition to each other but as intricately bound together. Central issues of the product cannot be understood outside their process qualities, and processes cannot evolve except by reference to products. Thus, with the shift, context, situat-edness, contingencies, choice, creativeness, and variation are not nice add-ons that can be addressed after the norm has been established; they *are* the norm.

For SLA the implications can hardly be more far-reaching. But because language plays such a central role in all human inquiry, the shift from prod-uct to process has important implications for the most fundamental notions of the Western scientific research tradition. In that positivist tradition, which dominates much of our inquiry, these notions, packaged and traded as fixed entities through the power of the decontextualized word (e.g., "theory and practice," "norm and variation," "truth and relativism," "objectivity and subjectivity," "fact and interpretation"), have become reified as building blocks for a rational fixed reality. They have been endowed with a literalness, a power, and a truth value that, as it turns out, are themselves subject to thorough questioning. In sum, through its understanding of the nature of language, SLA research is engaged in the same postmodernist critique that has generally been associated with literary criticism or philosophy (see, e.g., Candlin; Hall; Pennycook).

The Nature of (Instructed) Language Acquisition

If language now seems better understood in terms of situated multiple realities, that multiplicity is further heightened in language acquisition: an infinitely variable object (a language in use) is being acquired by learners who themselves are infinitely varied as both individual and social beings. To complicate matters more, in second language acquisition, particularly by adults, learners already possess a range of the socioculturally embedded capabilities that we call communicative competence in a language.

Small wonder that SLA researchers, despite a significantly expanded knowledge base, are increasingly self-conscious about central aspects of their theorizing. Ellen Bialystok remarks on "the enormity of the mystery of second language acquisition and a consequent modesty about what a particular theory is capable of explaining. Earlier theories did not have this virtue of humility" (157). From the standpoint of cognitive psychology, Judith Greene observes that ironically our richer knowledge base gives us all the more reason not to overstate the nature of representations of knowledge in the brain and the processes people engage in as they access memory stores in order to produce language (81; also see Greene and Coulson for an accessible overview).

SLA research affirms and attempts to capture the multiple situatedness of language, the learner, and the process of learning in its key construct of interlanguage. The work done in the last twenty years has made it possible for us to arrive at some important context-dependent generalizations. Those pertaining to the classroom are the focus of the following discussion. Bill VanPatten's essay in this volume gives a glimpse of the directions future inquiry in this area might take: orders of acquisition, developmental sequences, the lack of certain kinds of errors, and the limited effects of explicit grammatical instruction.

The Classroom as a Supportive Foreign Language Learning Environment

SLA research has expended significant effort on the relation between second language learning and first language learning. On the basis of that research it can now be stated that classroom SLA is distinct in nontrivial ways from naturalistic acquisition of a second language and also distinct in nontrivial ways from child or first language acquisition. The implications of that conclusion for curriculum and instruction are tremendous. Two issues, pointing to no longer necessary or defensible curricular and instructional practices, indicate the depth of the changes required in curricula and pedagogy if we followed through on those two major conclusions.

First, nearly all curricula and most methodologies thus far have been built on an analytic model of the formal system of language, a model that has turned out to be seriously flawed. Second, those curricula and methodologies that have not been so built, the experiential approaches, nevertheless arose from a theoretical context that produced its own powerful limitation: by placing the process of learning a second language into close proximity with the "natural" process of first language learning, they excluded the classroom as a legitimate environment for experiential learning.

In other words, both analytic and experiential approaches treated the classroom as an impoverished, nonreal environment for learning a second language. That fact alone accounts for foundational limitations in critical areas of curricular practice.

Curricula, materials, textbooks, and norm-referenced assessment instruments are given too much or, at the very least, entirely inappropriate power. Worse, in their form-centeredness, they construct and privilege a way of being a second language learner that makes an emphasis on meaning a near impossibility for many students. That this is true even for analytically oriented learners is amply demonstrated by the difficulties they encounter in moving from introductory and intermediate performance abilities to the thoroughly contextualized performance profile of the advanced learner.

Depending on which of the two approaches — the analytic or the experiential — teachers favor, they present two nearly opposite profiles of the teaching-learning activity. This conceptual discontinuity is most troubling and detrimental to program coherence in foreign language departments, all the way through the graduate level (see Swaffar, "Articulating"). When no curricular plan exists, teachers are free to consider their various classroom interventions (e.g., input enhancement, teaching of grammatical points through awareness-raising and multiple contextualizations, negotiated error correction, privileging of certain modalities at certain points) as enhancing students' learning or as irrelevant to such learning (for perspectives on this issue, see Doughty; Harley; *Learning Outcomes Framework*; Lightbown, Spada, and White; van Lier). One approach seems as good as another, because in many cases validation can be obtained only after long instructional periods and most curricula do not offer long instructional periods.

In the absence of comprehensive planning, one might expect the continuation of practices that emphasize a noncontextualized focus on form, though such practices ignore some of the most fundamental features of social interaction with language. Research has established that patterns of social interaction provide the basis for learners to acquire the complex interrelations between language forms and meanings. Classroom SLA research strongly suggests a near complete reversal of the approaches college programs generally practice in their curricula. The traditional sequencing begins with an emphasis on form that sets up highly problematic processing habits and a totally skewed set of expectations about the nature of the foreign language or, for that matter, any language. Students who persevere and graduate to content classes are often ill-prepared to succeed in that new environment. They have not learned to negotiate the many nonunique but contextually specified relations among meanings, functions, and forms (whether the forms are grammatical or lexical). Nor have those students been given the necessary scaffolding to develop, over time, the processing capabilities, foundational cognitive habits, and interpretive skills to deal with the considerably more complex literacy tasks that are now required of them in those content classes (James; Swaffar, Arens, and Byrnes).

To make matters worse, the students' inability to participate in the literacy practices of the second language is, unfortunately though not surprisingly, often diagnosed as insufficient accuracy. The remedy is formal accuracy training at the sentence level — the usual prescription is an advanced grammar review of the most traditional sort — a continued privileging of form over meaning. But that privileging was the problem to begin with: language taken to be best learned separate from meaning. Students' interlanguage profiles and slope are disregarded, and the dissonances this disregard creates for them as second language learners are formidable.

SLA research suggests that curriculum designers instead consider beginning instruction with a meaning focus, starting learners out with processing strategies directed toward the creation of meaning and knowledge on the basis of forms. There need not be a contradiction between communicative language teaching and form. Indeed, the accumulated research shows that certain ways of focusing on form support learners' continued interlanguage adjustment. A careful integration of meaning and form should be maintained, with meaning having primacy. Also, a focus on form in a generally communicative orientation might be more conducive to learning if that focus comes later rather than earlier. In any case, the study of form is always, as Catherine Doughty says in this volume, "contingent on rather than anticipatory of language learning problems" (Doughty's essay provides an exceptionally thorough yet accessible discussion of this issue).

Another problematic aspect of unarticulated language programs is their implied message that learners should be able to develop a broad performance profile in the short period of time generally allotted to language learning. Of course, nothing could be further from the truth. As a consequence, blame is assigned to teachers and to students, when the true culprit is an unrealistically short language learning sequence. An expectation of targetlike norms during the learning experience only aggravates this situation, contributing to an air of unreality.

Learners also receive signals from the classroom second language learning environment that they are not being taken seriously as whole persons. The sense of unreality, stemming from an inappropriate focus on formal properties and from interactions that fail to address central features of human learning (van Lier, this volume), is added to by the underestimation and underuse of the processing capabilities of learners (Hulstijn and Schmidt). As VanPatten states in this volume, "Long gone are the days when a learner was seen as a tabula rasa on which the new linguistic system could be written." Instead, learners follow both seemingly universal and highly individualistic cognitive processing mechanisms that are "responsible for processing input, accommodating new data and restructuring the linguistic system, or assembling utterances during production." Although we may not be able to change the order of acquisition, we may be able to enhance, under certain conditions, the speed with which certain features are learned (Pica, "Simplicity"; Pienemann). Teaching based on such insights can help learners construct their interlanguage systems with efficiency. Given a range of production and comprehension tasks, learners are encouraged to continue to adjust their systems toward the one that underlies the language being learned (Swain).

Another holdover from the audiolingual era and its structuralist-inspired curriculum is the inordinate primacy given to oral language, an emphasis that was easily transferred to communicative language teaching despite theoretical and practical reservations. SLA research now recognizes the benefits L1-literate adult learners can derive from that literacy as they encounter L2 texts in reading and writing, benefits that pertain not only to reading and writing abilities themselves but also to learning to speak and understand a language. Fixed sequences in a curriculum among the different language modalities (first listening, then speaking, then reading, and finally writing) are not only unsupported by research, they may even be detrimental for the adult learner in the collegiate environment, all the more so as language instruction is usually of such short duration. Understanding literacy as multiply constituted in function, personal empowerment, social status, and individual growth (see Ferdman and Weber), SLA research affirms collegiate learners as adults who come not only with a wealth of general knowledge but also with well-developed literacy skills in the first language. As Greene comments about first language processing, "It is genuinely impossible to distinguish between linguistic knowledge and general knowledge. What does seem indisputable is that language users bring to language processing a conceptual apparatus of knowledge, expecting language to conform to what is known about the world" (88). The ways that background knowledge facilitates or inhibits second language learning are infinitely varied and therefore not knowable ahead of time. But we can no longer question the centrality of meaning in a dramatically expanded understanding of language acquisition and the role of the learner. With the shift to meaning, many familiar terms and expectations that have driven curricular thinking in the past (e.g., error, error-correction, and fossilization; mastery or native-like performance; receptive and productive language use; oral and literate language; accuracy, fluency, and complexity) now take on totally different roles and significances. Swaffar, in her comprehensive and insightful overview of these issues, observes that foreign language departments have yet to work out "a consistent philosophy about the relationship between acquiring language and acquiring knowledge" ("Using" 78). That philosophy is the sine qua non for overcoming the piecemeal approach to language learning that characterizes nearly all college programs, including those that have made attempts to incorporate content.

It would be entirely too idealistic to expect the dramatic changes envisioned here to be readily embraced by foreign language departments. Curricula reside in multiple interdependencies, are even entangled in them, and must take them into account. Even when a department faces internal and external obstacles with a clear vision, cooperation, and energy, the complexity of curriculum construction and the long-term nature of the project are daunting. Also, changes that affect faculty members' lives must be handled with great care and professionalism. Fortunately, there is no need to change programs wholesale or in a short time to start reaping some of the benefits of the suggested redirection. What is indispensable are, first, an understanding that change is in order and, second, an understanding that faculty members need to craft a consensus about the nature of the program so that changes can be made coherently and over a realistic period of time. As Swaffar states, "The enterprise is worthy of our best efforts. Our profession's future may well depend on its ability to expand the mission of language study: to integrate theory, content courses, and language as coherent stages in *all* students' language acquisition" ("Articulating" 50). The scholarly basis and justification for a rigorously academic and educationally sound reorientation of foreign language programs are available. It remains for departments of foreign languages to seize the rich opportunities that this work has provided.

WORKS CITED

AAHE Teaching Initiative. Washington: Amer. Assn. for Higher Educ. 1994–.

Allen, J. P. B. "General-Purpose Language Teaching: A Variable Focus Approach." Brumfit 61–74.

Arens, Katherine. "Applied Scholarship in Foreign Languages: A Program of Study in Professional Development." *The Dynamics of Language Program Direction.* Ed. David P. Benseler. AAUSC Issues in Lang. Program Direction. Boston: Heinle, 1993. 33–63.

Articulation and Achievement: Connecting Standards, Performance, and Assessment in Foreign Language. New York: Coll. Examination Board, 1996.

Barr, Robert B., and John Tagg. "From Teaching to Learning: A New Paradigm for Undergraduate Education." *Change* Nov.-Dec. 1995: 13–25.

Berman, Russell A. "Global Thinking, Local Teaching: Departments, Curricula, and Culture." *ADFL Bulletin* 26.1 (1994): 7–11.

Bialystok, Ellen. "Analysis and Control in the Development of a Second Language." *Studies in Second Language Acquisition* 16 (1994): 157–68.

Brinton, Donna M., M. S. Snow, and Marjorie Wesche. *Content-Based Foreign Language Instruction.* New York: Newbury, 1989.

Brumfit, Christopher J., ed. *General English Syllabus Design: Curriculum and Syllabus Design for the General English Classroom.* Oxford: Pergamon, 1984.

Byrnes, Heidi. "Addressing Curriculum Articulation in the Nineties: A Proposal." *Foreign Language Annals* 23 (1990): 281–92.

———. "Issues in Foreign Language Program Articulation." Silber 6–28.

Byrnes, Heidi, and Michael Canale, eds. *Defining and Developing Proficiency: Guidelines, Implementations, and Concepts.* Lincolnwood: Natl. Textbook, 1987.

Canale, Michael, and Merrill Swain. "Theoretical Bases of Communicative Approaches to Second Language Teaching and Testing." *Applied Linguistics* 1 (1980): 1–47.

Candlin, Christopher N. "Syllabus Design as a Critical Process." Brumfit 29–46.

Crawford-Lange, Linda M. "Curricular Alternatives for Second-Language Learning." Higgs 81–112.

Cummins, Jim. "From Coercive to Collaborative Relations of Power in the Teaching of Literacy." *Literacy across Languages and Cultures.* Ferdman, Weber, and Ramírez 295–331.

Doughty, Catherine. "Second Language Instruction Does Make a Difference: Evidence from an Empirical Study of SL Relativization." *Studies in Second Language Acquisition* 13 (1991): 431–69.

Egan, Kieran. *Educational Development.* London: Oxford UP, 1979.

Ferdman, Bernardo M., and Rose-Marie Weber. "Literacy across Languages and Cultures." Ferdman, Weber, and Ramírez 3–29.

Ferdman, Bernardo M., Rose-Marie Weber, and Arnulfo G. Ramírez, eds., *Literacy across Languages and Cultures.* Albany: State U of New York P, 1994.

Grandin, John M., Kandace Einbeck, and Walter von Reinhart. "The Changing Goals of Language Instruction." *Language for a Multicultural World in Transition.* Ed. Heidi Byrnes. Lincolnwood: Natl. Textbook, 1992. 123–63.

Greene, Judith. "Language Processes and Models." Greene and Coulson 51–89.

Greene, Judith, and Mark Coulson. *Language Understanding: Current Issues.* 2nd ed. Buckingham: Open UP 1995.

Grosse, Christine U., and G. M. Voght. "The Evolution of Languages for Specific Purposes in the United States." *Modern Language Journal* 75 (1991): 181–95.

Hall, Joan Kelly. "A Consideration of SLA as a Theory of Practice: A Response to Firth and Wagner." *Modern Language Journal* 81 (1997): 301–06.

Harley, Birgit. "Effects of Instruction on SLA: Issues and Evidence." *Annual Review of Applied Linguistics* 9 (1988): 165–88.

Harley, Birgit, Patrick Allen, Jim Cummins, and Merrill Swain, eds. *The Development of Second Language Proficiency.* New York: Cambridge UP, 1990.

Henning, Sylvie Debevec. "The Integration of Language, Literature, and Culture: Goals and Curricular Design." *Profession 93.* New York: MLA, 1993. 22–26.

Higgs, Theodore V., ed. *Curriculum, Competence, and the Foreign Language Teacher.* Skokie: Natl. Textbook, 1982.

Hoffman, Ernst F., and Dorothy James. "Toward the Integration of Foreign Language and Literature Teaching at All Levels of the College Curriculum." *ADFL Bulletin* 17.3 (1986): 43–45.

Hornberger, Nancy. "Continua of Biliteracy." Ferdman, Weber, and Ramírez 103–39.

Hulstijn, Jan, and Richard Schmidt, eds. *Consciousness in Second Language Learning.* Spec. issue of *AILA Review* 11 (1994): 5–113.

Hyltenstam, Kenneth, and Manfred Pienemann, eds. *Modelling and Assessing Second Language Development*. Clevedon, Eng.: Multilingual Matters, 1985.

Hymes, Dell. "On Communicative Competence." *Sociolinguistics: Selected Readings*. Ed. J. B. Pride and Janet Holmes. Baltimore: Penguin, 1972. 269–83.

James, Dorothy. "Reshaping the 'College-Level' Curriculum: Problems and Possibilities." *Shaping the Future: Challenges and Opportunities*. Ed. Helen S. Lepke. Middlebury: Northeast Conf. Repts., 1989. 79–110.

Johnson, Carl H. "Choosing Materials That Do the Job." Phillips, *Building on Experience* 67–92.

Jurasek, Barbara S., and Richard T. Jurasek. "Building Multiple Proficiencies in New Curricular Contexts." Phillips, *Building Bridges* 89–121.

Jurasek, Richard T. "Integrating Foreign Languages into the College Curriculum." *Modern Language Journal* 72 (1988): 52–58.

Kramsch, Claire. "The Cultural Discourse of Foreign Language Textbooks." *Toward a New Integration of Language and Culture*. Ed. Alan J. Singerman. Middlebury: Northeast Conf., 1988. 63–88.

Kramsch, Claire, and Thomas Nolden. "Redefining Literacy in a Foreign Language." *Die Unterrichtspraxis* 27.1 (1994): 28–35.

Krashen, Stephen D., and Tracy D. Terrell. *The Natural Approach: Language Acquisition in the Classroom*. Oxford: Pergamon, 1983.

Krueger, Merle, and Frank Ryan, eds. *Language and Content: Discipline-Based Approaches to Language Study*. Lexington: Heath, 1993.

Kumaravadivelu, B. "The Postmethod Condition: (E)Merging Strategies for Second/ Foreign Language Teaching." *TESOL Quarterly* 28 (1994): 27–48.

Lambert, Richard D. *Language Instruction for Undergraduates in American Higher Education*. Washington: Natl. Foreign Lang. Center at Johns Hopkins U, 1990.

Lange, Dale L. "The Curricular Crisis in Foreign Language Learning." *ADFL Bulletin* 25.2 (1994): 17–22.

———. "Sketching the Crisis and Exploring Different Perspectives in Foreign Language Curriculum." *New Perspectives and New Directions in Foreign Language Education*. Ed. Diane W. Birckbichler. Lincolnwood: Natl. Textbook, 1990. 77–109.

Lantolf, James P. "Second Language Acquisition Theory Building?" *Language and Nation*. British Studies in Applied Linguistics 11. Eds. George Blue and Rosamond Mitchell. Clevedon, Eng.: Multilingual Matters, 1995. 16–27.

Larsen-Freeman, Diane, and Michael H. Long. *An Introduction to Second Language Acquisition Research*. New York: Longman, 1991.

The Learning Outcomes Framework: A Report of the Articulation and Achievement Project, 1995–96. New York: Coll. Board, 1995.

Lightbown, Patsy M., Nina Spada, and Lydia White, eds. *The Role of Instruction in Second Language Acquisition*. Spec. issue of *Studies in Second Language Acquisition* 15 (1993): 143–277.

Long, Michael. "A Role for Instruction in Second Language Acquisition: Task-Based Language Teaching." Hyltenstam and Pienemann 77–99.

Massy, William F., Andrea K. Wilger, and Carol Colbeck. "Overcoming 'Hollowed' Collegiality." *Change* July-Aug. 1994: 10–20.

Medley, Frank W., Jr. "Identifying Needs and Setting Goals." Phillips, *Building on Experience* 41–65.

Met, Myriam. "Learning Language through Content: Learning Content through Language." *Foreign Language Annals* 24 (1991): 281–95.

MLA Commission on Professional Service. "Making Faculty Work Visible: Reinterpreting Professional Service, Teaching, and Research in the Fields of Language and Literature." *Profession 1996*. New York: MLA, 1996. 161–216.

Mosher, Arthur. "The South Carolina Plan for Improved Curriculum Articulation between High Schools and Colleges." *Foreign Language Annals* 22 (1989): 157–62.

Munby, John. *Communicative Syllabus Design*. Cambridge: Cambridge UP, 1978.

National Standards in Foreign Language Education. Yonkers: ACTFL, 1995.

New London Group. "A Pedagogy of Multiliteracies: Designing Social Futures." *Harvard Educational Review* 66.1 (1996): 60–92.

Omaggio Hadley, Alice C. *Teaching Language in Context*. 1986. 2nd ed. Boston: Heinle, 1993.

Parsons, R. A. "Language, Literature, and Curriculum Revision in the 1980s." *Foreign Language Annals* 18 (1985): 213–18.

Peck, Jeffrey M. "Culture/Contexture: An Introduction." *Culture/Contexture: Explorations in Anthropology and Literary Studies*. Ed. E. Valentine Daniel and Peck. Berkeley: U of California P, 1996. 1–33.

Pennycook, Alastair. "The Concept of Method, Interested Knowledge, and the Politics of Language Teaching." *TESOL Quarterly* 23 (1989): 589–618.

Phillips, June K., ed. *Building Bridges and Making Connections*. Burlington: Northeast Conf., 1991.

———, ed. *Building on Experience—Building for Success*. ACTFL Foreign Lang. Educ. Series 10. Lincolnwood: Natl. Textbook, 1978.

———. "If Not Consensus, at Least Coherence and Transparency." *ADFL Bulletin* 26.3 (1995): 37–43.

Pica, Teresa. "Linguistic Simplicity and Learnability: Implications for Language Syllabus Design." Hyltenstam and Pienemann 137–51.

———. "Questions from the Language Classroom: Research Perspectives." *TESOL Quarterly* 28 (1994): 49–79.

Pienemann, Manfred. "Learnability and Syllabus Construction." Hyltenstam and Pienemann 23–76.

Reder, Stephen. "Practice-Engagement Theory: A Sociocultural Approach to Literacy across Languages and Cultures." Ferdman, Weber, and Ramírez 33–74.

Redfield, James. "The Politics of Language Instruction." *ADFL Bulletin* 20.3 (1989): 5–12.

Richards, Jack C. *The Language Teaching Matrix*. Cambridge: Cambridge UP, 1990.

Savignon, Sandra J. *Communicative Competence: Theory and Practice*. Reading: Addison, 1983.

Shohamy, Elana. "Connecting Testing and Learning in the Classroom and at the Program Level." Phillips, *Building Bridges* 154–78.

Shulman, Lee S. "Teaching as Community Property." *Change* Nov.-Dec. 1993: 6–7.

Silber, Ellen S., ed. *Critical Issues in Foreign Language Instruction*. New York: Garland, 1991.

Snow, Marguerite Ann. "Discipline-Based Foreign Language Teaching: Implications from ESL/EFL." Krueger and Ryan 37–56.

Snow, Marguerite Ann, Myriam Met, and Fred Genesee. "A Conceptual Framework for the Integration of Language and Content in Second/Foreign Language Instruction." *TESOL Quarterly* 23 (1989): 201–17.

Stern, H. H. "Toward a Multidimensional Foreign Language Curriculum." *Foreign Languages: Key Links in the Chain of Learning*. Ed. Robert G. Mead, Jr. Middlebury: Northeast Conf. on the Teaching of Foreign Langs., 1983. 120–46.

Swaffar, Janet K. "Articulating Learning in High School and College Programs: Holistic Theory in the Foreign Language Curriculum." *Challenges in the 1990s for College Foreign Language Programs*. Ed. Sally Sieloff Magnan. Boston: Heinle, 1990. 27–54.

———. "Curricular Issues and Language Research: The Shifting Interaction." *Profession 89.* New York: MLA, 1989. 32–38.

———. "Using Foreign Language to Learn: Rethinking the College Foreign Language Curriculum." *Reflecting on Proficiency from the Classroom Perspective.* Ed. June K. Phillips. Lincolnwood: Natl. Textbook, 1993. 55–86.

Swaffar, Janet K., Katherine M. Arens, and Heidi Byrnes. *Reading for Meaning: An Integrated Approach to Language Learning.* Englewood Cliffs: Prentice, 1991.

Swaffar, Janet K., Katherine Arens, and Martha Morgan. "Teacher Classroom Practices: Redefining Method as Task Hierarchy." *Modern Language Journal* 66 (1982): 24–33.

Swain, Merrill. "Communicative Competence: Some Roles of Comprehensible Input and Comprehensible Output in Its Development." *Input in Second Language Acquisition.* Ed. Susan M. Gass and Carolyn G. Madden. Rowley: Newbury, 1985. 235–53.

The Teaching of Literature. Spec. issue of *PMLA* 112 (1997): 7–112.

Tschirner, Erwin. "Scope and Sequence: Rethinking Beginning Foreign Language Instruction." *Modern Language Journal* 80 (1996): 1–14.

Valdés, Guadalupe. "The Teaching of Minority Languages as Academic Subjects: Pedagogical and Theoretical Challenges." *Modern Language Journal* 79 (1995): 299–328.

Valdman, Albert. "Authenticity, Variation, and Communication in the Foreign Language Classroom." *Text and Context: Cross-Disciplinary Perspectives on Language Study.* Ed. Claire Kramsch and Sally McConnell-Ginet. Lexington: Heath, 1992. 79–97.

van Lier, Leo. "Language Awareness, Contingency, and Interaction." Hulstijn and Schmidt 69–82.

Welles, Elizabeth B., ed. *Articulation.* Spec. issue of the *ADFL Bulletin* 26.3 (1995): 1–63.

Wesche, Marjorie Bingham. "Discipline-Based Approaches to Language Study: Research Issues and Outcomes." Krueger and Ryan 57–79.

Widdowson, Henry G. "Educational and Pedagogic Factors in Syllabus Design." Brumfit 23–27.

Yalden, Janice. "Syllabus Design in General Education: Options for ELT." Brumfit 13–22.

NOTES ON CONTRIBUTORS

KATHLEEN M. BAILEY, professor of applied linguistics at the Monterey Institute of International Studies, has done research in teacher development, second language acquisition, language assessment, and language classroom research. She is coauthor, with Dick Allwright, of *Focus on the Language Classroom,* an introduction to classroom research for language teachers (Cambridge UP, 1991). With David Nunan she edited *Voices from the Language Classroom,* a collection of qualitative research (Cambridge UP, 1996). She has worked with language teachers in Japan, Hong Kong, Singapore, Argentina, Brazil, Trinidad, Poland, Czechoslovakia, Italy, and the United States.

ELIZABETH B. BERNHARDT, director of the Language Center and professor of German studies at Stanford University, has spoken and written on second language reading, teacher education, and policy and planning for foreign and second language programs. She teaches German language courses and offers seminars on second language learning.

ROBERT J. BLAKE, professor of Spanish and chair of the Department of Spanish and Classics at the University of California, Davis, has published widely in Spanish linguistics on topics dealing with historical phonology and syntax, modern syntax (the Spanish subjunctive), and second language learning. A leader in the development of computer-assisted materials for the teaching of Spanish, he has written *Recuerdos de Madrid,* a ten-part computer adventure for the Macintosh (1991), and *Nuevos Destinos: CD-ROM for Spanish* (jointly sponsored by Annenberg CPB/Project, WGBH, and McGraw-Hill, Inc., 1998). He is currently working on a distance learning project, Remote Technical Assistance, that will run over the Internet across hardware platforms (IBM, Mac, UNIX). He is coauthor, with

Alicia Ramos and Martha Marks, of *Al corriente* (3rd ed., 1998), a second-year Spanish textbook based on authentic reading materials.

HEIDI BYRNES, professor of German at Georgetown University, is interested in classroom-based second language acquisition by the collegiate advanced learner, with an emphasis on literacy phenomena that pertain to reading and writing and the relation of those phenomena to acquiring academic-level performance in a second language. Her articles have appeared in a variety of journals and edited volumes, and she has presented widely at professional conferences and diverse faculty- and curriculum-development efforts.

CATHERINE DOUGHTY, associate professor of linguistics at Georgetown University, teaches courses in language acquisition, language assessment, and research methods. She does research in second language acquisition, particularly focus on form and the negotiation of meaning in classroom SLA. She has written articles on SLA and CALL for applied linguistics journals and for edited collections. Her most recent research projects investigate cognitive processing and SLA, implicit feedback in L2 classrooms, and the connection between negotiated comprehension and SLA. She is coeditor (with Jessica Williams) of *Focus on Form in Classroom SLA* (Cambridge UP, 1998).

THOM HUEBNER, professor of linguistics and language development at San Jose State University, has written articles for numerous journals in the fields of SLA, language minority education, and language policy and planning. He edited a selection of works of Charles Ferguson (Oxford UP) and is coeditor of the Series in Bilingualism (John Benjamins). He is currently working on a volume about language policy issue in the United States.

GABRIELE KASPER, professor of applied linguistics at the University of Hawai'i at Mānoa, teaches for the master's in ESL and the PhD in SLA programs. Her research focuses on sociolinguistic and psycholinguistic aspects of interlanguage pragmatics, especially pragmatic development, instruction, and research methods. Her recent books include *Interlanguage Pragmatics* (with S. Blum-Kulka, Oxford UP, 1993), *The Pragmatics of Chinese as Native and Target Language* (U of Hawai'i P, 1995), and *Communication Strategies: Psycholinguistic and Sociolinguistic Perspectives* (with E. Kellerman, Longman, 1997). For more information about her teaching and research, visit http://www.lll.hawaii.edu/esl/ and http://www.lll.hawaii.edu/nflrc/.

CLAIRE KRAMSCH, professor of German and foreign language education at the University of California, Berkeley, is author of *Culture and Context in Language Teaching* (Oxford UP, 1993) and *Redefining the Boundaries of Language Study* (Heinle, 1995). She has done research on the implications of discourse analysis and social and cultural theory for foreign language education and is currently finishing a monograph, *Language and Culture* (Oxford UP). Her next project will focus on the cultural politics of language study.

ELANA SHOHAMY, professor of language education at Tel Aviv University, has done research in the area of language testing and assessment, on oral testing, method effects, alternative assessment, the connection between testing and instruction, the washback effect, and the political and social dimensions of language tests. She is codirector, with Bernard Spolsky, of the Language Policy Research Center, which is researching and introducing a new language policy in Israel. She is also director of research at the National Foreign Language Center, Washington, DC. She is author of *Second Language Research Methods* (with Herbert Seilger, Oxford UP, 1989).

LEO VAN LIER, professor of educational linguistics at the Monterey Institute of International Studies, has worked in the Netherlands, England, Denmark, Mexico, and Peru and teaches graduate courses in educational linguistics and teacher development in the United States since 1984. His current interests are educational and ecological linguistics, complexity theory, and sociocultural learning. He is author of *Introducing Language Awareness* (Penguin, 1995) and *Interaction in the Language Curriculum: Awareness, Autonomy, and Authenticity* (Longman, 1996).

BILL VANPATTEN, professor of Spanish and second language acquisition and teacher education at the University of Illinois, Urbana, is author of *Input Processing and Grammar Instruction: Theory and Research* (Ablex, 1996) and coauthor, with James F. Lee, of *Making Communicative Language Teaching Happen* (McGraw, 1995). He does research in second language input processing and the effects of explicit instruction on the acquisition of grammar. He is currently exploring the application of capacity theory to second language acquisition.

NAME INDEX

Adams, John, 41, 42–43
Addams, Jane, 46, 47
Ahmad, Khurshid, 211, 214
Alderks, Cathy, 220
Alderson, Charles, 250
Allen, J. P. B., 265, 268, 272
Allen, Patrick, 263
Allwright, Richard L., 75, 76, 85, 91, 98
Andersen, Roger W., 64
Angiolillo, Paul F., 49, 50
Antonek, Janis L., 97
Appel, Gabriele, 192
Ard, Josh, 68
Arens, Katherine M., 23, 274, 278, 288
Argyris, Chris, 96
Armington, Susan, 229
Arndt, Horst, 199
Arteagoitia, Igone, 144, 147, 150
Aston, Guy, 172
Atkinson, J. Max, 173
Atkinson, Paul, 91
Au, Kathryn Hu-Pei, 90
Austin, John L., 65, 184
Axelrod, Joseph, 52, 53

Bachman, Lyle F., 184, 244, 246, 250
Bacon, Susan M., 97

Bailey, C. J., 66
Bailey, Kathleen M., 16, 75, 76, 83, 86–87, 90–91, 98, 178, 246
Bailin, Alan, 233
Baker, C., 152
Bakhtin, Mikhail M., 178
Ball, Martin, 200
Barasch, Ronald M., 27
Bardovi-Harlig, Kathleen, 186, 189, 194, 197, 202
Barnes, Douglas, 179
Barr, Robert B., 266–67
Barson, John, 224
Bates, Elizabeth, 142
Bateson, Gregory, 76
Bausch, Karl Richard, 31
Baycroft, Bernard, 129
Bayley, Robert, 66
Beauvois, Margaret Healy, 224
Beck, Maria, 118
Beebe, Leslie M., 66, 185, 188, 189, 194, 195, 196
Bell, Lawrence, 68
Berenz, Norine, 71
Beretta, Alan, 14
Bergman, Marc L., 188, 190
Berman, Russell A., 11, 12, 33, 36, 278, 283
Bernhardt, Elizabeth, 15

Bialystok, Ellen, 192, 286
Bickerton, Derek, 66
Bickes, Gerhard, 209
Bigelow, Donald N., 52, 53
Billmyer, Kristine, 201
Blake, Robert J., 19, 178, 229
Bland, Susan K., 228, 229
Bley-Vroman, Robert, 118
Bloch, Bernard, 49, 50
Block, David, 14
Bloomfield, Leonard, 49, 50
Blum-Kulka, Shoshana, 65, 185, 186,
    187, 188, 189, 195, 196, 200, 203
Bodman, Jean, 189, 196
Bogdan, Robert, 91
Bolinger, Dwight, 68
Bourdieu, Pierre, 29, 160, 161, 162, 168
Bouton, Lawrence F., 186–87, 201
Bowerman, Melissa, 135, 141
Bowers, C. A., 165, 174
Brandl, Klaus K., 213, 215, 229–30
Brazil, David, 159
Brecht, Richard D., 24
Brindley, Geoffrey, 132
Brinton, Donna M., 263
Brooks, Frank B., 175
Brown, Cheryl, 87, 90, 96
Brown, Gillian, 248
Brown, J. S., 244
Brown, James D., 76, 82, 203, 213
Brown, Penelope, 185
Brumfit, Christopher J., 14, 75
Bruner, Jerome, 166, 176, 177
Burt, Marina K., 108
Bush, George, 52, 54
Butterfield, Earl, 115
Byrnes, Heidi, 7, 9, 12, 23, 31, 35, 271,
    272, 277, 278, 288

Cadierno, Teresa, 124
Campbell, Cherry C., 87
Campbell, Donald, 82
Canale, Michael, 240, 244, 272, 285
Candlin, Christopher N., 265, 267, 285,
    286
Carr, Wilfred, 96
Carrell, Patricia L., 186
Carroll, Brendan J., 246
Carroll, Suzanne, 151
Carter, Jimmy, 52, 54
Carter, Ronald, 33, 34

Cassidy, Anthony, 96
Cazden, Courtney, 132
Chapelle, Carol, 216, 220, 222, 230
Chaudron, Craig, 65, 75, 76, 89, 90, 96,
    97, 160
Chomsky, Noam, 60, 69
Chun, Dorothy, 213, 215
Clahsen, Harold, 132
Clark, John L. D., 81, 240
Clarke, Mark A., 14, 34
Cleghorn, Ailie, 89
Clifford, Ray, 112
Clinton, Bill, 52, 54
Clyne, Michael, 64, 200
Coffin, Edna, 217
Cohen, Andrew, 189
Cohen, Louis, 94
Colbeck, Carol, 8, 280
Cole, Michael, 165, 166
Coleman, Algernon, 48–49, 50, 55
Collins, Allan, 244
Comrie, Bernard, 68
Cook, Guy, 34
Cook, Thomas D., 97, 238
Cook, Vivian J., 63
Corbett, Greville, 211, 214
Corder, S. Pit, 30, 62
Coste, Daniel, 36
Coulmas, Florian, 189
Coulson, Mark, 286
Coulthard, Malcolm, 163
Coupland, Justine, 192
Coupland, Nikolas, 192, 199, 200
Crawford-Lange, Linda M., 271
Crook, Charles, 178
Crookes, Graham, 96
Crystal, David, 69
Csikszentmihalyi, Mihalyi, 176
Cummins, Jim, 263, 280

Dahl, Merete, 202
Darder, Antonia, 165, 167
Dauphin, Gary, 234
Davidson, Fred G., 244
Davidson, Rosalind G., 139
Davies, Graham, 211
Davis, Kathryn A., 14, 34
Day, Elaine, 139, 145–46
DeCarrico, Jeanette S., 122
de Certeau, Michel, 29
Deci, Edward L., 167, 175

Delanshere, Ginette, 251
Denzin, Norman K., 84
Detmer, Emily, 203
DeVillar, Robert A., 225
Dickerson, Lonna, 66
Dickerson, Wayne, 66
Doi, Toshiyuki, 195
Donato, Richard, 97
Donitsa-Schmidt, Smadar, 248
Doughty, Catherine, 6, 7, 17, 132, 136,
    143, 144, 145, 147, 149, 150, 151,
    152, 172, 173, 288, 289
Douglas, Dan, 248
Duff, E. C., 96
Duff, Patricia A., 89, 134
DuFon, Margaret Ann, 189, 201
Dulay, Heidi C., 108
Dumais, Susan T., 121
Duncan, Starkey, 173
Dunkel, Patricia, 211

Ebbutt, David, 96
Eckman, Fred, 68
Edge, Julian, 75
Ediger, Anne, 217
Edmondson, Willis, 190
Edwards, Anthony D., 159
Egan, Kieran, 177, 269
Einbeck, Kandace, 264, 282
Eisenhower, Dwight, 52
Eisenstein, Miriam, 189, 196
Elbow, Peter, 90
Ellis, Rod, 63, 66, 75, 87, 106, 130, 160,
    174, 191
Ephratt, Michael, 222
Erickson, Frederick, 186
Eubank, Lynn, 118
Evans, Jacqueline, 149

Færch, Claus, 90, 115, 189, 194
Fairclough, Norman, 29, 33, 161
Fantuzzi, Cheryl, 14
Farrar, Michael, 135, 136
Farris, Michael, 234
Felix, Sasha, 31, 131
Ferdman, Bernardo M., 290
Ferguson, Charles A., 14, 59, 61, 64, 68,
    89
Feustle, Joseph A., Jr., 226
Ficksdal, Susan, 189, 197

Fife, Robert Herndon, 48, 50
Fillmore, Charles J., 248
Finkel, Jules, 233
Firth, Alan, 14, 18
Fletcher, Paul, 82
Flinders, David, J., 165, 175
Flores, Fernando, 214, 220
Flynn, Suzanne, 68
Forbes, James, 135
Fowler, Roger, 33–34
Franklin, Benjamin, 41, 42
Fraser, Bruce, 185, 186
Freed, Barbara F., 75
Freeman, Donald, 90
Freire, Paulo, 167
Fridman, Boris, 144, 147, 150
Friend, Margaret, 135
Frommer, Judith, 234
Frota, Sylvia, 87, 144
Fry, John, 90
Fujii, Yoko, 202
Fukushima, Saeko, 188
Furstenberg, Gilberte, 215, 222

Gaies, Stephen J., 75
Gale, Larrie E., 233
Gallimore, Ronald, 165
Garcia, Carmen, 189
Garfinkel, Harold, 169
Garrett, Nina, 212, 216, 228, 230, 233
Gaskill, William H., 88
Gass, Susan M., 59, 63, 67, 68, 109, 136,
    210
Gay, Geri, 229
Gazdar, Gerald, 60
Gee, James, 34
Genesee, Fred, 89, 137, 152, 283
Gibson, James J., 169, 174, 175, 179
Giddens, Anthony, 160, 177
Giles, Howard, 192, 199, 200
Goffman, Erving, 29
González-Edfelt, Nidia, 209, 233
Goody, Jack, 26
Gordon, Claire, 248
Goswami, Dixie, 96
Grandin, John M., 264, 282
Graumann, Carl F., 175
Green, Judith, 90
Green, Peter, 131
Greenberg, John H., 66
Greenblatt, Stephen, 23

Greene, Judith, 286, 290
Gregg, Kevin, 27
Grice, H. Paul, 190
Griffin, Peg, 165, 166
Grosjean, François, 200
Grosse, Christine U., 282
Grotjahn, Rüdiger, 14, 76, 90
Guba, Egon G., 82, 83, 91
Gumperz, John J., 169, 171, 173, 186, 197
Gunn, Giles, 23
Guthrie, Grace Pung, 90

Hahn, Angela, 31
Hainline, Douglas, 211
Hakansson, Gisela, 120
Hall, Joan Kelly, 14, 18, 286
Hall, Patrick J., 246
Halliday, M. A. K., 138
Hamilton, Jan, 250
Hammerly, Hector, 112, 139
Hammersley, Martyn, 91
Hancock, Charles, 244
Harley, Birgit, 139, 140, 149, 263, 288
Harren, David, 233
Hartford, Beverly S., 186, 189, 194, 197, 202
Hatch, Evelyn, 14, 34, 64, 82
Havelock, Eric, 26
Hawkins, Roger, 106, 119
Heath, Shirley Brice, 43
Hecht, Karlheinz, 131
Held, Gudrun, 185
Hendricks, Harold, 214
Henning, Sylvie Debevec, 271
Henze, Rosemary, 87
Heritage, John, 173
Herren, David, 234
Herron, Carol, 150
Heshusius, Lois, 76, 80, 83, 88, 96, 97
Higgins, Chris, 233
Higgins, John, 214, 215
Higgs, Theodore V., 112, 272
Higham, John, 46, 47
Hilles, Sharon, 70
Hilleson, Mick, 87
Hiraga, Masako K., 202
Hoffman, Ernst F., 271
Holland, V. Melissa, 220
Hornberger, Nancy, 279

Horwitz, Elaine K., 124
House, Juliane, 65, 185, 188, 189, 190, 194, 196, 198, 201
Hudson, Thom, 203
Huebner, Thom, 16, 31, 32, 63, 66, 68, 89
Hughes, Arthur, 82
Hulstijn, Jan, 144, 146, 148, 289
Hustler, David, 96
Hyland, John, 96
Hyltenstam, Kenneth, 66, 67, 68
Hymes, Dell H., 18, 138, 184, 240, 244, 285

Ikoma, Tomoko, 194
Inbar, Ofra, 248

Jaegar, Richard M., 82
Jahn, Gary R., 213
James, C. Vaughn, 27
James, Dorothy, 2, 3, 9, 271, 288
Jamieson, Joan, 216, 221, 230
Janney, Richard W., 199
Jarvis, Gilbert A., 94
Jefferson, Gail, 160, 169, 173, 175
Jefferson, Thomas, 41–42
Johns, Tim, 214, 215
Johnson, Carl H., 272
Johnson, Donna M., 82, 90
Johnston, Malcolm, 132
Jones, Randall, 246
Judd, Elliot, 202
Jurasek, Barbara S., 283
Jurasek, Richard T., 283

Kamhi-Stein, Lia, 96
Kamil, Michael L., 14
Kaplan, Abraham, 80
Kaplan, Jonathan D., 220
Kasper, Gabriele, 14, 17, 18, 65, 90, 115, 140, 173, 185, 186, 188, 189, 190, 191, 193, 194, 196, 200, 201, 202, 203
Kebir, Catherine, 96
Kemmis, Stephen, 93, 96
Kenyon, Dorrie M., 246, 248
Kinginger, Celeste, 165
Kitao, Kenji, 187
Klein, Ewan, 60

Klein, Wolfgang, 14, 63, 115
Knight, Susan, 229
Königs, Frank, 31
Kowal, Maria, 144, 145, 146
Kramsch, Claire, 8, 9, 14, 15, 23, 26, 28, 30, 31, 33, 34, 35, 39, 278, 279
Krashen, Stephen D., 27, 108, 113, 131, 138, 139, 144, 273
Kress, Gunther, 26
Krueger, Merle, 283
Kruger, Ann, 136
Kuhn, Thomas S., 16
Kumaravadivelu, B., 274
Kurth, Awino, 9

Labov, William, 66, 89
Lachman, Janet L., 115
Lachman, Roy, 115
Lagerman, Robert, 233
Lakshmanan, Usha, 70
Lambert, Richard D., 271
Lange, Dale L., 265, 271, 278, 285
Lantolf, James P., 14, 34, 192, 285
Lapkin, Sharon, 138, 139, 145, 146
Larsen-Freeman, Diane, 14, 63, 106, 111, 202, 264, 274
Lavine, Roberta Z., 124
Lazaraton, Anna, 14, 34, 82, 248
Leech, Geoffrey, 185
Leeman, Jennifer, 144, 147, 150
Lett, John A., Jr., 77
Levinson, Stephen D., 185
Lewin, Kurt, 94
Lightbown, Patsy M., 31, 68, 111, 113, 130, 138, 139, 140, 148, 151, 288
Lii, J. H., 161
Lincoln, Yvonna S., 82, 83, 91
Liskin-Gasparro, Judith E., 244
Long, Michael H., 14, 63, 64, 69, 75, 76, 106, 111, 136, 142, 144, 160, 264, 272, 274
Lopez, Marilyn, 250
Lörscher, Wolfgang, 201
Lunde, Ken R., 224
Lynch, Brian K., 244

MacWhinney, Brian, 142
Madden, Carolyn G., 198
Maeshibia, Naoko, 191
Magnan, Sally S., 76, 83, 98

Maisano, Richard, 220
Manion, Lawrence, 92, 94
Marcus, H., 175
Marisi, Paulette, 250
Marks, Elaine, 33
Marshall, Catherine, 91
Martin, Jeffery, 220
Massy, William F., 8, 280
Matsumoto, Keiko, 87, 90
Matsuo, Naoko, 168, 173
Matthews, Clive, 233
Maybin, Janet, 178
McCarthy, Michael, 34
McLaughlin, Barry, 121
McLean, K. P., 195
McLuhan, Marshall, 218
McNamara, Timothy F., 241, 246, 250
McTaggart, Robin, 93, 96
Medley, Frank W., Jr., 272
Mehan, Hugh, 163
Meisel, Jürgen, 31, 132
Merrow, John, 162
Messick, Samuel, 251
Met, Myriam, 283
Mey, Jacob L., 183
Michaelis, Kathleen, 200
Miller, Ted, 198
Mitchell, Rosamund, 75
Mizuno, Suesue, 230
Moerman, Michael, 173
Moore, Dorothea, 46
Morgan, Martha, 274
Morgenstern, Douglas, 215, 222
Morrow, Keith E., 240
Mosher, Arthur, 282
Moss, Pamela, 251
Munby, John, 272
Murray, Janey H., 215, 220, 222, 233
Myers, Cynthia L., 198

Nattinger, James R., 122
Neil, Deborah, 200
Nelson, Diane, 68
Nelson, Keith, 135
Nemser, William, 62, 141
Neuwirth, Christine, 220
Nevo, David, 253
Newman, Denis, 165, 166
Newman, S. E., 244
Nixon, John, 96
Noblitt, James S., 26, 228, 229

Nolden, Thomas, 278, 279
Nunan, David, 82, 85, 90, 92, 95, 96
Nyyssönen, H., 190

Ochs, Elinor, 192
Ochsner, Robert, 34, 86, 90, 97
Oja, Sharon Nodie, 95
Oller, John, 240, 244
Olshtain, Elite, 185, 187, 188, 189
Omaggio Hadley, Alice C., 76, 83, 98,
     112, 121, 272, 273
O'Neal, Wayne, 68
Ong, Walter, 26
Oscarson, Mats, 246
Otto, Frank M., 81
Oxford, Rebecca, 124

Palmer, Adrian, 244
Pangle, Lorraine Smith, 40, 41
Pangle, Thomas L., 40, 41
Parker, Katherine, 65, 160
Parsons, R. A., 271
Passeron, Jean-Claude, 161, 162, 168
Patrikis, Peter C., 11, 26
Pavesi, Maria, 112
Peck, Jeffrey M., 11, 33, 278, 280
Pederson, Kathleen Marshall, 233
Peirce, Bonny Norton, 33, 34
Pelletier, Luc G., 167
Pennycook, Alastair, 14, 286
Perrault, Charles, 29
Perrone, Charles, 129
Pertosky, Anthony, 251
Peters, Ann, 115
Phillips, June K., 276
Phillipson, Robert, 43
Pica, Teresa, 136, 137, 160, 172, 173,
     174, 274, 284, 290
Pienemann, Manfred, 31, 111, 112,
     119–21, 132, 145, 290
Piirainen-Marsh, Arja, 199
Pinker, Steven, 118
Platt, Elizabeth, 175
Platt, John, 61
Polio, Charlene, 134
Pomerantz, Anita, 173
Poole, Deborah, 192
Porter, Patricia, 136, 160
Preston, Dennis, 66

Pullum, Geoffrey K., 60
Putnam, Robert, 96

Quinn, Robert, 209, 213, 218

Rardin, Jennybelle P., 81
Rathunde, Kevin, 176
Reddy, Michael J., 14
Reder, Stephen, 279, 280
Redfield, James, 271
Rehbein, Jochen, 197
Reichardt, Charles S., 97
Richards, Jack C., 61, 88, 129, 267
Richards, Keith, 75
Riggenbach, Heidi, 248
Rintell, Ellen, 187
Rivers, Wilga M., 87
Roberge, Yves, 151
Robinson, Mary Ann, 144, 188, 189,
     195, 196
Roblyer, Margaret D., 209, 215, 230, 232
Roche, Jörg, 9
Rodgers, Theodore, 129
Rogers, Margaret, 211, 214
Roitblat, Herbert, 187
Rommetveit, Ragnar, 170
Roosevelt, Theodore, 47
Rose, Kenneth R., 201, 203
Ross, Steven, 191, 197
Rossman, Gretchen B., 91
Rubin, Joan, 87, 217
Rudduck, Jean, 172
Rudolph, Frederick, 24, 42
Ruschoff, Bernd, 215
Rutherford, William, 146, 174
Ryan, Frank, 283
Ryan, Richard M., 167, 175

Sacks, Harvey, 160, 169, 173, 175
Sag, Ivan, 60
Sajavaara, Kari, 246
Salumets, Thomas, 10
Samaniego, Fabián A., 223
Samimy, Keiko K., 81
Sams, Michelle R., 220
Samway, Katherine Davies, 90
Sanders, Ruth H., 27
Sanz, Cristina, 144

Sato, Charlene J., 195
Savignon, Sandra J., 285
Saville-Troike, Muriel, 83, 89
Sawyer, Mark, 191
Schachter, Jacquelyn, 59, 68, 143
Schegloff, Emanuel, 160, 169, 173, 175
Scherer, George A. C., 81
Schieffelin, Bambi B., 192
Schmidt, Richard W., 85–86, 87, 88,
    115, 122, 144, 146, 190, 191, 289
Schneider, Walter, 121
Schulze, Rainer, 201
Schumann, Francine E., 87
Schumann, John H., 85, 87, 99, 132
Schwartz, Bonnie D., 113
Schwartz, Joan, 88
Schwerdtfeger, Ingeborg C., 26
Scollon, Ron, 29, 189, 197
Scollon, Suzanne, 29, 189, 197
Scott, Andrew, 209
Searle, John, 65
Seliger, Herbert W., 89
Selinker, Larry, 62, 63, 141, 184, 185,
    248
Shapiro, Rina, 64
Shapson, Stan, 139, 145–46
Sharwood Smith, Michael, 115, 144,
    145, 146, 147, 150
Shavelson, Richard J., 82
Shaw, Peter A., 84
Shea, David P., 192
Sheffer, Hadass, 200
Sheridan, Eileen, 250
Shi, Austina Yi-Peng, 194
Shiffrin, Richard T., 121
Shimura, Akihiko, 195
Shirai, Yasuhiro, 14
Shohamy, Elana, 19, 243, 244, 248, 254,
    282
Shor, Ira, 165
Shulman, Lee S., 273
Schultz, Jeffrey, 186
Shuy, Roger, 165
Silber, Ellen S., 271
Simpson, David, 40
Simpson, Paul, 33, 34
Sinclair, John M., 159, 163
Slobin, Dan, 142
Smith, Diane McLain, 96
Smith, John K., 76, 80, 83, 88, 96, 97
Smith, Karen, 230, 233

Smith, Phillip D., 81
Smith, William Flint, 211
Smulyan, Lisa, 95
Snow, Catherine E., 7–8, 136, 139
Snow, M. S., 263
Snow, Marguerite Ann, 96, 271, 283
Spada, Nina, 148, 288
Spolsky, Bernard, 14, 238
Spradley, James P., 91
Spring, Joel, 41, 44
Stanley, Julian C., 82
Stansfield, Charles W., 246, 248
Stern, H. H., 40, 48, 50, 271
Stevens, Vance, 211
Stillman, Peter R., 96
Strickland, Dorothy S., 96
Stoks, Gé, 215
Sugiura, Masayoshi, 232
Suppes, Patrick, 211
Sussex, Roland, 211, 214
Swaffar, Janet K., 4, 10, 23, 76, 83, 98,
    265, 271, 274, 278, 288, 290–91
Swain, Merrill, 115, 138, 139, 140, 144,
    145, 146, 151, 240, 244, 263, 285,
    290
Swann, Philip Howard, 211
Szostek, Carolyn, 93, 96

Tagg, John, 266–67
Takahashi, Satomi, 187, 189, 196
Takahashi, Tomoko, 185, 188–89, 194,
    195, 196
Tanaka, Noriko, 188
Tannen, Deborah, 200
Tanner, Daniel, 44, 45
Tanner, Laurel, 44, 45
Tarone, Elaine E., 66
Taylor, Steven J., 91
Terrell, Tracy D., 129, 273
Tharp, Roland, 165
Thomas, Jenny, 185, 186, 198
Todd, Jody, 136
Tomasello, Michael, 136, 150
Tomlin, Russel S., 146, 148
Towell, Richard, 106, 119
Trager, George L., 49, 50
Trahey, Martha, 119
Trim, J. L. M., 53
Trosborg, Anna, 191
Trueba, Henry J., 90

Tschirner, Erwin, 272
Tsui, Amy B. M., 96
Tucker, G. Richard, 97
Tuckman, Bruce W., 82
Tuman, Walter Vladimir, 211
Turner, Joan M., 202
Twitchin, John, 178
Tyler, Andrea, 198

Uliss-Weltz, Robin, 194
Underwood, John, 211, 213–14, 220

Valdés, Guadalupe, 3, 263, 269
Valdman, Albert, 282
Valette, Jean Paul, 223
Valette, Rebecca M., 223
Vallerand, Robert J., 167
Van Campen, Joseph, 211
Van Handle, Donna, 217
van Lier, Leo, 7, 14, 17, 34, 75, 80, 83,
    84, 89–90, 91–92, 94, 95, 96, 98–99,
    163, 164, 165, 167, 168, 169, 173,
    175, 178, 288, 289
van Manen, Max, 177
VanPatten, Bill, 6, 7, 17, 106, 107, 108,
    114, 116, 124, 144, 147, 286, 289
Varela, Elizabeth, 151
Varonis, Evangeline, 136, 210
Villa, Victor, 146, 147, 148
Voght, G. M., 282
von Hoene, Linda, 33, 34
von Reinhart, Walter, 264, 282
Vygotsky, Lev S., 18, 92, 124, 166, 174,
    176, 192

Wagner, Johannes, 14, 18
Wagner-Gough, Judy, 64
Waizer, Ronit, 248
Wallat, Cynthia, 90
Walters, Richard, 225, 227, 233
Walton, A. Ronald, 24
Warschauer, Mark, 224
Watson-Gegeo, Karen A., 83–84, 90
Watts, Richard J., 198
Webber, Mark J., 10, 33

Weber, Heidi, 61
Weber, Rose-Marie, 290
Webster, Noah, 41, 42, 43
Weinbach, Liora, 189
Welles, Elizabeth B., 5, 10, 282
Wells, Gordon, 163, 166, 179
Wertheimer, Michael, 81
Wertsch, James V., 167, 178
Wesche, Marjorie Bingham, 241, 246,
    247, 263, 271, 281
Wesley, Edgar Bruce, 45
Westgate, David P. G., 159
Whalen, Samuel, 176
Whiskeyman, Ann, 217
White, Joanna, 132, 145
White, Lydia, 70, 113, 117, 118, 119,
    143, 288
Whitehead, Alfred North, 20
Wickens, Christopher D., 115
Widdowson, Henry G., 33, 34, 266
Wiemann, John M., 199, 200
Wildner-Basset, Mary, 201
Wilger, Andrea K., 8, 280
Williams, Jessica, 143, 149
Wilson, Guy, 233
Winograd, Terry, 214, 220
Wittgenstein, Ludwig, 160, 178
Wolfram, Walt, 66
Wolfson, Nessa, 202
Wong-Fillmore, Lilly, 64
Woods, Anthony, 82
Worth, Fabienne, 33
Wyatt, David, 211

Yalden, Janice, 265
Yamashita, Sayoko, 198, 203
Yeh, Jody, 194
Yoshinaga, Naoko, 191
Young, Dolly J., 124
Young, Richard, 66, 136, 172, 173, 249
Young, Robert, 167, 168
Yu, Janet Harclerode, 96
Yule, George, 172, 173, 178

Zajonc, R. B., 175
Zuengler, Jane, 66

SUBJECT INDEX

access, SLA processing and, 114
accessibility, hierarchy of, 67–68
accommodation (adjustment), 61, 64, 114
acculturation. *See* model, acculturation
accuracy
   development of, 121–22, 140
   and fluency, 141–52, 290
   role of, 5, 8–9, 288–89
   See also interlanguage
achievement
   CALL and, 230
   definition of, 240
   distinguished from proficiency, 240, 245
   evaluation of, 137, 243
   in language knowledge, 244–45, 256
   multiplism and, 242, 256
   predicting, 8
acquisition
   of aspect, 130–31, 139
   distinguished from learning, 27–28
   incomplete, 118
   logical problem of, 69, 117, 152n3
   natural process of, 273, 287
   of negation. *See* negation, acquisition of
   orders of, 106–07, 110–11, 264
   patterns of, 70

second language. *See* second language acquisition
   stages of, 111, 120–21. *See also* acquisition, orders of
   of tense, 139
   time required for, 134–36
   See also first language acquisition
ACTFL. *See* American Council for the Teaching of Foreign Languages
advertising, language of, 61
affective variables, 80, 81, 87, 93, 124, 167
affordance, 175, 176, 179n5
A la rencontre de Philippe (software), 215, 222–23, 224, 233
alterity, construction of, 11
America 2000, 52
American Council for the Teaching of Foreign Languages (ACTFL), 2, 5, 32, 53, 54, 245, 250, 259
   See also Oral Proficiency Interview
Americanization, and the teaching of language, 46–47
analysis
   contrastive, 63, 108, 193
   conversational, 61, 87–88, 248–49
   discourse, and SLA research, 31, 64–65, 76
   ethnomethodological, 173

analysis (*cont.*)
  functional, 129
  interaction, 76, 136–38
  multiple perspectives, 97
  in naturalistic inquiry, 84, 88, 89
  statistical, 96
  variation, 61
  See also data, analysis; research, quali-
    tative; research, quantitative
anxiety, 90, 124
apology, strategies of, 190–91
Apple Media Kit (software), 219, 233
Applied Linguistics (journal), 32, 61
appropriateness, 162, 188
  See also sociopragmatics
approximative system. *See* inter-
    language
aptitude, 77, 80, 124, 230, 264
Army Specialists' Training Program
    (ASTP), 48, 49–50, 54
articulation, 5, 276, 282
assessment
  alternative, 239, 241–42, 247
  and CALL, 228
  formative, 243
  informal, 247
  interview as, 246, 247
  items for, 247–49
  main-points, 248
  of politeness, 187, 189
  procedures for, 246–47, 248, 251–52,
    255–56, 257
  process of, 242–54
  program, 2, 5, 282
  purposes of, 243–44, 251–52, 254
  quality of, 251–52
  tasks for, 247–49
  See also proficiency movement; self-
    assessment; testing
Atajo (software), 223–24, 233
Athena Project (MIT), 222
attention
  capacity for, 115, 147
  to form. *See* form, attention to, in SLA
  input processing and, 114–16
  to meaning. *See* meaning, attention to
  as a psycholinguistic mechanism,
    142
attitude, 146, 192
  See also motivation
audiolingualism, 40, 51, 108, 273, 277,
    290

Australian Second Language Proficiency
    Ratings, 245
Authorware (software), 219, 233
autonomy, IRF and, 167
awareness. *See* attention

baby talk, 64
backsliding. *See* regression
behaviorism, 51, 83
bilingualism, 46, 61, 62, 171, 200, 269,
    279
bounding node, 70
Brigham Young University, Mission
    Training Center, 87
bulletin board, electronic, 225, 226,
    232

CAI. *See* instruction, language,
    computer-assisted
Calis (software), 219, 233
CALL (computer-assisted language
    learning) software
  creating, 218–19
  database of programs for, 234
  effective, 215–16, 220–21, 230,
    232n2
  evaluated, 221–24
  hardware for, 216–18, 231
  implementation and, 218–19
  learning paradigms for, 213–15
  and research on SLA, 228–32
  for teaching language, 210, 212,
    227
camera, digital, 217
Canadian Modern Language Review, 32
case study
  first-person. *See* diary study
  as naturalistic inquiry, 83, 85–86
  one-shot, 85
  resources for, 90
Center for Information on Language
    Building and Research (London),
    233
Center of Applied Linguistics, testing
    by, 246
child language. *See* first language acqui-
    sition
chunking, 122, 142, 191
  See also fluency
class, social, and communication, 61

classroom
communicative language teaching in, 135
constraints of, for learning, 160–62
electronic. *See* classroom, virtual
inadequacy of, for SLA, 134–35
interaction in, 158–59
pragmatic transfer and, 195, 201
research in. *See* research, classroom-centered
resource of, for learning, 162
SLA and, 31, 287–91
virtual, 224–28
classroom talk, 6, 159, 163–69, 175, 177
See also interaction
clause, relative, 67–68
cloze tests. *See* testing, cloze
coconstruction, learning as, 164–68
cognitive code, 51
cognitive development, 192. *See also*
zone of proximal development
cognitive processing, 120, 228, 289
acquisition and, 116–19
See also development, sequence of;
second language acquisition, processes in
attention and, 115–16, 147
constraints in. *See* constraints, second language acquisition; speech processing, and access
mechanisms of, 141–42, 147, 289
pragmatic transfer and, 197
speech acts and, 65, 186–87
Coleman Report, the (1929), 48–49
collegiality, hollowed, 8, 280
Committee of Ten, 45, 48
communication
across genders, 61
breakdown of, 8–9
competence in. *See* competence, communicative
cross-cultural, 61, 69
equality in, distinguished from symmetry, 168–69
and foreign language curricula, 201, 282
language as, 6
natural, 27
strategies. *See* learner, strategies
Communicative Gap Software, 215
Community Language Learning (methodology), 273

comparison, as a psycholinguistic mechanism, 142
competence
age and, 136
communicative, 9, 18, 28, 85, 134, 136, 240, 244
of computers, 220
curriculum and, 272, 285
defined, 184, 240, 286
form and, 138
as the goal of language instruction, 183–84, 285
multiplism and, 242
discourse, 285
grammatical, 244, 285
linguistic, 32, 189, 196, 240, 244, 277–78
organizational, 184
performance and, 285
pragmatic, 184, 190–92, 244
sociolinguistic, 240, 244, 285
strategic, 285
textual, 32, 244
transitional, 62
See also interlanguage
written, SLA research and, 33
complexity, 140, 290
comprehension
assessing, 247–48
checks, 64–65, 172
data for research on, 202
of nonliteral utterance, 186–87
pragmatic, 186–88, 202
computers
hardware for, and language teaching, 211–12, 216–18
intelligence in, 219, 220–21
software for. *See* CALL
See also technology
conferences, 243
on applied linguistics, 32, 63
electronic discussion groups as, 226, 230–31
on language teaching, 55
consciousness, 191–92, 201
raising, in SLA. *See* form, attention to; noticing
constraints
of classroom settings, 160–62, 176–77
first-language transfer, 109
and focus on form, 145

constraints (*cont.*)
  phrasal, 122
  second language acquisition, 105,
     106, 110, 113, 120, 123–25, 191
  speech processing and, 119–23
content, in second language acquisi-
     tion, 3, 6, 270, 288
context
  dependency. *See* language, context-
     dependent
  and form, 66
  sociopragmatics and, 185–86
  and task, 241
contextualization
  assessment and, 257
  cues, 171, 173, 186
  in interaction, 169, 171–72, 178
contingency
  described, 179n4
  foreground and background and, 170
  interaction and, 169–72, 173, 175–76,
     178
control group (experimental group), 77,
     78, 79
  See also research, empirical, approaches
     to
conversation
  analysis, 64–65, 87–88
  as contingent language, 170–72
  instructional, 165
  online, 231
  pragmatics and, 184
  See also coconstruction, learning as;
     repair, conversational; style, con-
     versational
correction. *See* error
Council of Europe, 53
Course Builder (software), 219, 233
Course of Action (software), 219, 234
criteria, 88, 94, 250–52
critique, postmodernist, 33, 286
cues. *See* contextualization, cues
culture
  academic, and foreign language cur-
     ricula, 276–78
  canonical (high), 29
  and competence, 281
  departmental, and curriculum design,
     263
  everyday, 29
  high. *See* culture, canonical

  and language, 26, 35, 43, 46, 80, 279
  studies of, 3, 24, 33–36
curriculum
  Americanization through, 46–47
  analytic model of, 287
  ASTP, 49
  the Coleman Report and, 48–49
  college-level, 7, 10, 13, 35, 262–91
  communicative approach and, 282
  construction of, 262–91
  content-based instruction and, 84, 140
  core, foreign languages and, 275–76
  default position and, 269, 270–71
  defined, 265
  design, 58, 266–67, 270, 274–75
  development of, 264–91
  external challenges for, 280–84
  in foreign language education, 262–91
  functionalism in, 42, 51, 54, 129, 134
  functional-notional, 272
  K–12, 4, 45
  language across the curriculum (LAC)
     and, 136
  methodology as, 273–74
  natural growth hypothesis of, 272–73
  role of CALL in, 224
  scope of, 268
  secondary school, 41, 45
  sequence in, 284
  and social change, 281
  substitutions for, 271–74
  textbooks as, 271–73
  traditional, 23–24, 44, 131, 132, 277

data
  for action research, 92, 93
  analysis, 16, 75–76, 82, 83–84, 85,
     185, 264
  for case studies, 86
  collection, 16, 75–76, 83–84, 185
  defined, 76
  for diary studies, 87
  elicited, 18, 89
  in experimental research, 81–82
  mentalistic, 89, 90
  in naturalistic inquiry, 84, 88, 89
  negative evidence as, 109, 143, 152n3
  not quantified (qualitative), 75, 97
  for pragmatics research, 202
  quantified, 75, 81–82

De orilla a orilla (software), 225
department, foreign language, 3, 8,
    9–13, 26–30
development, cognitive, 192. *See also*
    zone of proximal development
development, language
  sequence of, 107, 108, 109, 111, 118,
    132–33
  studies on, 190–92
  See also competence, communicative;
    interlanguage; proficiency
dialogue, 167, 213, 217, 253, 256
  computer-based, 215
  deficiencies of CAI in, 214
dialogue journal, assessment and, 247
diary study
  assessment and, 247
  as naturalistic inquiry, 83, 84, 86–87,
    89, 90–91
dictionary, online, 229
difficulty, level of, and assessment,
    252
Digital Chisel (software), 219, 234
Dime (software), 223, 234
directness, 185, 187, 188–89
discourse
  analysis, and SLA research, 31, 64–65,
    76
  authentic, and pragmatics research,
    202
  as a basis for pedagogy, 33
  between native and nonnative
    speakers, 64–65, 168–69, 170–71,
    173, 175
  boundaries, 25, 221
  child-directed, 136
  domains, 221
  therapeutic, 61
  See also accommodation (adjustment)
Discovering French Interactive (software),
    223, 224, 234
discussion group. *See* bulletin board,
    electronic
divergence, pragmatic, 197, 198–99
doctor-patient communication, 61
dummy subjects, 70

education
  decentralization of, and foreign lan-
    guage curricula, 275–76

  goal of, 266
  the origins of public, and language
    teaching, 44–46
  reform in, 44, 48, 177
Educational Action Research (journal),
    94
elicitation
  methodology, 89, 98
  in testing, 12, 242, 245–52
elitism, language study as, 49, 54
e-mail, language teaching and, 224–25,
    228, 232
emic, distinguished from etic, 83, 88
English
  as an international language, 24, 31,
    281
  as a second language (ESL), 31,
    129–30, 158–59, 171, 186–87, 230
English Only movement, 51, 54
English Plus movement, 51
enrollment, in foreign language pro-
    grams, 4, 10
error, 109, 110, 140, 145, 151, 290
  analysis, 221
  correction, 140, 229, 290
  cultural fault lines as, 35
  lack of, 107–10, 113
  transfer, 108–109
ethnography
  of communication, 61
  defined, 83
  emic principle of, 83, 88, 90, 95
  holistic principle of, 83
  interview for, 91
  as naturalistic inquiry, 83–85
  research and, 76, 98
  resources for, 89–91
ethnomethodology, 88
  analysis, 173
  conditional relevance in, 169
  reflexive tying in, 169
etic, distinguished from emic, 83, 88
evidence, negative and positive, 142–43
exhibition, assessment and, 242, 247
Exito (software), 233n10, 234
explicit/implicit. *See* acquisition, dis-
    tinguished from learning; instruc-
    tion, language, explicit;
    instruction, language, grammar
    and; instruction, language, im-
    plicit; knowledge

faculty, of foreign language depart-
    ments, 9, 11, 276–77
as designers of the curriculum, 274–75
failure, pragmatic, 197–99
feedback, 150–51, 215
    See also error
feminism, studies of, 30, 33, 34
field notes, 90
FIPSE (Fund for the Improvement of
    Postsecondary Education), 4
first language acquisition, 30, 106,
    135–36, 287
and linguistic theory, 60
FlanNet, 226, 233n16
flooding, 145, 147
fluency, 27, 121–23, 139
    and accuracy, 141–52, 290
    and communicative language teach-
        ing, 136
    theories about, 122–23
    and traditional teaching, 133
focus on form (FonF), 50, 129–31,
    138–40, 144–51, 270, 272, 282, 287
    defined, 144
FonF. *See* focus on form
force, illocutionary, 65, 185
    See also meaning
foreigner talk, 64
Foreign Language Annals, 32, 53
foreign language education, 45–46,
    48–54
    and applied linguistics, 62
    curriculum in, 262–91
    goals of, 4–7, 268, 282–83
    native language literacy and, 3
Foreign Service Institute, 54
form
    attention to, in SLA, 115–16, 128–38.
        See also focus on form
    defined, 115
    developmental sequence and, 118–19
    and immersion programs, 139–40
    impermanence of learned, 6
    linguistic. *See* grammar, as linguistic
        form
    overlearning of, 111–12
    in the traditional syllabi, 131–32, 140
    and variation theory, 66
formula, routine, learners' uses of, 189,
    190
fossilization, 112, 290

generalization, 79, 94, 95, 264
    and accessibility, hierarchy of, 67–68
Goals 2000, 55
government and binding. *See* theory,
    government-binding
grammar
    hierarchy of accessibility of. *See* acces-
        sibility, hierarchy of
    as linguistic form, 6, 128
    linguistic theory and, 60
    restructuring of, 113–14, 116–19, 121
        See also interlanguage
    structuralist, 50, 129, 131
    teaching of, 6, 106, 110–13, 128–38,
        148
        See also instruction, language, gram-
            mar and
    traditional, 128–29, 144
        See also Universal Grammar
grammaticality judgments. *See* research,
    grammaticality judgments in
grammaticalization, language learning
    as, 174, 175
group work, 84, 136

handover, scaffolding and, 166, 177
heritage language, 3
hierarchy of accessibility. *See* accessibil-
    ity, hierarchy of
homework, assessment and, 247
Hypercard (software), 219, 234
hypermedia, 213, 219, 221–24
HyperMedia Shells (software), 219, 234

idiomaticity, 140
IL. *See* interlanguage
illocution, 65, 185–86
ILP. *See* interlanguage, pragmatics
immersion programs, 136, 137–39
immigration, and language instruction,
    42, 46–47, 53–54
implicational hierarchy, 67, 68
indirectness, 185, 189, 196
initiation-response-feedback (IRF),
    163–69, 175, 177
    continuum, 163
    limits of, 164–68, 169
input, 87, 107, 113–16, 139, 142, 145
    adjustment in, 147

input, adjustment in (*cont.*)
   See also baby talk; foreigner talk; in-
      take, described; interaction
   effects of, for SLA, 141–44
   enhancement, 144, 145
   See also flooding; focus on form
   negotiation of. *See* intake, described;
      interaction; output
inquiry, naturalistic, 76, 82–91, 98
instruction, language, 131
   as beneficial, 112–13
   the Coleman Report and, 48–49
   college-level, 4–5, 24
   communicative, 5–9, 290
   computer-assisted (CAI), 212, 214
      See also CALL
   content-based, study of, 84
   as detrimental, 111–12
   effects on SLA, 110–13, 132
   explicit, 17, 106, 110–13, 129, 133,
      142, 144–49, 177, 287
   focus of. *See* focus on form; meaning
   grammar and, 110–13
   implicit, 142
   innovation in K–12, 4
   institutional contexts of, 7–9
   K–16, 5
   and literary research, 3
   marginalization of, 3, 277
   necessity for, 112, 131
   and SLA research, 35–36
   traditional, 6, 8, 277
   See also teaching, of language
intake, described, 114
interaction
   analysis. *See* analysis, interaction
   between native and nonnative speak-
      ers, 137, 173, 175
   between nonnative speakers, 170–71
   CAI and, 213, 233n3
   contingency in, 169–76
   equality in, 168–69
   learner-learner, 158, 159–60, 168,
      176
   research on, 76
   resources for, 173–74
   social, and learning, 175, 285
   symmetry in, 168, 169, 170, 175, 178
   and symmetry in ILP, 192
   teacher-learner, 158–59, 161–62,
      163–65, 177, 192

turn-taking in. *See* initiation-response-
      feedback
   See also input, adjustment in; negotia-
      tion, of meaning
InterChange (software), 234
interdisciplinarity, 12, 62
interface, CAI instruction and, 212–13,
      223
interference. *See* transfer
interlanguage (IL), 8, 62, 264, 286, 289,
      290
   communicative language teaching
      and, 136–37, 139
   described, 184
   development, 65, 137
   and grammar. *See* grammar
   and language universals, 66–67
   learned forms and, 6, 289
   model of, 141–43
   pragmatics (ILP), 65, 183, 184
   stages of, 132
   transfer in, 65, 109
   variation in, 66
Internet, the, language instruction and,
      216–17, 225, 226, 227, 228
interpretation, and information,
      28–29
intersubjectivity, 170, 173
interview
   as assessment, 246, 247
   Oral Proficiency (OPI), 8, 54
introspection, 87, 89, 90
IRF. *See* initiation-response-feedback
items, for assessments, 247–49, 251–52,
      256
ITS. *See* system, intelligent tutoring

jigsaw reading, 84
journals
   for SLA research, 32, 63, 94
   See also diary studies
Juegos Communicativos (software), 215

knowledge
   analysis of, 192
   metalinguistic, 129, 133, 145
   retrieval. *See* processing
   and systematic interlanguage varia-
      tion, 66, 71

knowledge (*cont.*)
  See also acquisition, distinguished
    from learning; attention; instruc-
    tion, language, explicit; instruc-
    tion, language, grammar and;
    instruction, language, implicit;
    knowledge; language, knowledge;
    research, grammaticality judg-
    ments in

L1. *See* first language acquisition
L2. *See* second language acquisition
language
  ability, 5
  academic, 10
  as action, 192
    See also speech acts
  authentic use of, 184
  authoring, 218–19, 221, 233n17
  change in, and variation, 66
  content and, 276–78
  context-dependent, 7, 115, 130, 185,
    241, 249, 254
  contingent, 170
  development. *See* development, lan-
    guage
  functions of, speech acts and, 65
  as information processing, 28–29
  instruction. *See* instruction, language;
    teaching, of language
  knowledge
    acquiring, 291
    criteria for evaluating, 238, 249–51,
      256–57
    defined, 243–45, 254–55
    unschooled, academia and, 27–28,
      29
    See also attention; competence
  laboratory, ideal, 216–17
  natural, 220
  nature of, 59, 134, 265, 285–86
  non-Western, 35
  patterns of use in, 34
  principles of, 69
  production, 290
  reception, 290
  role of, in early America, 40–44
  structural conceptualization of, 50
  study of, and linguistics, 30
  teaching of. *See* teaching

  universals. *See* universals
  See also foreign language education
language centers, 11
Language in Society (journal), 32
language laboratory, 51
Language Learning (journal), 32, 62
learnability, 132
learner
  advanced, 186, 189–90, 191, 196, 200,
    249
  changing perceptions of, and SLA re-
    search, 34
  role of, 212, 266–67, 289–90
  and SLA, 113–23
  strategies, 89, 120, 229–30
  training, 84
  variables, 230
learner talk, 160
learning
  as coconstruction, 164–68
  content-based, 136
  cooperative, 93
  curriculum design and, 266–67
  experiential, 287
  social interaction and, 157
  talk (talk for language learning),
    160–61
  theme-based, 136
  unrealistic expectations for, 289
Learn to Speak Spanish (software), 223,
  234
Libra (software), 219, 234
linguistics
  applied, 31–32, 33
    definitions of, 61–62
    and linguistic theory, 63
    scope of, 61–62
    and the teaching of language, 35–36,
      58–59
    and theory construction, 62
  and language study, 30, 240
literacy
  academic, and vernacular orality,
    26–27
  cultural, 11–12
    See also culture, studies of
  first language, 3, 278, 290
  as a goal, in college-level instruction, 9
  multiple, 12–13, 262, 278–80, 283
  predictors of, 8
  second language, 31

literature
  separation of, from language teaching,
    270, 276–78
  teaching of, in translation, 270–71

MacroMind Director (software), 219, 223,
    234
mapping, as a psycholinguistic mecha-
    nism, 142
materials
  authentic, 213–14, 233n4
  development, 271–72
meaning, 50
  attention to, 114, 116, 147–48
  focus on, for SLA, 148, 289, 290
  force as, 65
  and form, 115, 287
media, electronic, 26–27
  See also multimedia, in language in-
    struction
Mellon Foundation, 71
memory, 114, 121, 142
  See also processing
methodology
  comparative, in ILP research, 185
  as curriculum, 273–74
  in research. *See* research, methodology
    of
  in teaching, 51, 277
  types of, 273
microworld, computer tutoring and,
    220, 221
Middlebury College Language Schools,
    226
Minnesota, second language instruction
    in, 4, 5
miscommunication, 197–99
mistakes. *See* error
model
  acculturation, 63, 85–86
  of collaborative action research, 95
  of communicative language ability,
    184
  input-output, of communication, 174
  linguistic theory, 60
  monitor, 63
  multidimensional, 63
  of multiplistic assessment, 255
  of pragmatic development, 192, 199
  of SLA, 141, 191, 287

of Universal Grammar theory, 69
Modern Language Association (MLA), 5,
    12–13, 40, 52–53
  Advisory Committee on Foreign Lan-
    guages and Literatures, 2
  Commission on Professional Service,
    276
  Committee on Computers and Emerg-
    ing Technologies in Teaching and
    Research, 219
  The Teaching of Literature (spec. issue
    of *PMLA*), 278
Modern Language Journal, 32
monolingualism, 49, 200
monologue, extended, 8
Monterey Institute of International
    Studies, 84
morpheme, acquisition of, 106–7
morphology, 31, 66, 119
  of verb, 106, 116–17, 118–19, 139–40
morphosyntax, and transferability,
    195
motivation, 80, 136, 167, 175, 192
multilingualism, 200
multiliteracy, 278–79
multimedia, in language instruction,
    210, 212–13, 216
multiplism, 251–52, 254–58
  described, 238, 242

National Defense Education Act
    (NDEA), 51, 52–53
National Education Association (NEA),
    45, 48
*National Standards in Foreign Language
    Education,* 276
National Standards in Foreign Language
    Education Project, 5
nationhood, and language, 43, 46
native speaker (NS), 3, 32, 64, 117–18,
    122, 132, 137
  and assessment of politeness, 168,
    187–89
  norms of, 194–95, 277
  and ILP, 199–200, 250–51, 264, 290
Natural Approach (methodology), 273
natural order. *See* development, lan-
    guage, sequence of
NDEA. *See* National Defense Education
    Act

NEA. *See* National Education Association

negation, acquisition of, 107, 108, 109, 122, 132

negotiation, of meaning, 136, 168, 169, 174, 285

network, computer, for CAI, 210, 216, 224–25

New London Group, 14, 278, 279

NNS. *See* nonnative speaker

nonnative speaker (NNS), 32, 64, 137, 168, 170–71

No recuerdo (software), 222–23, 224, 234

norm, pragmatic, 199–201

noticing, 142, 192, 201

NS. *See* native speaker

observation
   assessment by, 242, 247, 255, 256
   participant, as naturalistic inquiry, 90, 91

observer's paradox, 89

orality, 26–27, 29–30, 290

Oral Proficiency Interview (OPI), 8, 54

output, 114, 123, 146

pair work, 136, 192

paradigm, instructional, for CALL lessons, 214–16

parameters. *See* principles, and parameters
   pro-drop, 70–71

pedagogy
   discourse-based, 33
   and the electronic classroom, 227–28
   language, and applied linguistics, 30–31, 58–59
   SLA research and, 31
   thoughtfulness in, 177

peer, assessment by, 242, 247

Pennsylvania Foreign Language Project, 51, 81

performance
   and competence. *See* competence, performance and
   criteria for quality of, 250–52
   profile, 289
   testing, 239, 241

phonology, 66, 195

phrase
   institutionalized, 122
   lexical. *See* chunking

PICS. *See* Project for International Communications Studies

pidginization, 63, 139, 140, 143

PLATO. *See* Programmed Logic for Automated Teaching Operations

policy
   curriculum design and, 265–66
   language, 31

politeness, 187, 189, 198

polyword, 122

portfolio, assessment and, 242, 247, 255, 256

pragmalinguistics, 185, 186, 192

pragmatics, 31, 61
   cross-cultural, 185
   interlanguage (ILP), 183, 184
   research on, 202

President's Commission on Foreign Language and International Studies, 5, 51–52, 54, 55

principles, and parameters, 69–71

process, and product, 285

processing
   controlled distinguished from automatic, 121–22
   control of, 192
   See also cognitive processing

pro-drop. *See* parameters, pro-drop

production
   assessing, 247–48
   psycholinguistic strategies and, 120
   and reception, distinction of, 124, 139

professionalization, of language teaching, 3

proficiency
   CALL and, 230–31
   defining, 238–39, 240
   guidelines for, 5
   pragmatic transfer and, 196–97
   studies of, 190–91
   teaching oriented to, 51
   testing, 5, 245

proficiency movement, 4, 5–6, 7–8, 9

program, computer, for language instruction, 211–13
   See also CALL, evaluated

program coordination, 23, 35–36

Programmed Logic for Automated
Teaching Operations (PLATO),
211–12
project, assessment by, 247
Project for International Communications Studies (PICS), 233n4, 234
pronoun, resumptive, 67
pronoun copy, 109, 112
psychoanalysis, and academic scholarship, 30
psycholinguistics, 31, 51
psychology, 115, 286
psychometrics. *See* research, psychometric

qualitative/quantitative. *See* research,
qualitative; research, quantitative
questionnaire, 202, 248
QuickTime (software), 234
Quota Act (1921), 47

rating scales, of language knowledge,
245, 250
reading, importance of, 48–49, 51, 52,
54
recall, 89, 90
redundancy, 140
reflection, assessment and, 247
register, 64
classroom, 139, 143
extended, 140
regression (backsliding), 111
reliability, in assessment, 251–52
religion, and the teaching of foreign
languages, 44
Remote Technical Assistance (software),
226, 227, 233n15
repair, conversational, 88, 173–76
as interactional modification, 172–73
self-repair, 173
by students, and IRF, 165
research
action, 75, 76, 77, 91–96, 98
approaches to, 76–77
CALL and, 228–32
case study in. *See* case study
changing focus of, 30–32, 263–64
classroom-centered, 35, 75, 264
collaborative, 95

commonalities in, 96–98
and communicative ability, 6
and curriculum development, 262–91
design, 76, 78–79
in discourse analysis. *See* discourse,
analysis, and SLA research
emergence of, 30–33
empirical, approaches to, 75–99
on English as a second language, 31
ethnographic, 76
experimental, 75, 76, 77–82, 98
goals of, 80, 92–93
grammaticality judgments in, 131–32
hermeneutic (interpretive), 97
individuals and, 124
interactional, 76
interpretive. *See* research, hermeneutic
and linguistic theory, 63–71
literary, and the teaching of foreign
languages, 3
and literary-cultural studies, 32–36
longitudinal, 86, 87, 191
mentalistic data in, 90, 93
methodology of, 30–31, 32, 88, 91,
185, 264
multidisciplinary, 24–45, 62–63
multimethod, 202
naturalistic. *See* inquiry, naturalistic
and the nature of language, 285–86
nomothetic (theory-driven), 97
and non-Western language, 35
outcomes, criteria for significance of,
88, 94,
paradigms of, 76
participatory. *See* research, action
postmodernism in, 286
on pragmatics, 202
preexperimental, 85
process, 76, 285–86
process-product, 76
product, 76, 285
proposal, 91
psychometric, 76, 257
publication of, 32
qualitative (relativist), 34, 76
quantitative (positivist), 34, 76, 80
recall in. *See* recall
on testing procedures, 248–49
theory-driven. *See* research, nomothetic
traditional, 76, 157

research (*cont.*)
  triangulation in, 84–85
  universals and, 124
researcher, objectivity in, 81
resources
  for case study research, 85
  in classrooms, for learning, 162
  for experimental research, 82
  for interaction, 173–75
  for naturalistic inquiry, 89–91
  technological, 210, 233–34
rhetoric, comparative, 32
role play, assessment and, 246, 247, 248

Satellite Communications for Learning
    (SCOLA), 234
scaffolding, 166, 176, 177, 288
scale, rating language knowledge on,
    245
scanner, digital, for CAI, 217
scholarship, academic, 30
SCOLA. *See* Satellite Communications
    for Learning
second language acquisition (SLA), 51,
    69
  constraints and, 105, 106, 109, 113,
    116
  faculty's knowledge base in, 275
  linguistics and, 30, 58–71
  multiple literacies and, 283
  nature of, 69, 286–87
  patterns of, 67
  processes in, 114–23
  research. *See* research
  and theories of language, 60, 64, 70
  theory of, 5, 62–63
Second Language Research Forum, 63
self-assessment, 242, 246–47, 255,
    256
sentence. *See* syntax
sentence builder, 122
sequencing, and instruction, 6, 265,
    288, 290
  See also acquisition
setting, social, and learning, 157–59,
    175–76
Silent Way (methodology), 273
skill, teaching of, and academia, 28–29
SLA. *See* second language acquisition
social distance, perception of, 188

society, change in, and college curric-
    ula, 281
sociolinguistics, 31, 51
sociology, in SLA research, 30
sociopragmatics, 185–86, 187, 188,
    194–95, 198
software, language-teaching, 212–13,
    214–15, 218–19
  See also CALL
speech acts
  of learners, 188–90
  theory of, 65, 66
speech processing, and access, 119–23
stages of acquisition. *See* acquisition,
    stages of
standards. *See* teaching, of language,
    standards and
statistics. *See* data, quantified
strategies, 120
  See also learner, strategies; universals
Strength through Wisdom (President's
    Commission on Foreign Language
    and International Studies), 5, 54
students
  demands of, and the foreign language
    curriculum, 281–84
  technology and, 211, 213, 219
Studies in Second Language Acquisition
    (journal), 32, 62–63
style
  cognitive, 124, 230, 264
  communicative, 197, 199, 200
  conversational, 249. *See also* prag-
    matics
  intercultural, pragmatics and, 195
stylistics, 31, 34
subjacency, principle of, 69
Suggestopedia (methodology), 273
SuperCard (software), 219, 222, 234
SuperMacLang (software), 219, 234
syllabus, 129, 267
  See also curriculum
symmetry
  defined, 179n4
  See also interaction, symmetry in
syntax, 31, 66
  acquisition of. *See* grammar; instruc-
    tion, language, grammar and
system, intelligent tutoring (ITS), 215,
    220
Système-D (software), 223–24, 234

task, 241
  assessment and, 245, 247–49, 251–52,
    256
  in SLA research, 66, 92, 123, 124, 149
  in teaching, 124, 136, 149, 150
  and variation theory, 66
teachability, hypothesis about, 63
teacher
  learners and, 158–59, 161, 163–65,
    177
  role of, 177, 225–26
  traditional, 128, 129–31, 134, 161,
    162, 210
  training, 231–32
Teachers of English to Speakers of Other
    Languages (TESOL), 32, 51
teacher talk, 135, 160, 162, 177, 225
teaching, of language
  applied linguistics and, 61
  and apprenticeship, 176
  approaches to, 287–88
  communicative (CLT), 5–6, 51, 128,
    240
  dichotomy in, 24, 51, 55–56, 270–71,
    276–78
  learner-centered, 212
  and pragmatic development, 201
  responsive, 165
  second language as distinguished
    from foreign language, 54
  seniority and, 58
  sociohistorical phenomena affecting,
    51–52
  standards and, 54–55
  in the United States, 39–56
  See also technology, and teaching
technology
  role of, 210, 215
  and teaching, 28–29, 161, 178n2,
    209–32
  venue for, 209–10
telephone, assessments by, 248
TESOL. *See* Teachers of English to Speak-
    ers of Other Languages
TESOL Quarterly, 32, 34
testing, 32, 77, 238–59
  administration of, 249
  assessment of, 256
  cloze, 239–40, 248
  communicative, 239, 240–41
  and curriculum, 253, 255

direct, 240–41, 246
discrete-point, 129, 239
integrative, 239–40
interpreting results of, 253, 257
objective/multiple-choice, 239
performance, 239, 241, 245, 246
placement, 243, 245
portfolio. 242, 247
proficiency, 245
purposes of, 243–44, 253
results of, 253–54, 257–58
semidirect, 246
simulation, 246, 247, 248
standardized, 249
work-sample, 246
See also assessment
text, orientation toward, in CAI, 212,
    230–31
textbooks
  and computer programs, 223, 231
  as curriculum, 271–73
textualization, schooled literacy and, 30
theory
  accommodation, 61, 192
  acculturation, 63, 85–86
  cognitivist, 192, 277
  communicative accommodation,
    192
  complexity, 80
  construction of, and SLA research,
    69
  critical, 30, 33
  curriculum, and foreign languages,
    268–69
  educational, 25
  environmentalist, 63
  functional-typological, 63
  government-binding, 69–70
  interactionist, 63
  of language, 51, 59–63
  language socialization, 192
  linguistic
    and applied linguistics, 63
    defined, 59–60
    and SLA research, 63–71
  nativist, 63
  of pragmatic development, 191–92
  probability, and experimental re-
    search, 78–79
  processability, 120–21
  of SLA, 5, 62–63

theory (*cont.*)
    sociocultural, 34, 192
    speech-act, 65, 66
    structuration, 177
    variation, 63, 66
    See also Universal Grammar
thoughtfulness (tact), pedagogical,
    177
Toolbook (software), 219, 234
Total Physical Response (methodology),
    273
transfer
    and assessment of politeness, 187
    pragmatic, 65, 193–97
    and proficiency, 196–97
    See also interlanguage, transfer in
transferability, 195–96
transformation
    innovation and, 177
    IRF and, 167–68
translation, 31
triangulation of data, 84–85, 89, 93
turn-taking, 160, 165
    See also interaction
tutorials, CAI and, 214, 220

UG. *See* Universal Grammar
underdetermination, paradox of, 117
uniqueness principle, 118–19
Universal Grammar (UG), 31, 69–71,
    116, 118
    and first language acquisition, 60,
        116–17
    parameters, 69, 118
    and second language acquisition,
        117–19

universals, 105
    constraints on. *See* constraints, speech
        processing and
    implicational, 67
    language, 66–68
    of language acquisition, 105, 106–13
    pragmatic, 193
    typological, 66–68
University of Colorado, research pro-
    gram at, 81
University of Minnesota, 4–5
US English movement, 51

validity
    and assessment, 251, 252
    criterion measures of, 88, 94, 251–52
    external, 79
    internal, 78
values, social, and pragmatic diver-
    gence, 198–99
variables, 80–81
variance, and assessment, 252, 257
variation, 61, 66, 105, 123–24, 264, 285
video, for language teaching, 219, 224
VideoLinguist (software), 234
vocabulary, acquisition, research on, 31

Web, World Wide, 210, 225
workplace, language of the, 61
WorldScript (software), 226
writing, process approach to, 84

zone of proximal development (ZPD),
    166, 174, 176, 192